Photography

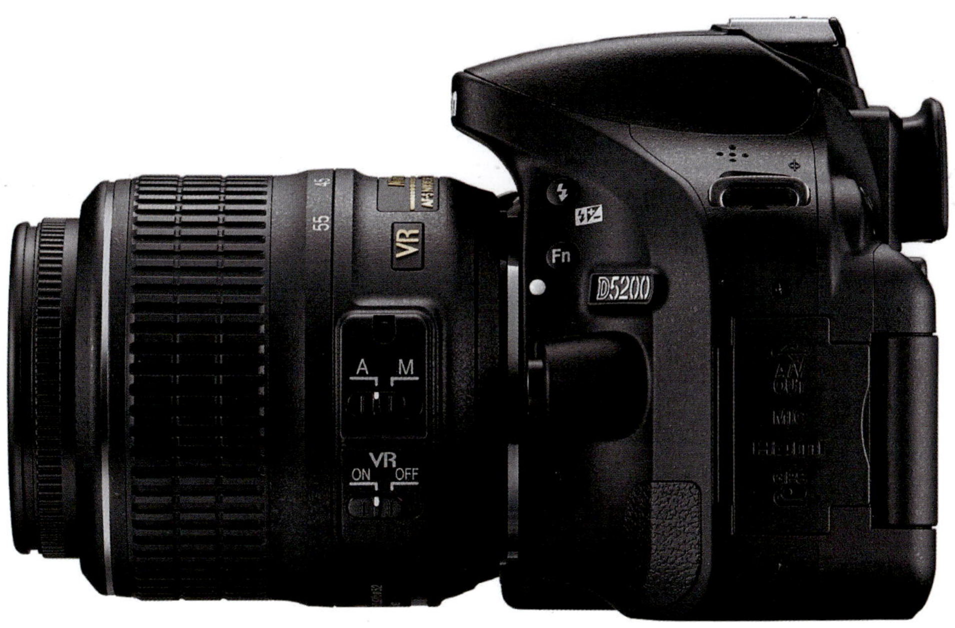

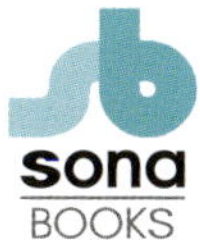

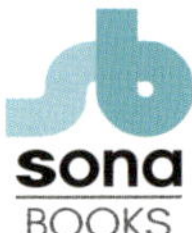

sona
BOOKS

© Danann publishing limited 2024

**First published in the UK 2019 by Sona Books
an imprint of Danann Media Publishing Ltd.**

Design rights © Danann publishing limited 2024

WARNING: For private domestic use only, any unauthorised Copying,
hiring, lending or public performance of this book is illegal.

Published under licence from Future Publishing Limited a Future PLC group company.
All rights reserved. No part of this publication may be reproduced or stored in
a retrieval system or transmitted in any form or by any means without the prior
written permission of the publisher.

© 2018 Future Publishing PLC

CAT NO: SON0437
ISBN: 978-1-915343-62-8
Made in the UAE.

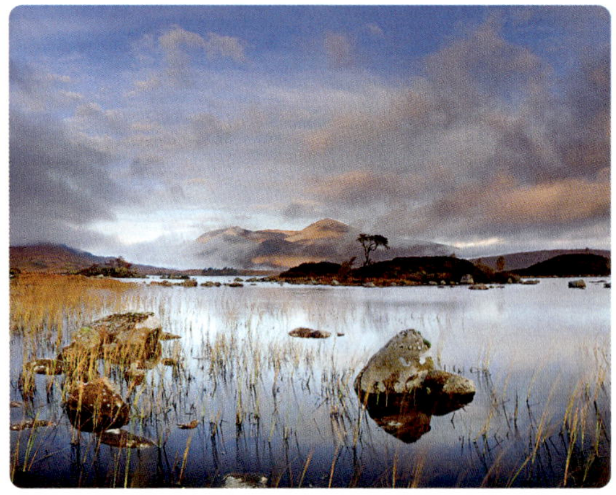

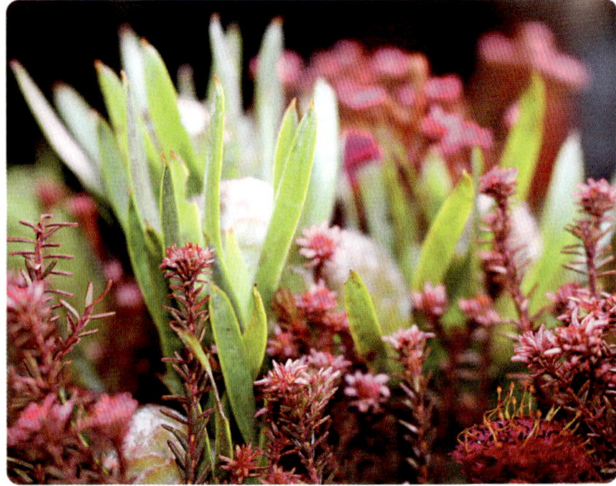

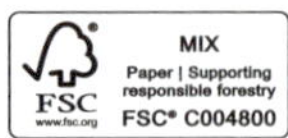

Welcome to

The Compact Beginner's Guide to
Photography

Compared with camera phones and compact cameras, modern DSLRs can seem terribly over-complicated to the novice photographer. The truth is, they have to be over-complicated to satisfy the needs of a diverse range of users, despite the fact that most photographers will only use a small percentage of the features on a regular basis. What the beginner photographer really needs, then, is a no-nonsense guide to the most important features on DSLRs written by experts that reveals in plain English exactly what they need to know and nothing more. This is that book.

The Compact Beginner's Guide to Photography explains all the photography concepts beginners need, such as how to balance exposures, how to get sharp shots, and how to maximise image quality.

Once you've mastered these basics, you can then move on to our more advanced skills section at the end of the book featuring practical how-to guides for shooting a range of core subjects. Take your photography to the next level and start learning today!

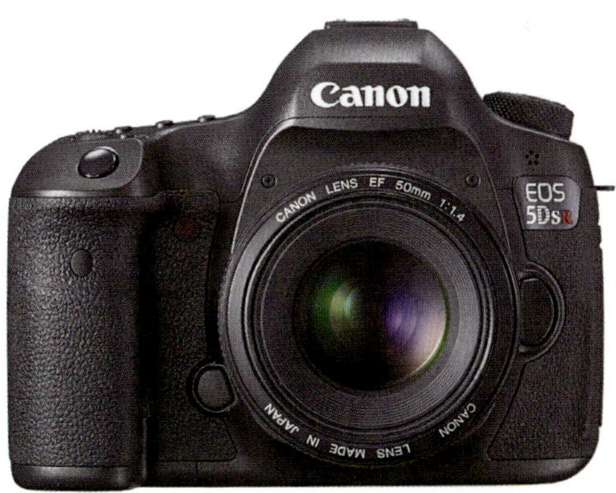

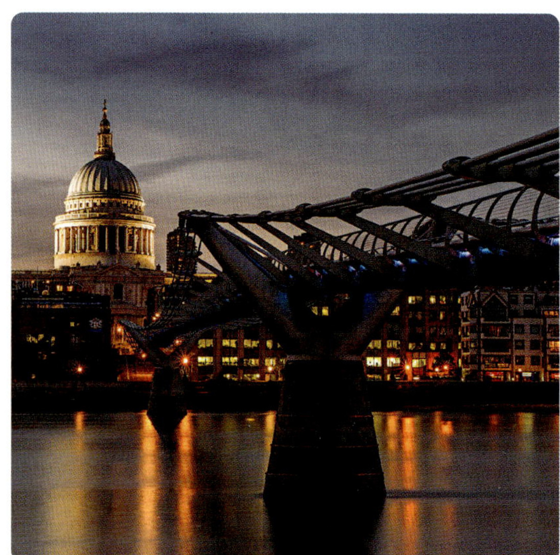

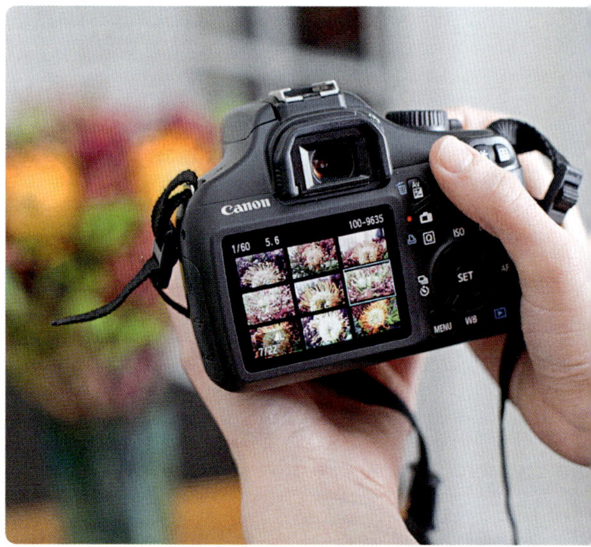

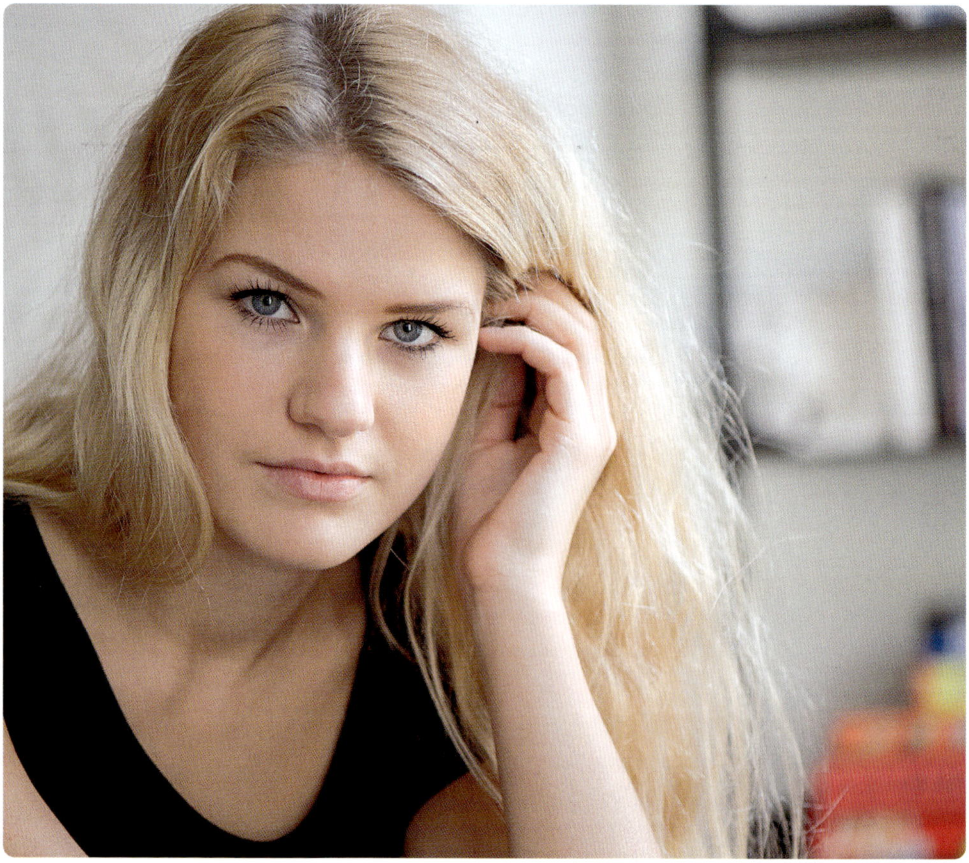

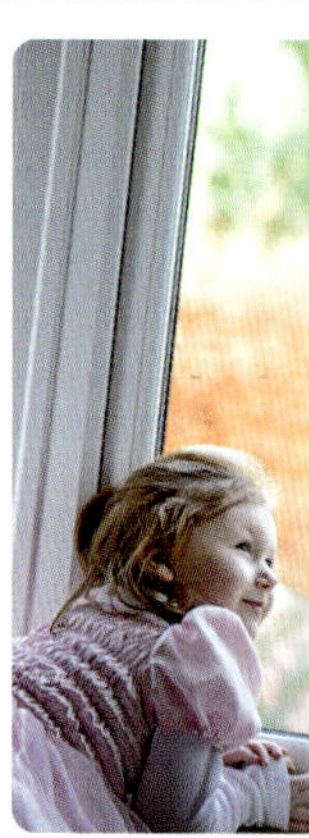

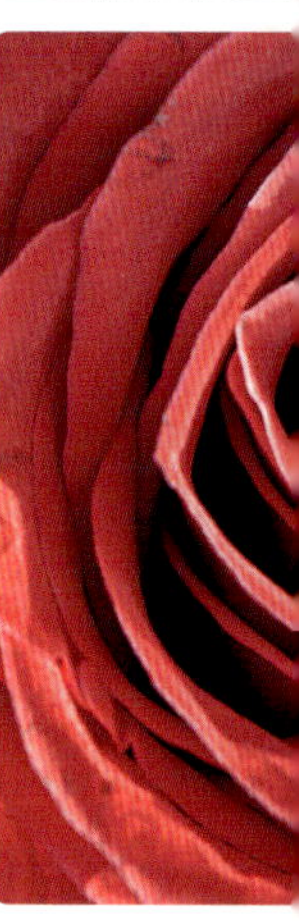

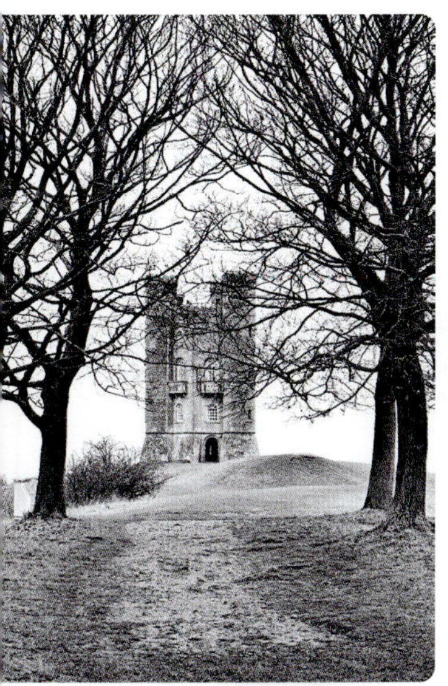

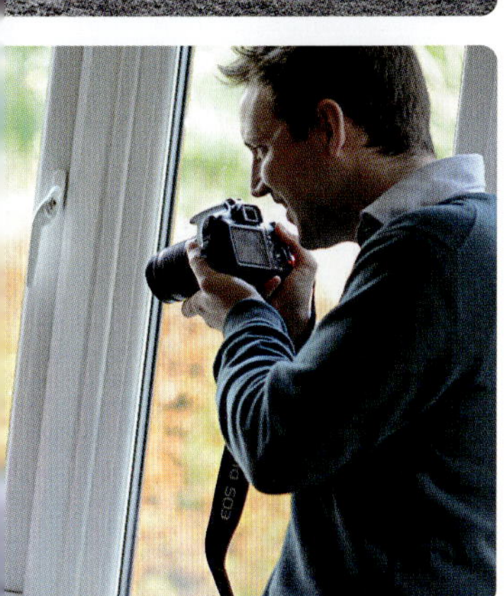

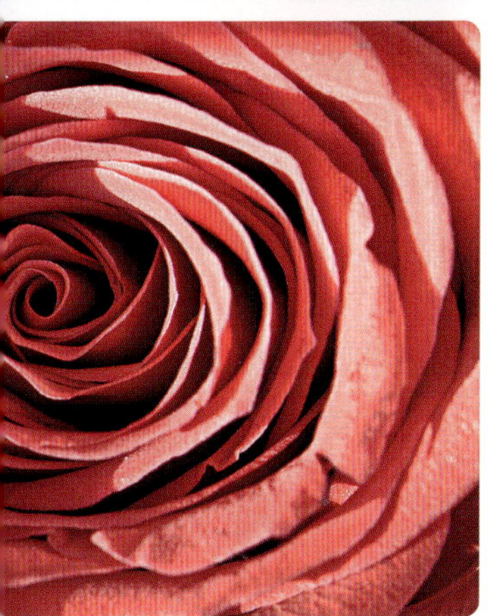

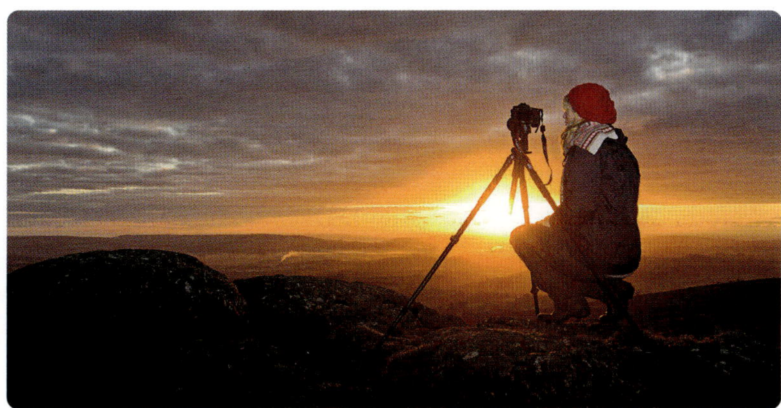

The Camera

We take a digital SLR camera and accessories out of the box to show you how to set it all up

08 Unbox your SLR
Take the first steps in setting up your digital SLR, and get familiar with the accessories that accompany it

12 Power up!
Learn everything you need to know about your SLR's built-in battery and included charger pack

14 Memory cards for cameras explained
We take a look at the various types of memory card so that you know which one is right for your camera model

18 How to fit a lens to your camera
Our easy-to-follow guide reveals all you need to know about attaching lenses to an SLR and removing them

20 A guided tour of your digital SLR camera
Get to know your camera better by understanding where all of the main controls and dials are positioned and what they are for

24 A guide to your SLR's menu system
Discover how to access the most important camera settings in your SLR's menu, and customise the features

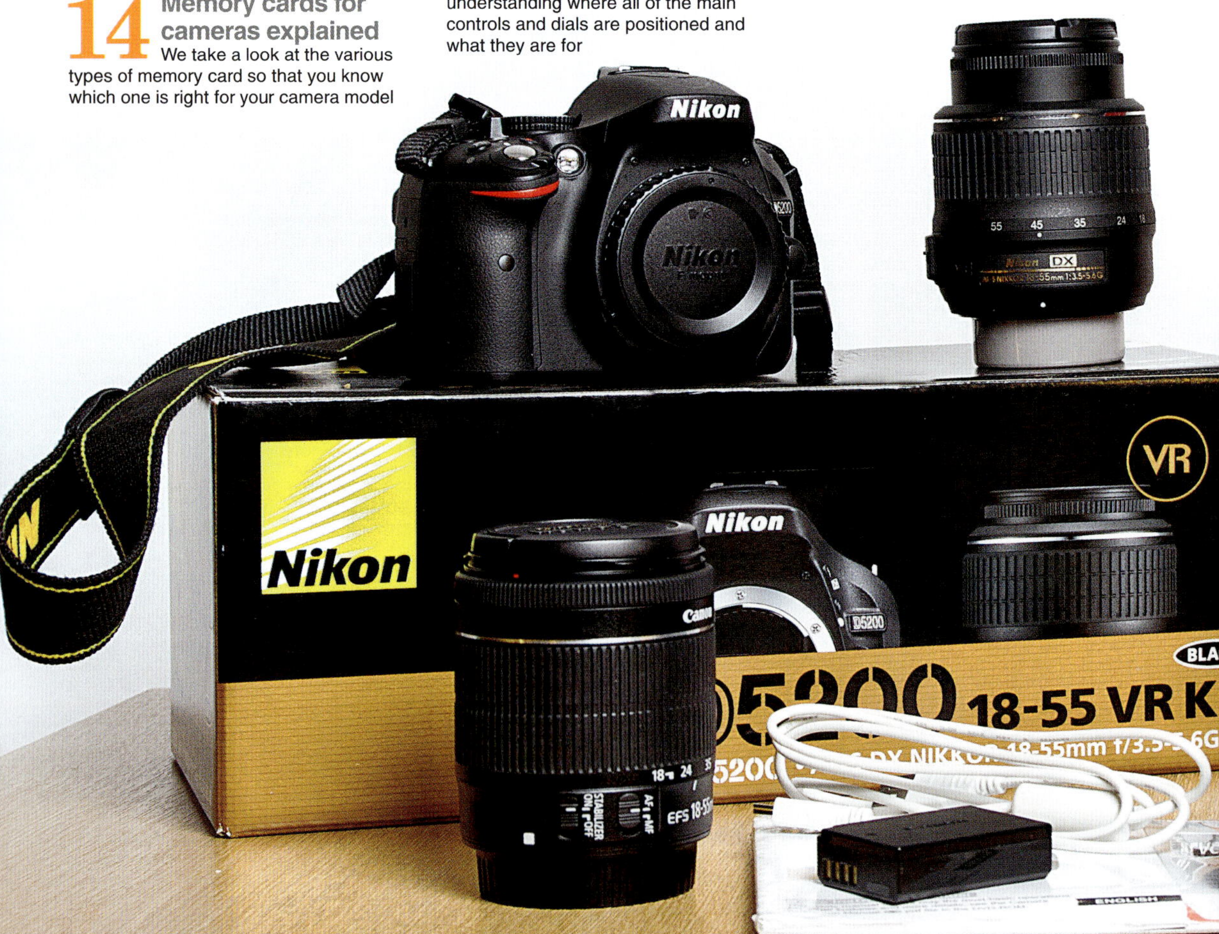

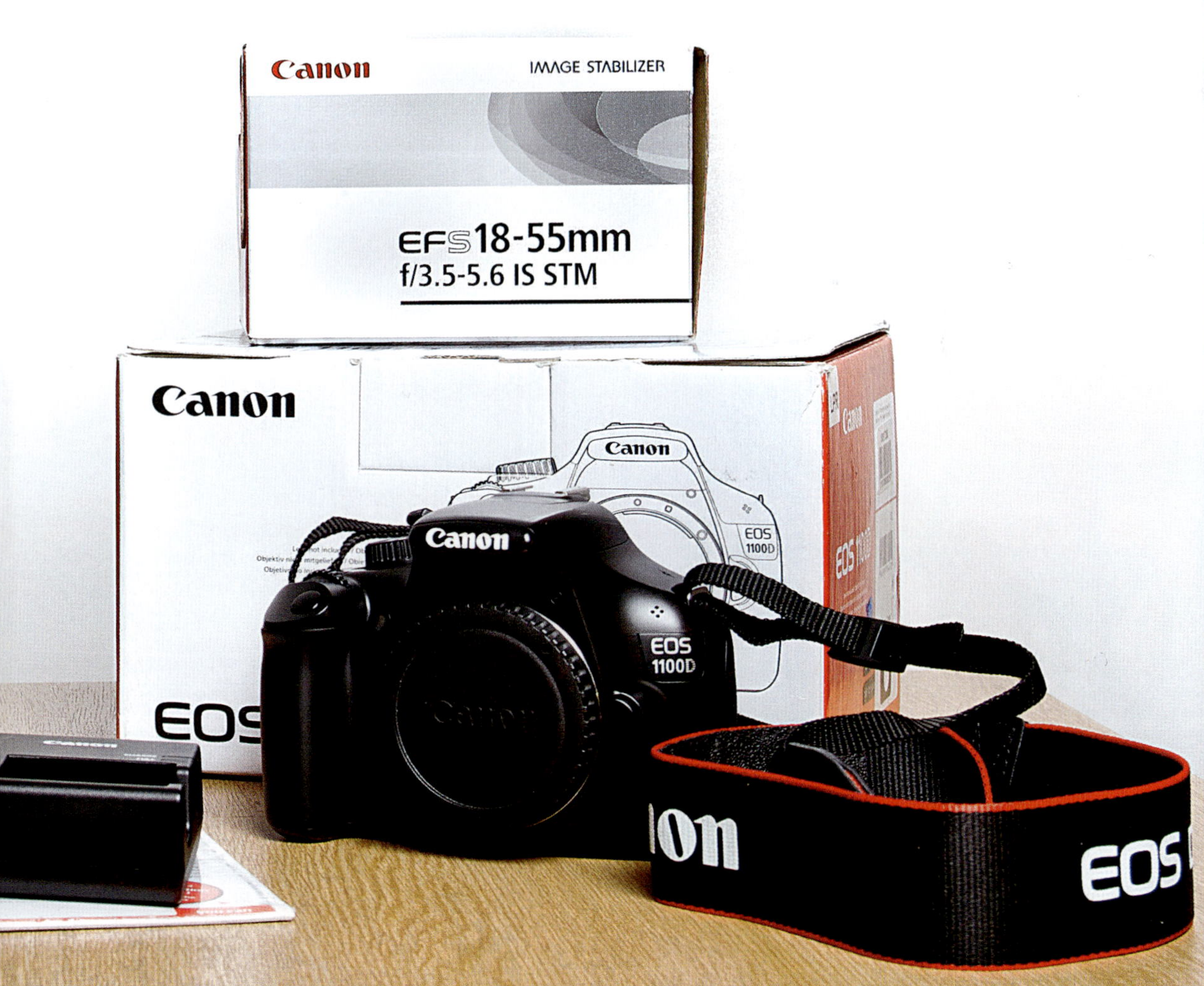
Canon
IMAGE STABILIZER
EFS18-55mm
f/3.5-5.6 IS STM
Canon
Canon
EOS
1100D
Canon
EOS
1100D
EOS
Canon
EOS

Unbox your SLR

Take the first steps in setting up your digital SLR, and get familiar with the accessories that accompany it

I t's always the same when you buy something new (whether it's new-new or secondhand) — as soon as you get your new DSLR home you'll want to start using it straight away. And that's fine. But for the very best results it's well worth spending some time familiarising yourself with your new camera and its accessories before you start shooting. So, to ensure that you know what's what from the outset, here we'll give you a quick guide to the basics.

To take and save pictures, you'll need a memory card that's compatible with your camera, and these aren't often supplied as standard. Not sure what to buy? We'll be covering memory card types and requirements later on in this chapter.

For now, though, we suggest you go and grab your camera box and follow along with us so you can be sure your camera is set up properly before you head out to take pictures.

1 USB cable

The USB cable enables you to connect your camera directly to your computer or tablet, so you can transfer, look at, file and back up images without the need for a card reader.

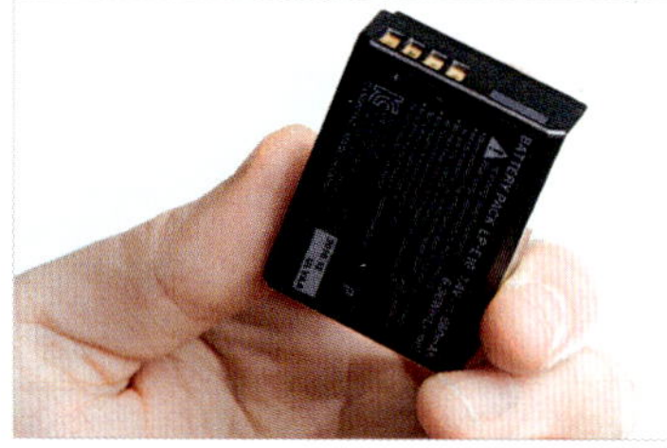

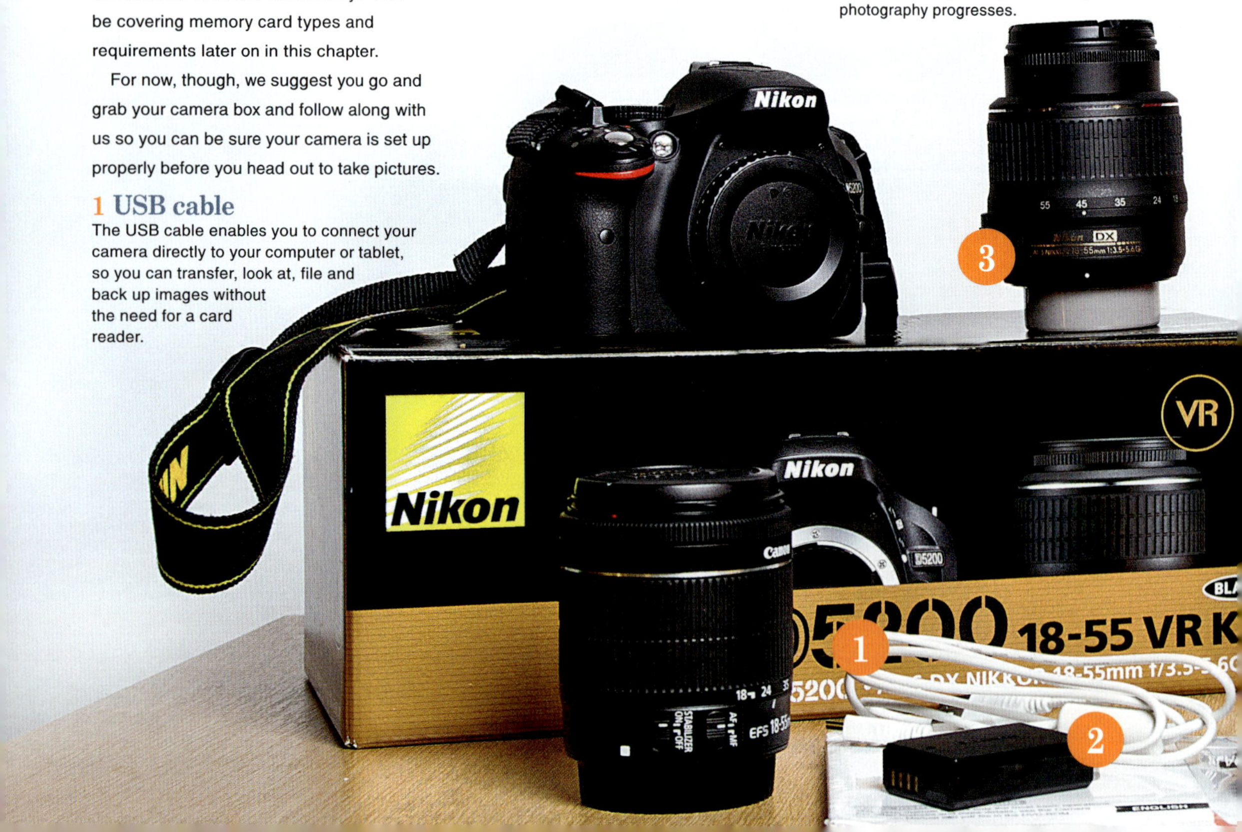

2 Battery

Your camera will be powered by a Lithium-ion rechargeable battery, which slots neatly into the battery compartment. Different camera models will need a different battery type. If you need to buy a spare, check the battery body for the model number.

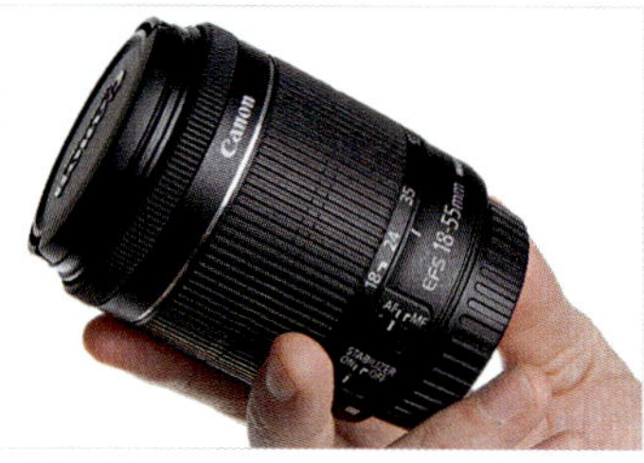

3 Lens

If you haven't already done so, you'll need to purchase a lens. Many entry-level DSLRs are sold with a kit lens included in the price, and this is a good way to get started. A standard zoom lens, such as an 18-55mm model, is perfect for beginners, and you can invest in more flexible (and expensive) lenses as your photography progresses.

Software and manual

Your camera's instruction manual might not seem the most interesting read, but it will prove very handy if you ever get stuck, so make sure it's always in your kit bag. If you're unsure where to find certain features or your camera is doing something you weren't expecting, the manual will most likely provide a solution. You can also download a digital version of your camera's manual from the manufacturer's website.

You'll notice, too, that your camera comes with free software that will help you to organise and edit your shots, and it's a good idea to install this right away. Simply insert the disc into your computer and follow the on-screen instructions. Keep the software running smoothly by downloading regular updates from your camera manufacturer's website.

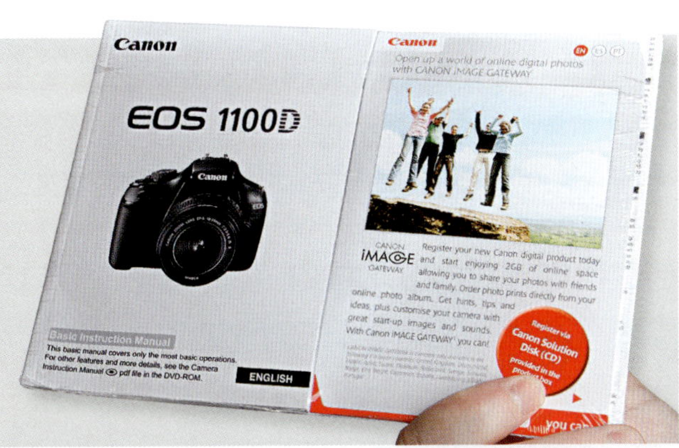

4 Battery charger

The battery charger will come with a cable that attaches to a power supply. A small LED light will let you know when the battery is fully charged. It's worth charging your battery each time you return from a shoot so that your camera is always powered up. It's worth carrying a charged spare too.

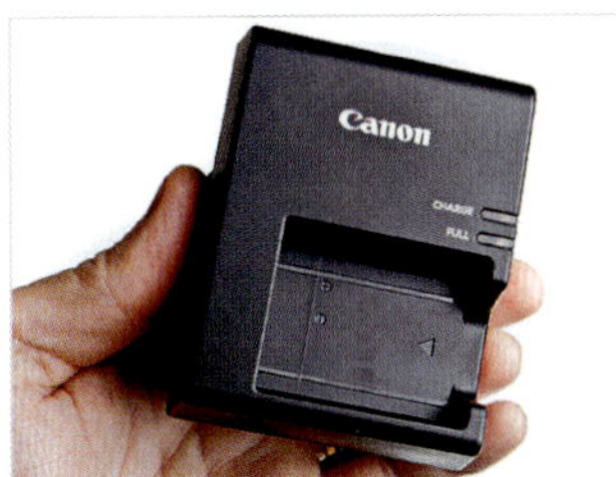

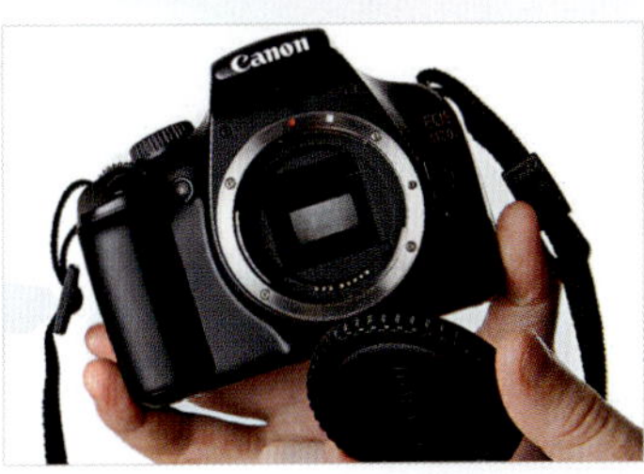

5 Main camera body

The first and most important thing is the body itself. Your camera will arrive with a protective body cap that should always be fitted when you don't have a lens attached. This prevents dust and dirt entering your camera and sitting on the sensitive image sensor inside. These 'sensor spots' will decrease the quality of your images.

6 Neck strap

To hang your camera securely around your neck, and ensure your camera is always there and ready to shoot, you need to attach the neck strap (see our step-by-step guide on the next page to find out how).

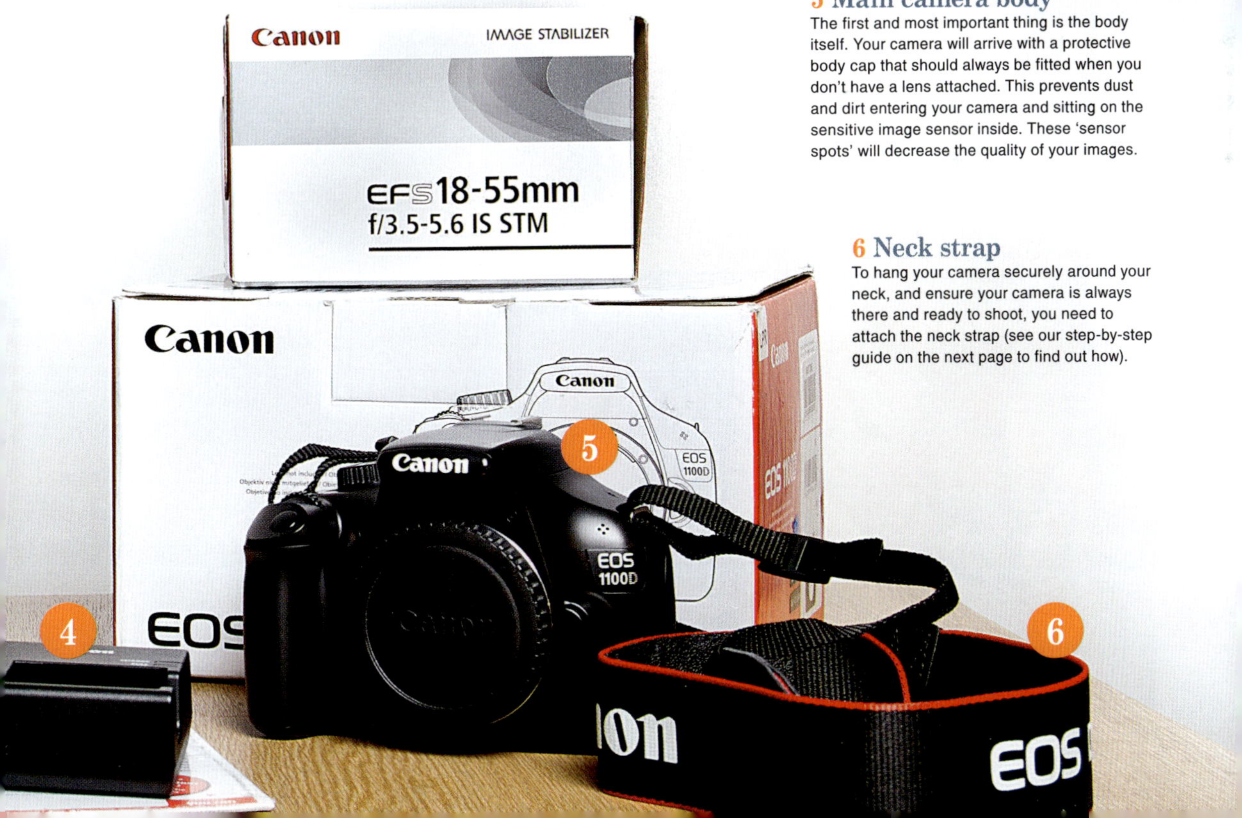

Fit the camera strap

Attach the neck strap supplied with your DSLR to the body of the camera securely with our step-by-step guide

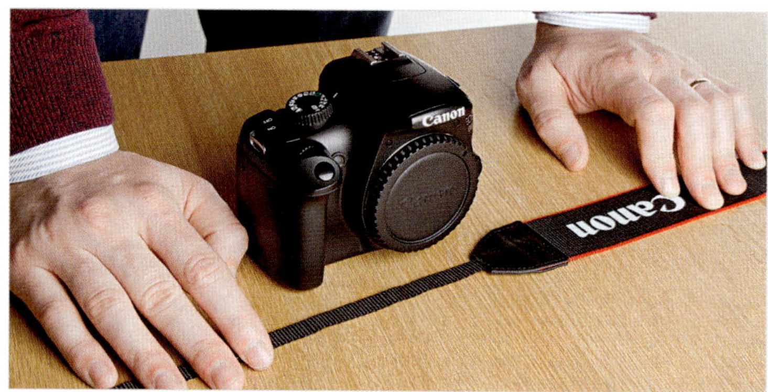

01 Lay out the strap

Take the strap out of the box and lay it down on a flat surface in front of the camera body. Make sure the writing on the strap is facing upwards and is the right way around.

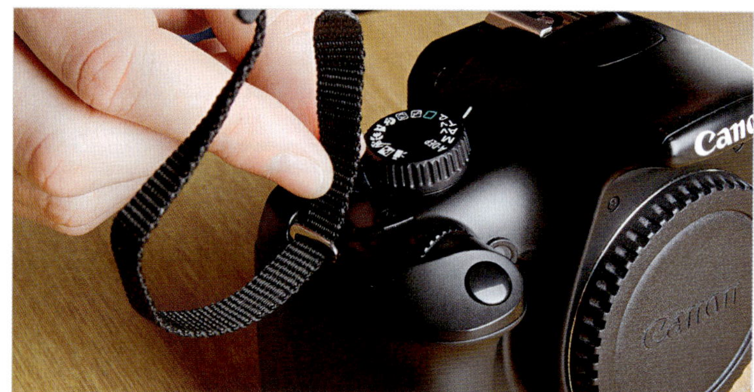

02 Place in the loop

Grab the small end of the strap and thread it underneath and through the bar on the side of the camera body. Pull about 10cms of the strap through.

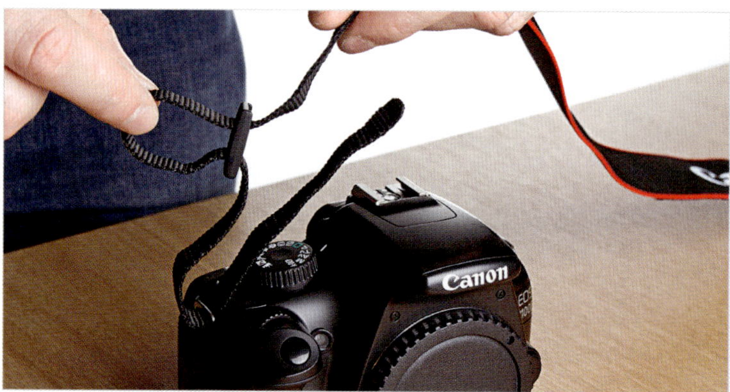

03 Adjust the buckle

Now grip the plastic buckle and pull out a few inches of the strap to make a loop. The next step can be a bit fiddly, so ensure you pull out enough slack now to make the next stage easier.

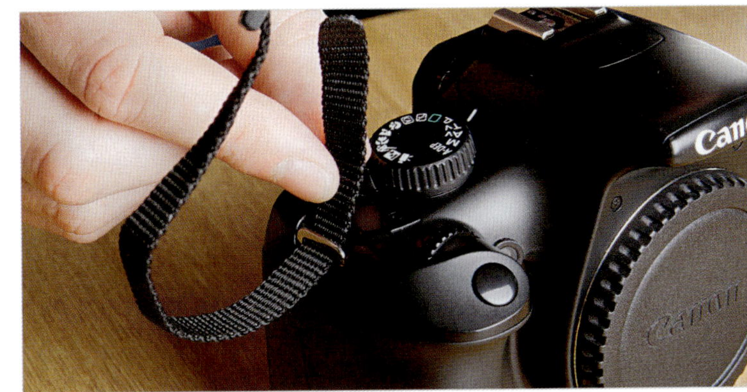

04 Pull it tight

Carefully thread the end of the strap up and down through the buckle so that it locks into place (see the image). You can now pull the strap tight.

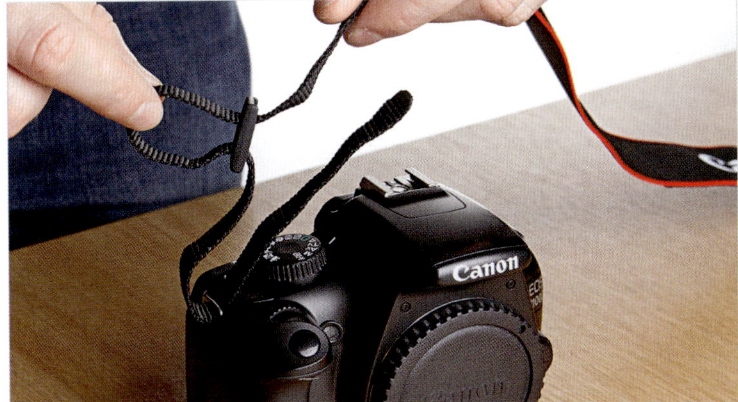

05 Repeat the process

Repeat this process on the other side and give each side a firm pull to test it's secure. You can now hang your camera around your neck knowing it's fully protected. Some photographers prefer to wrap the strap around their wrist and grip the camera in the hand.

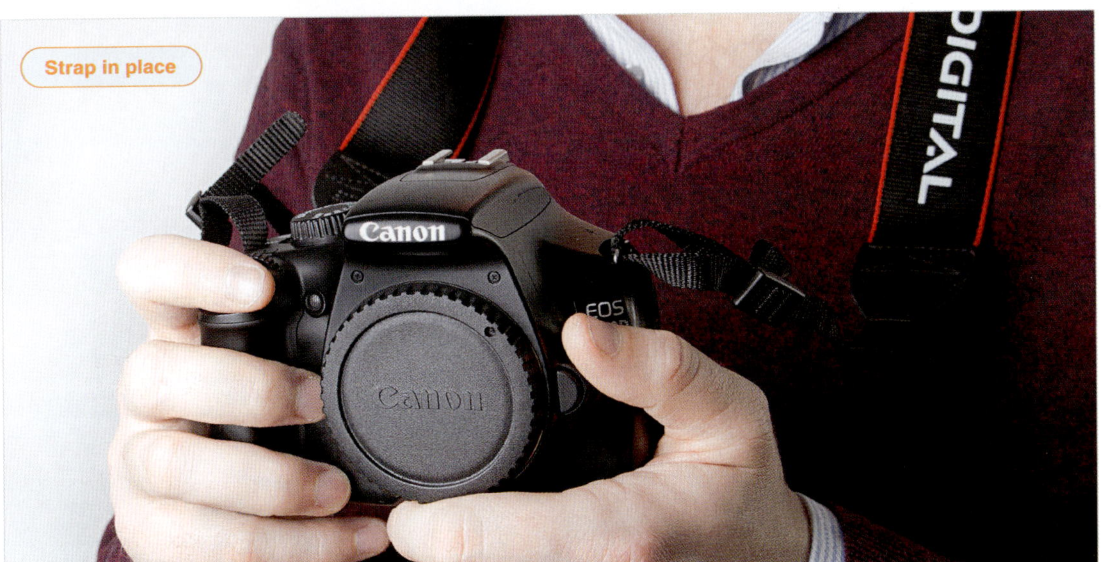

Power up!

Learn everything you need to know about your SLR's built-in battery and included charger pack

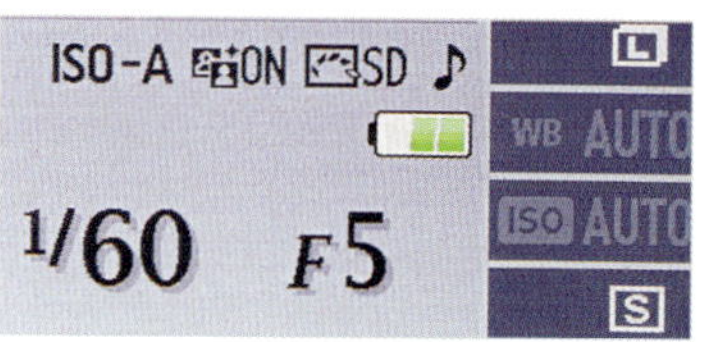

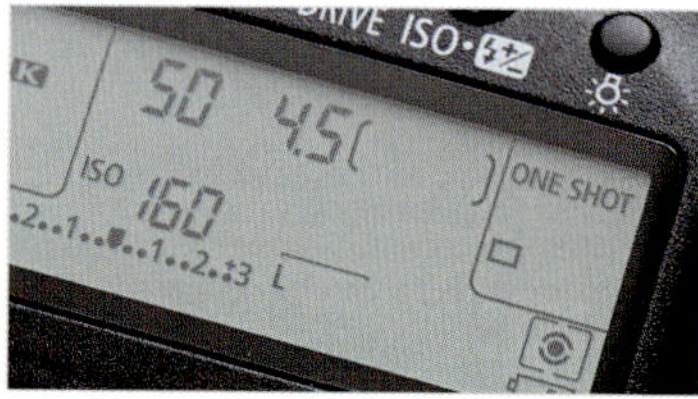

Before you even think about delving into your camera's endless menus and features, you'll need to charge the battery and insert it. Each camera is supplied with a battery and charger in the box, and your battery will be a Lithium-ion rechargeable type.

Some older DSLRs still take AA batteries, but the modern Lithium-ion batteries supplied with the vast majority of new cameras last far longer, and are easier to recharge. To charge the battery, simply insert it into the charger slot, plug in the charger, and switch on the power.

The battery is the lifeline to your DSLR. Unlike film cameras, where everything could be controlled manually, digital cameras need batteries to power everything from the on switch to the autofocus.

So, before you get started, here's how to get the best out of your rechargeable battery.

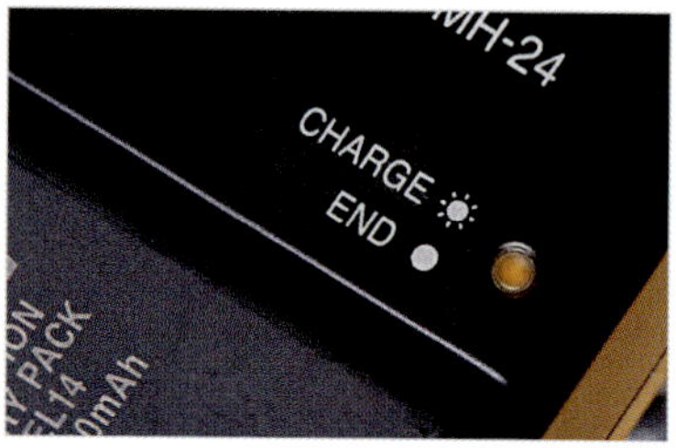

How do I know when the battery is fully charged?

Your charger will have an indicator light that changes colour or stops flashing when your battery is full.

How do I know how much charge is in my battery?

Your camera's LCD screen will feature a battery icon that lets you know at a glance how much juice is left. When power gets really low it will start flashing. Some DSLRs also include a top panel LCD with a small battery icon in the corner.

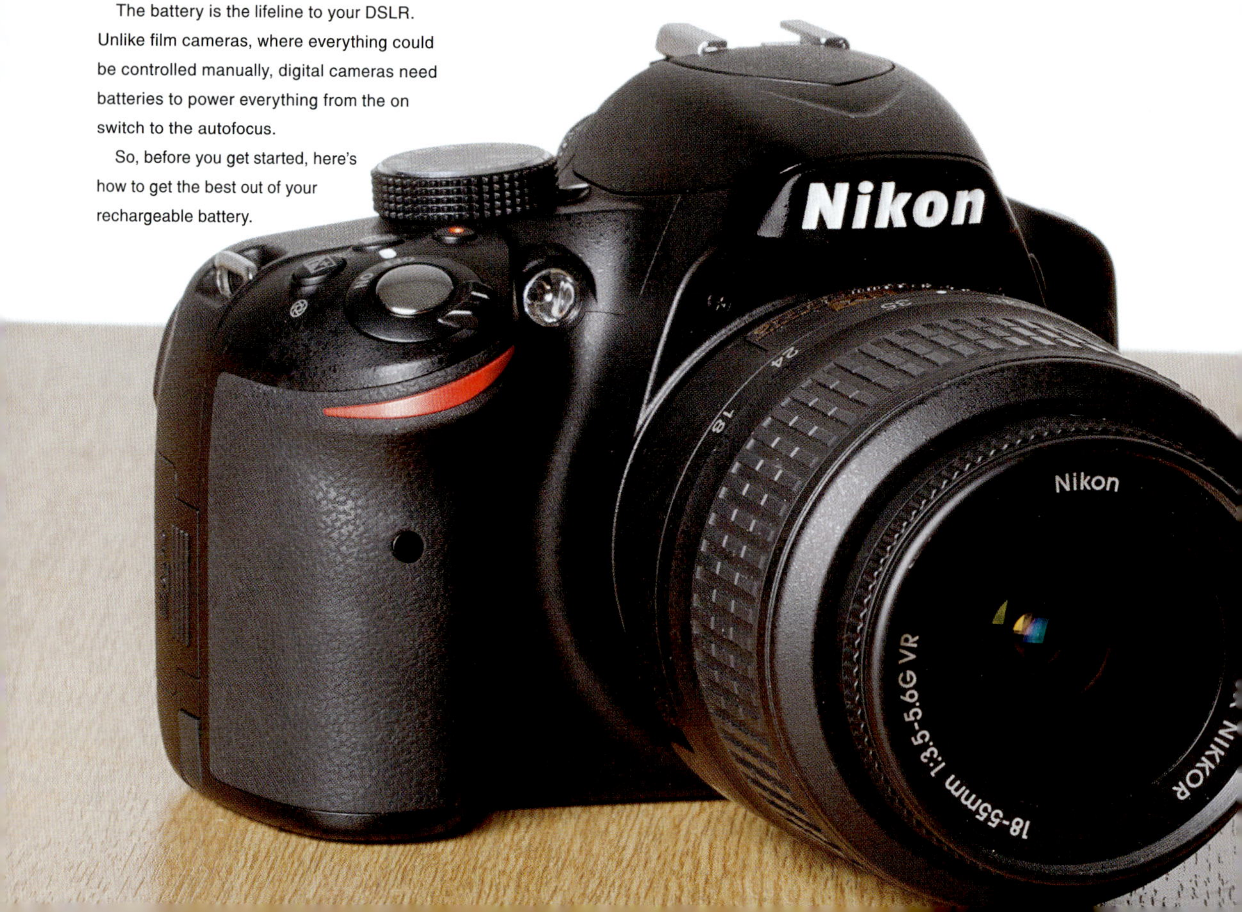

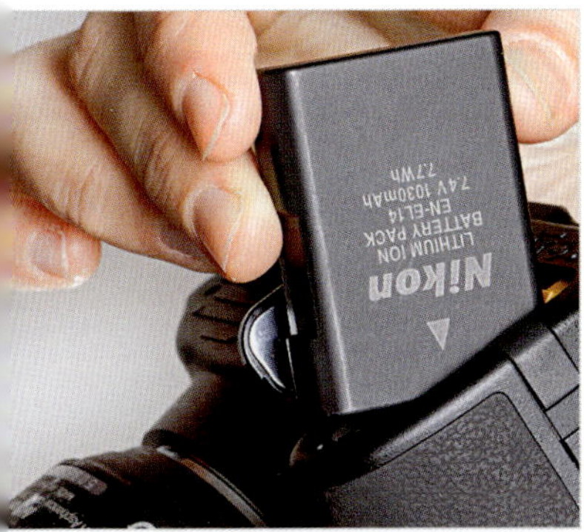

How do I insert the battery into my camera?

There's a battery slot on the bottom of your camera. To open it you need to flick the safety catch and lift the door. Carefully insert the battery with the connection points facing down and it will click into place. Your battery will only fit into your camera one way, so don't force it!

How do I know what type my battery is?

Check the battery body for details of the type. Every battery includes a code. A Canon battery, for example, will start with the letters LP, and Nikon batteries with the letters EN. The battery for the Canon EOS 1100D is called an LP-E10.

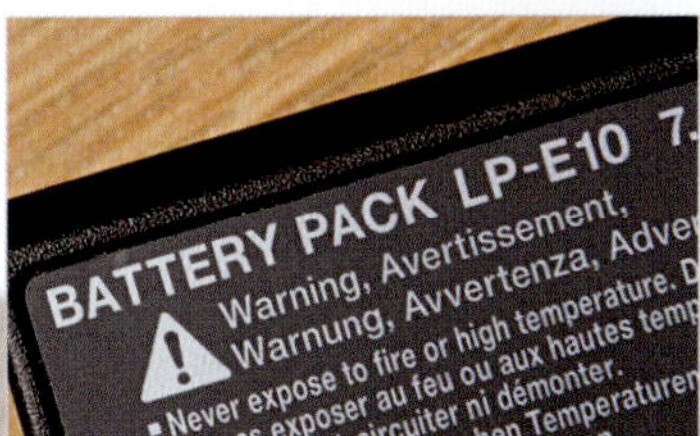

Five ways to make your battery last longer

1 Keep it warm

Your battery's power will drain much faster in the cold, so keep it (and any spares) as warm as possible. Carry multiple batteries when shooting in freezing temperatures, and keep your spares in a pocket next to your body.

2 Avoid draining features

There are some functions that will drain your battery faster than others. Live View, autofocus, pop-up flash and image review will all use up power. If you're running low on battery life, resist the temptation to check your images on screen. It's amazing how much longer you can keep your camera going with a strict 'no review' policy.

3 Get a spare

A spare battery is always a sound investment. That way you can be sure you'll never get caught without power as an amazing photo opportunity presents itself.

4 Store your camera and battery separately

If you don't use your camera for a long period of time — and we're talking a couple of months or more — it's best to take the battery out and store it separately. This will make your battery last longer.

5 Use a battery grip

A battery grip is essentially an additional battery compartment that doubles up as a secondary grip for the camera. This provides double the amount of battery life, and can make the handling of smaller cameras easier for those with large hands. With some cameras, the grip fits into the empty battery compartment when the battery door is removed; in other cases, it connects to multiple pins on the base of the camera. Many models also feature an additional shutter release button that's more conveniently placed for portrait-orientation shooting.

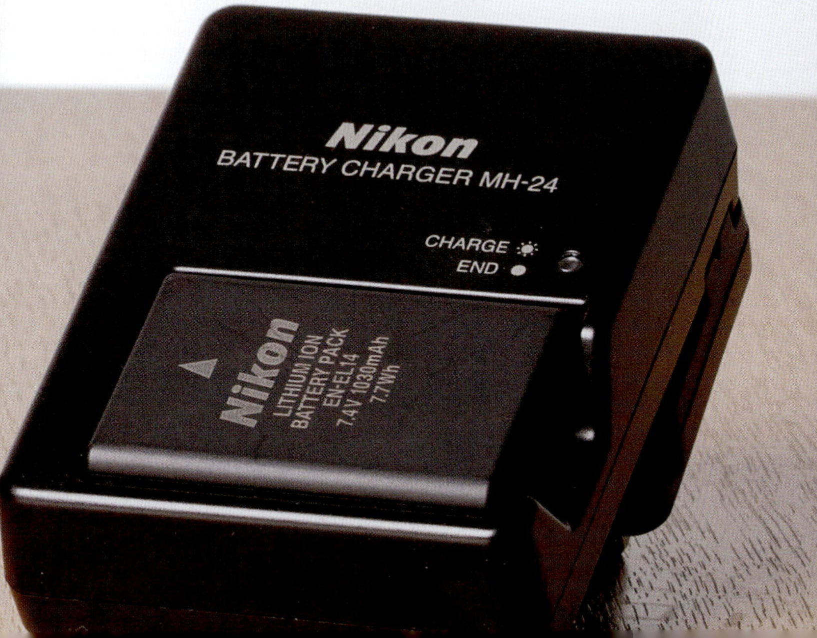

Memory cards for cameras explained

We take look at the various types of memory card so that you know which one is right for your camera model

One important item that won't be supplied with your DSLR is a memory card, so here we'll take a look at the basic types of memory cards, and what you need to know before you head out to buy one.

A memory card is a small device that's slotted into your camera and is used to record and store images as you shoot. With so many types of memory card on the market, getting the right one for your camera can be tricky, so to make it easier we've split the options into chunks. There are three things to consider — card type, size (or capacity) and speed.

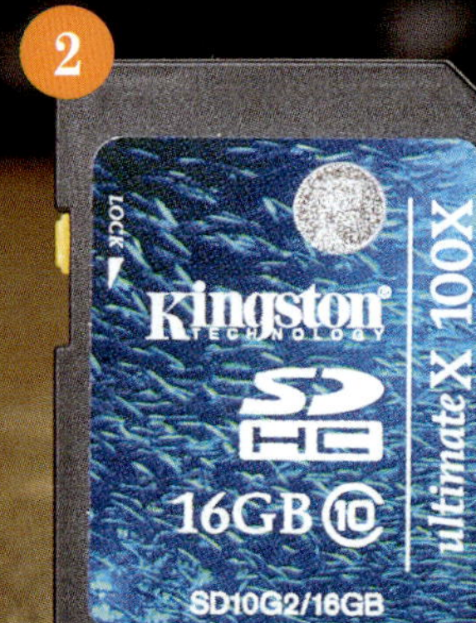

01 CompactFlash

The CompactFlash (or CF) card has the largest dimensions of all the cards available. You're most likely to need a CompactFlash card if you have an older or high-end DSLR.

02 SD, SDHC, SDXC

This is the most common type of memory card, used by most entry-level DSLRs. SD, SDHC and SDXC cards all look exactly the same, but there are differences, which come down to how many images they can hold (see the Capacity box overleaf). These cards are flat and rectangular, with one angled corner.

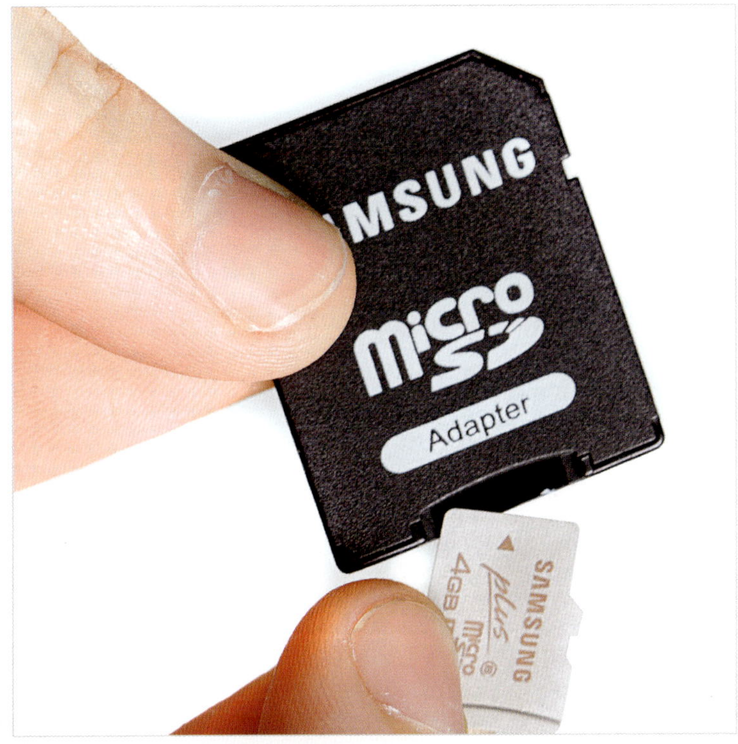

03 Micro SD and Adaptor

To use a Micro SD card in your DSLR, you'll need a Micro SD card adaptor. Insert the Micro SD card into the adaptor, then insert this into your camera. Mini SD cards are also available, but again you'll need the right type of SD adaptor to insert it into your camera.

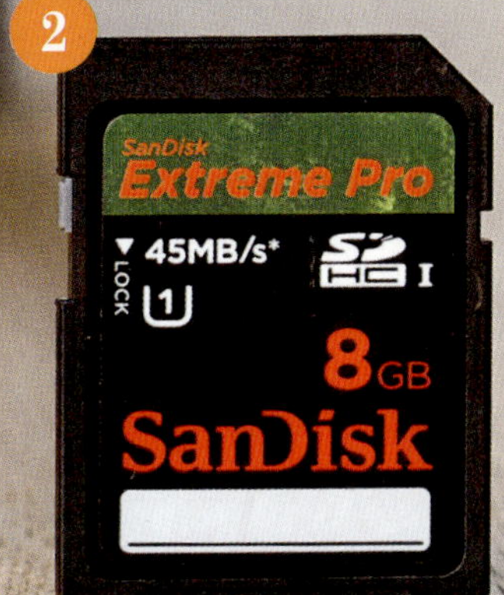

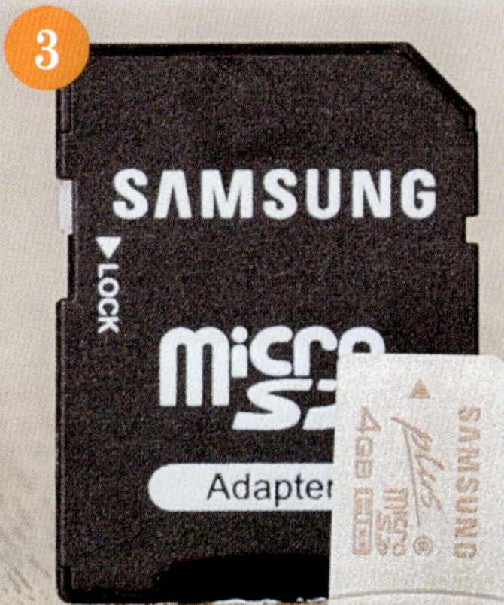

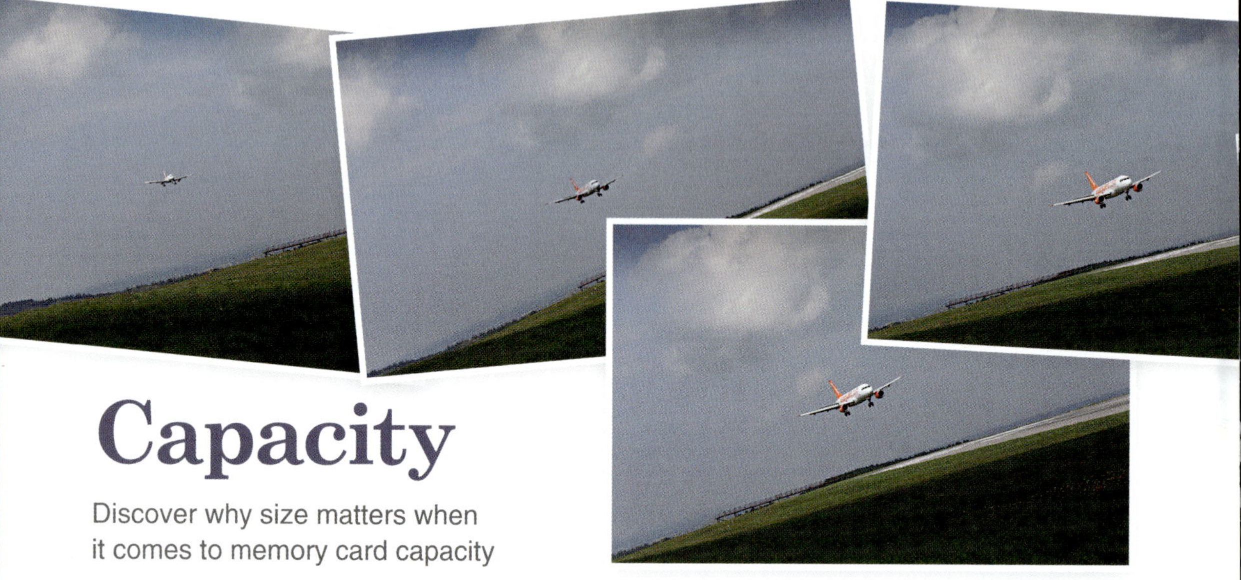

Capacity

Discover why size matters when
it comes to memory card capacity

Once you've worked out which type of memory card you need, you'll need to consider the capacity. The capacity of a memory card is measured in gigabytes (GB), and this capacity dictates how many images or video files it can hold. The size of each image captured by your camera depends on the resolution of its sensor, and the file type you choose to shoot. As mentioned, SD, SDHC and SDXC cards all look the same, but their capacities vary. The advantage of using an SDHC or SDXC card, for example, is that these can come in much larger sizes. An SDHC card can hold up to 32GB of images, and an SDXC can store as much as two terabytes (TB). This makes an SDXC card ideal if you plan to shoot lots of video footage.

CompactFlash cards also come in a range of sizes — up to 256GB, but the chances areyou won't need anything as large as this — it's better to carry several smaller cards, anyway, so that you have less to lose should a single, larger card fail or go missing. Cards with around 8GB or 16GB of space can be picked up for around £20-30.

Insert the card into your camera
Bought the right card? Here's how to use it…

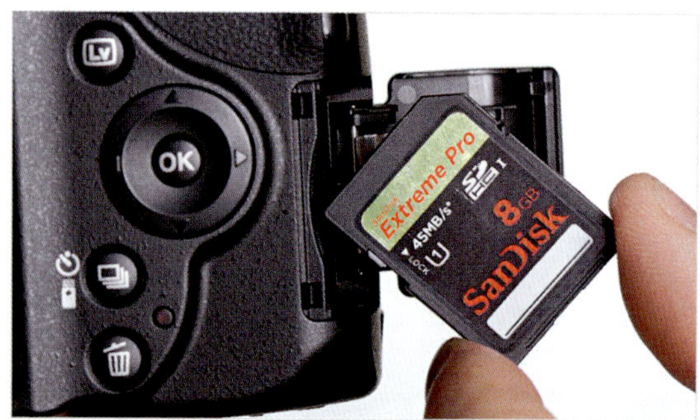

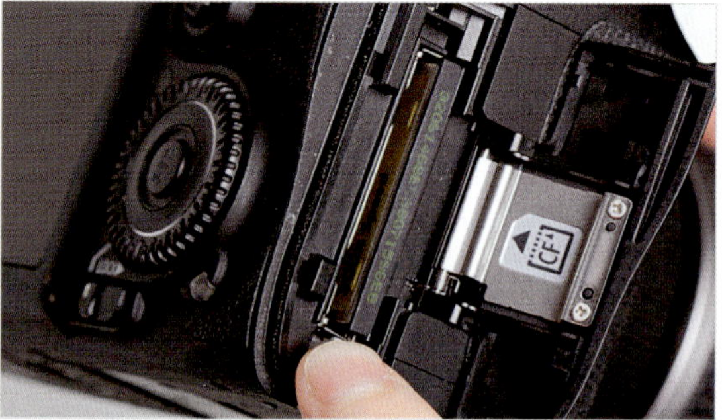

01 Find the card slot
Find your camera's memory card slot. Most have a mechanism that you push forward to make the slot spring open; some have a catch system, where you need to push a button or twist a catch to open it. Push the card into the slot. It will only click into place when inserted the right way, so be careful not to damage the camera's delicate pin connectors.

02 How to remove a card
There are different ways to eject a memory card, depending on the type you're using. For an SD-type card, for example, you simply push it inwards and allow it to spring out of the slot. To eject a CompactFlash card, press the small button next to the card slot, then ease it gently out. Either way, ensure you power down your camera before you attempt to remove the card.

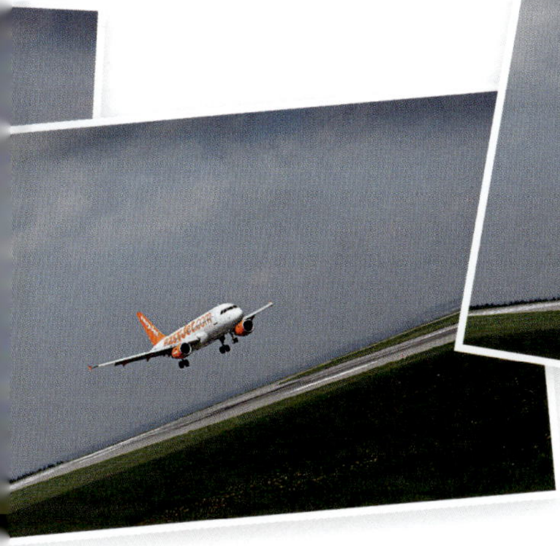

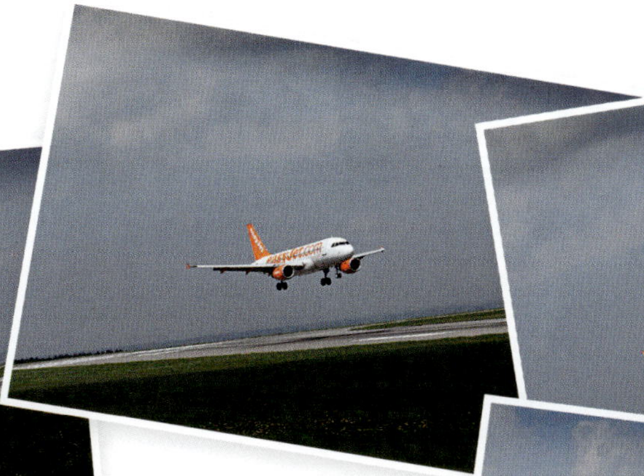

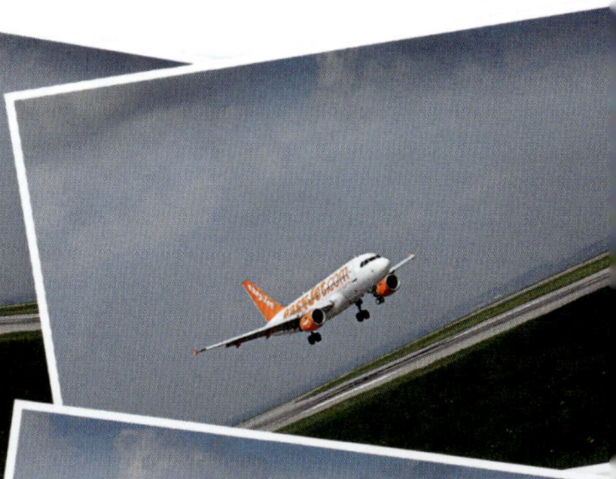

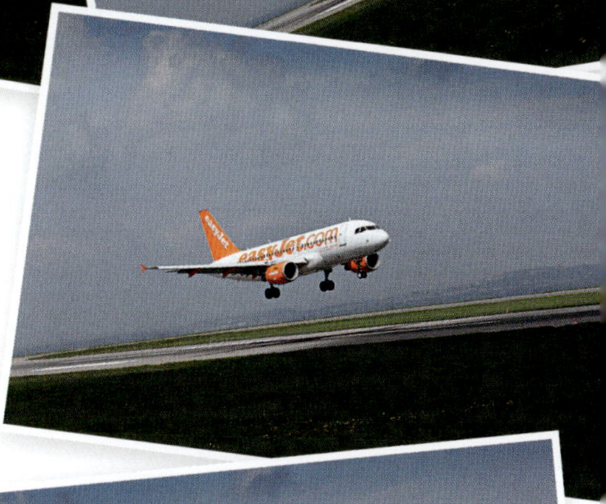

Recording in progress...

When recording a fast action sequence such as this, the speed of the memory card and your camera's processor plays a key part in how many images you can capture in quick succession before the camera's buffer freezes to catch up. A small red LED light will flash while your camera is processing images. Don't switch off your camera or eject the memory card during this time.

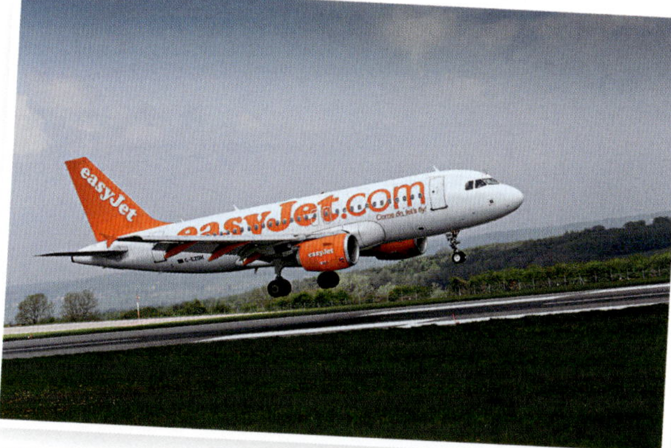

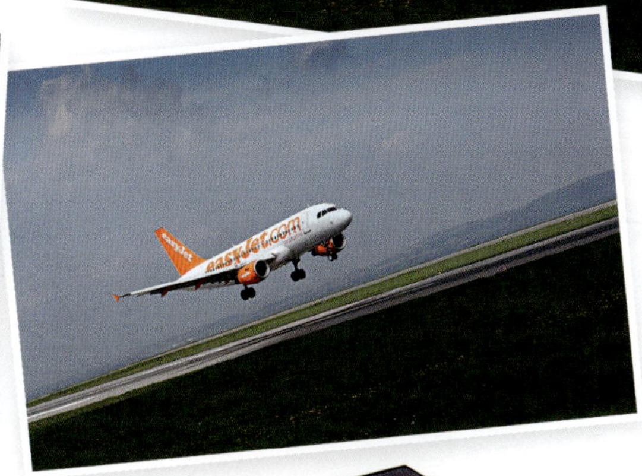

The need for speed
Buy a fast card for the ultimate performance

When buying memory cards, speed refers to how quickly the card and camera can process and record the images as you shoot. For example, if you're recording a high-speed action sequence or video, a fast card is a must.

The speed of your memory card is measured in megabytes (MB) per second, and refers to the speed at which the card can 'read' and 'write' your images, that is, how fast data can be retrieved and saved. The slowest cards start at about 5MB/s, and anything above 30MB/s is probably fast enough. Not all cards have their speed written on the body, and different manufacturers use different systems.

If you're just starting out, a fast card (which could cost considerably more than a standard card) isn't essential. However, they're certainly worth the investment should you choose to capture raw files for maximum quality, or take an interest in shooting action, fast-paced sports or videos.

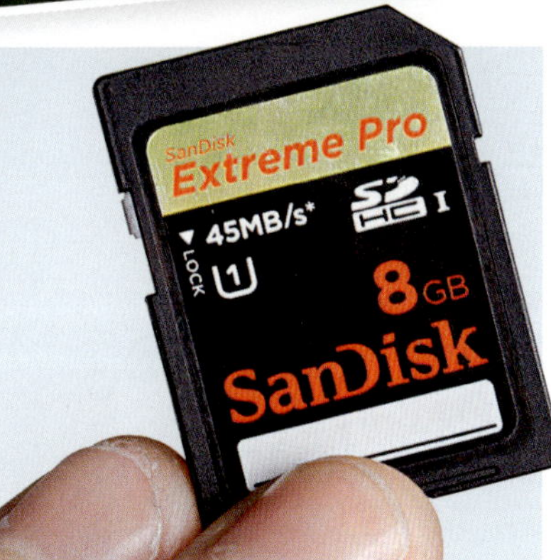

How to fit a lens to your camera

Our easy-to-follow guide reveals all you need to know about attaching lenses to an SLR and removing them

The beauty of owning a DSLR is that you can change the lens. This is one of the greatest advantages, and makes your camera much more versatile — you can shoot up close or further away from your subject, alter the angle of view, and get creative with blur. And when you come to upgrade your camera, you may still be able to carry on using the old lens.

Lenses come in a variety of shapes, sizes and prices. You'll most likely have a standard kit lens when starting out. They're often bundled with entry-level DSLRs, which offers a versatile focal range (18-55mm) for an affordable price. But once you become more experienced, you'll want to experiment with the differing focal lengths of other lenses. Although at first it may feel a bit unnatural to change your lens, once you've done it a few times it will become second nature to you.

Each lens make and manufacturer has an alternative mounting system. This means you can only fit a lens with a certain mount onto your make of camera body. If you have a Canon camera, a Nikon lens won't fit. However, there are a lot of third-party lenses on the market — just ensure they have the correct fitting for your camera before you buy.

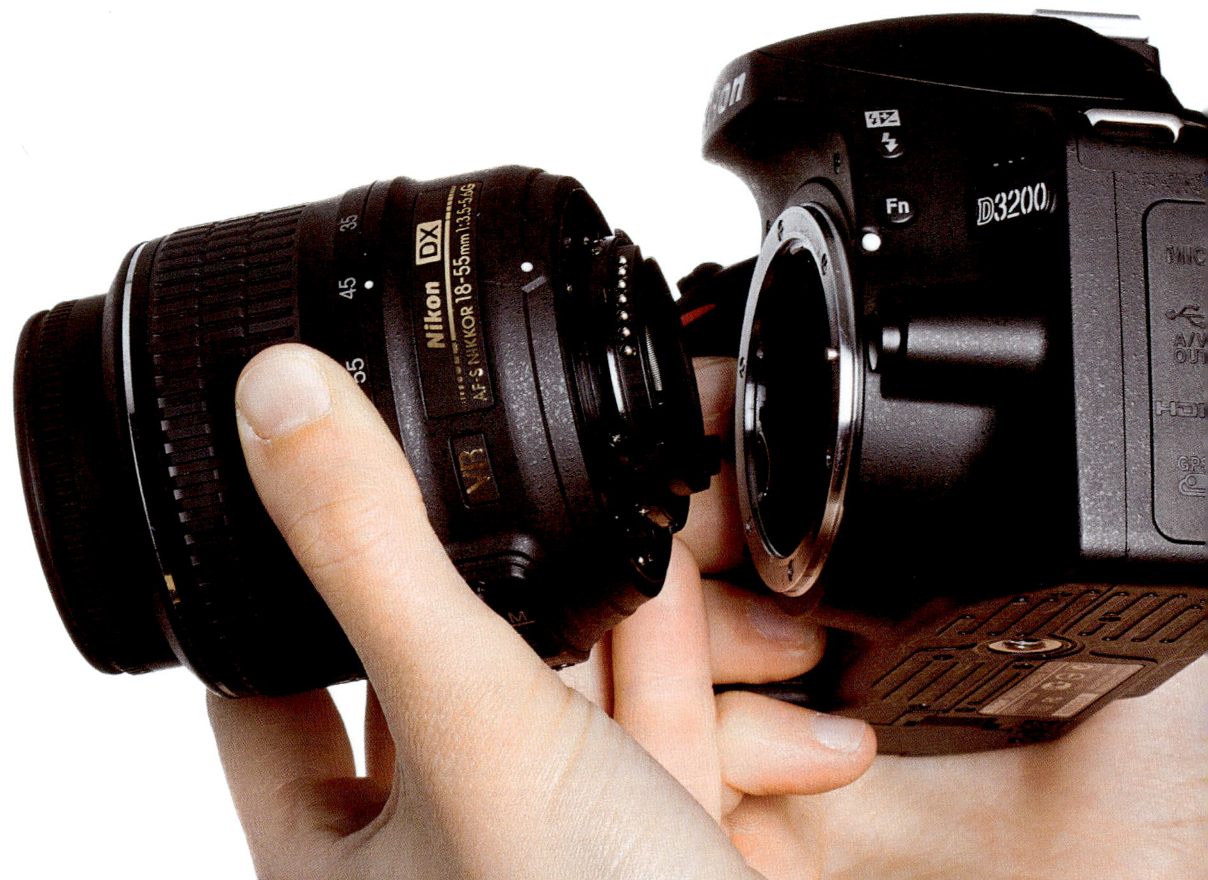

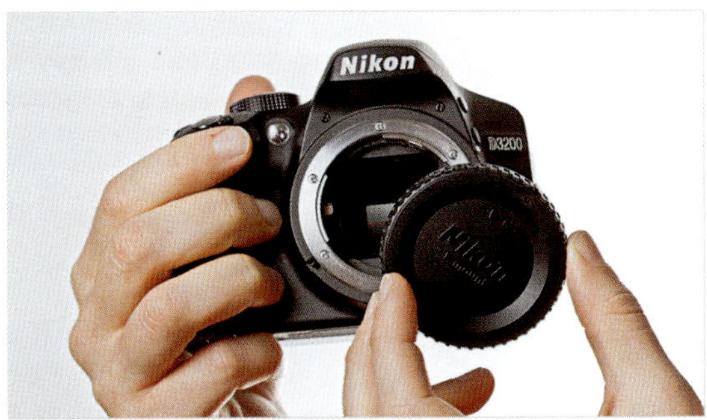

01 Remove the body cap

With your camera facing downwards (to prevent dust and dirt falling into the camera body and onto the sensor) twist the protective body cap to remove it from the camera. You should attach a lens or replace this cap quickly to minimise the chances of compromising the camera's vulnerable mirror and sensor.

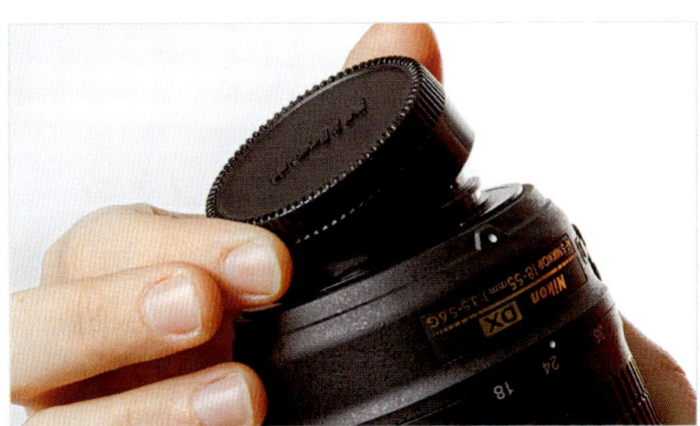

02 Remove the rear lens cap

Next, remove the protective cap from the back of the lens you want to attach. Again, try to keep this cap on at all other times — the connection points that control the lens's autofocus system must stay clean and protected when not in use. Place both of the removed caps back into their boxes for safe keeping.

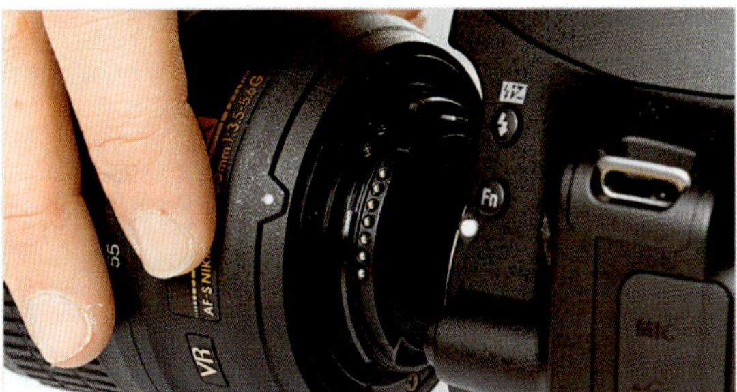

03 Line up the dots

You'll notice two dots — one on the lens and one on the body of your camera, which you'll need to line up. If you have a Canon camera with an APS-C sensor, you'll notice two dots — one red, one white. This is because Canon produces two types of lenses for different cameras. Line up white with white or red with red.

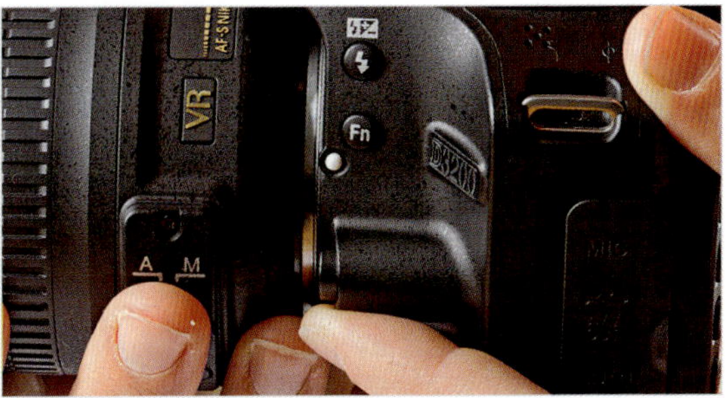

04 Twist it into place

Once the dots are lined up, push the lens gently into place, then twist to lock it into position (your lens will only twist in one direction, so don't force it). You'll feel the lens click into place. To remove the lens, press the lens-release button on the front of the camera and twist the lens in the opposite direction.

Top tips for lens care

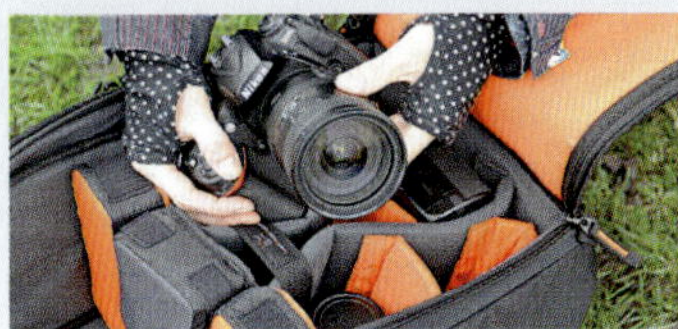

01 Change in a bag

When you remove the lens you expose your camera's sensor to the elements. If you're changing your lens outdoors, make sure you pick a sheltered spot to do it in. You can use the inside of your camera bag to stop the wind blowing in unwanted dust and dirt. If in doubt, however, leave the lens on!

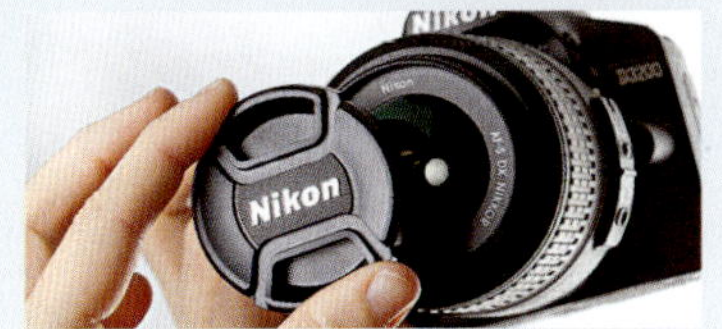

02 Protect your glass

Make sure you keep the glass end of your lens protected by attaching a lens cap when your camera's not in use. If you're worried about scratching the glass, you could invest in a UV filter, which you can leave attached in most situations. The filter size you need will be written on your lens.

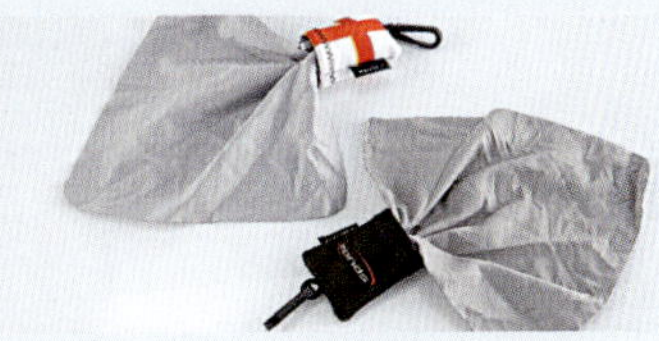

03 Use a lens cloth

A lens cloth is a must-have accessory. Before you shoot, make sure you check for rain spots or marks on your lens that could ruin the final result. If you wipe your lens with a sleeve or tissue, before long fine scratches will ruin the quality of your shots. A dedicated lens cloth will leave the front element spotless.

A guided tour of your digital SLR camera

Get to know your camera better by understanding where all the main controls and dials are positioned

On these pages, we'll give you a guided tour of an entry-level DSLR, the kind of camera you're likely to own if you're new to SLR photography. Of course, every make and model of camera will vary slightly in layout, but the basic features are all the same (your camera's instruction manual will tell you exactly what's where). Once you know where all the main features and controls are, it's much easier to get your head around how everything works. Read on to find out more…

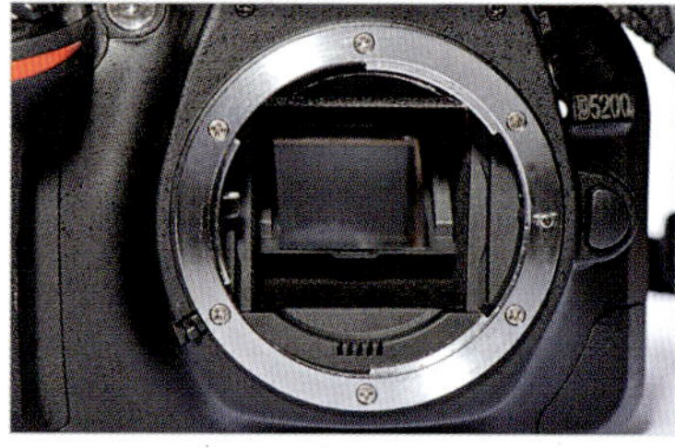

3 Mirror and sensor

When you take a photograph, the mirror inside your camera lifts out of the way to reveal the sensor behind it. This is where the image is recorded.

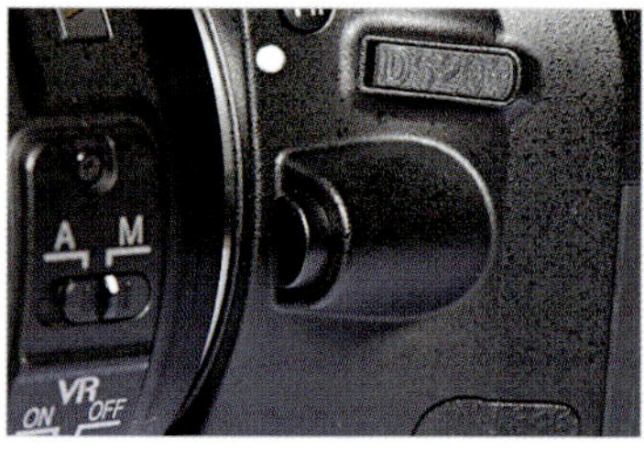

4 Lens release

To change your lens you need to press the lens-release button and then gently twist the lens itself to remove it. Depending on the make of your camera, you may need to twist it in a clockwise direction; others should be twisted anti-clockwise.

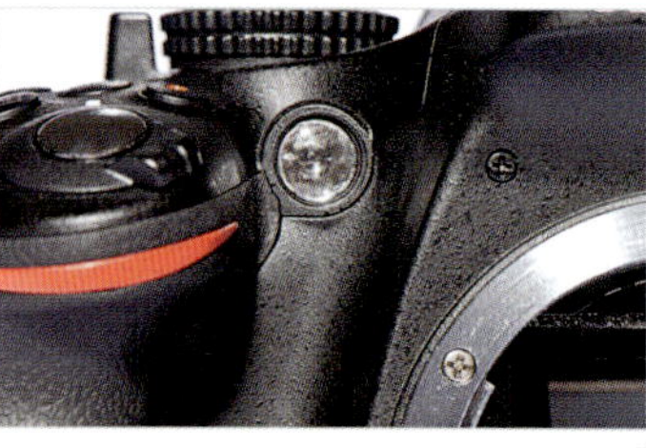

1 Focusing light

When light levels are low, some cameras use an assist beam or IR light to help achieve accurate focus.

2 Lens

The lens is the camera's eye. This is where the image is projected through to the sensor. Make sure you keep the glass element clean (using a soft lens cloth) and avoid accidental damage by replacing the lens cap when the camera's not in use.

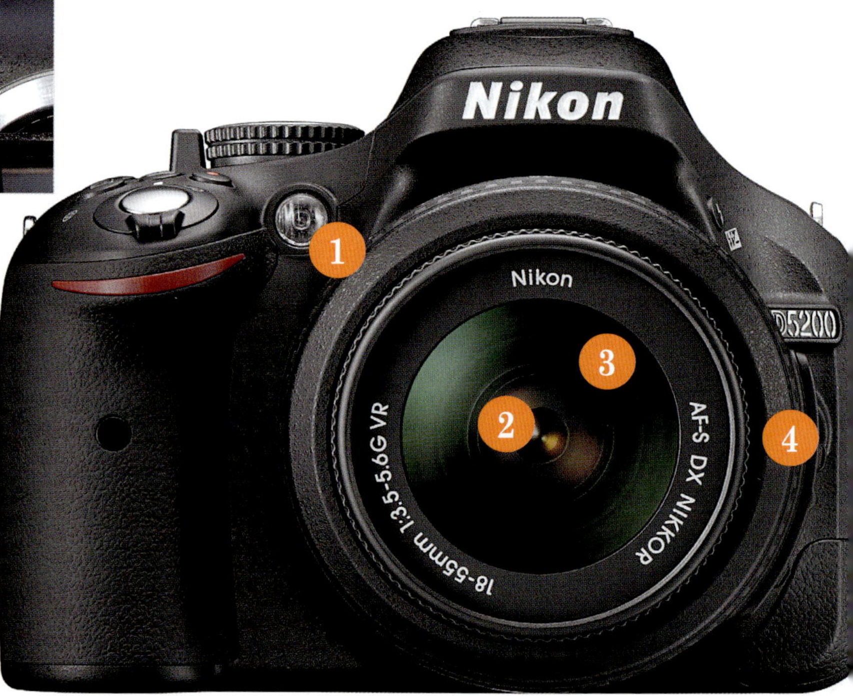

The top panel

You'll find the mode dial, shutter release, pop-up flash and hotshoe mount on top of your camera

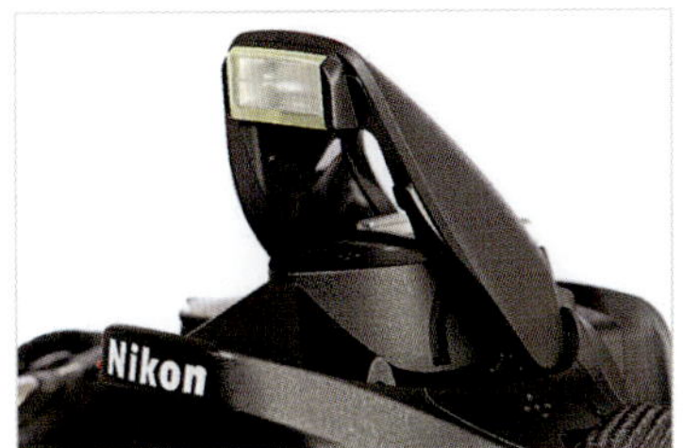

1 Pop-up flash

Most entry-level DSLRs have a pop-up flash unit built in. To activate it, press the small button next to the flash symbol. In your camera's Auto mode, the flash will engage automatically when light levels drop.

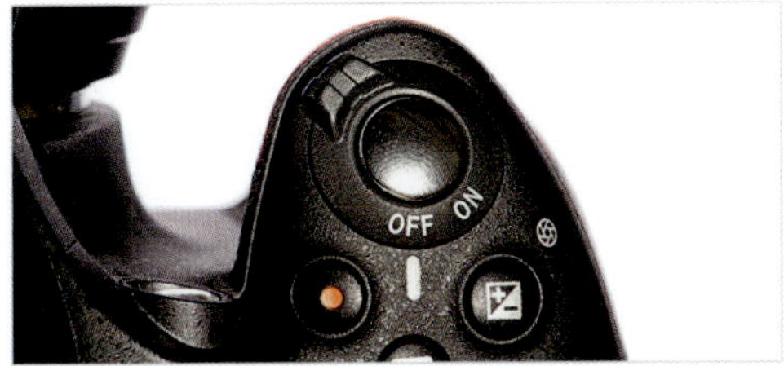

2 Shutter release

Here you'll find the on/off switch and the shutter-release button. To focus, half press the shutter release; press it fully to take the picture.

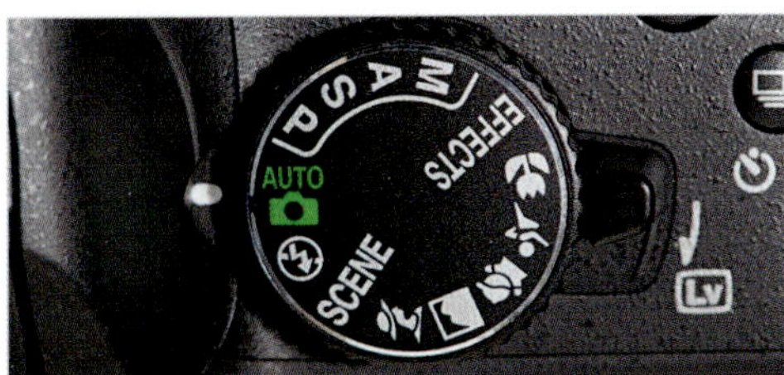

3 Mode dial

The mode dial features your camera's shooting modes, including Full Auto, various Scene modes, semi-automatic and fully manual options. Simply turn the dial to select. Some mode dials have a lock button in the centre that you must press before you turn the dial.

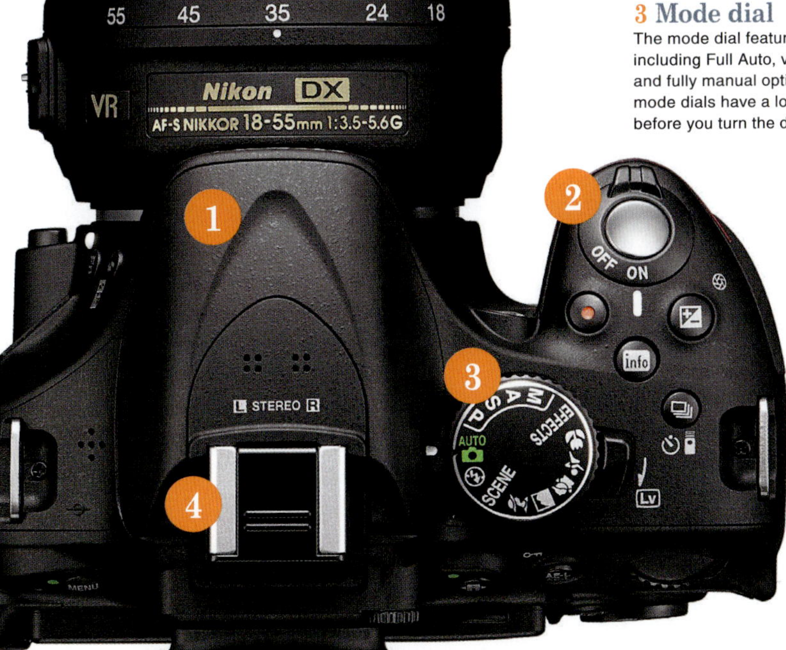

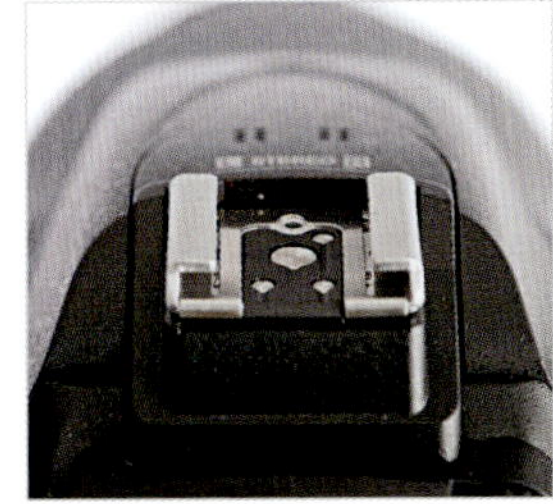

4 Hotshoe

The hotshoe enables you to attach an external device to your camera, such as a flashgun or a remote shutter release trigger.

Around the back

The back of the camera contains a range of viewing options and quick-access buttons and dials

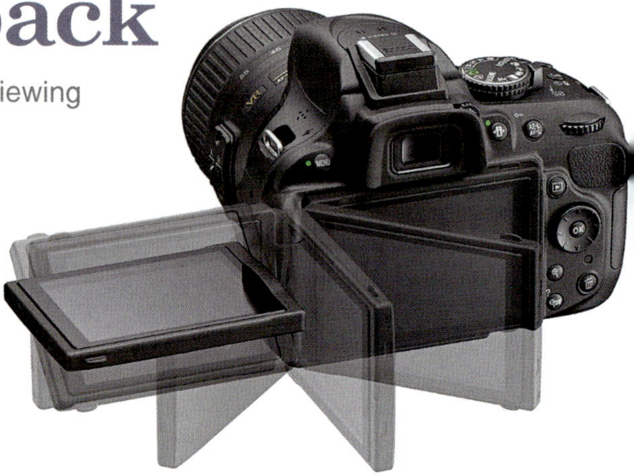

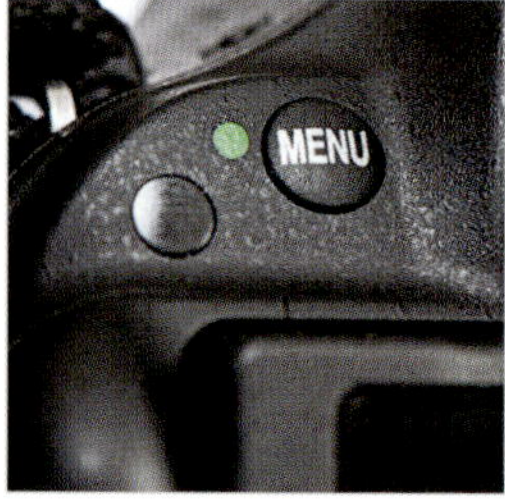

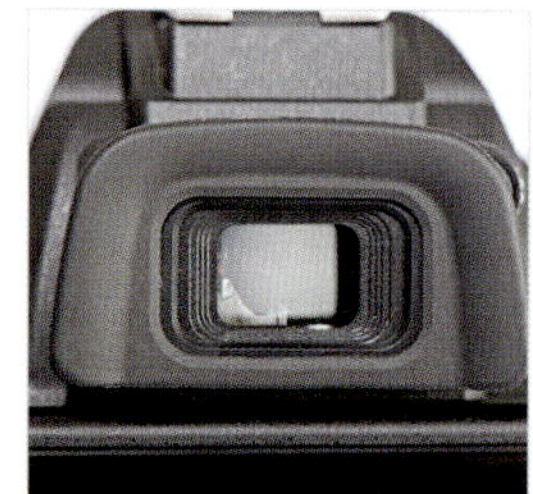

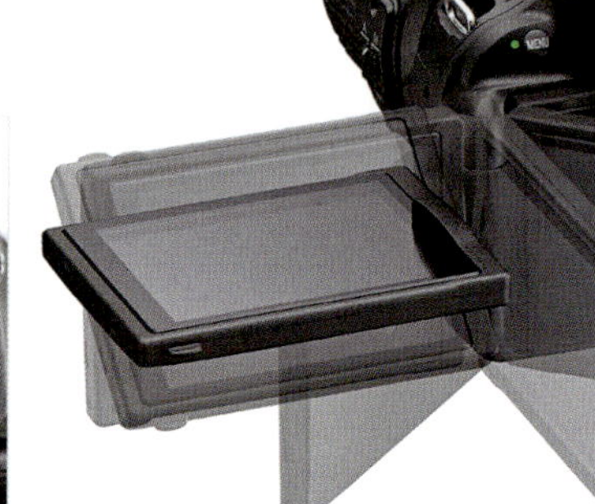

1 Menu button

Use the Menu button to access your camera's numerous features and functions.

2 Viewfinder

When you take a photograph, the mirror inside your camera lifts from the camera's internal mirror up to the viewfinder, where you can carefully frame your shot. This is what sets DSLRs apart from other cameras, because you see exactly what the lens sees.

3 LCD screen

The LCD screen has multiple uses, with some offering touchscreen control of menu settings and some simply enabling you to look at images and menu options or get a real-time view in Live View as you shoot. Some models come with a vari-angled screen, so you can twist it away from the camera body if you want to shoot from unusual angles.

4 Back panel control

On the right-hand side you'll find a control panel of sorts. Use this to navigate around your camera's main menu.

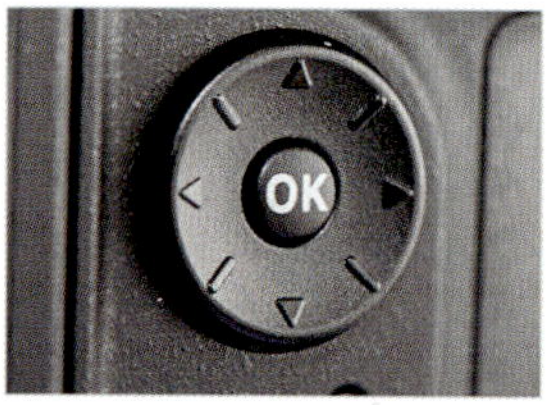

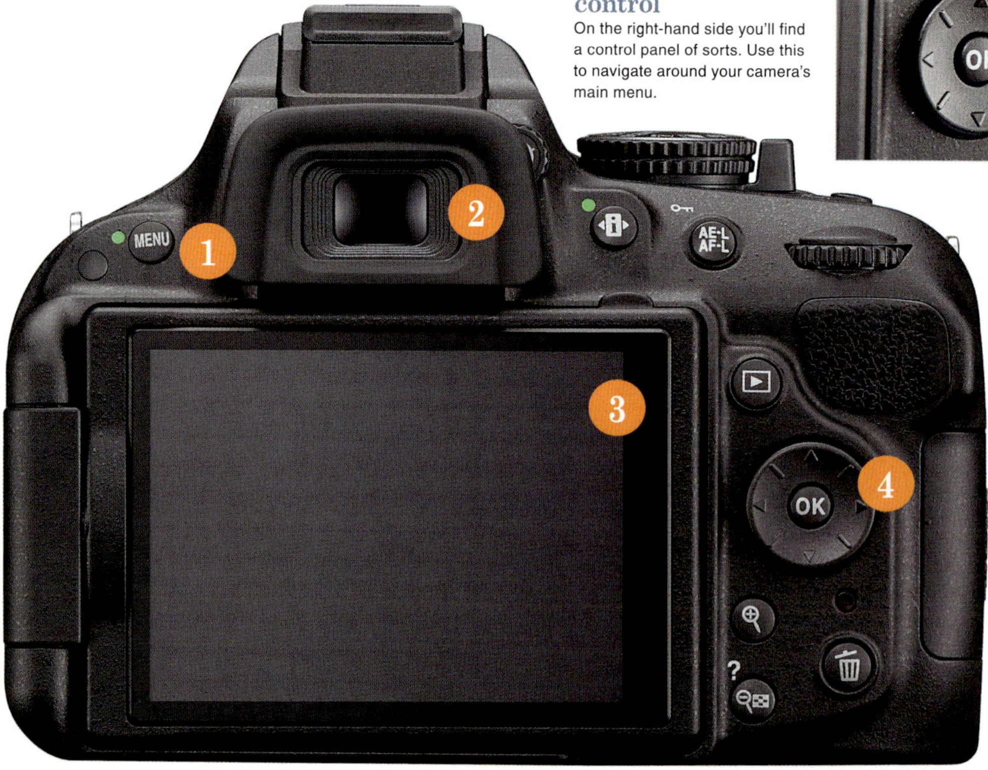

Side view

Head to the side panel of the camera to access your camera's connection points

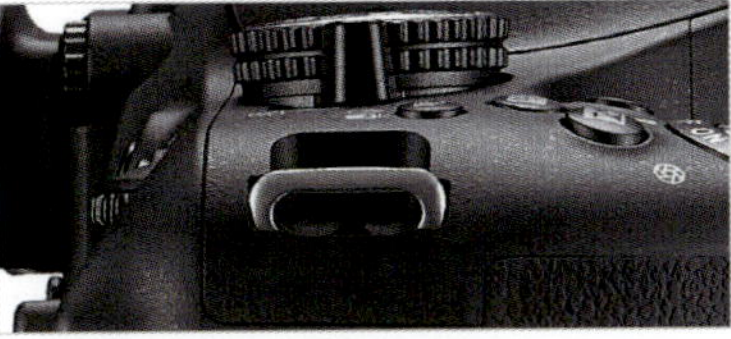

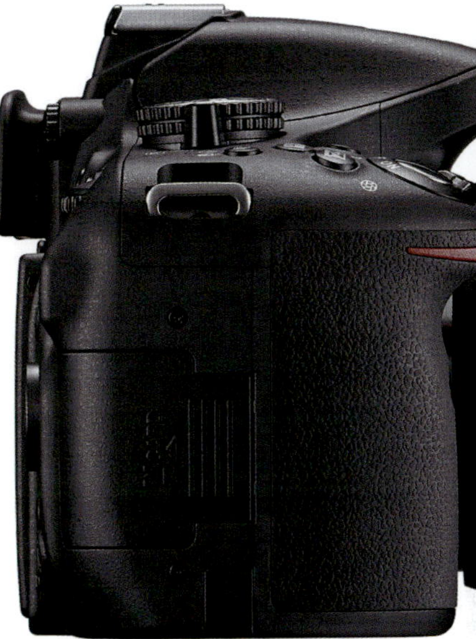

1 Neck strap attachment points

Thread your neck strap through these small attachment points so you can hang your DSLR securely around your neck.

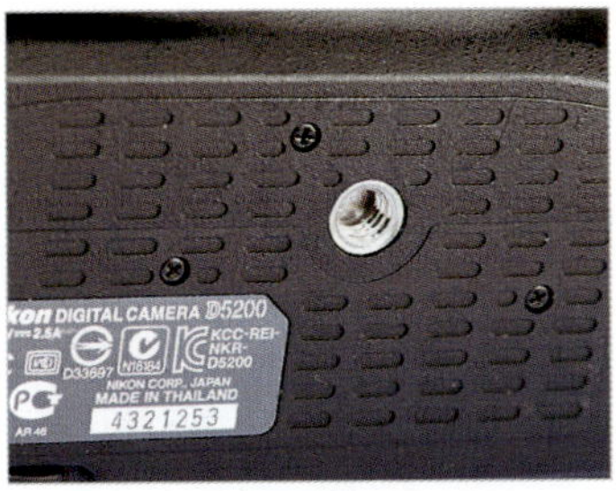

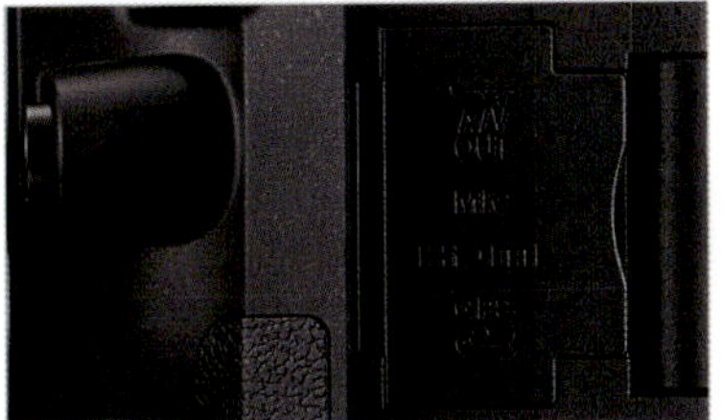

3 Tripod mount

Flip the camera over and you'll see a small threaded hole. This enables you to attach your camera to a tripod. You'll also find the battery compartment and memory card slot here (although some are positioned on the camera's side panel).

4 Memory card flap

Insert the correct memory card and your images will be recorded and saved as you shoot them.

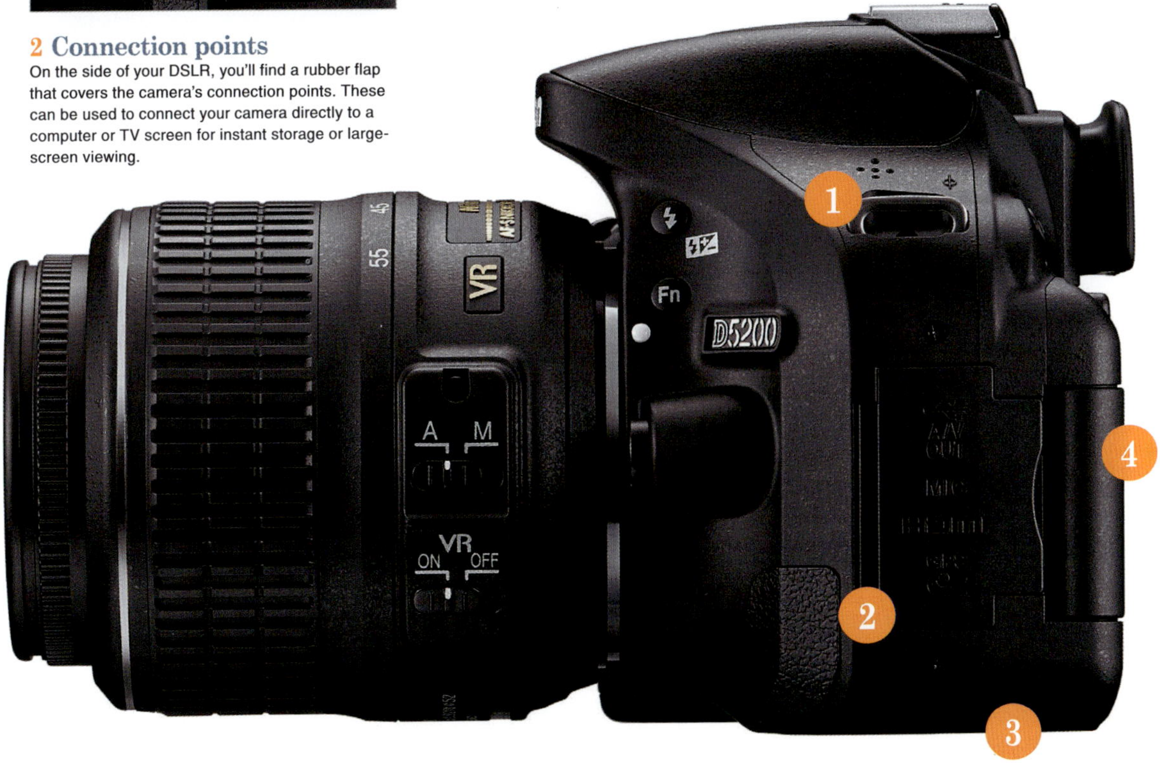

2 Connection points

On the side of your DSLR, you'll find a rubber flap that covers the camera's connection points. These can be used to connect your camera directly to a computer or TV screen for instant storage or large-screen viewing.

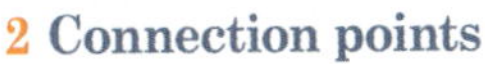

A guide to your SLR's menu system

Discover how to access and customise the most important camera settings in your camera's menu system

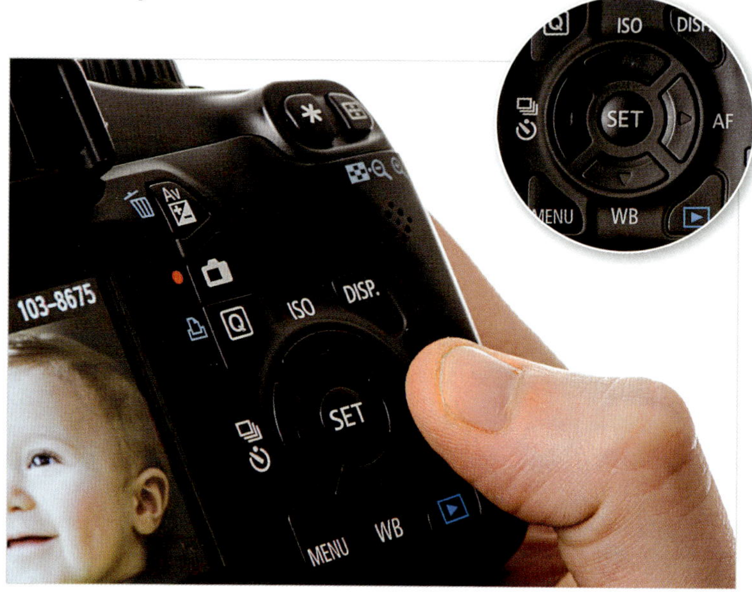

01 Menu button and controls

On the back panel of your DSLR, you should see a Menu button. Press it and you'll gain access to all your camera's most useful features and functions. Your camera will also have a Display or Info button, and Set or OK controls that enable you to find and select features. The control buttons on the back panel (usually on the right-hand side in easy reach of your right thumb) can be used to navigate through the menu system, making it quick and easy to make changes to settings on the fly.

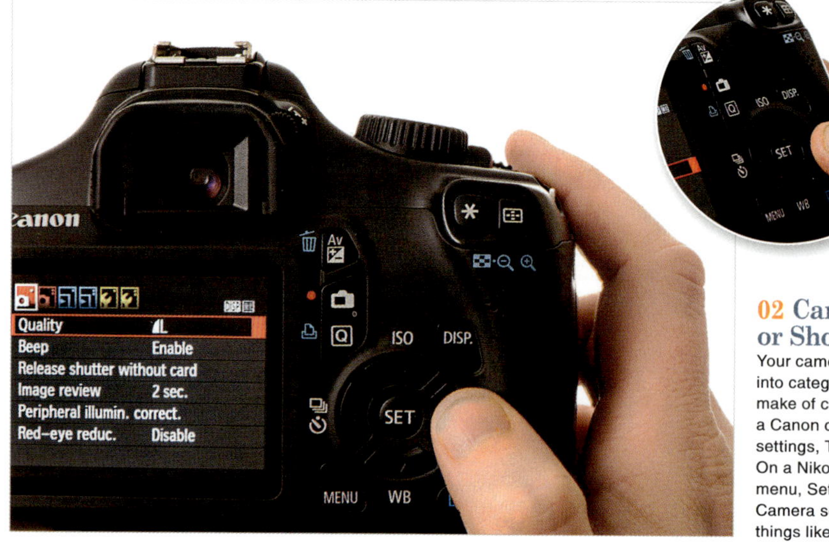

02 Camera settings or Shooting menu

Your camera's menu system will be divided into categories — how many depends on the make of camera you own, but the basics on a Canon camera, for example, cover Camera settings, Tool settings and Playback features. On a Nikon these are labelled as Shooting menu, Setup menu and Playback menu. The Camera settings menu can be used to alter things like Image Quality and flash control.

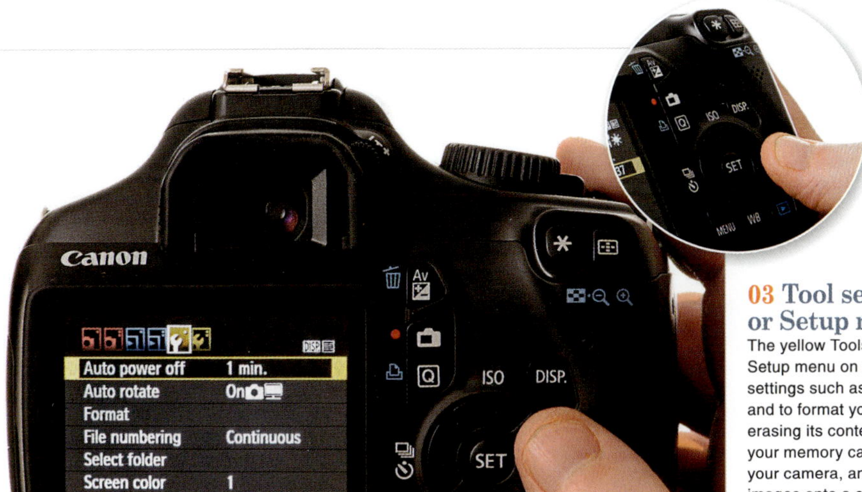

03 Tool settings or Setup menu

The yellow Tools menu on a Canon, or the Setup menu on a Nikon, enables you to change settings such as the LCD screen's brightness, and to format your memory card (permanently erasing its contents). It's a good idea to format your memory card as soon as you put it into your camera, and each time you transfer your images onto a computer for safekeeping.

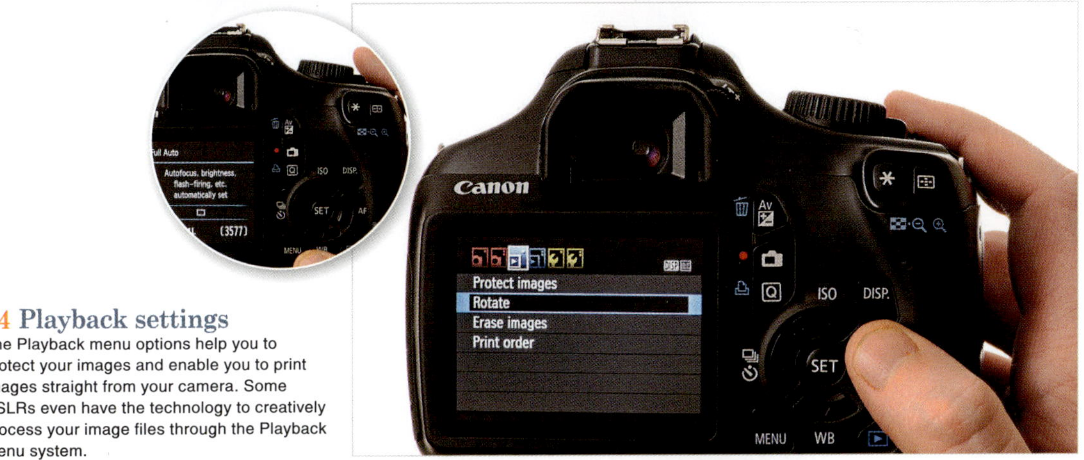

04 Playback settings

The Playback menu options help you to protect your images and enable you to print images straight from your camera. Some DSLRs even have the technology to creatively process your image files through the Playback menu system.

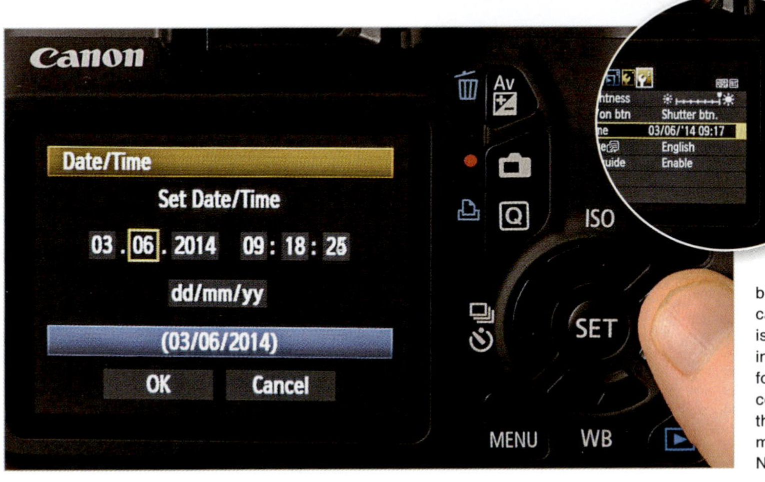

05 Time and date

Setting the time and date should be one of the first things you do with your camera when you take it out of the box. This is because time and date information is saved into every image file, making it easy to search for images by date later. You can also apply copyright information to images here. To set the date and time, navigate to the yellow Tools menu on a Canon or the Setup menu on a Nikon, then follow the on-screen instructions.

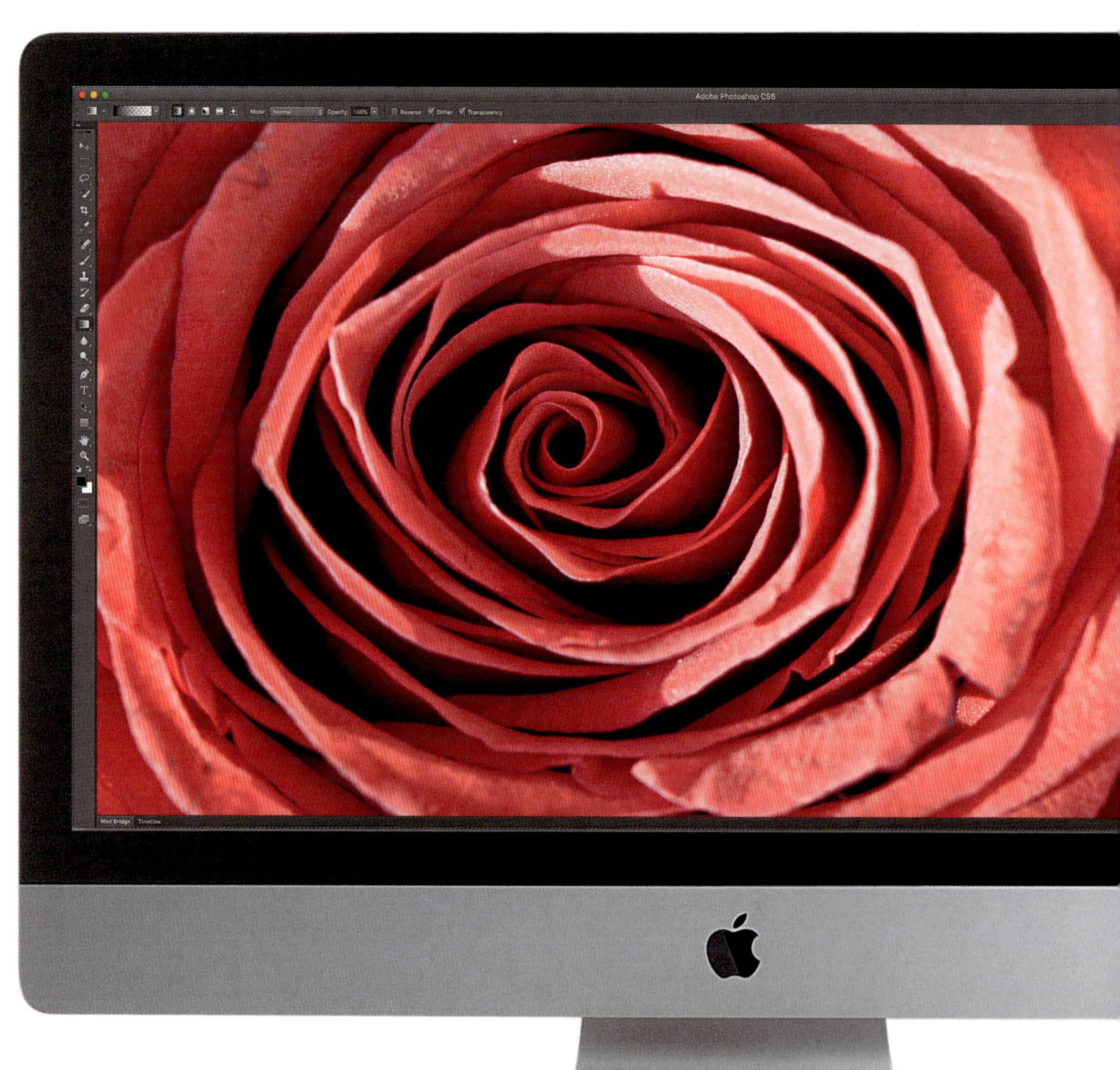

Getting Started

Learn how to hold your camera correctly, choose the right lens, get images onto your computer and more…

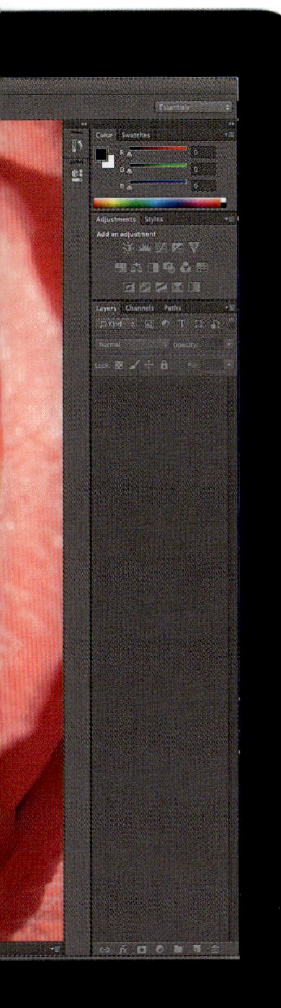

Learn how to hold your SLR correctly

Get it right from the start and produce better quality results by minimising the risk of accidental camera shake

You may think there's only one way to do it, but in fact the way you hold your camera can have an instant effect on the quality of the pictures you take, and it's amazing how many photographers get it wrong. Here, we'll show you how to manoeuvre the camera, control the buttons comfortably, and minimise the chance of introducing the kind of camera shake that will make it impossible to keep your shots sharp. By placing your feet, arms, legs and hands in the right position, you'll be amazed at how much easier it is to get great results — plus you'll really look the part!

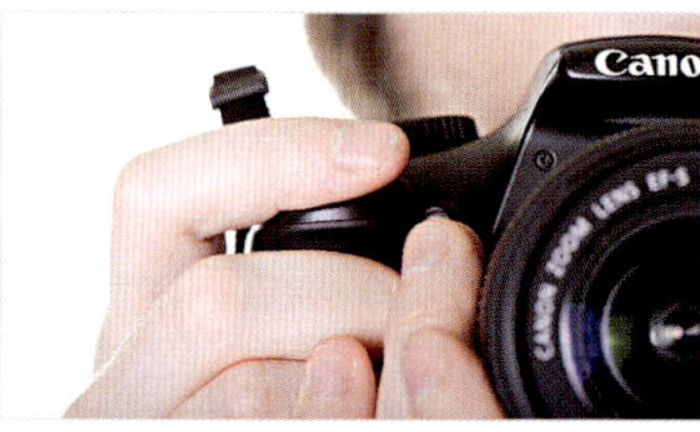

2 Shooting finger

Your DSLR is designed to be held in your right hand, so your right index finger should be used to press the shutter-release button on the camera's top plate.

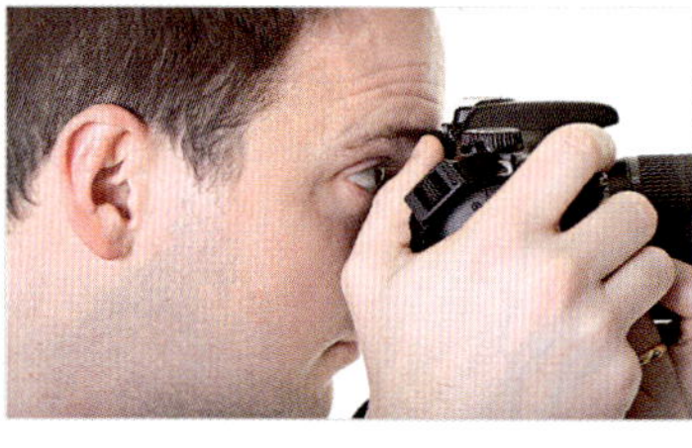

3 Eyebrow

When the camera is lifted up to the eye, press the viewfinder against the eyebrow, as shown. This makes another point of contact on your body, and instantly increases stability.

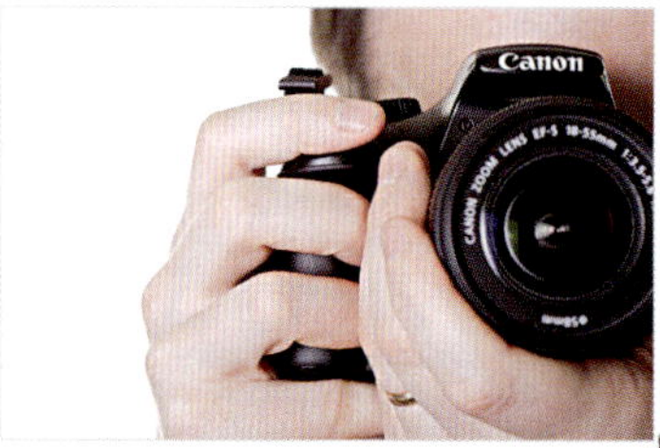

1 Right hand

The right hand should be used to grip the camera body. Curl your fingers around the camera's rubber (or textured) grip panel, and leave your thumb free to operate the rear controls.

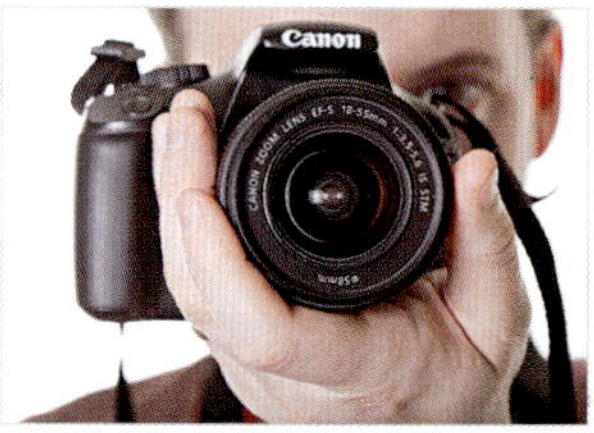

4 Left hand

Put your left hand out. Place the lens in this hand, cupping the lens gently from below, and the weight of the lens and camera immediately becomes supported. You can twist the barrel of the lens with this hand to zoom or focus manually.

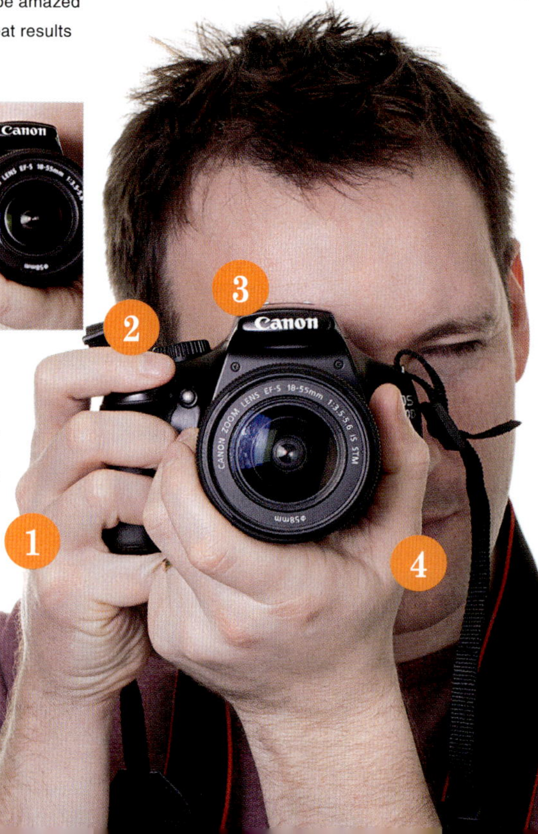

Shoot in the portrait position

The principles for shooting in the portrait orientation remain the same as for landscape shooting

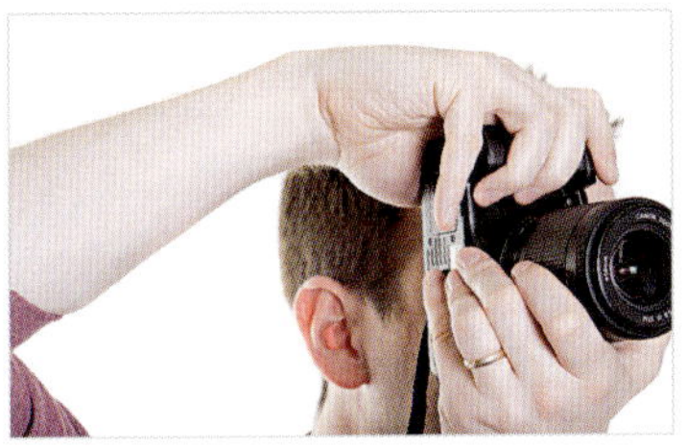

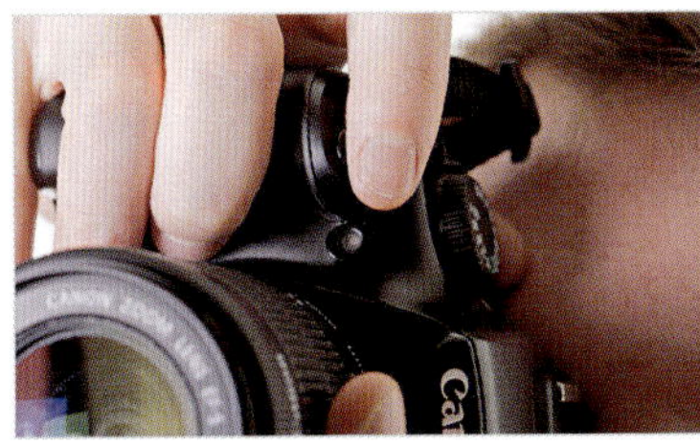

2 Shutter at the top

Turn the camera anti-clockwise so that the shutter button is at the top, as shown. Don't turn it the other way around, because you'll get your arms in a twist and find it much harder to shoot.

1 Right arm

When you move the camera around, your right arm will immediately come up. Keep it as steady as possible.

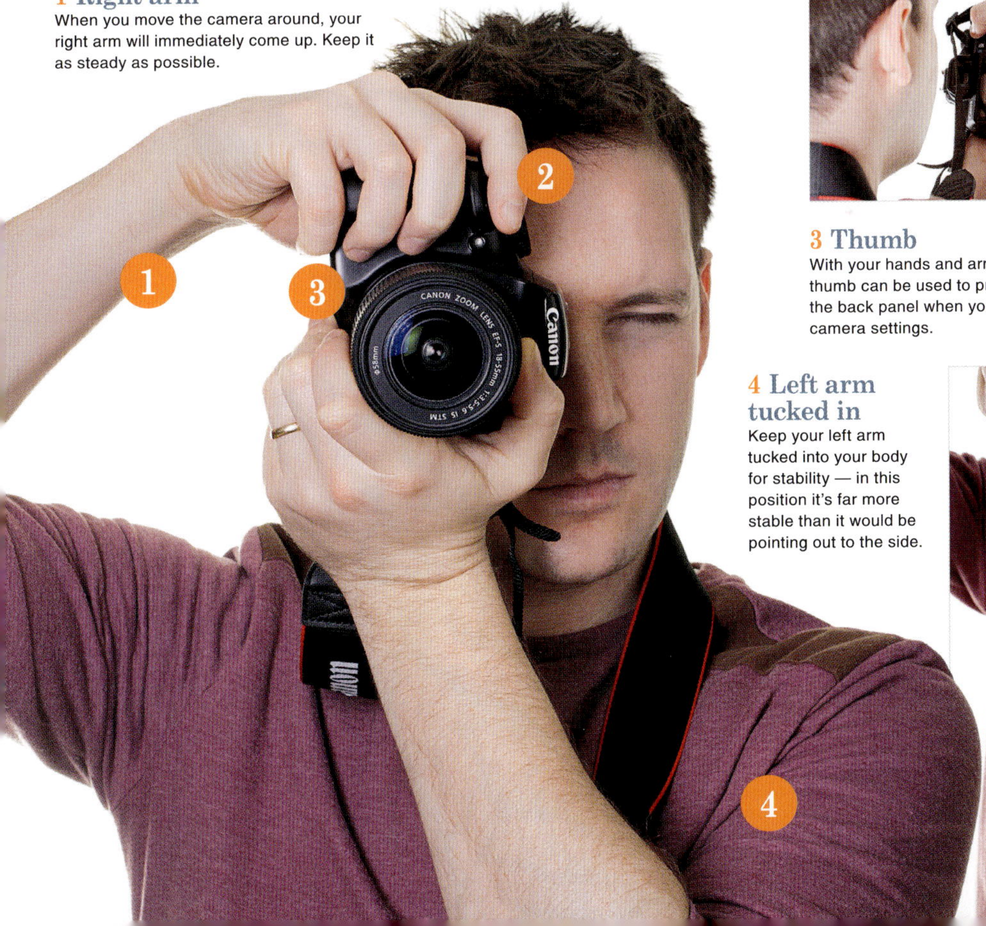

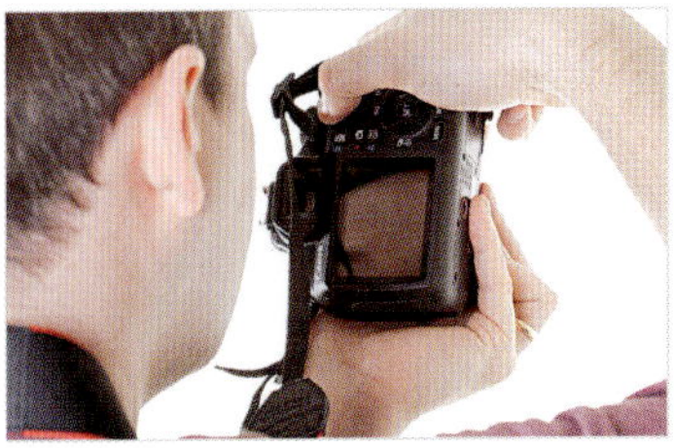

3 Thumb

With your hands and arms in this position your thumb can be used to press the buttons on the back panel when you want to adjust the camera settings.

4 Left arm tucked in

Keep your left arm tucked into your body for stability — in this position it's far more stable than it would be pointing out to the side.

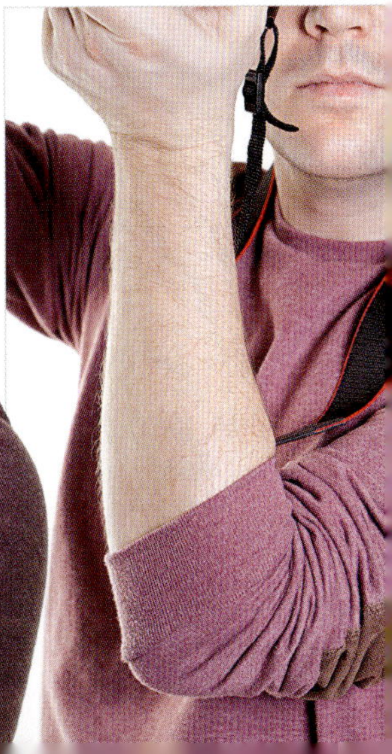

Four ways to stay steady

Control your breathing and stance, or lean against nearby fixtures for steadier shots

1 Breathing

Breathe out as you take the photo — you'll move around far more if you hold your breath. Practise makes perfect here. You'll be amazed at the effect that controlled breathing has on your shots.

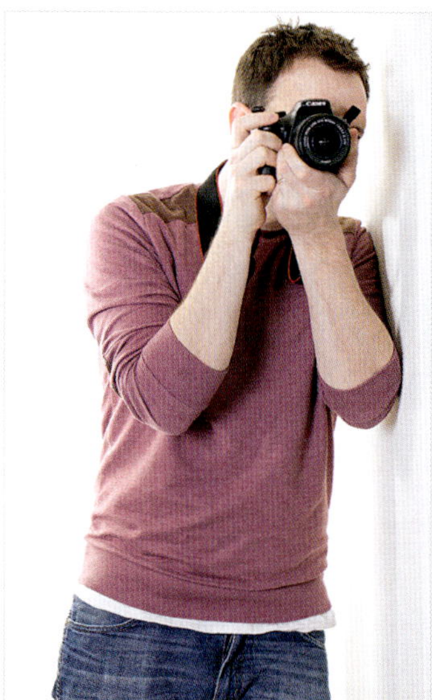

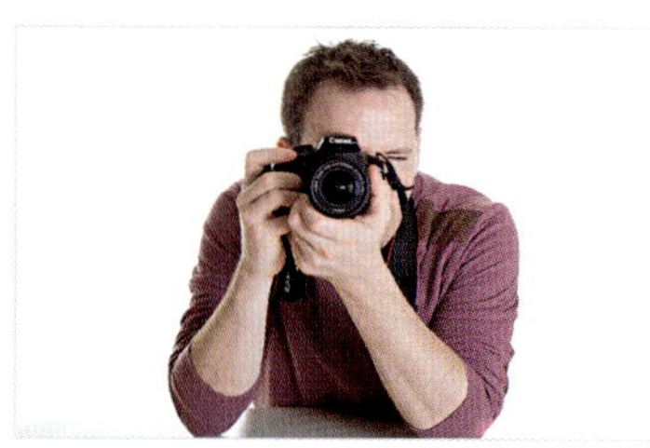

2 Elbows

If you have a surface area in front of you, lean your elbows onto it to steady yourself.

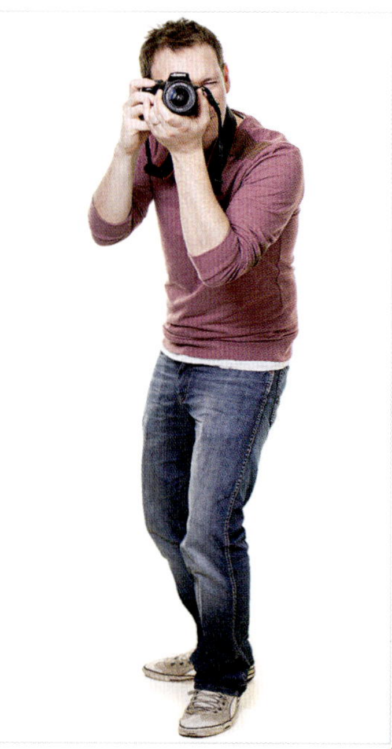

3 Arms

Another good way to keep your camera sturdy is by bracing yourself against something solid and immovable, such as a tree, wall or car.

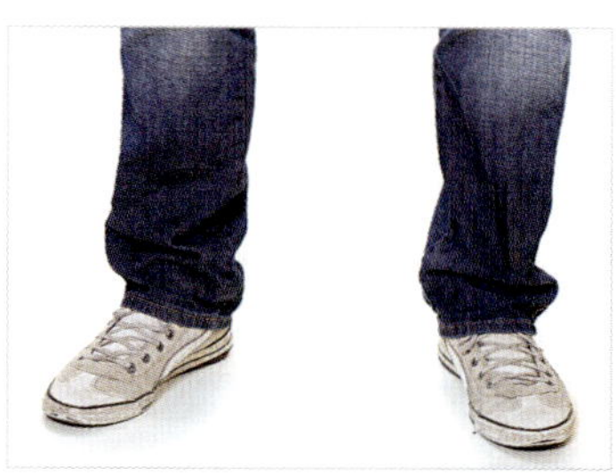

4 Legs

Place your feet a little apart so that you're balanced. If you're leaning in to take a shot, move one foot forward to create a body position that remains stable.

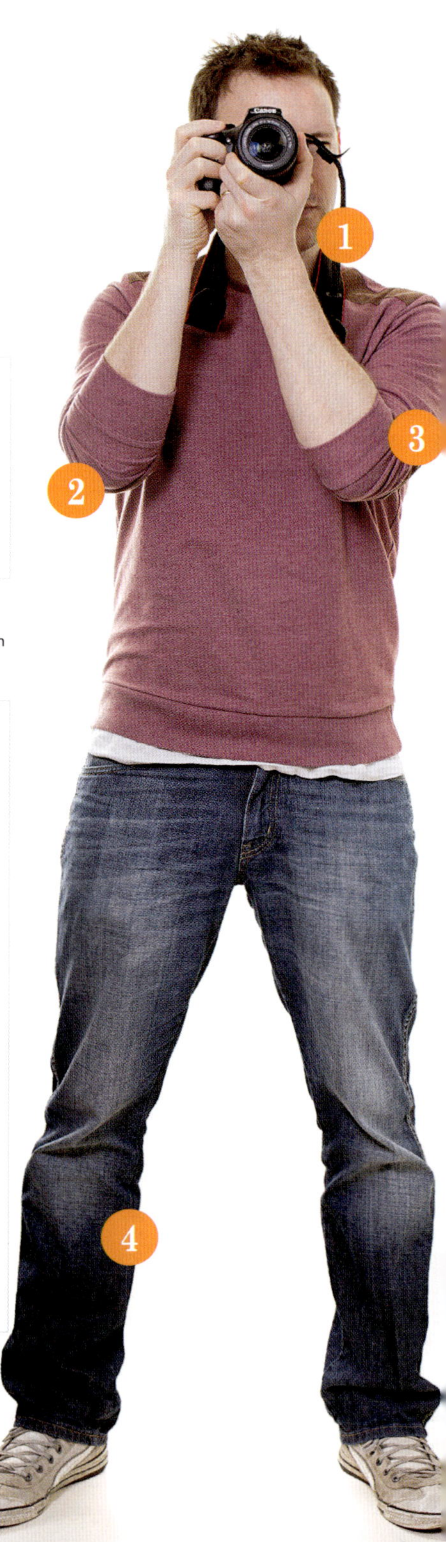

Be a human tripod

If all else fails, get down on one knee
to take the weight off your feet

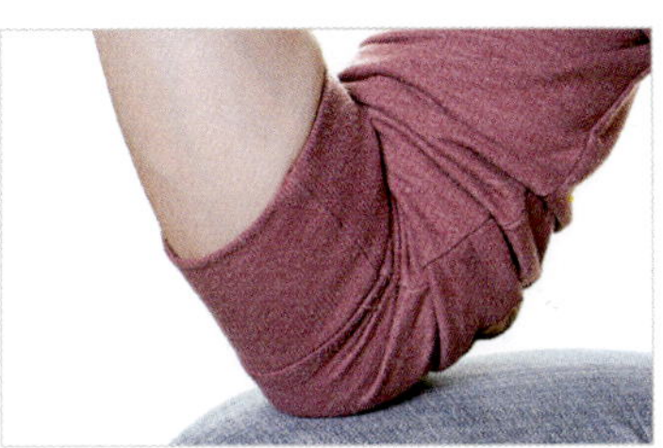

1 Connect arm and knee

Bring your arm up and place your elbow
on your knee to connect your leg and arm
together. This creates a braced position so
you don't move around.

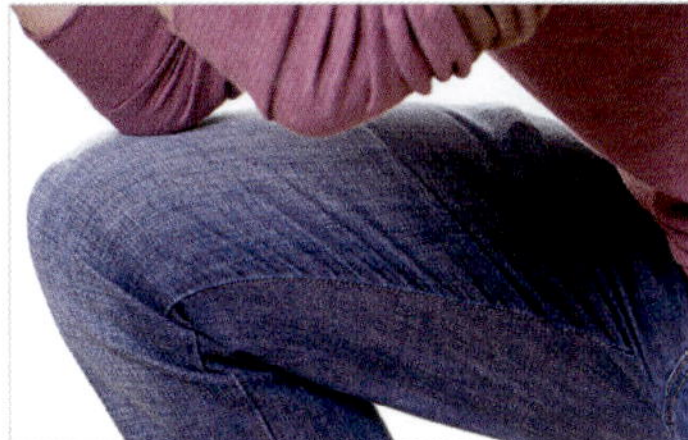

2 Raise a leg

By coming down into a crouching position
and bringing your leg up, you can turn your
body into a human tripod that supports
your camera effectively.

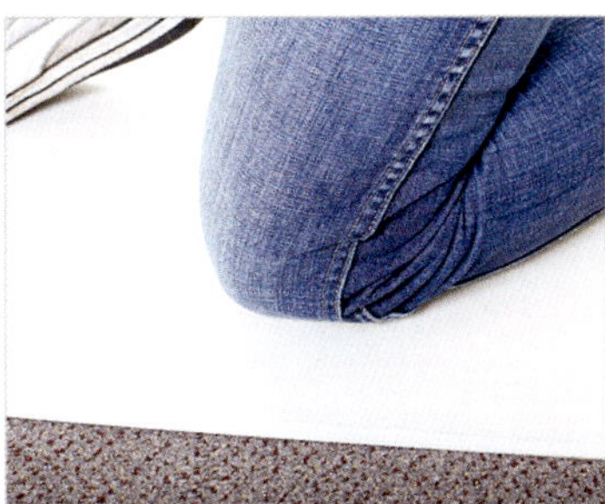

3 Take a mat

When shooting outdoors in this body position,
you might get a wet or dirty knee. Take a mat
or a plastic bag to kneel on so that you don't
ruin your clothes.

4 Core strength

Try to keep the core of your body still.
If you're steady through your centre,
you'll find it easier to control your legs
and arms.

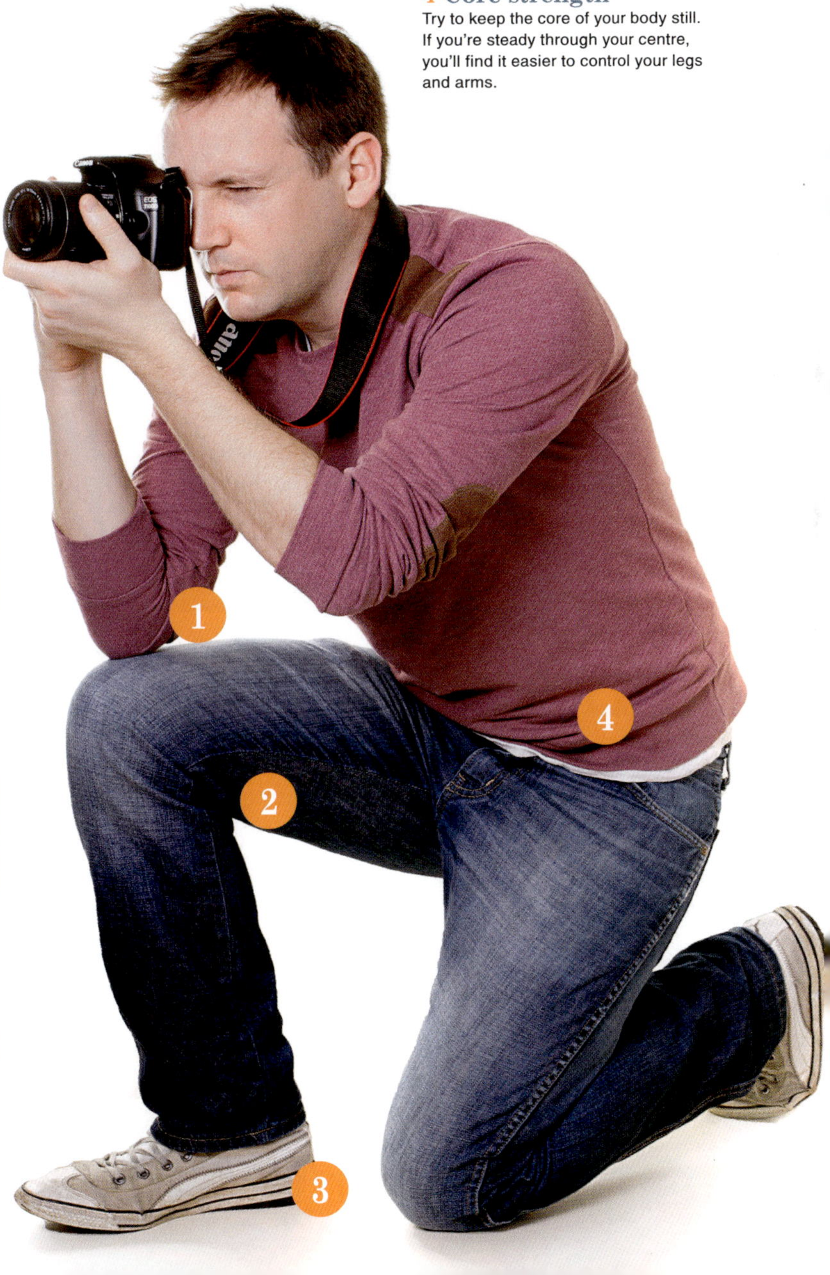

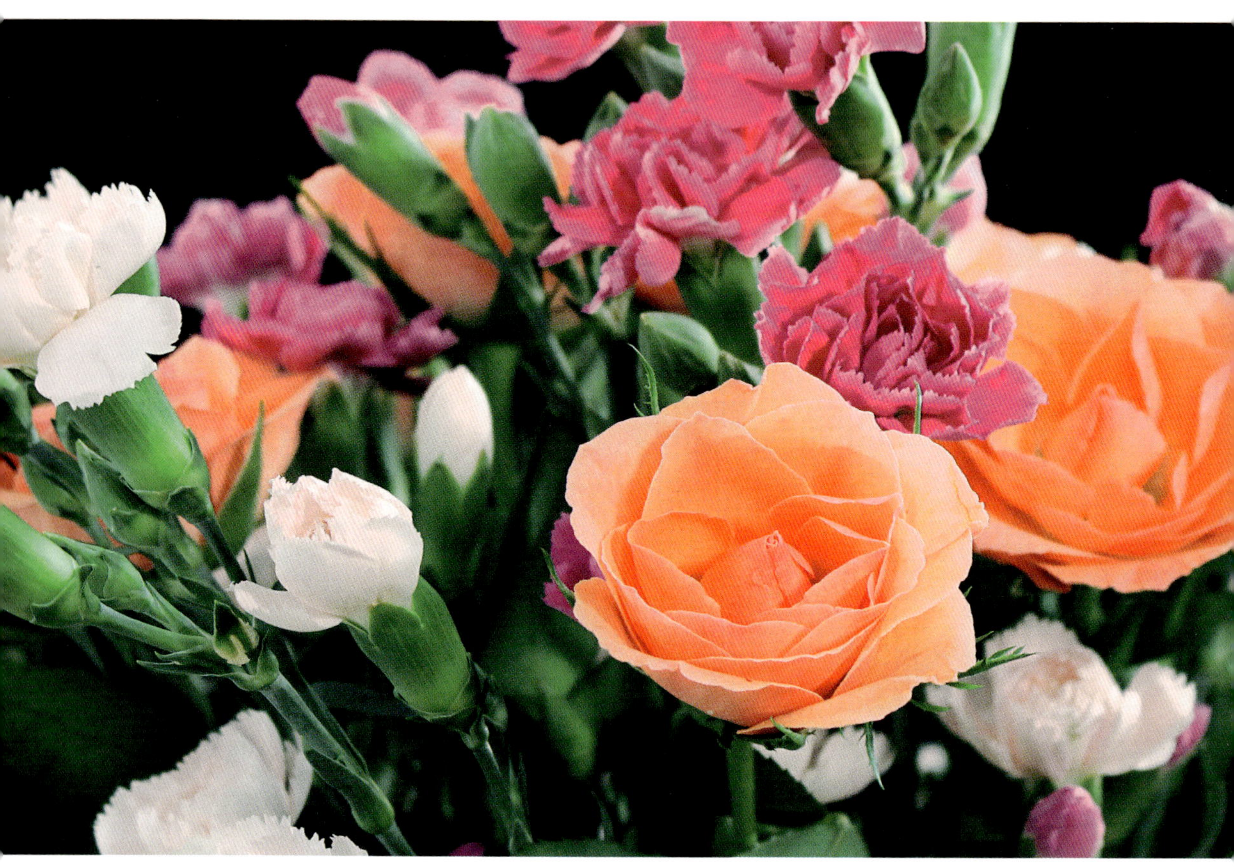

Lenses explained

A big advantage of digital SLRs over compact cameras is that you can change the lens for greater flexibility — here's a quick guide to using your optic

One of the biggest advantages of owning an SLR is that you can change the lens, which opens up a whole new world of opportunities for the creative photographer. Lenses come in a huge array of sizes (or focal lengths) that cover a range of viewing angles, from super wide to very long zooms. Whichever lens you use, it will be made up of a few components that work together to help you compose the scene you see through the viewfinder. Some lenses have a fixed focal length, but most — including the kit lens you may have bought with your camera — enable you to zoom in.

The numbers printed on your lens show you its focal length. Take a standard zoom lens. At its widest focal length it reads 18mm, but at its furthest zoom setting it reads 55mm. These figures may vary from lens to lens, so yours could be 24mm at the widest setting and 70mm when zoomed in. Just remember, the lower the number, the wider the view, and the higher the number, the more you can zoom in.

"You should keep stabilisation switched on while shooting with the camera handheld"

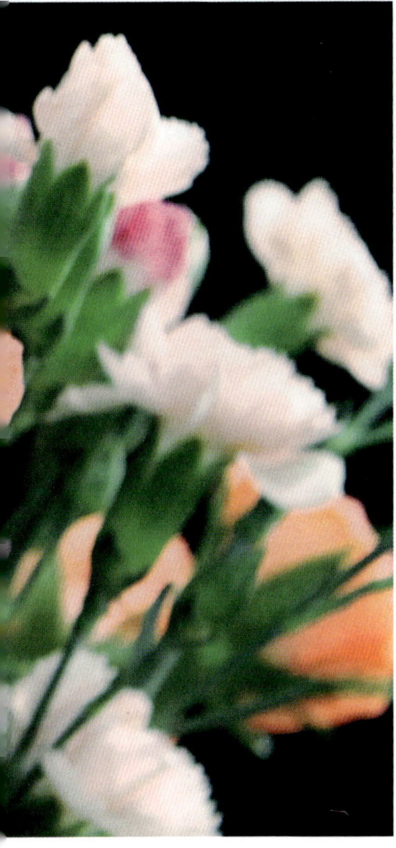

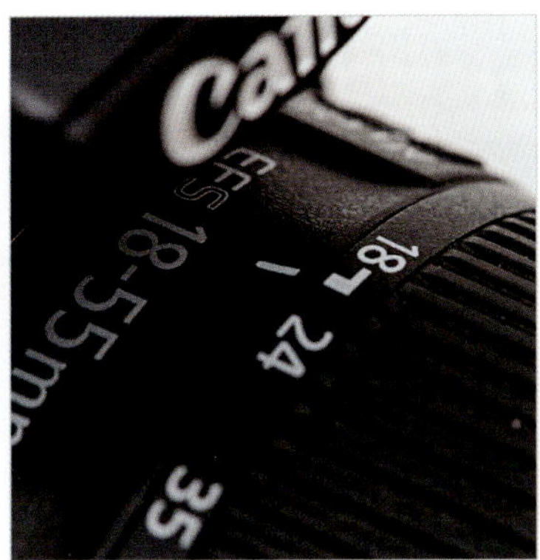

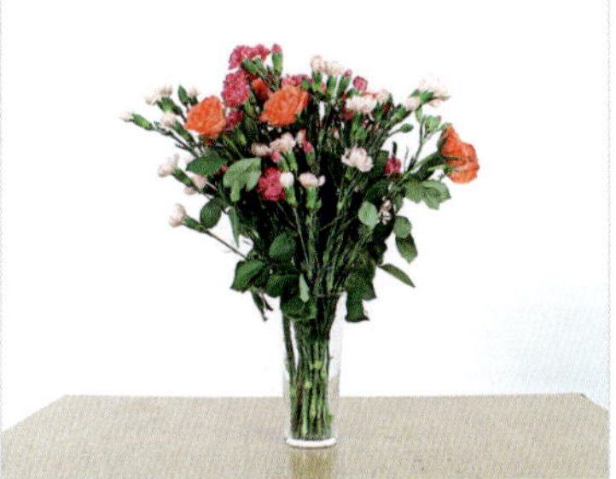

Above: With our 18-55mm kit lens fully zoomed out at the widest angle (at its 18mm setting), this is the most we can fit into the frame

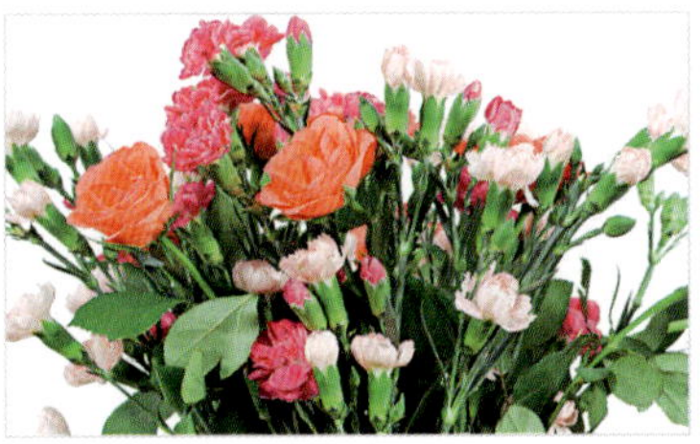

Right: If we keep the camera in the same position, but twist the lens barrel to 55mm, we're now fully zoomed in, and unless we move the camera physically forward, we can't get any closer to the subject

STEP BY STEP: How to zoom in with your lens

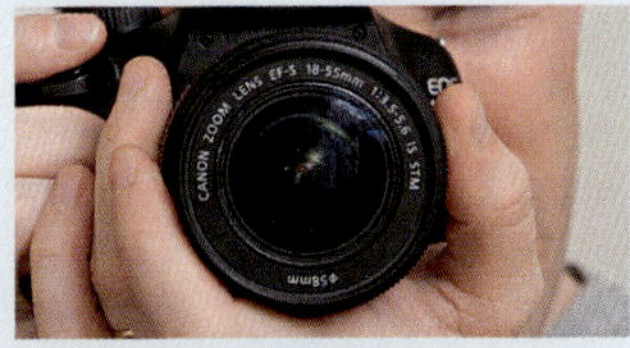

01 Do the twist

Put your left hand out and place the lens in this hand. To zoom in to a subject you need to twist the main barrel of your lens. This is the moving part that's situated closest to the camera body. There are numbers marked just above the moving barrel, and these numbers dictate how close or distant the lens is to your subject. So, for example, at the widest angle, our lens will be in this position, at a focal length of 18mm.

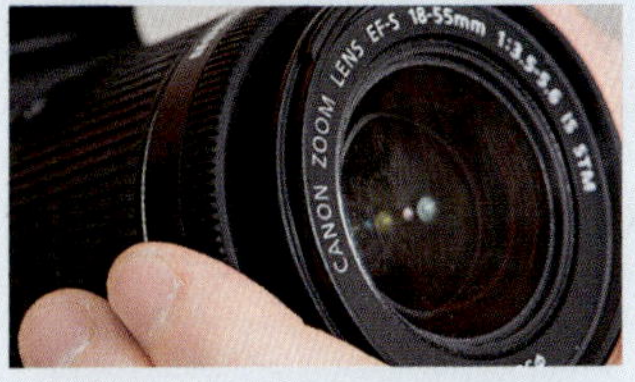

02 Get some focus

To focus your lens you need to twist the front ring on the lens barrel. If you're in the manual focus mode it moves freely. By moving it you can select the exact point in the image you want to make sharp. When using autofocus there's no need to touch the lens — the camera will do the focusing for you when you half press the shutter release. You just need to point the camera at the point you would like to appear in focus.

Your lens may also have image stabilisation (IS) or vibration reduction (VR) technology built in. This means that your lens will try to compensate for any movement created when holding your camera to prevent blur in the resulting images. You should keep stabilisation switched on while shooting with the camera handheld. If you mount your camera onto a tripod, however, you will need to turn it off.

The AF/MF switch

Lenses are essential for focusing, and accurate focusing is the key to a successful photo. You'll find a switch on your lens that has the letters AF and MF (or A and M) written on it. AF stands for autofocus and M stands for manual. If you want your camera to do the focusing for you, then move the switch to AF. If you're shooting a subject where you want to take full control of the focusing, use the manual setting instead.

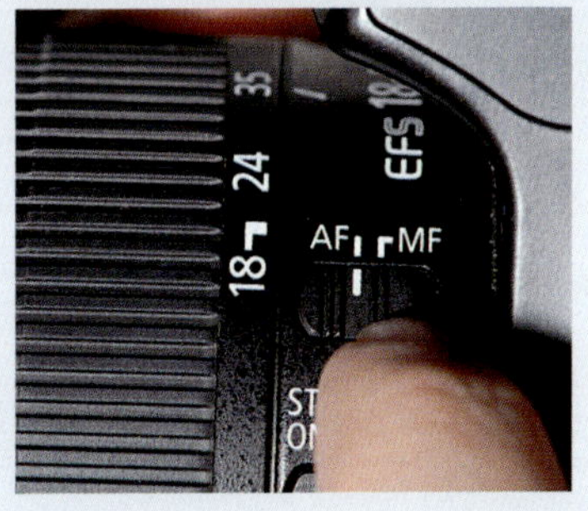

Which lens should you use?

Whatever subject you choose to shoot, there will
be a type of lens that's perfect for the job

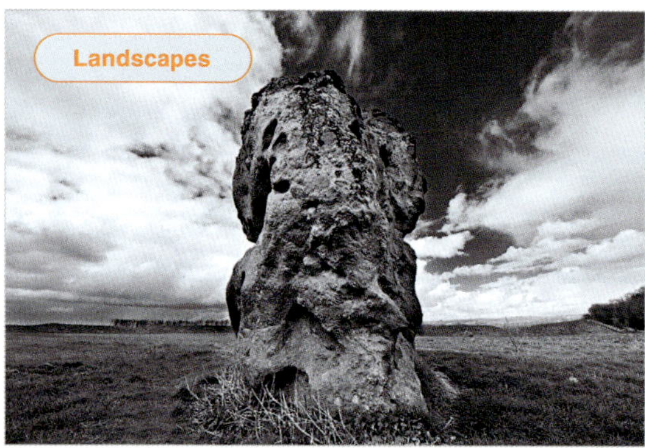

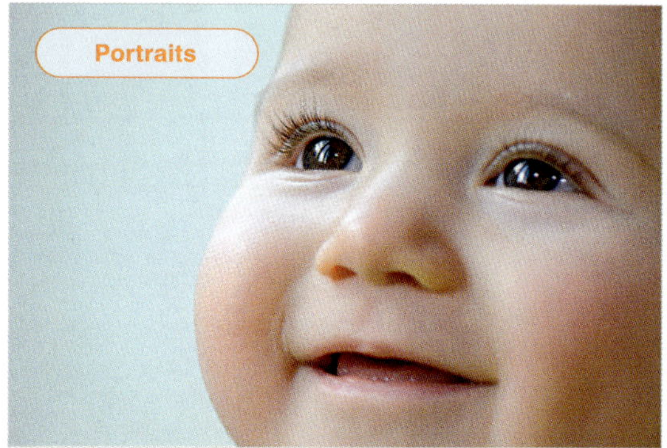

Which lens do you need?

When shooting landscapes, a wide-angle lens enables you to fit
as much of a scene as possible into the frame.

What's the typical focal length?

Wide-angle lenses range from 10mm to 35mm. Remember, though,
that wide angles can make objects appear smaller in the frame, so
you'll need to compose the image carefully.

Which lens do you need?

A fixed focal length lens will flatter your subject, and help you to get
creative with focus and blur. Without a zoom, however, you'll need to
move yourself forwards or backwards to adjust the composition.

What's the typical focal length?

Usually around 35mm, 50mm or 85mm. These lenses produce a high-
quality result, and are really lightweight.

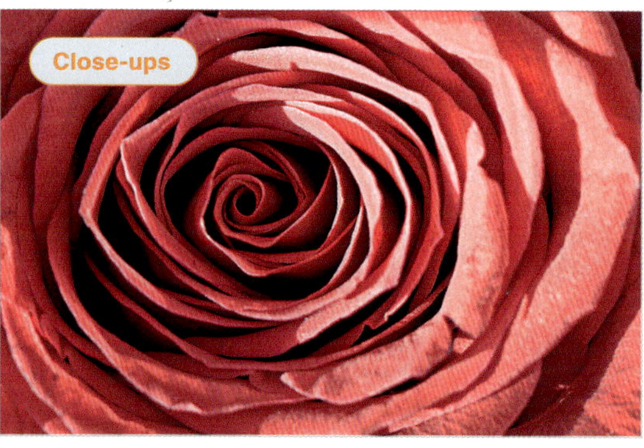

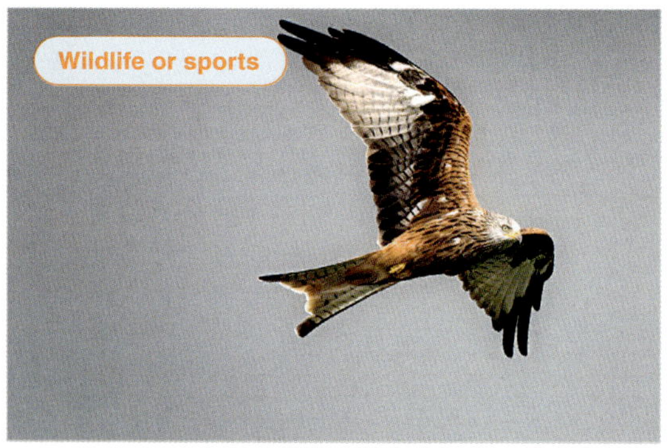

Which lens do you need?

If you want to capture the detail of an object at a one-to-one ratio
or closer, a macro lens is a must.

What's the typical focal length?

They vary, but 100mm is a popular focal length. Macro lenses can be
quite pricey, so only invest in one if you're serious about this kind of
photography. A cheaper alternative is to buy an extension tube, which
sits between a camera body and a standard lens.

Which lens do you need?

For wildlife and spectator sports (or any other genre that requires
you to shoot from a distance), you'll need a telephoto zoom.

What's the typical focal length?

Telephoto lenses usually start at around 70mm, and go up to
around 800mm. They can be heavy and expensive, due to the
complex glass construction, but if you need that extra reach, they
are well worth the investment.

Learn how to take your first photo

Learn all you need to know about how the shutter release button works, and start taking inspiring photos in Auto mode

Once you've familiarised yourself with your new camera and set it up to suit the way you shoot, you'll be keen to head out and start taking pictures. But if you're completely new to SLR photography, it's worth taking a few test shots in the comfort of your own home before you head out into the great outdoors. That way you can be sure that you're comfortable with holding your camera, zooming your lens in and out, and getting the focus right, rather than fiddling around on location and missing the perfect shot. To take an image, you need to press the shutter-release button, which is found on the right-hand side of your camera at the front. The shape of the camera has been designed so that you can comfortably grip your fingers around the body and use your index finger to press the button.

Here, we'll show you a straightforward way to take an image using your camera's Full Auto shooting mode, and with the focus mode set to automatic

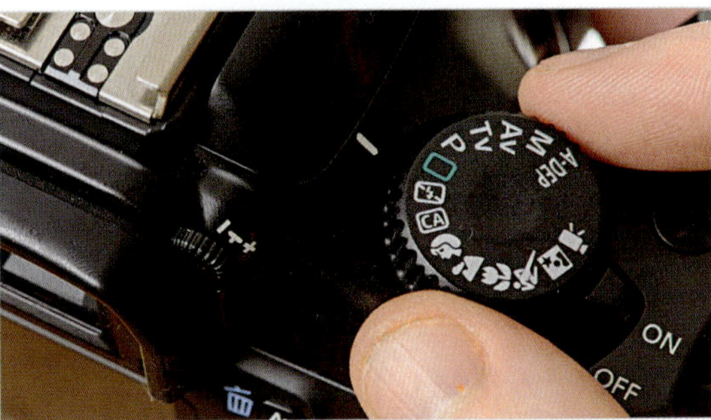

01 Turn to Full Auto mode
Turn your camera on, and then turn the Mode dial to the Full Auto setting (usually represented by a green, rectangular icon or similar). In this automatic setting your camera will control all of the settings for you. If there isn't enough light, it will engage the pop-up flash.

02 Compose the image
Hover your right index finger over the shutter-release button and bring the camera up to your eye. Look through the viewfinder, composing your image carefully and moving the camera around, or changing your position, until you're happy with what you see.

03 Half press to focus
With your lens set to AF (autofocus) mode, half press the shutter-release button and you'll feel and hear your lens focus automatically. Your camera will beep when the lens has locked focus, and the active focus points will be highlighted in red in the viewfinder.

04 Now shoot!
In one continuous movement, press the shutter-release down fully. In a fraction of a second the mirror inside your camera will flip up out of the way of the sensor, allowing light to pass through and on to the sensor. The image will now be stored on the memory card.

Learn the different ways of framing

We take a closer look at your SLR's Live View and viewfinder features to identify when each should be used to compose images

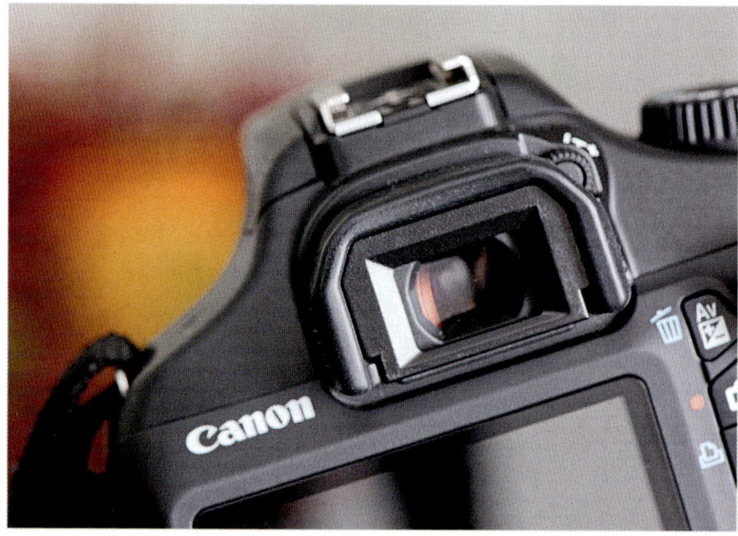

01 Viewfinder

The viewfinder is a small eyepiece on your camera's back panel. To use it simply pull it up to one eye and then close the other. The advantage of a viewfinder is that you can eliminate distracting elements around you and see exactly what you're about to capture. The disadvantage? It can be hard to get your eye to the viewfinder when shooting from awkward angles.

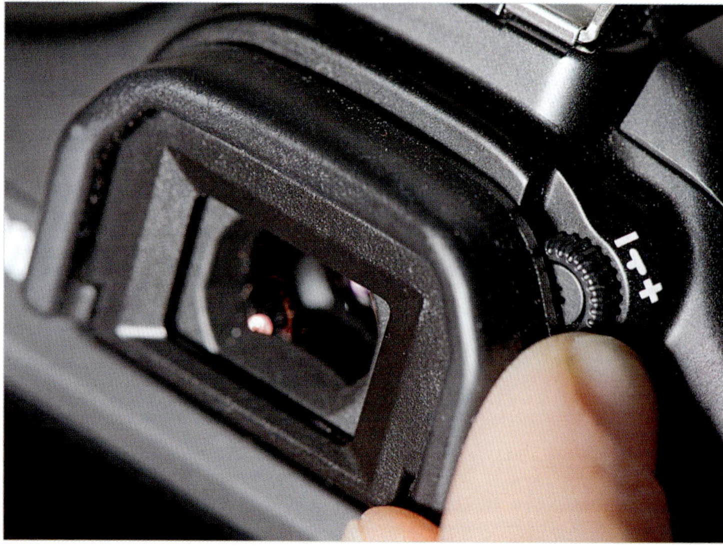

02 Dioptre

If you look through the viewfinder and the image seems blurry, don't panic. You'll notice a small dial to the side of the viewfinder that has a small + and - control. This is called the dioptre, and you can use it to bring the screen into sharp focus — particularly useful if you don't have 20:20 vision. This adjustment won't affect focusing; it simply makes it easier for you to see what the camera sees.

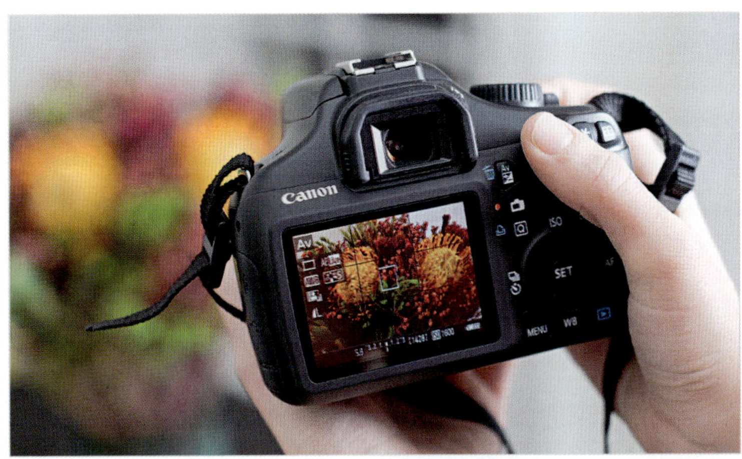

03 Live View

Your camera's Live View feature enables you to view the scene in front of your lens on the camera's rear LCD screen — like you would on a compact camera. It can also help with accurate focusing. You can change the screen display set-up by pressing the Display or Info button on the back panel — most DSLRs have the option to include an overlay grid on screen, for example, which can be used to aid composition. Beware, though, as Live View will drain your battery, fast.

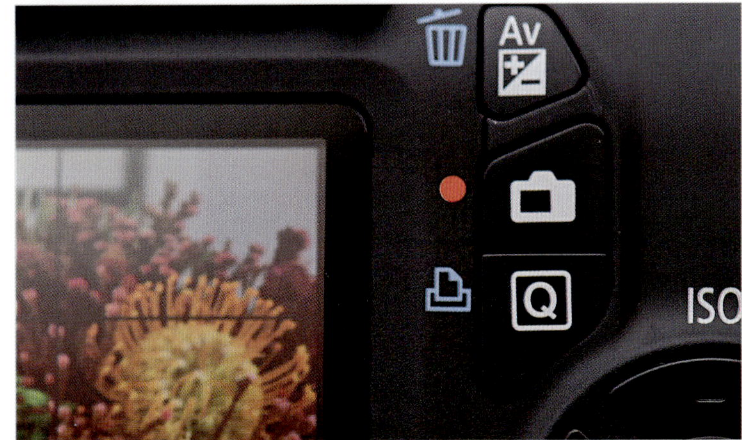

04 Live View button

Most DSLRs have a Live View button somewhere on the camera body so you can activate the feature without delving into the menu system. Some models have a lever on the top panel that you need to flick to activate. If you're struggling to find Live View, refer to your manual.

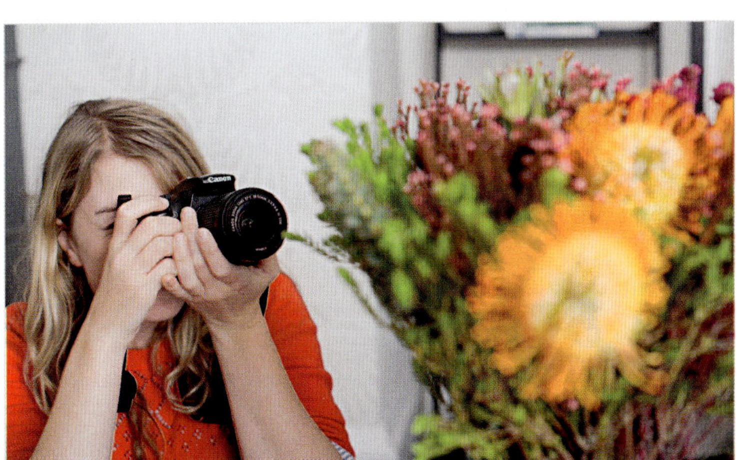

05 But which should you use?

The choice is yours — both options come in handy in different shooting situations. For example, when shooting landscapes or a still-life set-up it can be easier to use Live View, whereas the viewfinder makes it easier to keep up with fast action or focus accurately on a headshot. Live View is your only option in Movie shooting mode, and it's never possible to use the viewfinder with Live View activated — the mirror, which enables you to see through the viewfinder, has to flip out of the way for Live View to work.

Automatic shooting modes

Get started quickly by giving your SLR control of the basic settings and letting it do the hard work for you

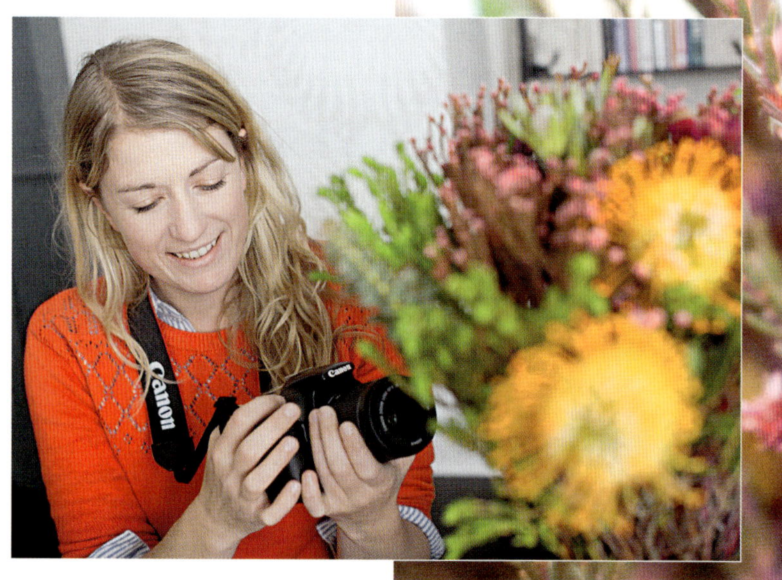

When you're ready to take a shot you'll need to decide which shooting mode to use. There are multiple options — including fully automatic, semi automatic, manual and scene modes — that can be accessed via the mode dial on your camera's top plate. Right now the options might seem bewildering — not least because they're represented only by icons and letters, but we'll make it easy for you.

The Full Auto mode is a good starting point for beginners. By handing over control of key settings to the camera, you can concentrate on careful framing. However, you will soon uncover its limitations. We'd recommend you shoot with it until you feel comfortable taking pictures, then switch to one of the more advanced shooting modes that we will cover on the following pages.

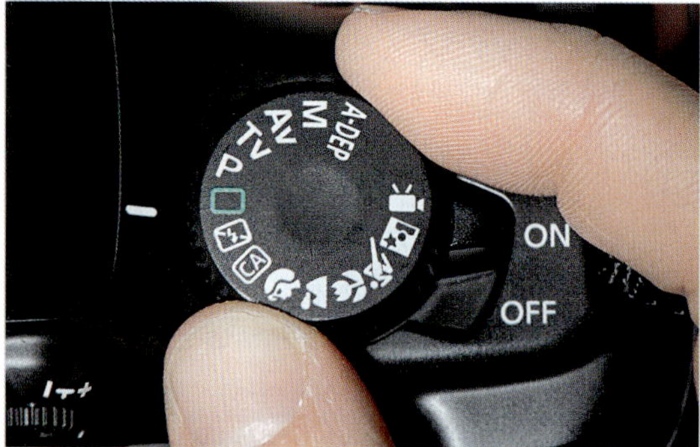

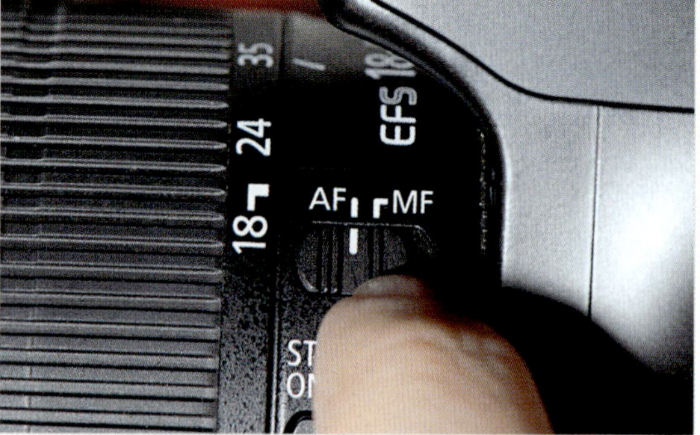

01 Select Auto

The Full Auto mode on a camera usually appears on the mode dial as a green rectangular icon, or something similar. Turn the dial around to this point to activate it. Make sure you're stood in a sturdy position with your finger hovering over the shutter release, and your left arm tucked tightly into your body.

02 Focus carefully

Make sure your lens is set to its autofocus (AF) mode. Now your lens will take care of the focusing for you, as long as you half press the shutter release, and you'll hear a beep when focus is achieved. In manual focus (MF) you are in complete control — simply turn the focus ring until your subject appears sharp.

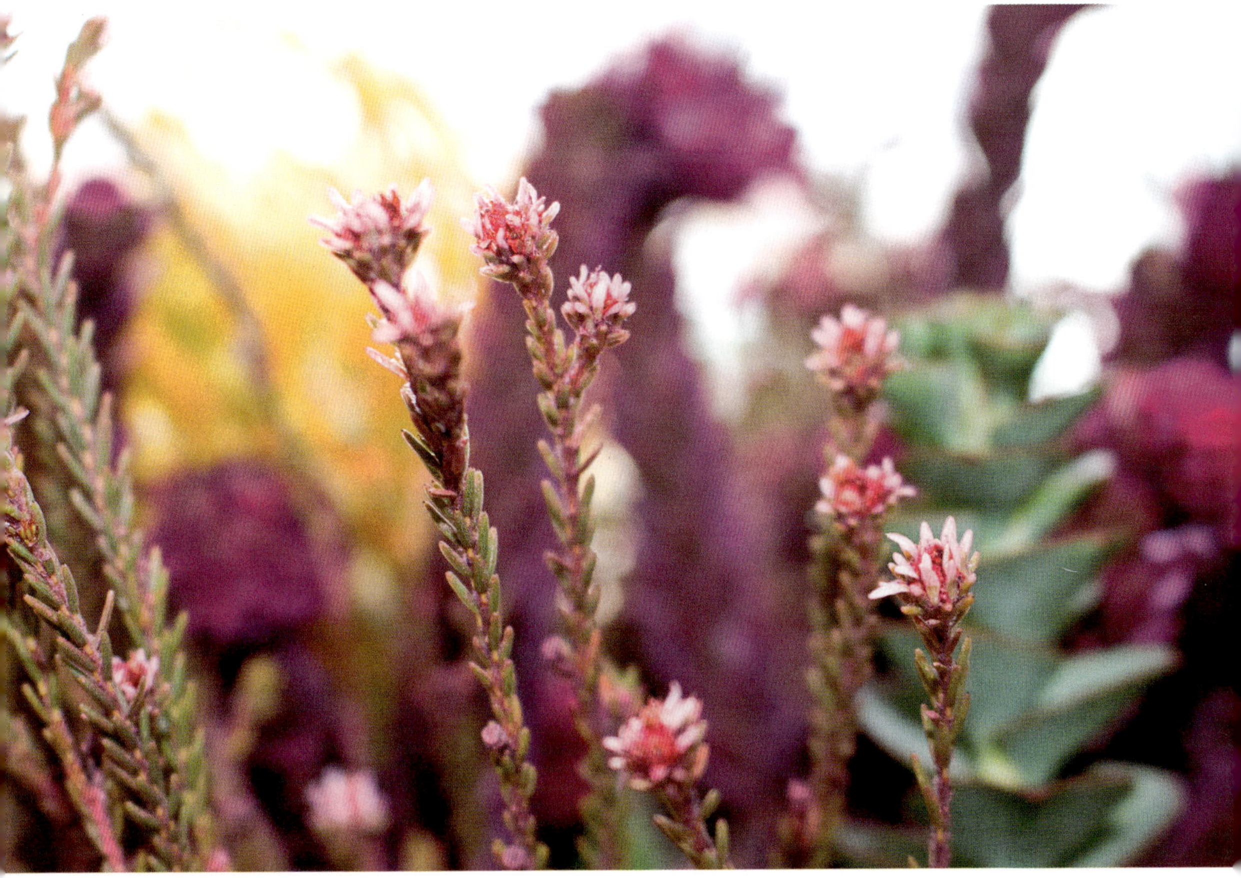

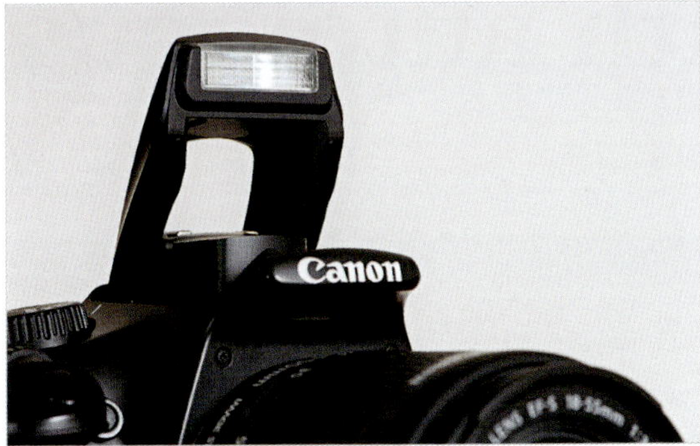

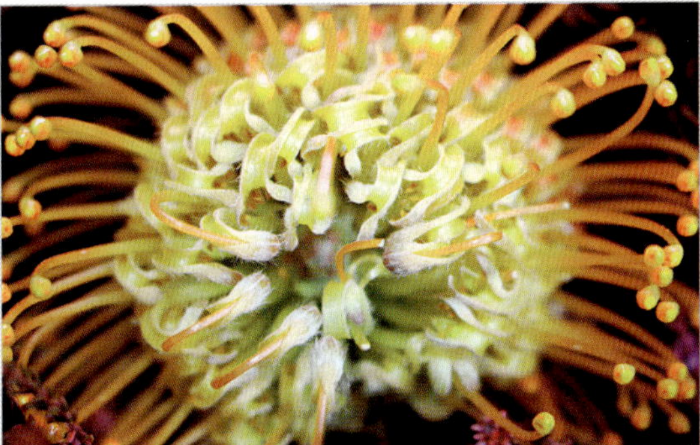

03 Flash light

If light levels drop when shooting in Auto mode, or you're taking pictures indoors, the pop-up flash will automatically engage to throw extra light on your subject. Flash is also useful when shooting a subject with dark shadows against a bright background, sometimes referred to as 'fill-in' flash, as used in the image above.

04 Take a different view

Now place your finger over the shutter button. Half press the button to activate the autofocus and fully press the button down to take the shot. Try having a go at shooting a flower yourself, varying your angle of view, and zooming in and out, for more creative results. You could shoot just the centre of the flower, for example.

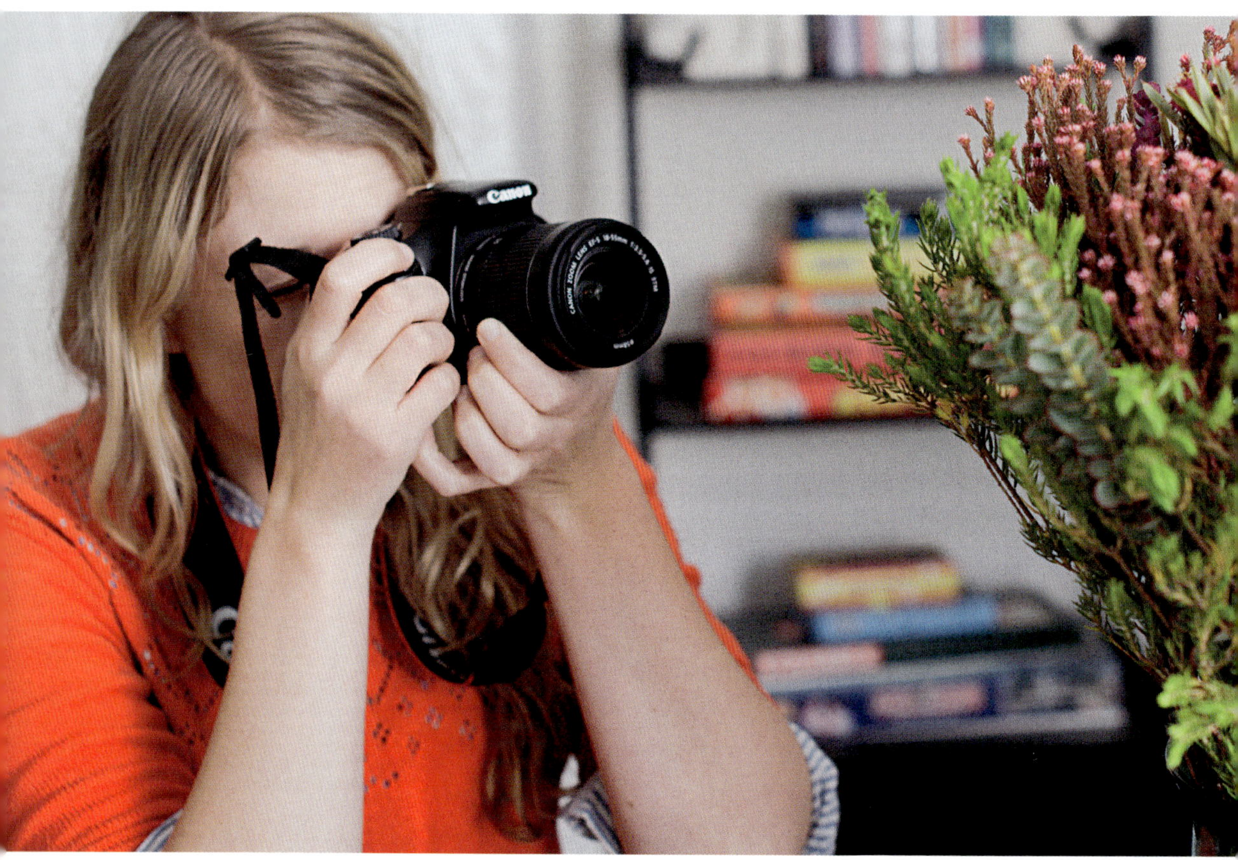

Stay sharp with autofocus

Let your camera take control of the focus,
so you can concentrate on the composition

As we've explained on the previous pages, autofocus is brilliant for beginners. If you're trying to master a new SLR camera, by leaving your camera to focus accurately on your subject, you're left free to focus (no pun intended!) on other things, such as positioning and composition.

You now know how to get started — ensure the switch on your lens barrel is set to AF, then actuate focus by half-pressing the shutter-release button and wait for the beep. As with all things, however, there are ways to get more from this feature, and things you should watch out for, as we explain here.

The pros and cons of autofocus

- *Great for beginners it takes full control of your focus setup, leaving you free to be creative*

- *It's very fast, and it's accurate most of the time*

- *Your camera might not focus on the part of the image you actually want to be sharp — it generally focuses on the closest object*

- *If there's not enough light, your camera will struggle to lock on to a focus point*

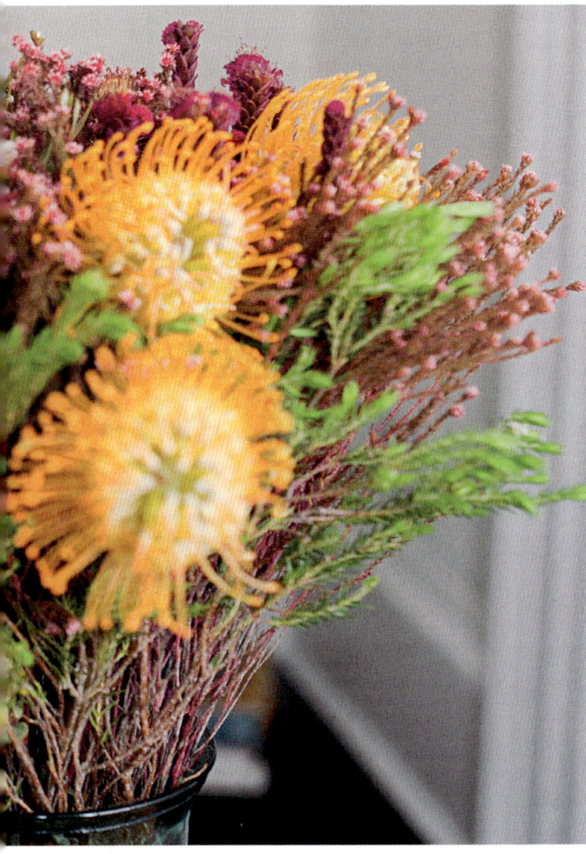

Autofocus grid

Your camera has a grid of autofocus points built in — you can see them as you look through the viewfinder. The number of focus points a camera has varies from model to model — high-end SLRs, for example, can have up to 51, making accurate focus far easier to achieve. In this example, our camera includes a nine-point AF grid, and in autofocus mode the camera will decide which of these points corresponds with the area you want to be sharp.

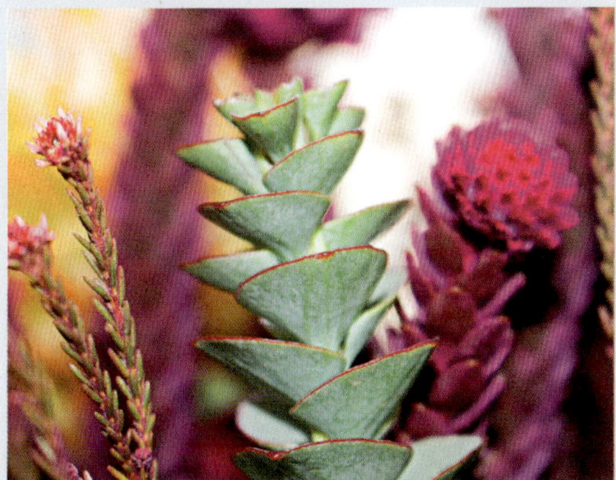

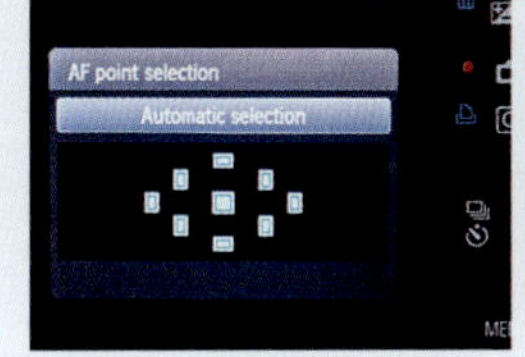

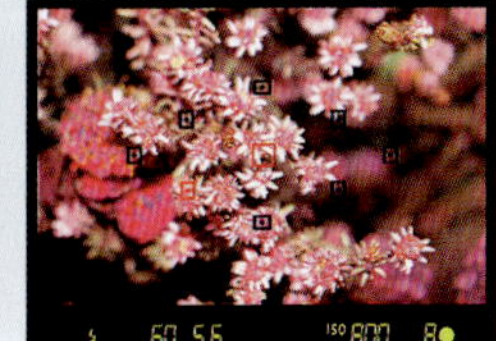

Problems focusing?

If your camera is struggling to lock focus (you'll hear the autofocus hunting backwards and forwards, struggling to lock on), it could be because there's not enough light. If this is the case, your camera won't let you fully press the shutter release down. To fix this problem, bring in some extra light by either shining an external light source such as a lamp, or moving your subject closer to natural light.

Your lens may also struggle to focus if it's too close to the subject. The solution? Simply move yourself back and recompose the shot. Just remember, if your lens can't lock focus you won't be able to press the shutter button down.

If you want to blur your photo on purpose and the AF setting won't let you, switch your lens to its manual focus (MF) setting and move the focus ring with your fingers until you get the desired effect. Just remember to switch back to AF when you've got your shot.

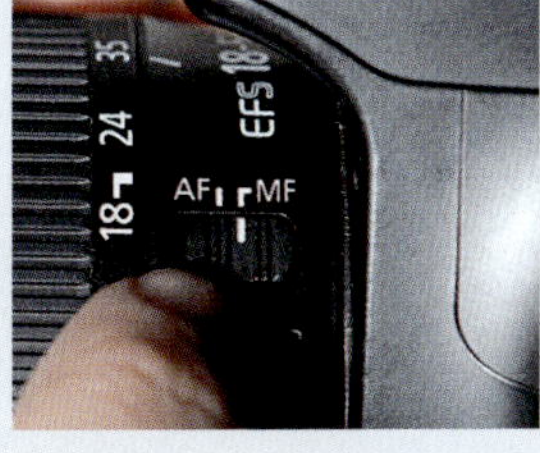

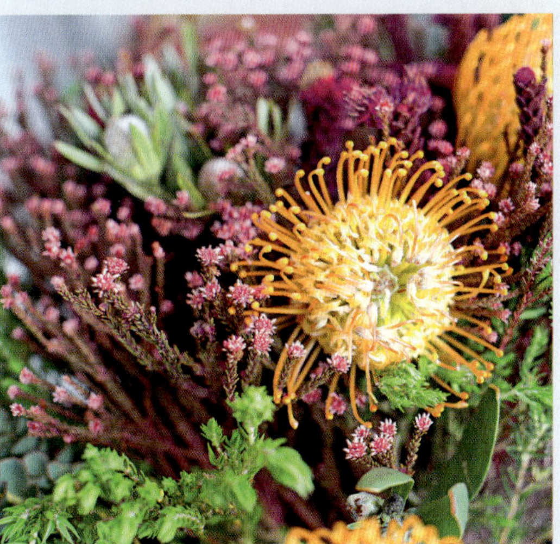

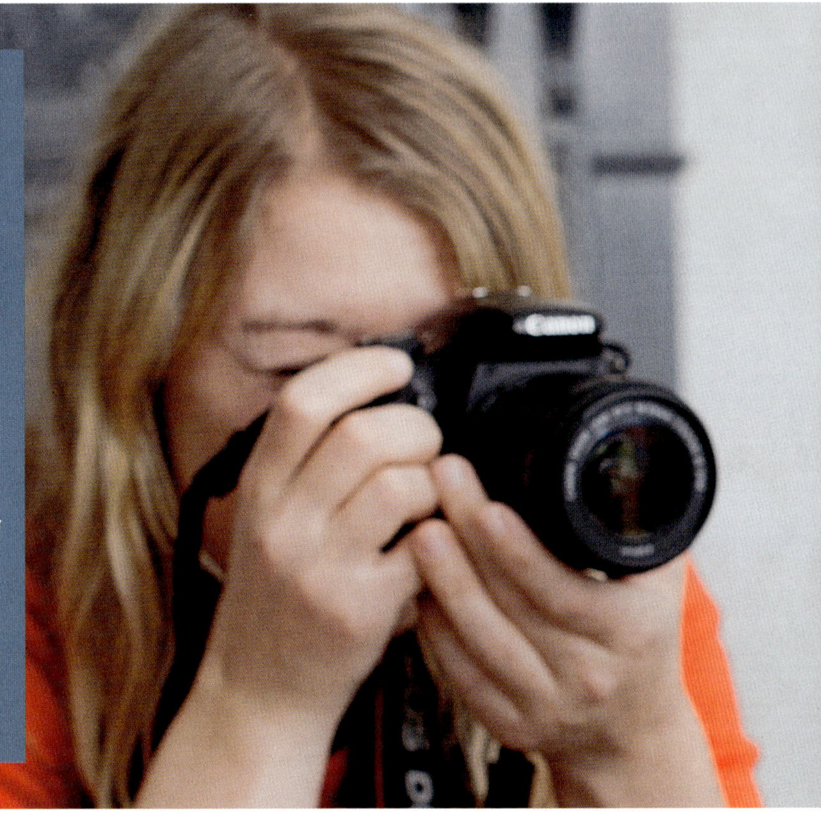

Maximise your picture quality

Discover how to adjust your camera's image quality to ensure you get the best possible photos in any situation

Before you start shooting, it's worth taking a second to think about image quality. Your camera enables you to select a number of different file formats, each resulting in images with varying file sizes, resolutions and quality levels. You'll be able to save your images as either JPEGs or raw files — in fact, on many cameras you can shoot both at the same time.

JPEGs are a universal file format recognised by all computers. They're small, and great if you want to quickly print or upload images to the internet. But if you plan to process your images in an image editor later, the quality will deteriorate as you work, and your editing options will be restricted.

Raw files are a little more complicated; they're the camera manufacturer's own format, and they contain uncompressed data. It's essential to process these files on your computer before you can edit them, print them, or share them online. Most DSLRs come bundled with editing software that can be installed on a computer and used to process raw files. A raw file containing this unprocessed data doesn't usually look quite so good straight out of the camera, but it will be packed with detail and offer much more flexibility when it comes to finessing or manipulating your images on a computer. Raw files are larger than JPEGs, so they will take up more space on your memory card.

When you're starting out with SLR photography it's best to select the High Quality JPEG option if you're unlikely to spend time editing them. You'll also fit more images on to a single memory card. As your shooting and editing skills progress, however, raw will guarantee better results.

How to change the file format

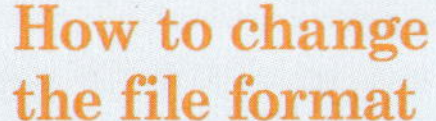

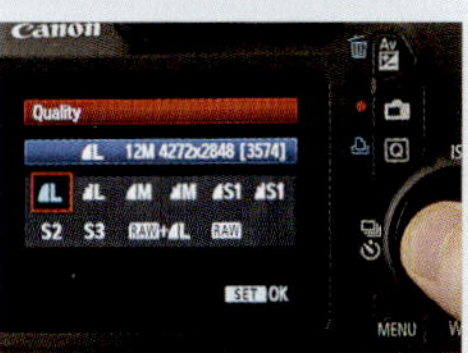

To set, or change, the file format (and therefore the image quality), first access your camera's main menu and navigate to the Image Quality section. You can now simply scroll to your desired setting — here we've selected the big L with the smoothed curve symbol, which stands for Large JPEG. See your camera's manual for more about the other file formats on offer. Just remember that you can always reduce your image sizes later on the computer, but you can't increase it if you've chosen to shoot at a lower quality.

Raw-processing software

If you're keen to edit your images, then it's always best to shoot in raw — after all, they contain the maximum amount of image data, so they look far better when processed carefully. You should think of the raw editing process as similar to developing film — you take the images, then you process the final results as you would in the darkroom.

Your camera will come with free raw-processing software in the box, which you'll need to install on your computer. With this software, you can tweak the exposure, colour, tone, contrast and sharpness — and that's just the start.

JPEG image quality up close

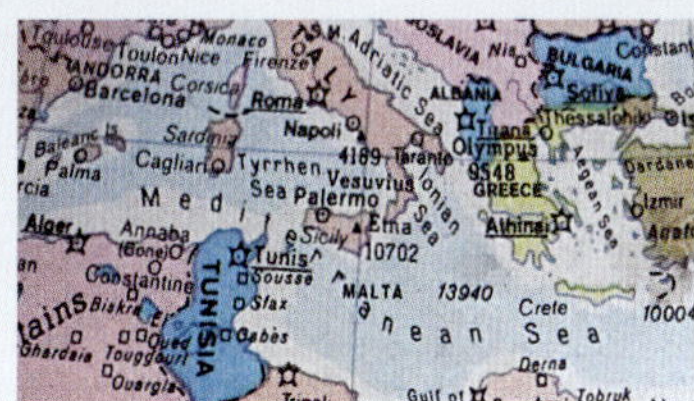

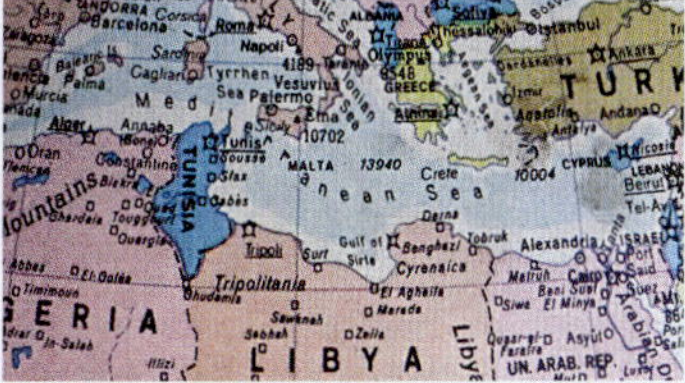

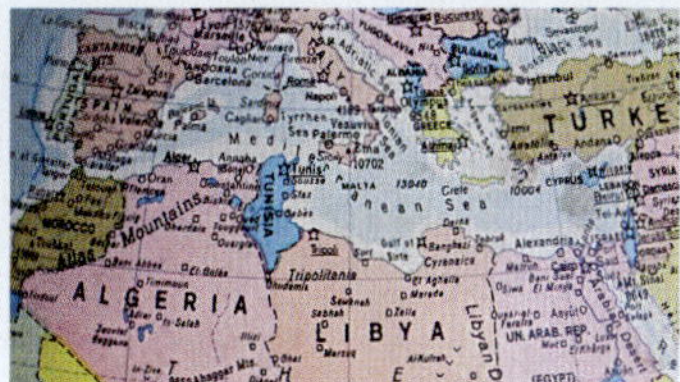

High-quality JPEG
In the high-quality example we can zoom in much further. This is the setting we'd recommend you shoot in.

Medium-quality JPEG
Sitting in the middle, this setting is useful when you need to save on memory card space but don't want to compromise too much.

Low-quality JPEG
You won't be able to print the low-quality images very big, but they are adequate if you only intend to upload to the web.

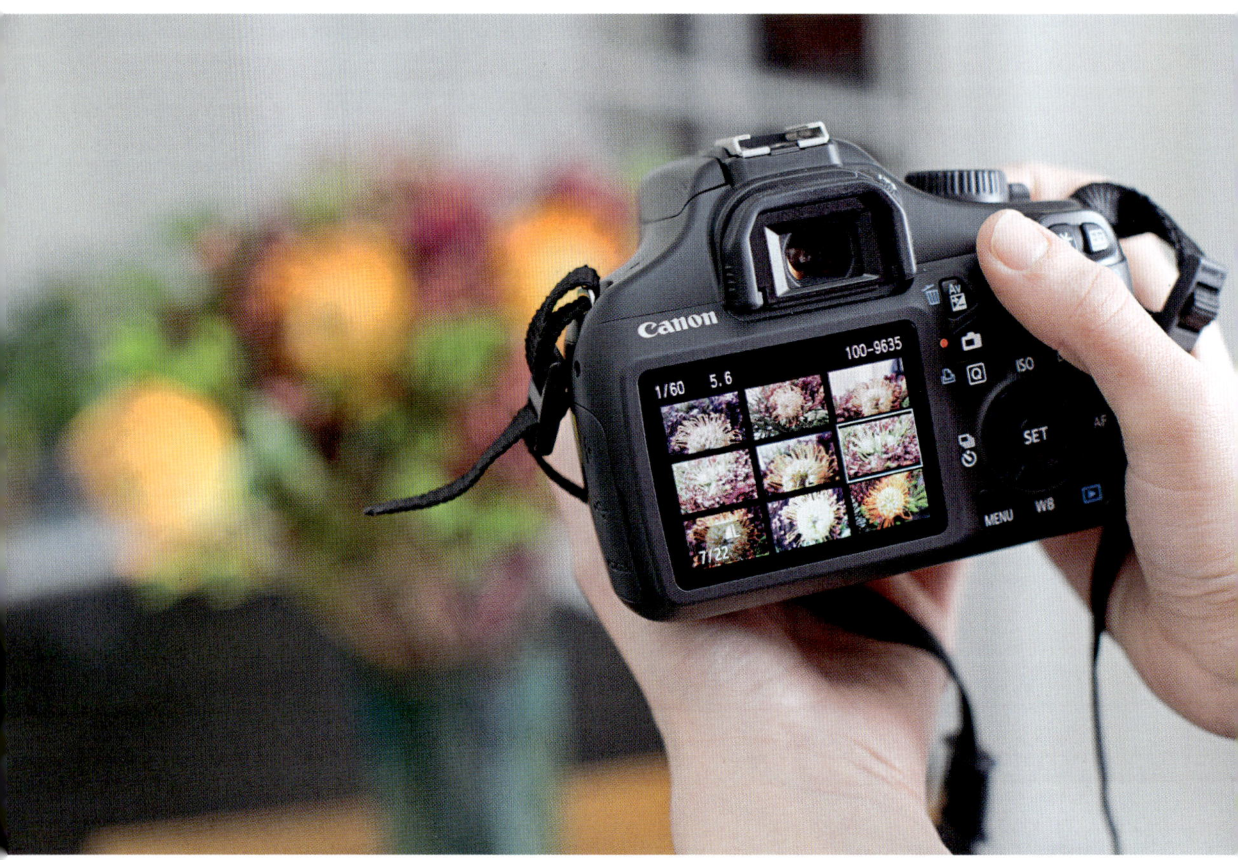

Review your photos on screen

Learn how to use your SLR's Preview mode to check
your photos on the LCD as soon as you've taken them

The beauty of digital photography, as opposed to film, is that you can take a few images, then view them on screen to see if you've got what you hoped for. Not happy with what you've taken? You can simply delete the images and try again.

To review your images, just press the playback button — this is usually marked with a play symbol on the back panel of your camera — and your images will appear. Use the navigation keys to scroll through them one by one. You can also access the image data, so you can see at a glance which settings you used — shutter speed, aperture, ISO etc.

Although it's useful to view images as you shoot, don't take for granted that what you see on screen is what you've actually captured. It's always best to view your images on a computer screen, as the colours will be more accurate and the image much clearer to see.

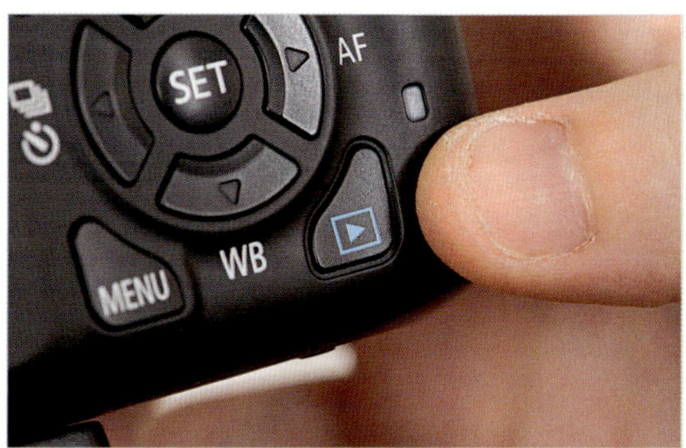

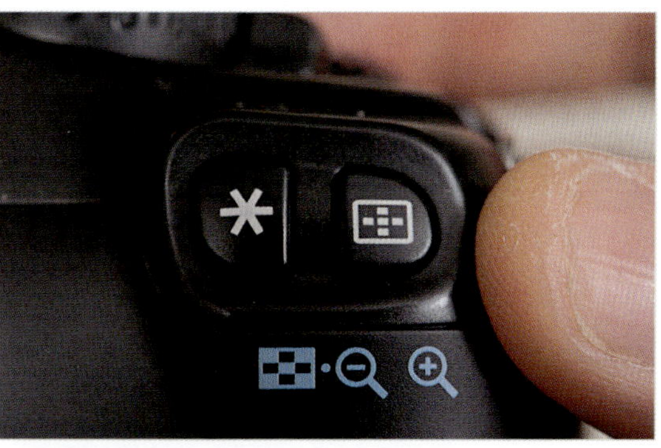

01 Play it again

Press the playback button and the last image that you shot will appear on screen. To scroll through all of your captured images, use the navigation keys on your camera's back panel control. On some DSLRs you can use the scroll dial to scroll through ten images at a time.

02 Zoom in

One of the best things about having a playback feature is that you can zoom right into the image to check that your focus is spot-on. To do this, press the zoom button (often represented by a magnifying glass) until you have the magnification you want.

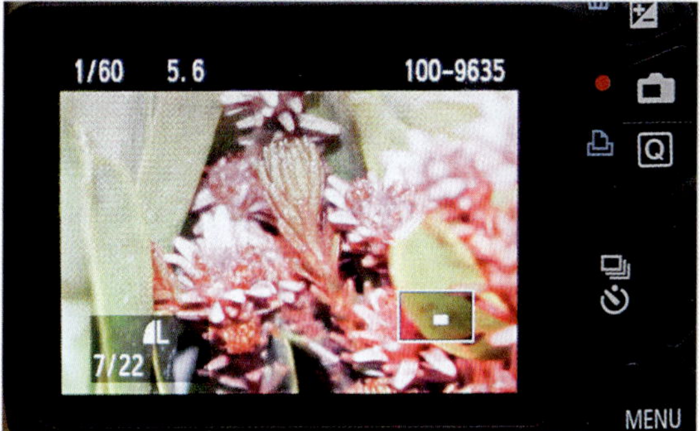

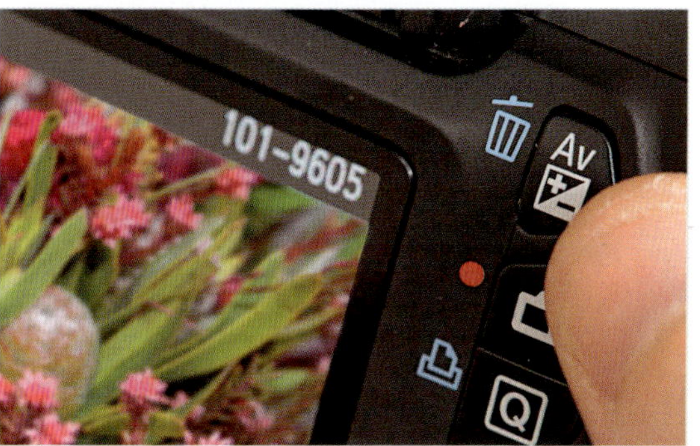

03 Check for sharpness

Using the back panel control, navigate around the image to check it's in focus. Make sure you zoom over the main focus point (if it's a portrait, ensure the eyes are sharp). Once happy, you can press the zoom out button to return to the normal view.

04 Deleting images

You have the option to delete images on your camera. You'll find a delete button situated on the back panel. Press the button and your camera will bring up a warning message, double-checking that you're sure you want to delete. Press OK to confirm.

Zoom out for more pictures

Your camera is capable of performing quite a few different tasks in playback mode. You can zoom out of your images so you can view them in a grid formation, for example, so that you can assess many similar images at once.

The more you zoom out, the smaller the icons will become, and the more images will fit on the screen. This is a far quicker way to find a single image from a whole day's shoot than checking each picture individually.

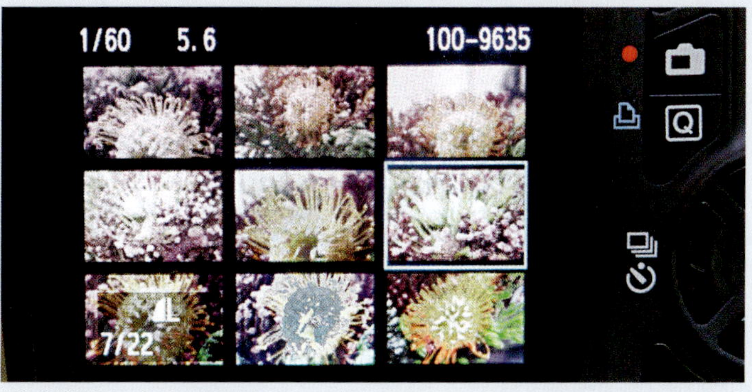

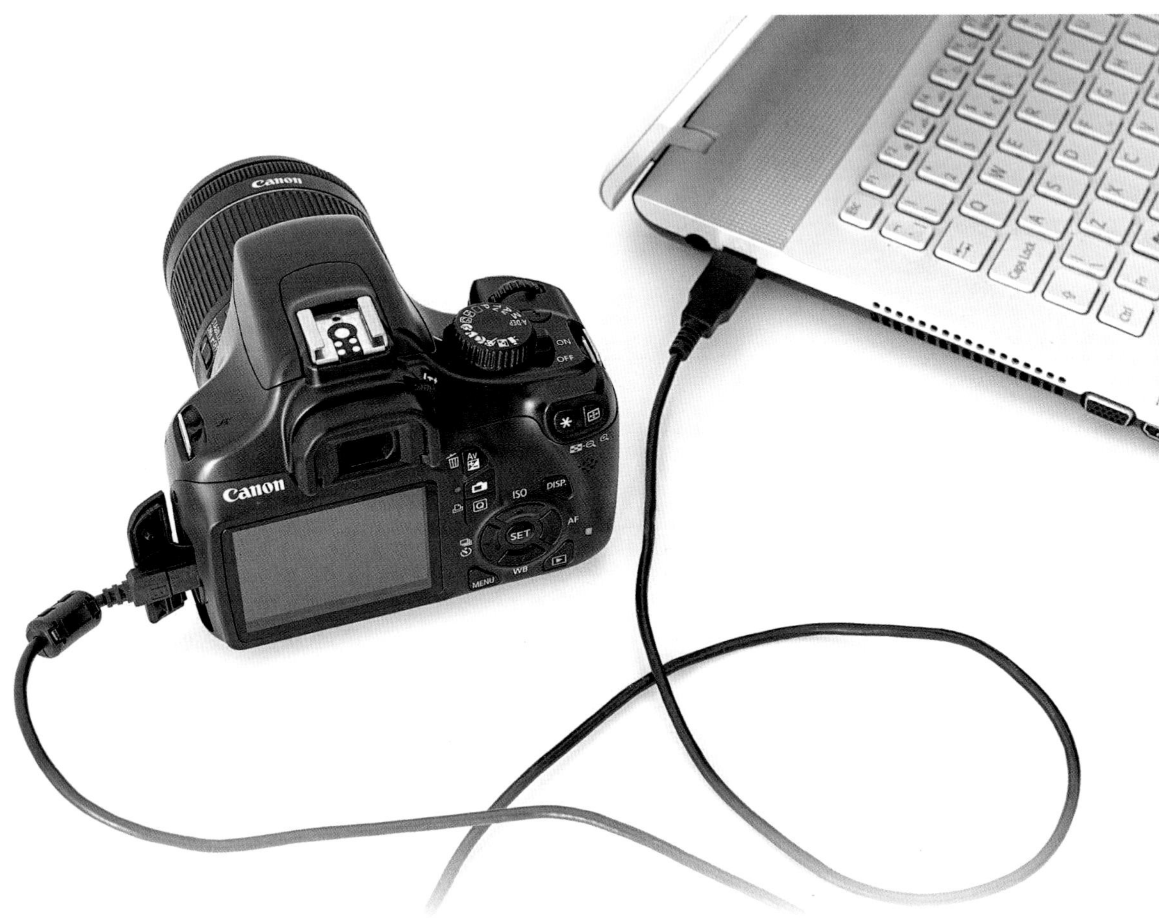

Transfer photos to your computer

See your images on the big screen by connecting and downloading them directly from your SLR to your PC

Once you've taken a few photos, don't let them languish on your memory card. By downloading them to your computer, you can sort, check and edit, then save your images to your hard drive.

Once downloaded, you can delete the images from your memory card, freeing up precious space so you can head out and shoot more. It helps if you devise a filing system from the start, so that your images are easy to find at a later date. Try putting them in folders labelled with the date they were taken, their subject, or even both.

There are different ways to get your images on your computer. The first is to connect your camera to your computer using the USB cable that came in the box. The second is to use a memory card reader, which is more efficient. The third option, if your camera has wireless connectivity, is to transfer images wirelessly.

Plug in with a USB
Connect camera to computer

Your DSLR comes with free image-editing software. Install this first by inserting the CD and following the on-screen instructions, or by downloading the software from your camera manufacturer's website.

Next, use the USB connection cable that came with your camera to physically link your DSLR and your computer. The small end plugs into your camera's USB connection point around the side.

Once connected, turn your camera on. Your computer should recognise your camera and open a program to download your images. Make a new folder on your hard drive and export all of your images into it. Name your folder — with the date, for example — so your images are easy to find later. Disconnect the cable once you've finished downloading everything.

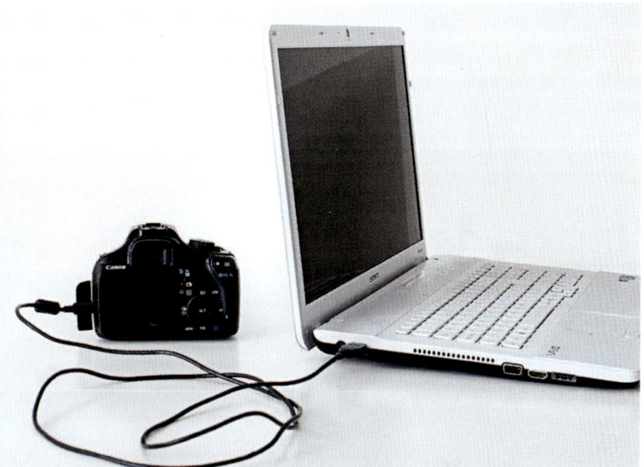

Use a card reader
Save wear and tear on your expensive camera

A memory card reader is a small device that plugs into your computer via a USB connection point. You then simply eject your memory card from your camera and insert it into the correct slot on the reader. Your computer will recognise the device, and present you with a folder from which you can drag your images into a folder for safekeeping on your computer's hard drive.

Try wireless options
The fast technology is growing

Some modern cameras come with built-in wireless connectivity such as Bluetooth, NFC and even Wi-Fi, enabling you to transfer images without cables. These work in different ways, often involving pairing with an app on your tablet or smartphone so you can upload images to social media or to cloud storage services.

If your camera doesn't have wireless built in, you could buy a Wi-Fi memory card that connects to your smartphone, tablet, PC or Mac, via a desktop or mobile app that enables you to transfer your images.

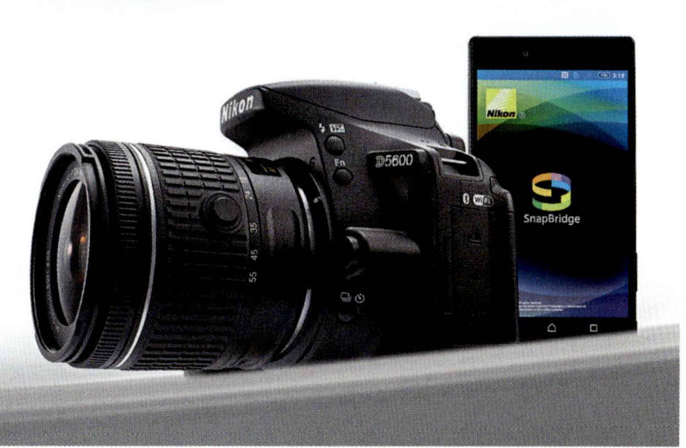

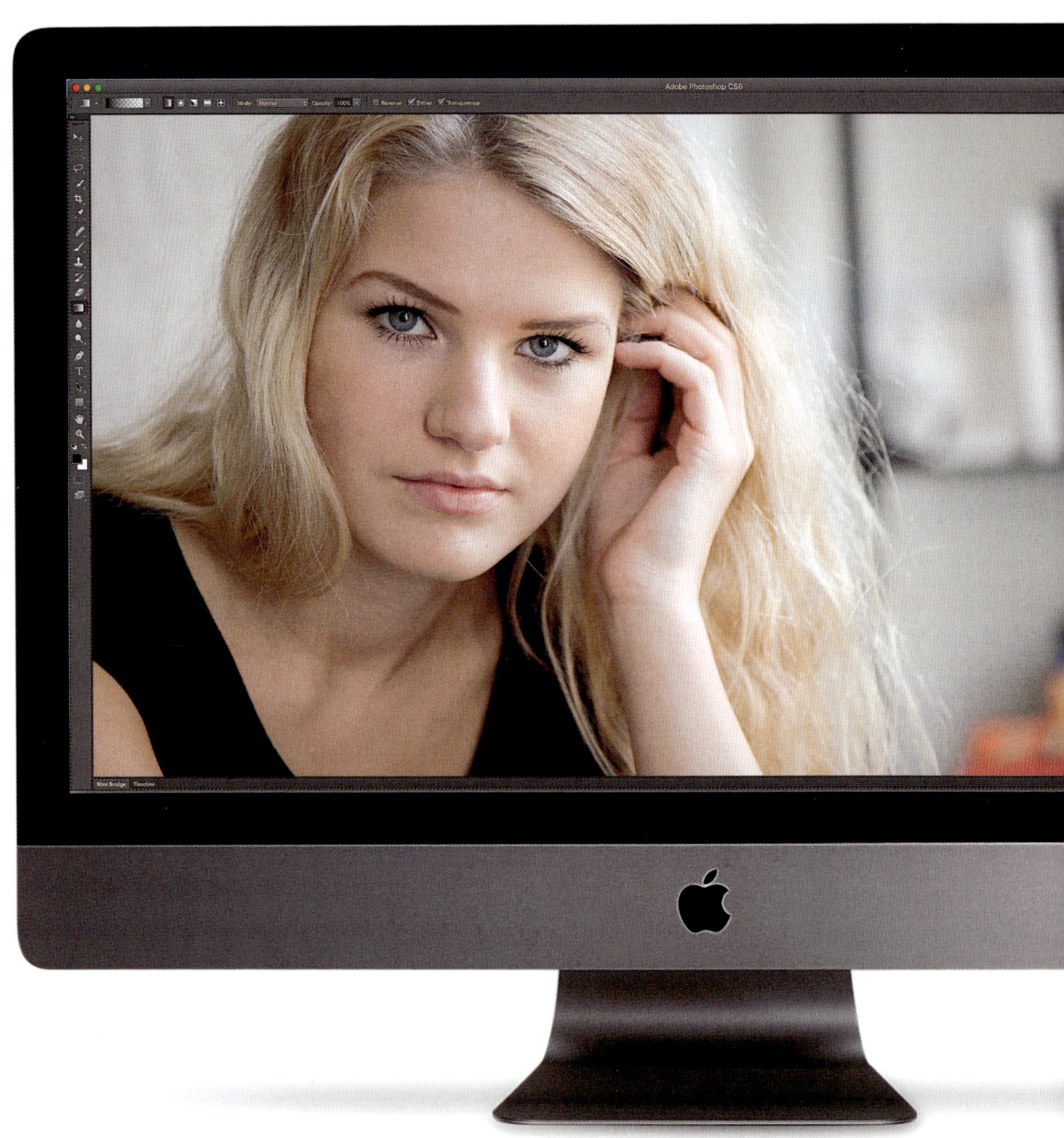

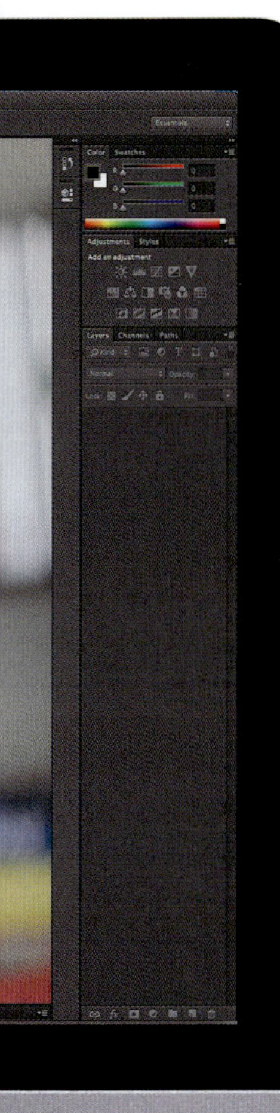

Portraits

Learn how to compose fabulous-looking portraits and start applying photographic effects for amazing results

50 A guide to your SLR's Scene modes
Ensure you capture great photos by selecting the appropriate scene mode for your subject

52 Produce picture-perfect portraits
Follow our guide to portrait composition and instantly take better shots of your friends and family

60 Discover how to blur a background
Learn how to simplify your portrait compositions with a beautiful blurred background using a wide aperture

62 Use AF points for sharper shots
Start taking more control of the sharpness of your images by selecting the autofocus points manually

64 Get natural lighting right
The right lighting is vital for shooting good portraits, so we reveal all you need to know to get started

A guide to your SLR's Scene modes

Get the most from any scene by selecting the appropriate Scene mode from the mode dial

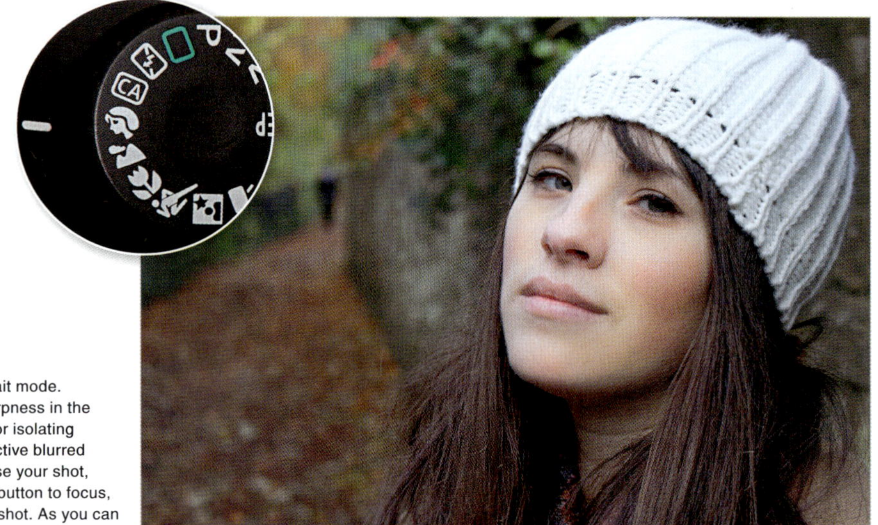

01 Portrait

The head icon indicates Portrait mode. This will keep the band of sharpness in the scene narrow, which is ideal for isolating your subjects against an attractive blurred background. To use it, compose your shot, half press the shutter-release button to focus, then press it fully to take your shot. As you can see, the background here is nicely blurred.

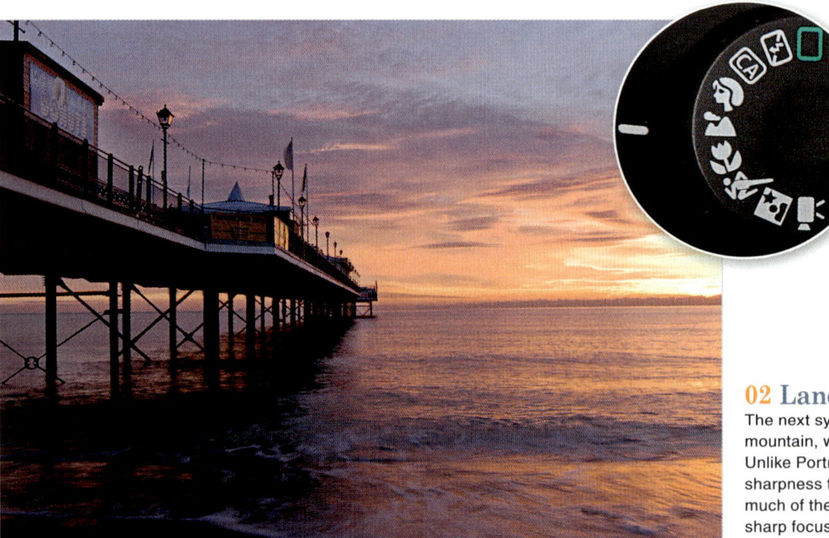

02 Landscape

The next symbol on the mode dial is a mountain, which stands for Landscape mode. Unlike Portrait mode, this will maximise sharpness throughout your image, so as much of the scene as possible is captured in sharp focus. Landscape mode will also boost colours and add contrast to your image.

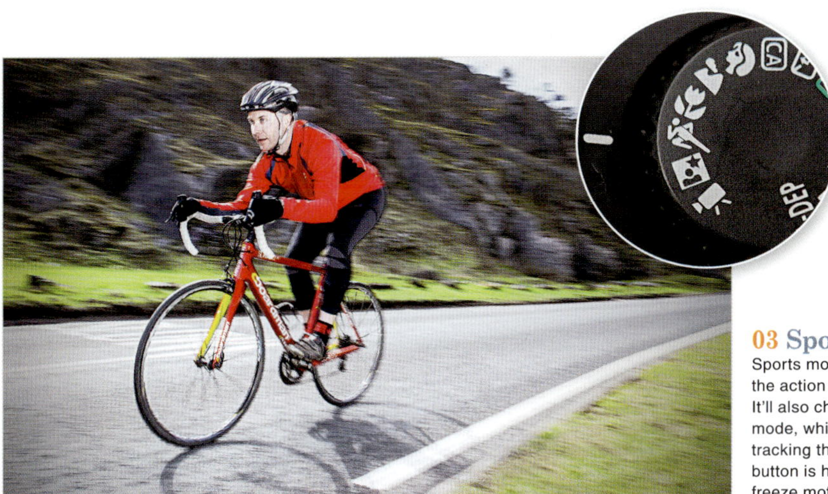

03 Sports

Sports mode will set up the camera to freeze the action when capturing moving subjects. It'll also change the focusing to Continuous mode, which means the autofocus will keep tracking the subject as long as the shutter button is half-pressed. This enables you to freeze motion and get the focusing spot-on.

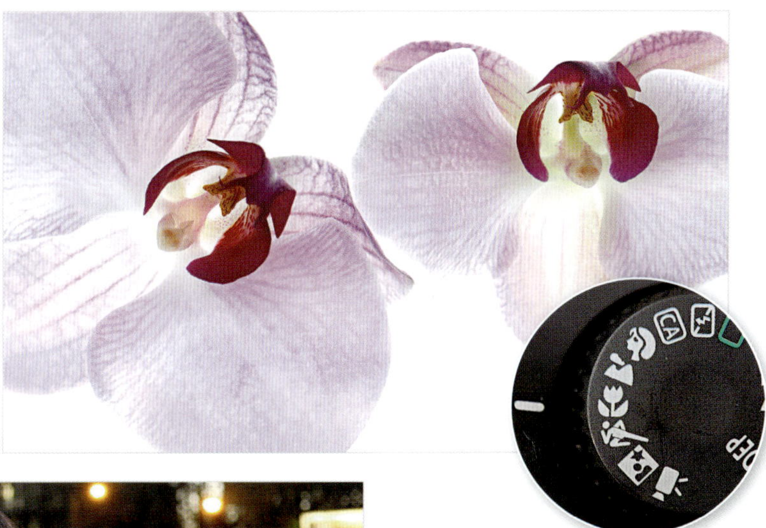

04 Close up

Close up mode, indicated by the flower, will set the camera up for macro-style photography. It'll sharpen the fine details and allow for a larger area of focus, which is important when shooting close-up images like this.

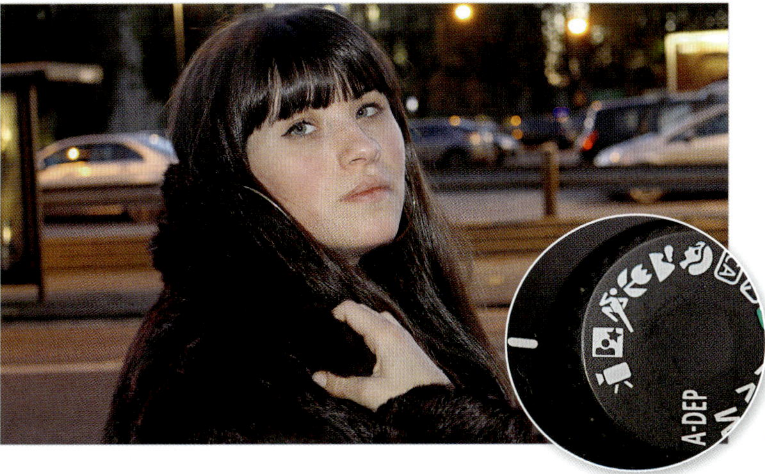

05 Night Portrait

In this mode your camera will try to balance out the light from the flash with the background scene, so the flash pops up to light the person in the foreground, then the camera balances out the exposure to record detail in the background too.

Produce picture-perfect portraits

Follow our guide to portrait composition and instantly take better shots of your friends and family

Your DSLR is the perfect tool for composing photographs. Its combination of viewfinder and lens make it much more suited to quick and precise composition than a point-and-shoot compact. But all the technical knowledge and camera controls we photographers obsess over count for nothing unless you know what you want to photograph, and how to position it within the frame.

There's never one 'correct' way to compose portraits, but here we'll give you a few pointers that are pretty much guaranteed to improve your results. Over the next eight pages,let us guide you through the basics of good portrait composition, so you can shoot your friends and family with confidence. We'll uncover the pitfalls you should avoid, and where to place your model in the frame for people shots that really wow!

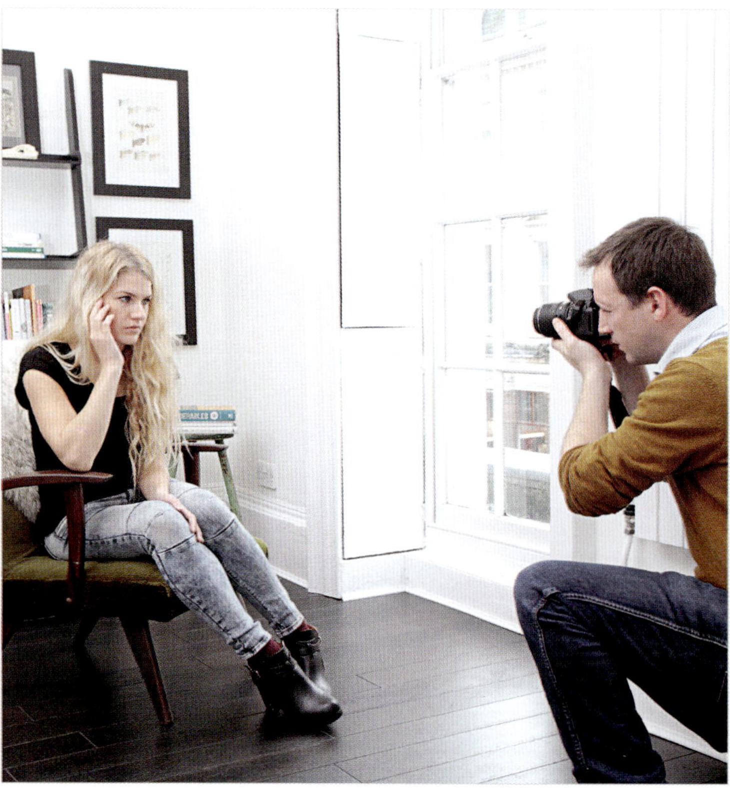

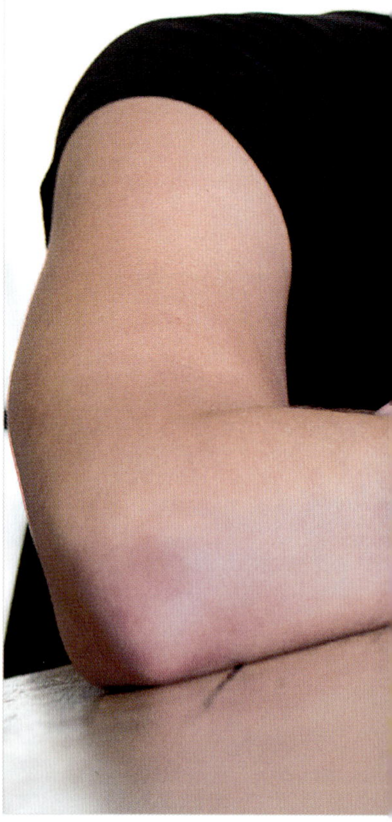

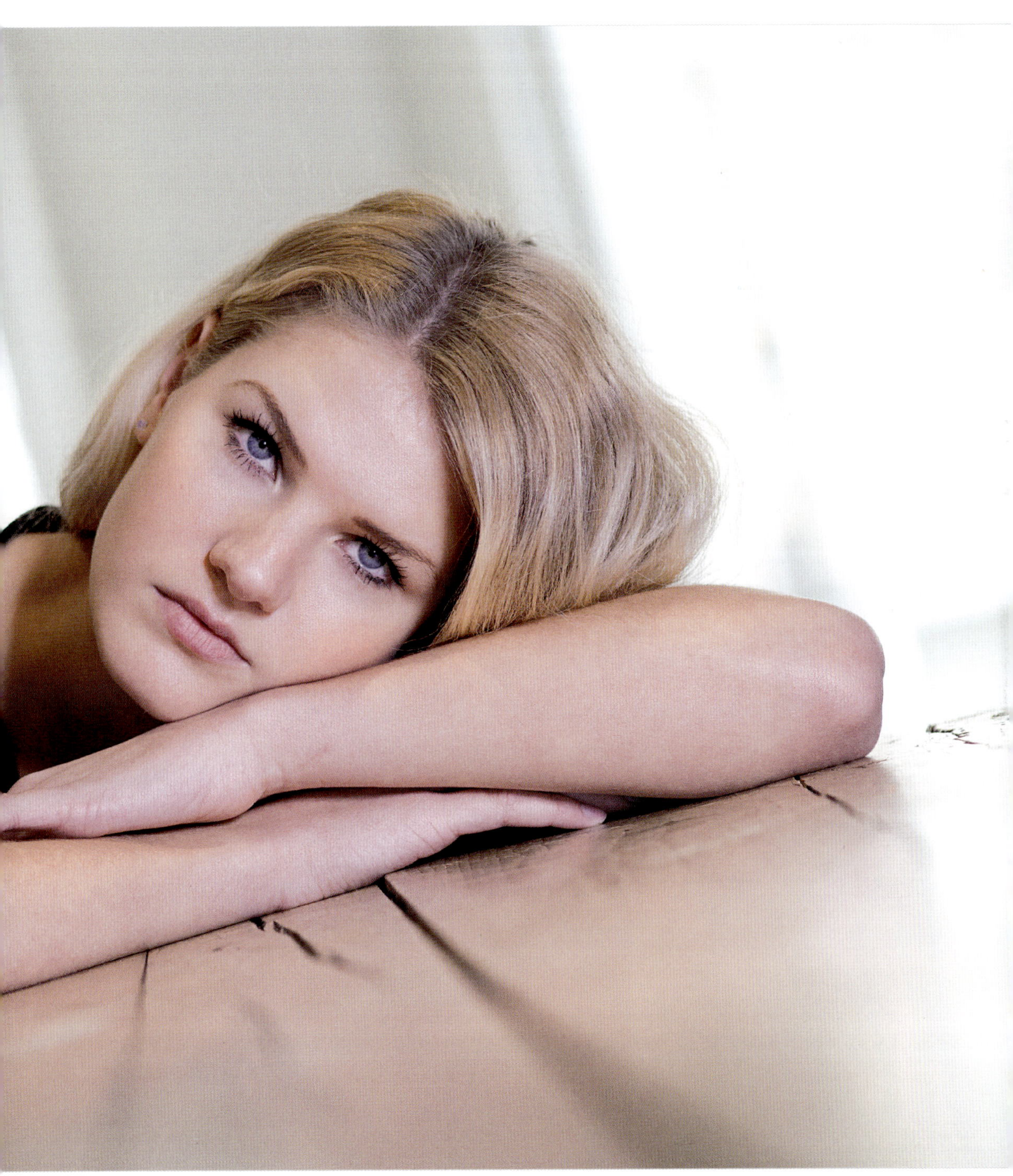

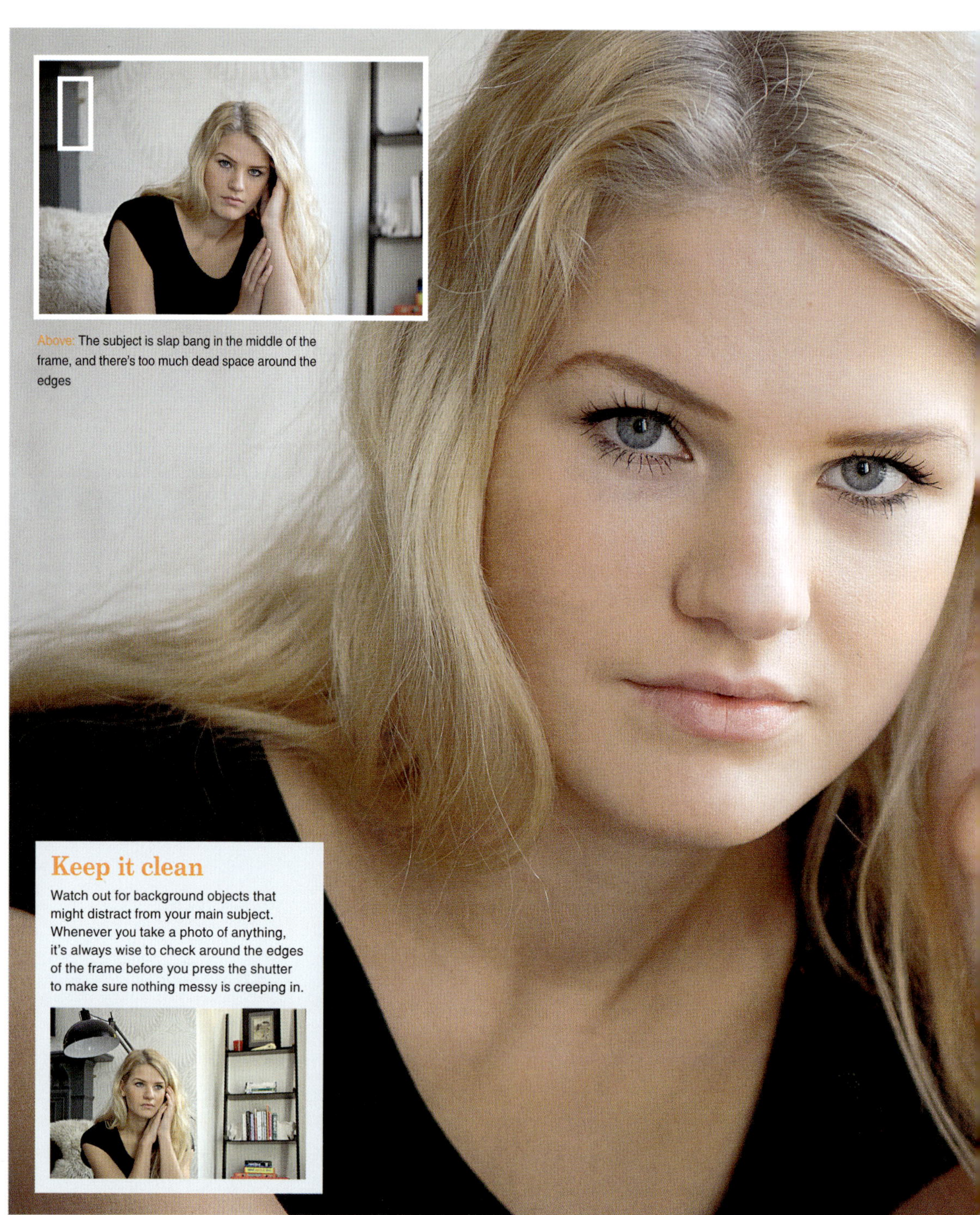

Above: The subject is slap bang in the middle of the frame, and there's too much dead space around the edges

Keep it clean

Watch out for background objects that might distract from your main subject. Whenever you take a photo of anything, it's always wise to check around the edges of the frame before you press the shutter to make sure nothing messy is creeping in.

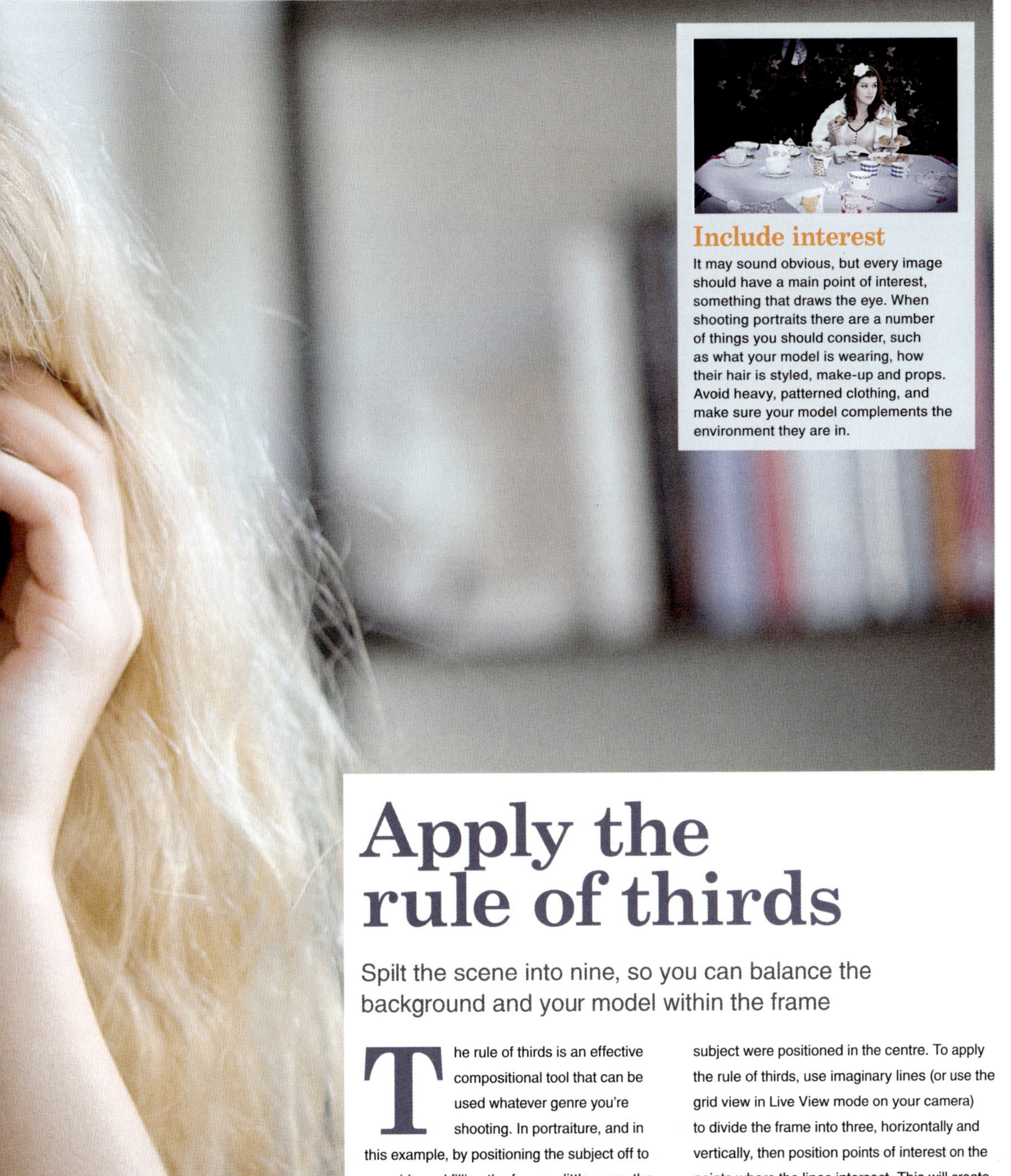

Include interest

It may sound obvious, but every image should have a main point of interest, something that draws the eye. When shooting portraits there are a number of things you should consider, such as what your model is wearing, how their hair is styled, make-up and props. Avoid heavy, patterned clothing, and make sure your model complements the environment they are in.

Apply the rule of thirds

Spilt the scene into nine, so you can balance the background and your model within the frame

The rule of thirds is an effective compositional tool that can be used whatever genre you're shooting. In portraiture, and in this example, by positioning the subject off to one side and filling the frame a little more, the composition is far stronger than it would be if the subject were positioned in the centre. To apply the rule of thirds, use imaginary lines (or use the grid view in Live View mode on your camera) to divide the frame into three, horizontally and vertically, then position points of interest on the points where the lines intersect. This will create stronger, more vibrant compositions.

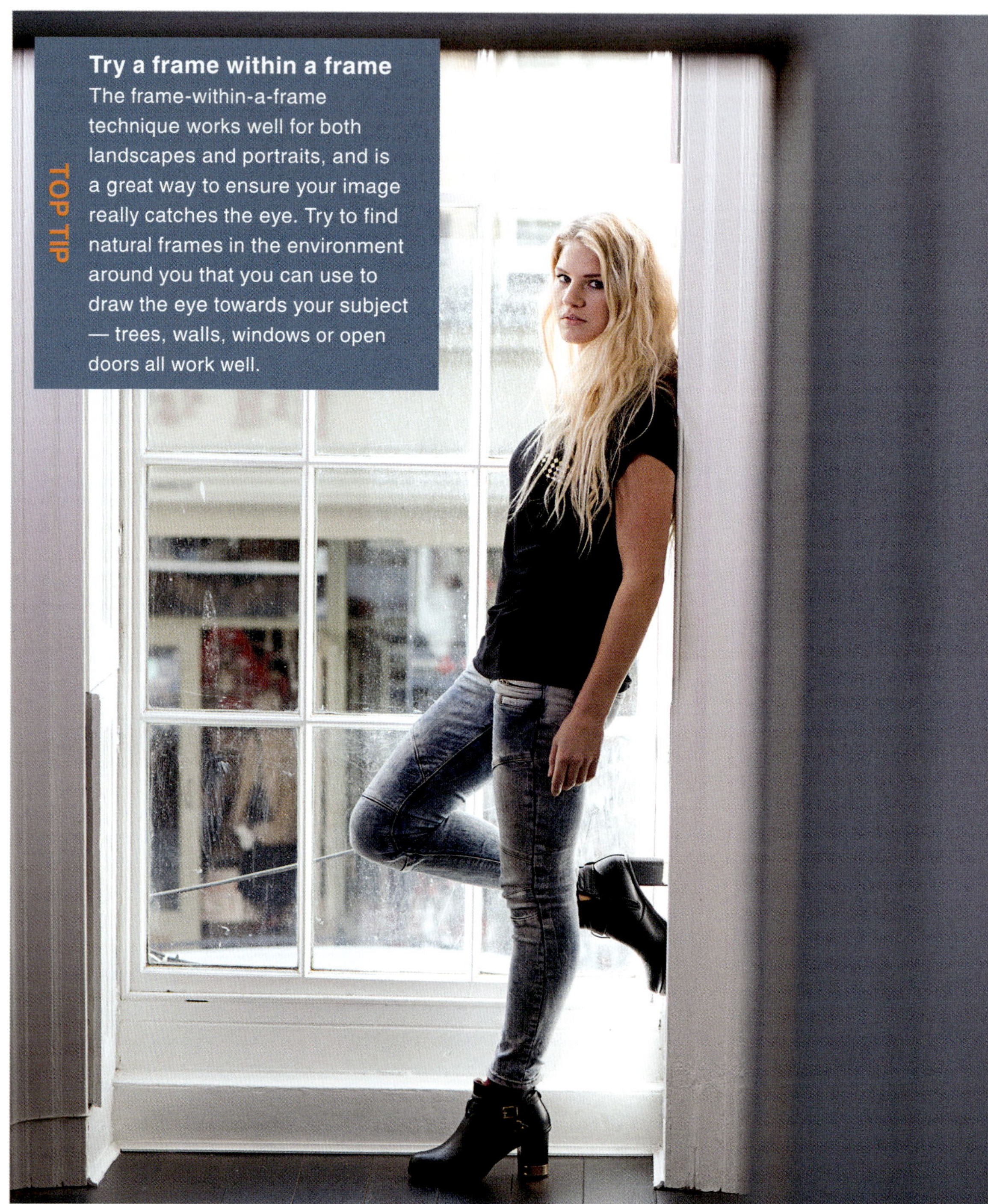
TOP TIP
Try a frame within a frame
The frame-within-a-frame technique works well for both landscapes and portraits, and is a great way to ensure your image really catches the eye. Try to find natural frames in the environment around you that you can use to draw the eye towards your subject — trees, walls, windows or open doors all work well.

Frame your masterpiece

Careful framing can transform an image from
a simple snap to a stylish showstopper

Where to crop

With portraits, unless you want the
whole body in the shot, you'll need
to decide what parts of the body to
include or exclude (also known as
cropping out, which can be done
in-camera or post-shoot).

Don't crop off at the hands or the
feet, because this will make for an
awkward composition. If you need to
lose the limbs, however, try to crop
half way between joints — above
the elbows or above the knees, for
example. If you want to crop in tight
to a headshot, try cropping the top
of the head out completely, drawing
attention to the eyes. Just remember
to apply the rule of thirds (see the
previous pages).

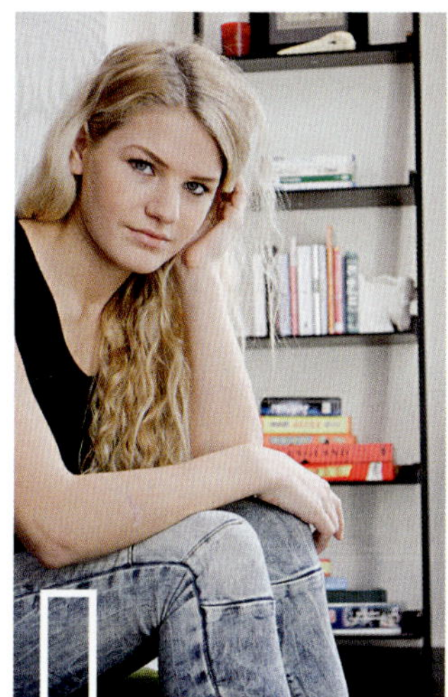

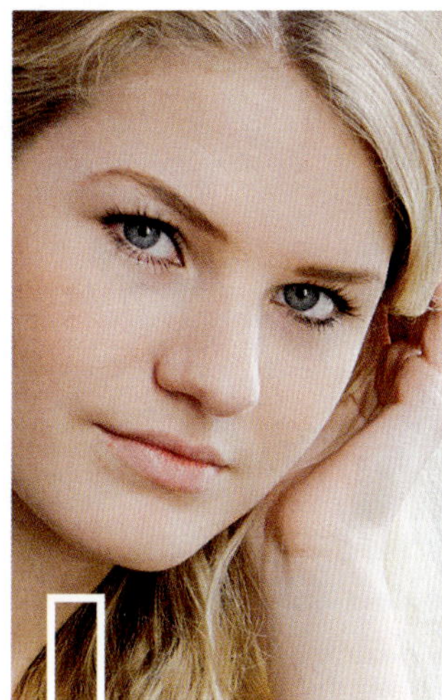

Left: It's fine to chop
into limbs, but make
sure you crop about
half way up and not
right next to the hands,
feet or elbows. The
close-up creates a
completely different
result. The left eye
rests a third of the way
in and down, which
really strengthens the
whole portrait

Leading lines

By including what is
known as a leading line
— natural or otherwise
— in your frame, you
can effectively draw
the eye of the viewer
through your image and
straight towards your
main subject. Here, the
leafy path leads the eye
up to the model. Always
look for elements in
the space or natural
environment you're
shooting in, such as
fences, walls, streams
and so on, to help you
do this.

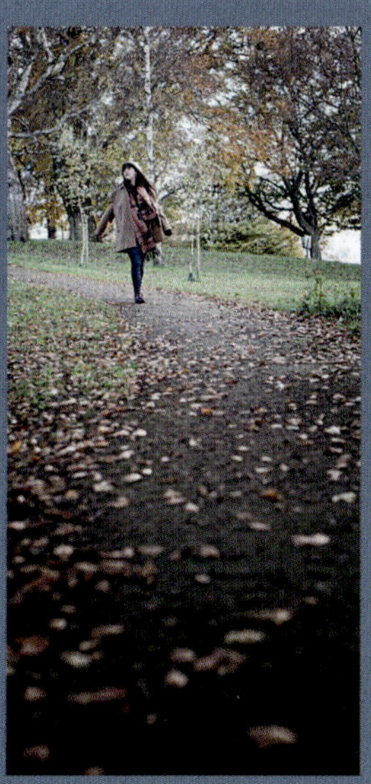

It's all about the eyes

If your model is looking
straight into your lens,
make sure their eyes are
pin sharp, as this is the
easiest way to connect the
viewer to the image. Just as
effective, though, is to ask
your model to look away
from the camera. This can
be suggestive and create
narrative. If your model is
looking to the side of the
frame, include space on that
side for them to 'look into'.

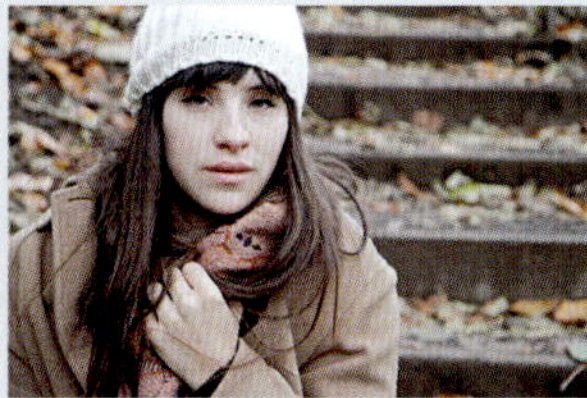

Above: You can make an instant connection by
getting your model to look directly into the lens

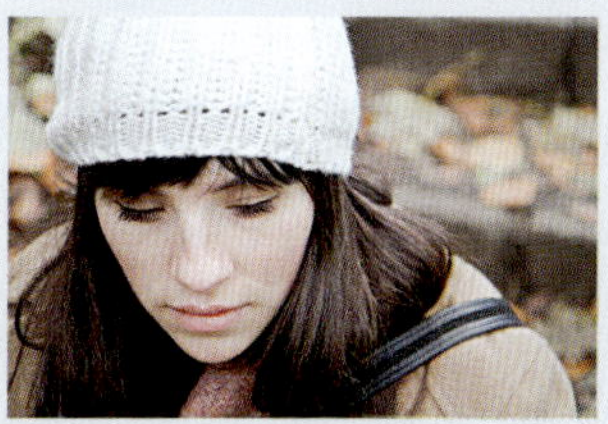

Right: Even when the eyes aren't
looking straight at the camera,
here they make the image. Note
there is more space on the right-
hand side of the frame, as the
eyes are pointing in that direction

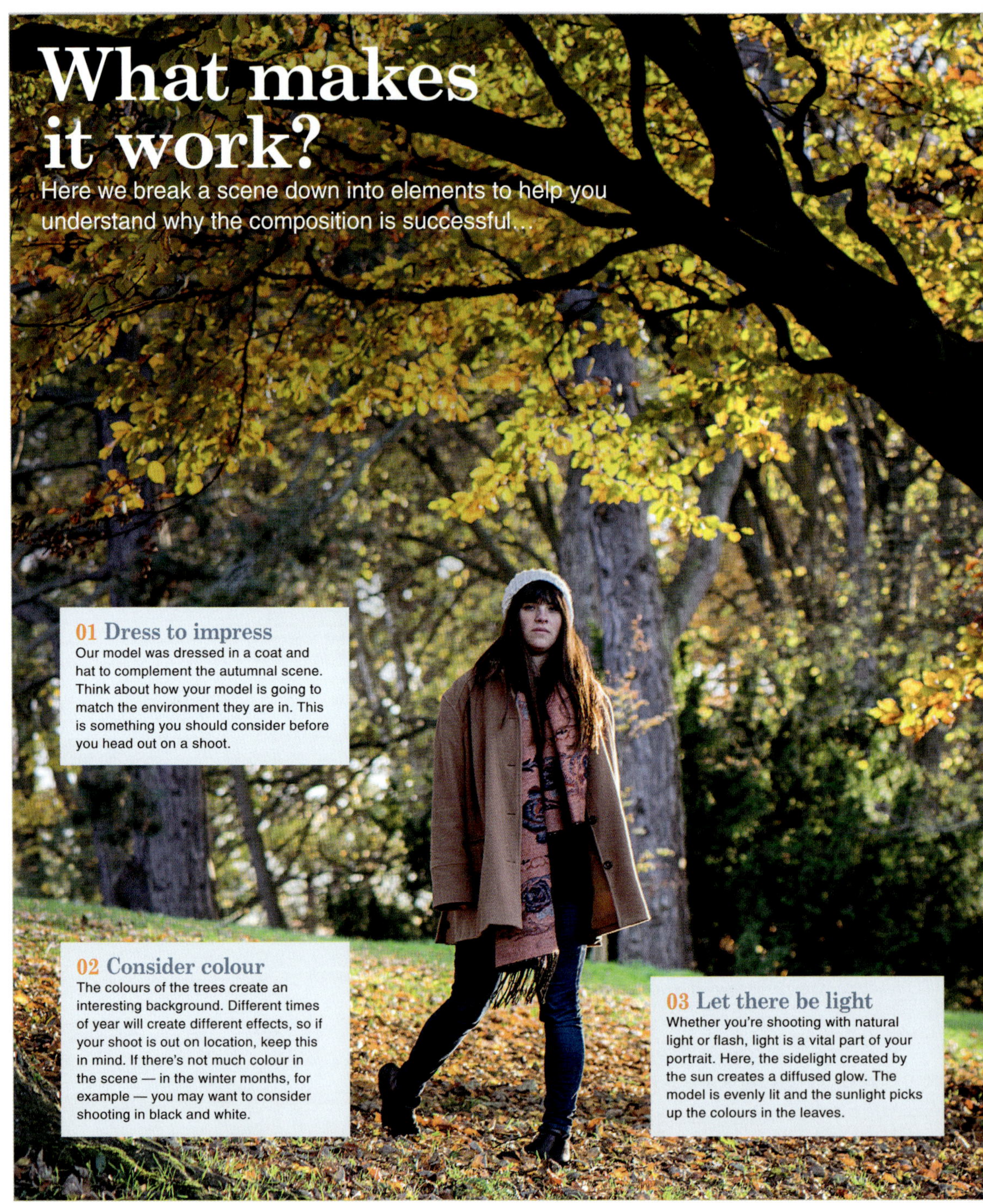

What makes it work?

Here we break a scene down into elements to help you understand why the composition is successful…

01 Dress to impress

Our model was dressed in a coat and hat to complement the autumnal scene. Think about how your model is going to match the environment they are in. This is something you should consider before you head out on a shoot.

02 Consider colour

The colours of the trees create an interesting background. Different times of year will create different effects, so if your shoot is out on location, keep this in mind. If there's not much colour in the scene — in the winter months, for example — you may want to consider shooting in black and white.

03 Let there be light

Whether you're shooting with natural light or flash, light is a vital part of your portrait. Here, the sidelight created by the sun creates a diffused glow. The model is evenly lit and the sunlight picks up the colours in the leaves.

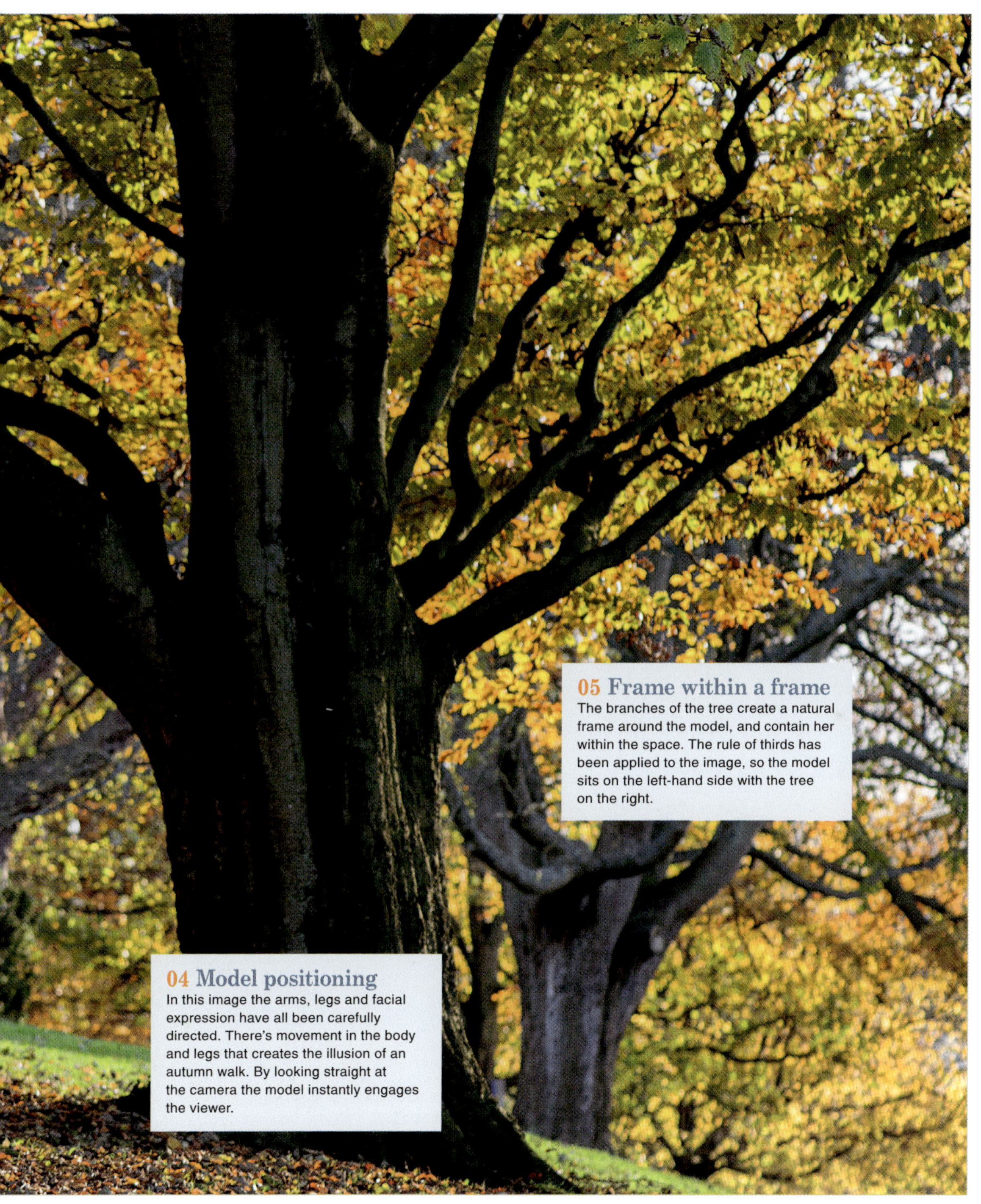

05 Frame within a frame
The branches of the tree create a natural frame around the model, and contain her within the space. The rule of thirds has been applied to the image, so the model sits on the left-hand side with the tree on the right.

04 Model positioning
In this image the arms, legs and facial expression have all been carefully directed. There's movement in the body and legs that creates the illusion of an autumn walk. By looking straight at the camera the model instantly engages the viewer.

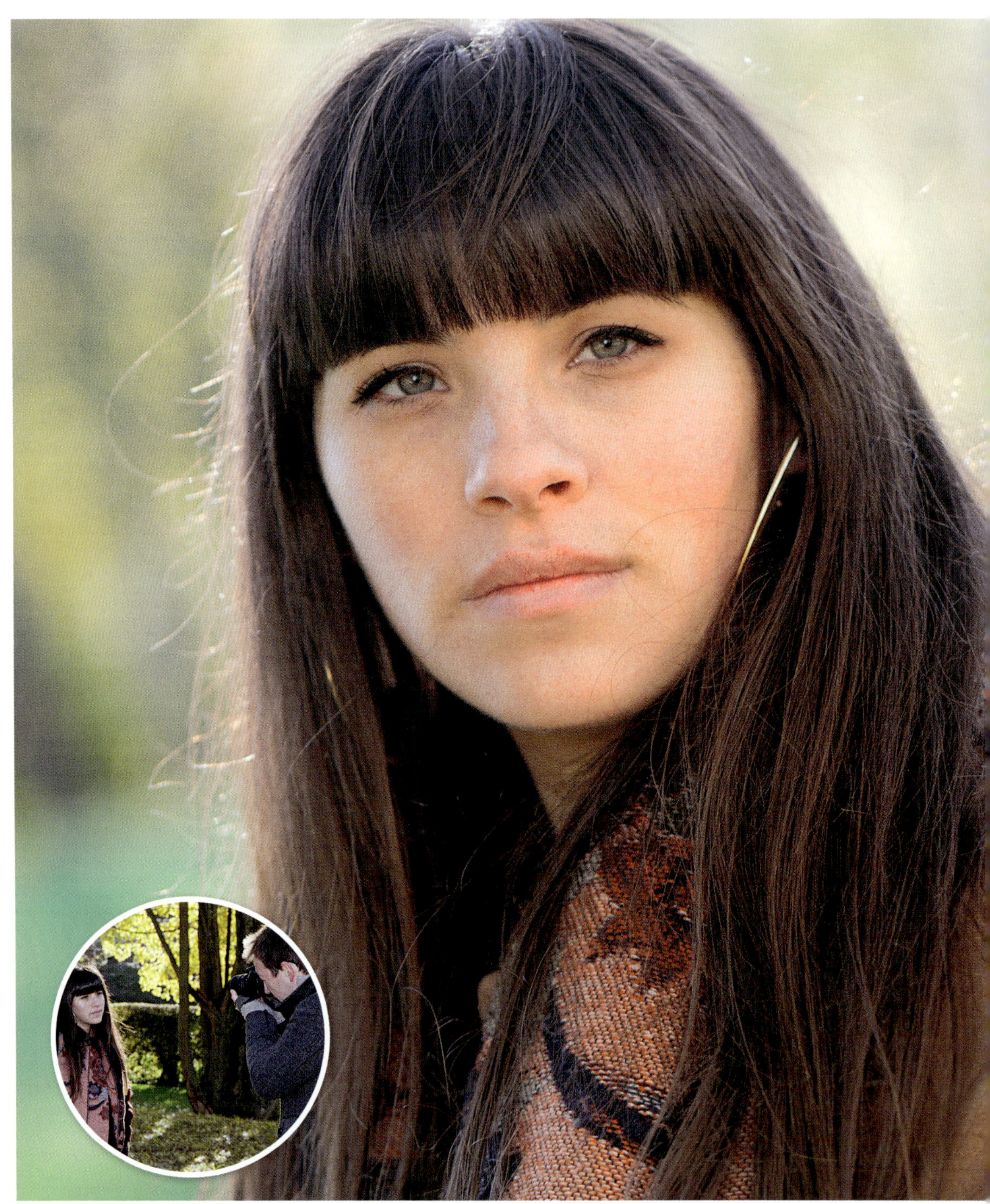

Discover how to blur a background

Learn how to simplify your portrait compositions with a beautiful blurred background using a wide aperture

Simplicity is one of the keys to good portraits, and one of the best ways to achieve this is by blurring out busy backgrounds. Not only does this focus attention firmly on your subject; it also gets rid of distracting background detail and gives your portraits a professional edge. To achieve a blurred background you'll need some parts of your image to be sharp, and others soft. When you focus on a single point in a scene it is captured in sharp focus, but you can also control how much of the image in front of and behind that point of focus that is recorded sharply. This area of sharpness could be very wide, or very narrow, and is called the depth of field.

So how do you make your subject sharp and transform the background into attractive blur? One easy way is to use your camera's Portrait mode, which will automatically choose an aperture setting that will keep the area of sharpness fairly narrow — anything outside of this area will be nice and soft. Here, we'll show you how it's done…

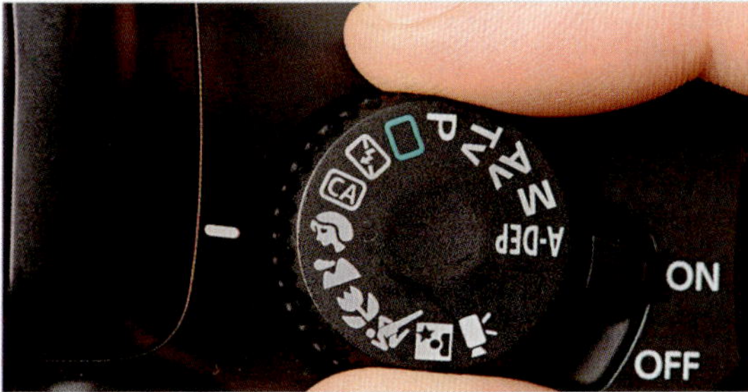

01 Select Portrait mode

Select Portrait mode by turning your camera's mode dial or accessing it via the menu. This mode chooses exposure settings that will capture your subject in sharp focus and throw the background into blur. The strength of this blur will be determined by how far your lens is zoomed in.

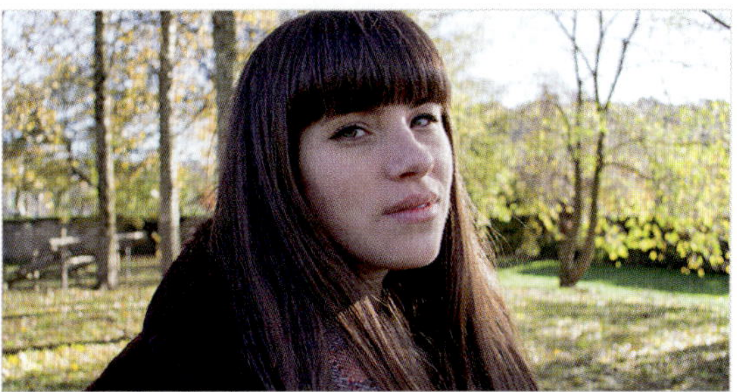

02 Too close

Make sure you focus carefully on your model, and not on anything in the background. If you shoot using one of your lens's widest focal lengths (the smaller number on your lens) you'll get unflattering results and the background won't blur enough, as in the image shown here.

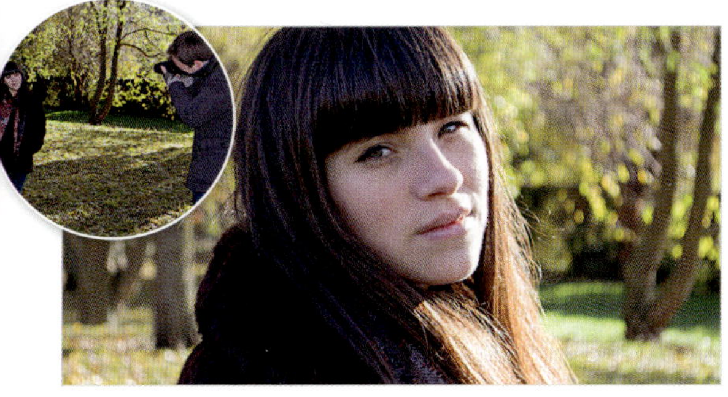

03 Step back

If you're close to your subject and using a fairly wide zoom setting, you may need to step back to stop the background appearing too sharp. Now you can zoom in with your lens (using a focal length with a larger number), so the area of sharpness will be narrower.

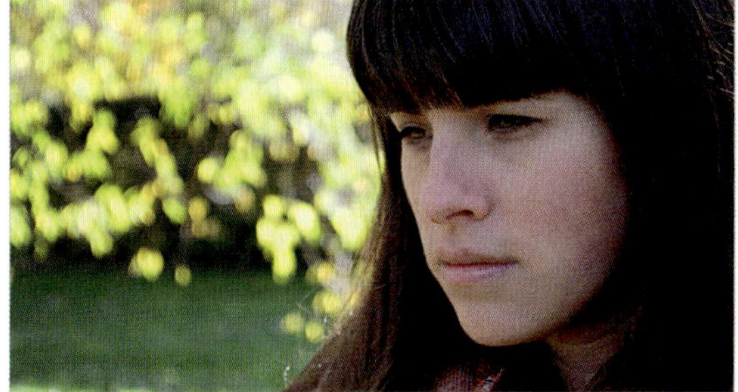

04 Add impact

Although we're blurring the background, it's still important to consider how it's going to appear in the frame. For extra impact, think about how the background blur will look. For example, bold colours or dappled light through trees can be very pretty when thrown out of focus.

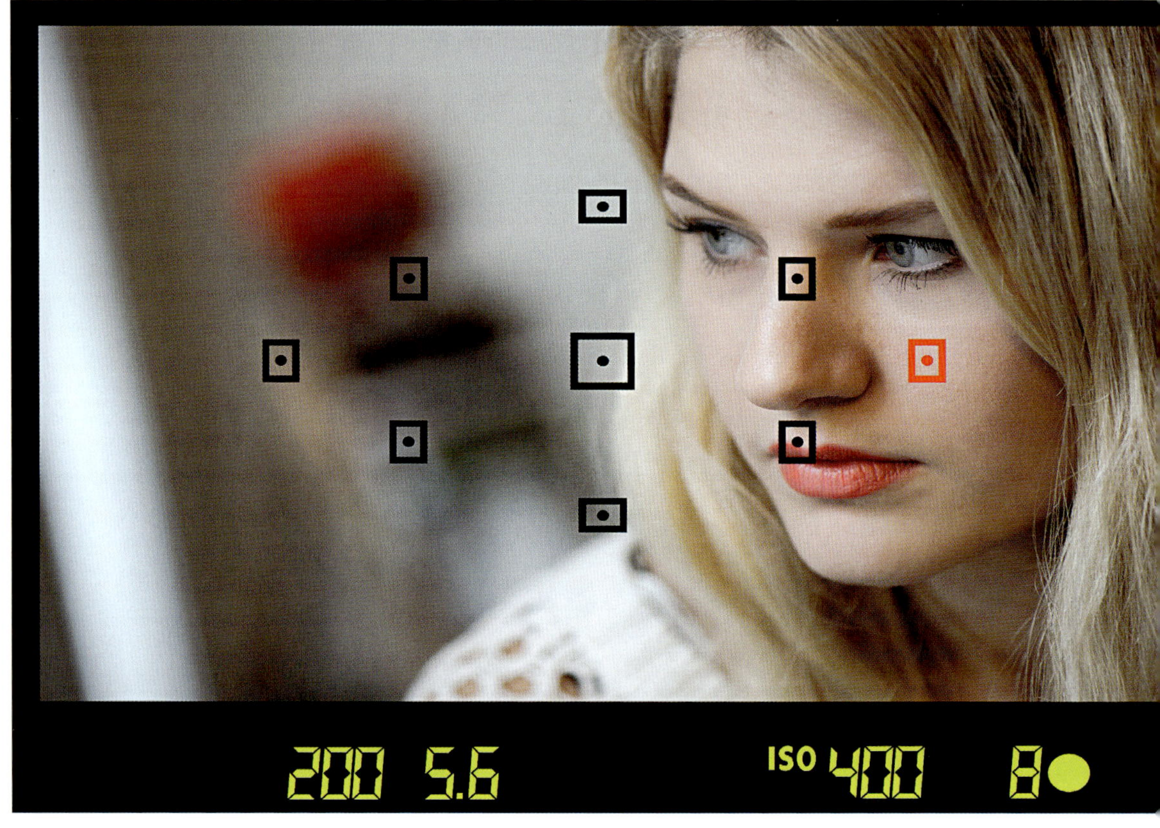

Use AF points for sharper shots

Start taking more control of the sharpness of your images by selecting the autofocus points manually

As we've already explained, to capture professional-looking portraits you need to blur the cluttered backgrounds. This focuses attention on the person in your shot, and helps to soften distracting background details. This means you need to control precisely which areas of your scene are in focus, or sharp, and which are soft.

For this reason, accurate focusing is vital. In portraits, the subject's eyes must be sharp, but that plane of sharpness will usually be quite narrow, so there isn't much margin for error. By default your camera's autofocus system is set up to snap onto objects in the centre of the frame, and often those closest to the camera. But what if your subject's eyes and face aren't in the centre of the frame?

Left to its own devices, autofocus will snap on to the centre of the scene, therefore throwing the eyes and face out of focus and ruining the shot. Even if your subject is in the centre of the frame, the central focus point will more than likely focus on the nose because it's closer to the camera. In situations like this you need to take control of the autofocus system, by telling the camera where to focus. Here's how it's done…

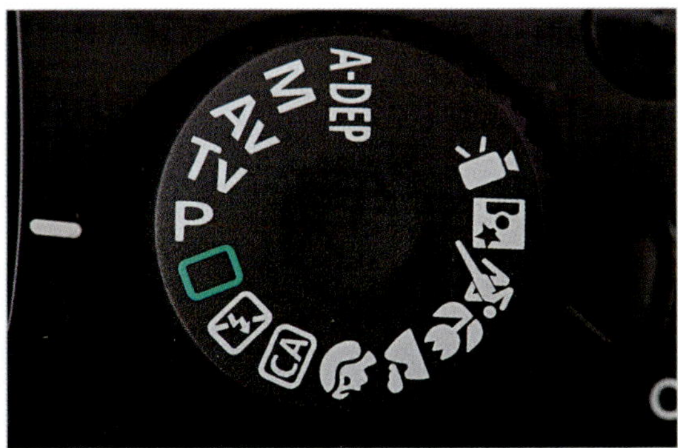

01 Switch to P mode

To select different focus points, you'll first need to select Program mode, marked with a P on the mode dial. This is a semi-automatic exposure mode that suggests ideal settings, but lets you take some control — perfect for beginners looking to experiment. Now make sure your lens is switched to AF (autofocus).

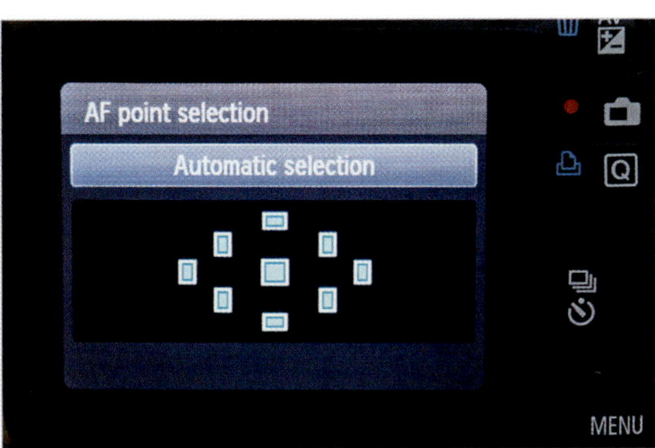

02 Available focus points

If you look through your viewfinder you'll see a faint grid pattern with one square in the middle surrounded by a selection of others. This is the focus grid. It allows you to see which focus point is currently active — it illuminates when focus is achieved. You can also move the focus point when shooting in Live View (see the box below for details).

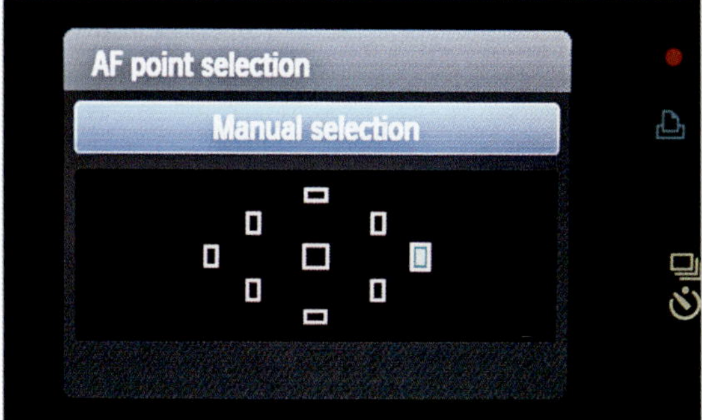

03 Get to the point

Each camera is different, so you'll need to find the button that enables you to bring up your focus points on screen (refer to your manual if necessary). Set the AF grid to its Single Point selection setting, and use the navigation keys to move the focus point around. In this case, we want to select the point on the right of the frame.

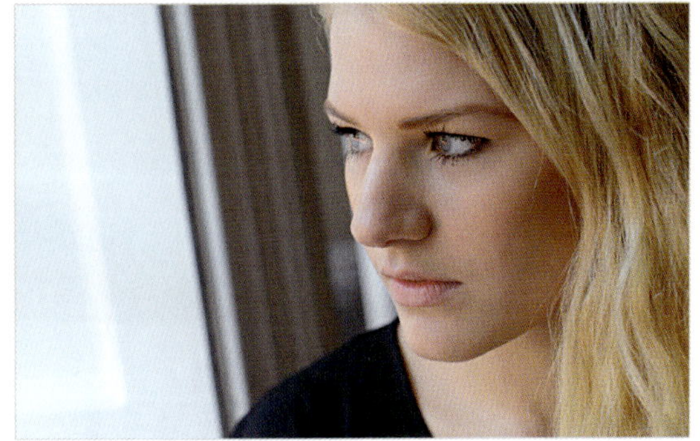

04 Now shoot!

Once you've decided which point to use, press the shutter-release button halfway to trigger the autofocus, and if you're happy that the lens has focused in the right spot, press the button fully to take your shot. Review the image on the LCD screen, zooming in to check that the eye is perfectly sharp.

Do it in Live View

You can use Live View to do exactly the same thing; the only difference is you won't see the nine-point grid, but a white box that sits in (and can be moved around within) the frame. Using the back-panel navigation controls, move it until it sits over the main subject, then simply half press the shutter-release button to focus.

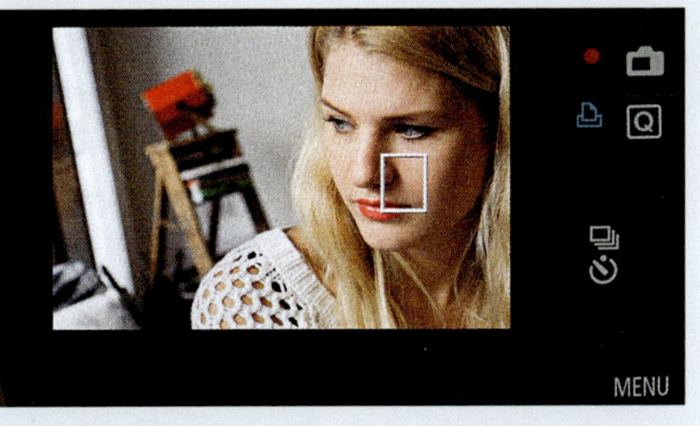

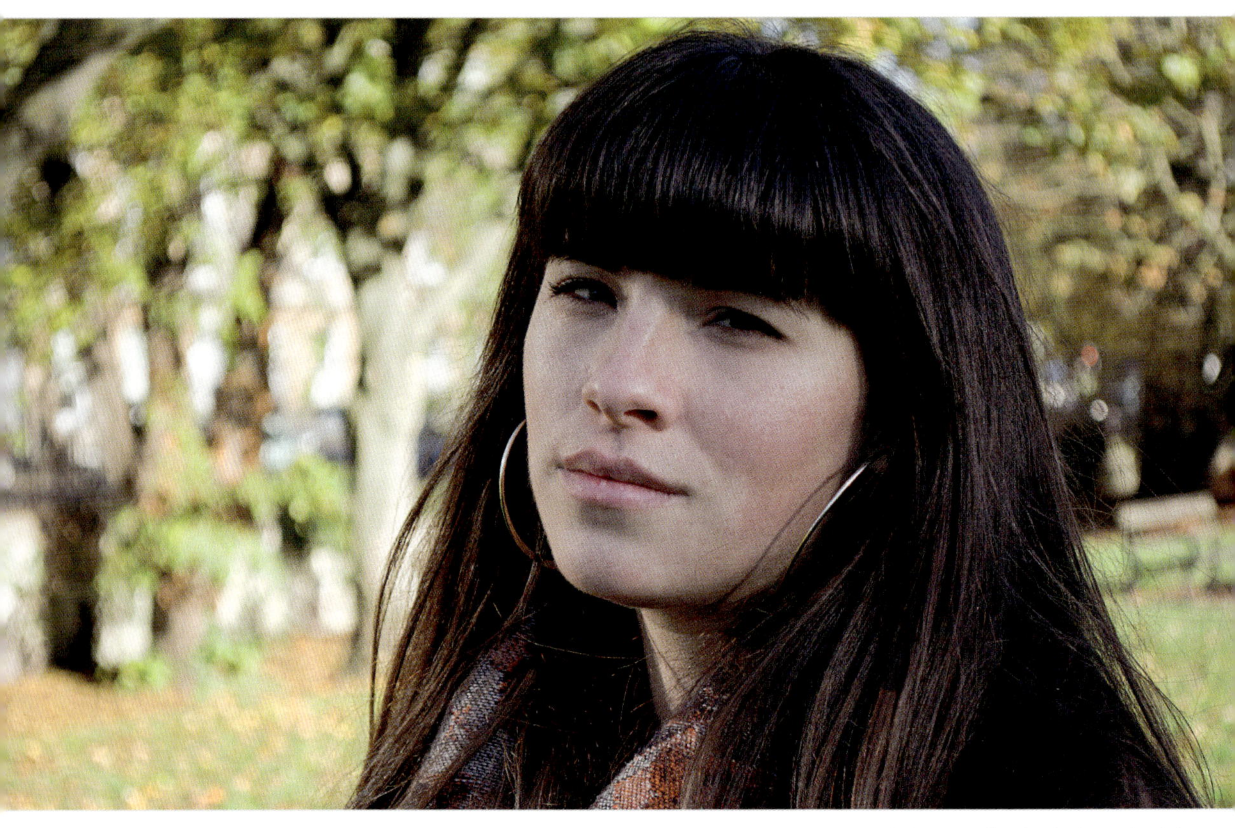

Above: Avoid harsh, unflattering shadows and squinting eyes by placing your model in the shade

Get natural lighting right

Avoid harsh sun and nasty shadows by placing your model in the shade

Photographers tend to classify light in one of two ways: hard and soft. Hard light comes from small light sources — a bare light bulb, for example. If you shone the light from a bare light bulb across your face, your nose would cast an unsightly shadow. But if you put a lampshade over the bare bulb, the light would be diffused and the shadow less harsh. The same principle is applied to flashguns with diffusers or studio flash units with softboxes attached.

When the sun is shining, the quality of light is hard — just like the bare lightbulb — because it comes from a small source, relatively speaking. That's not to say that the sun is small, but because it's so far away we see it as a small spot in a big sky. Shoot under a cloudy sky and the light is much softer, just like the lampshade-covered bulb. You'd be forgiven for thinking that a sunny day is best for taking pictures of people outdoors, as everything is bright and colourful, but when in comes to portraits, soft light is actually much more flattering.

> *"Shoot under a cloudy sky and the light is much softer, just like a lampshade-covered bulb"*

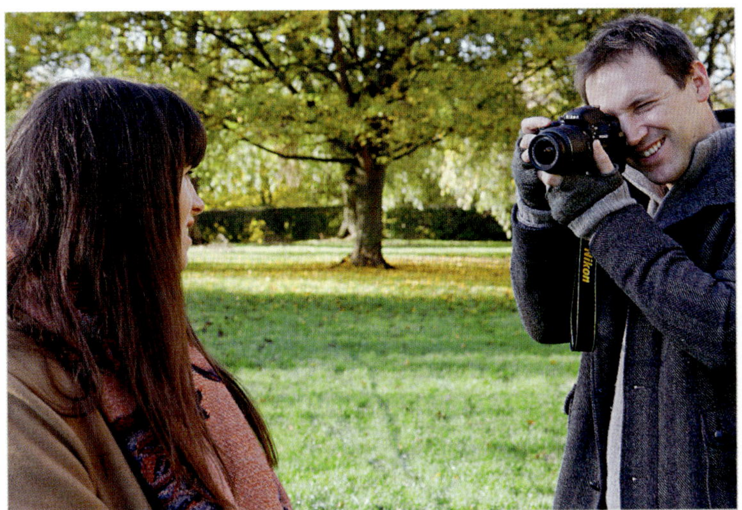

Above: By finding a spot like this the model is comfortable and you don't need to worry about your image being too bright

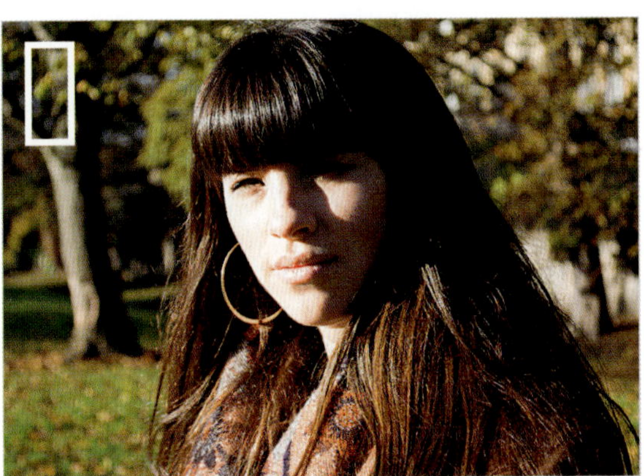

Left and below: As these images clearly show, harsh sunlight produces strong, ugly shadows on the model's face

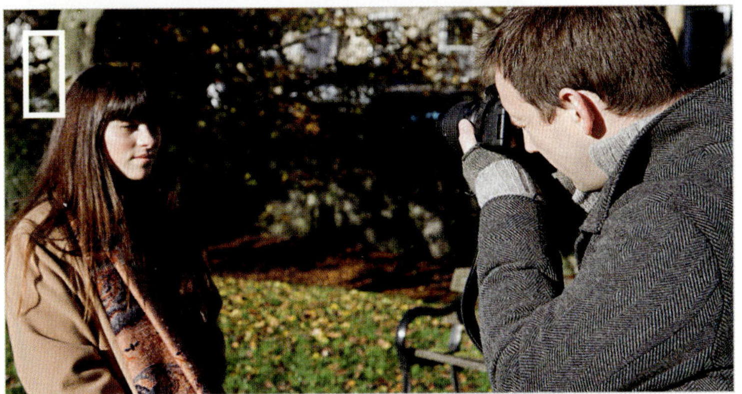

STEP BY STEP: how to get great portraits outdoors

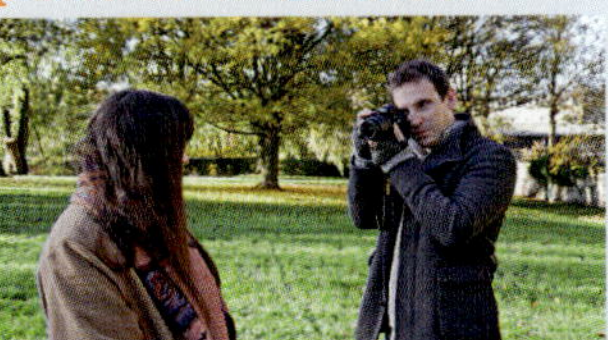

01 Find the right spot

Find the right location. If you're shooting in overcast conditions you don't need to worry about the sun; if you're shooting on a clear day find a shady spot. Remember to consider the background space behind your model. You don't want to include anything that is distracting in the frame.

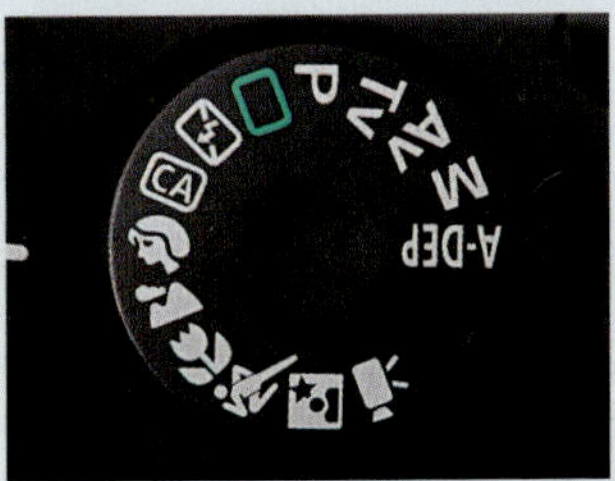

02 Essential settings

Select your camera's Portrait shooting mode. This will keep your model sharp and softly blur the background space. If you have a very bright background, then you may struggle to get the exposure of your image correct. If this is the case, move your model around until the background doesn't look so bright.

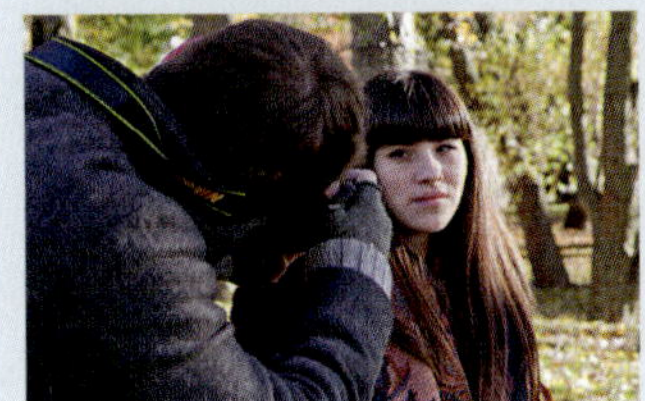

03 Get eye contact

For maximum impact, get your model to look directly into your lens. Keep talking, and keep the positive feedback coming so they feel relaxed in front of the lens. Position the main focus point on the eyes, and make sure your subject doesn't squint.

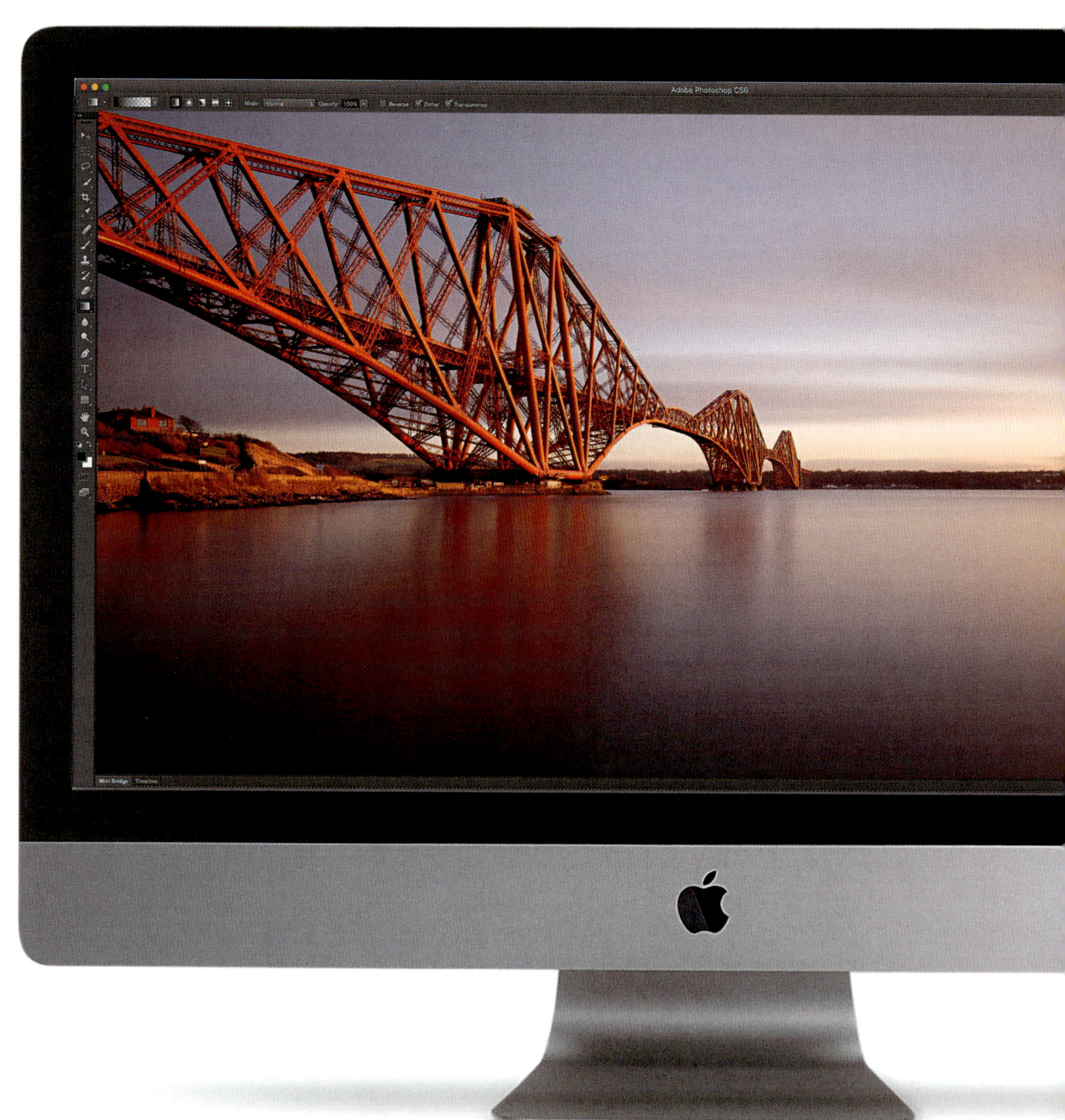

Landscapes

Everything you need to know to get started with landscape photography, from composition to exposure

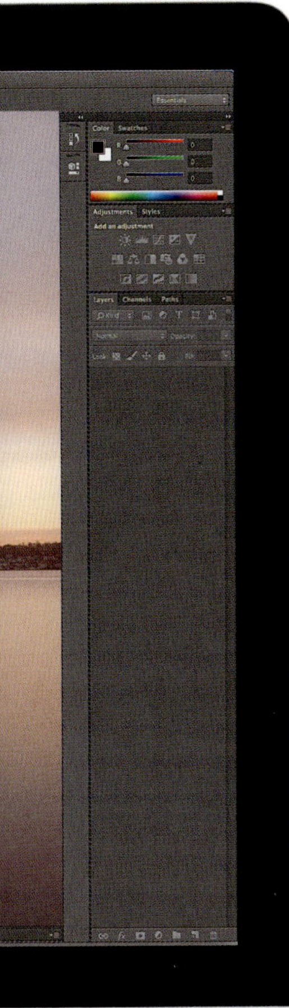

68 Master landscape composition

Get to grips with the basics of composition and start improving your own landscape pictures

76 Make the most of natural light

When it comes to landscapes, timing is everything, so ensure great results by being in the right place in the right light

82 Maximise your depth of field

Discover how to control the focus in your landscapes so that they're sharp where you want them to be

86 Take control of your exposures

Use your camera's exposure compensation feature to make images lighter or darker as you shoot them

Master landscape composition

Get to grips with the basics of composition and start improving your own landscape pictures

For those who love the outdoors there's nothing better than heading out on a landscape shoot with your DSLR. Landscape photography gives you the chance to capture spectacular scenes and get back to nature, but it can be frustrating if what you see in front of you is not what you capture on camera. Try and fit too much into the frame, for example, and impressive structures can appear very small in the final result. This is why you have to break the scene up and consider what's going on in the background and foreground — otherwise known as careful composition. Over the next ten pages, we'll guide you through the basics of landscape composition so that you can improve your results in an instant. We'll show you how to apply the 'rule of thirds' and use simple tricks such as leading lines, foreground interest and reflections to strengthen the shots you take. Once you've got to grips with the basics, the rest of your landscape photography will fall into place. Remember, you need to learn what works and what doesn't by doing, then reviewing!

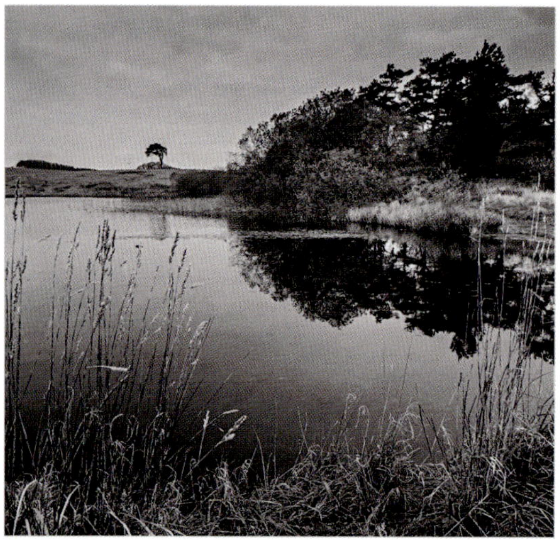

01 How to use the rule of thirds

The rule of thirds can be used in all genres of photography, but it's especially useful for landscapes. By splitting the scene into virtual thirds, vertically and horizontally, you can balance the composition, carefully positioning your main point of interest (a tree in this example) on a point where the lines intersect to draw the eye into the scene.

You should also aim to split the sky and ground in this way, including either one-third ground to two-thirds sky, or vice versa. If you're shooting on a day with nice colours in the sky, or there are interesting textured clouds above, for example, it would be best to include two-thirds of sky.

Above: In this image, the tree is in the centre and the sky and ground are evenly spilt

Above: Here, the eye is lead through the space and the tree occupies the left-hand side. The ratio of sky to land is also more pleasing

Apply the rule of thirds

Split the scene into nine sections to create a more pleasing landscape composition

02 How does the rule of thirds work?

Both artists and photographers use the rule of thirds to enhance their compositions because it really works. But how? If you place your main subject slap bang in the middle of the frame it will appear static — you create empty surrounding space that is rarely interesting. By using the rule of thirds, however, you use the space more effectively and draw the eye through the image.

You'll also find if you use the rule of thirds to split the sky and ground that the ratio of light (sky) and dark (ground) is more effective. This comes down to the fact that generally we don't like to view things in equal measures. That said, rules are made to be broken, so experiment with composition and see what works for you in a given scene.

Left: This simplistic image uses the rule of thirds to great effect

03 Frame it up

When you arrive on location, have a good look around before you even think about taking your camera out of your bag. Take your time and consider the space you're working with, moving around to decide on the best vantage point to shoot from. Use your fingers to mock up a frame so you can see what works and what doesn't. Many photographers will return to the same location on multiple occasions and in different lights to get the results they're after.

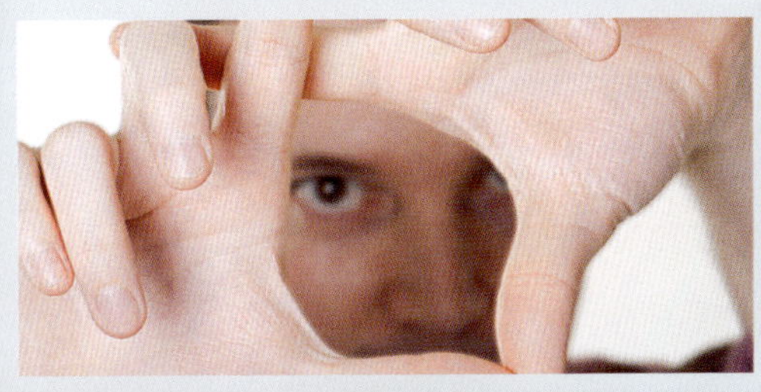

05 Use Live View to compose

Live View is a great feature that's guaranteed to help when it comes to composition. The Live View feature on most DSLRs comes with a grid overlay option that you can use to apply the rule of thirds. Simply line up the horizon in the top or bottom third and place your main subject at a point one-third of the way in — a simple yet effective setup.

04 Take a tripod

A tripod is a must-have accessory for all landscape photographers. When capturing scenic shots you'll often be shooting in low light at the start or end of the day, or using small aperture settings to capture as much of the scene as possible in focus, so you'll need to use a slow shutter speed, making it impossible to get sharp shots handheld.

Using a tripod also helps you to get composition right, as it forces you to slow down and think about how your subject is working in the frame. The best way to get better results is to shoot, review, tweak and then shoot again. It may take you a few attempts to get it right, so keep practising.

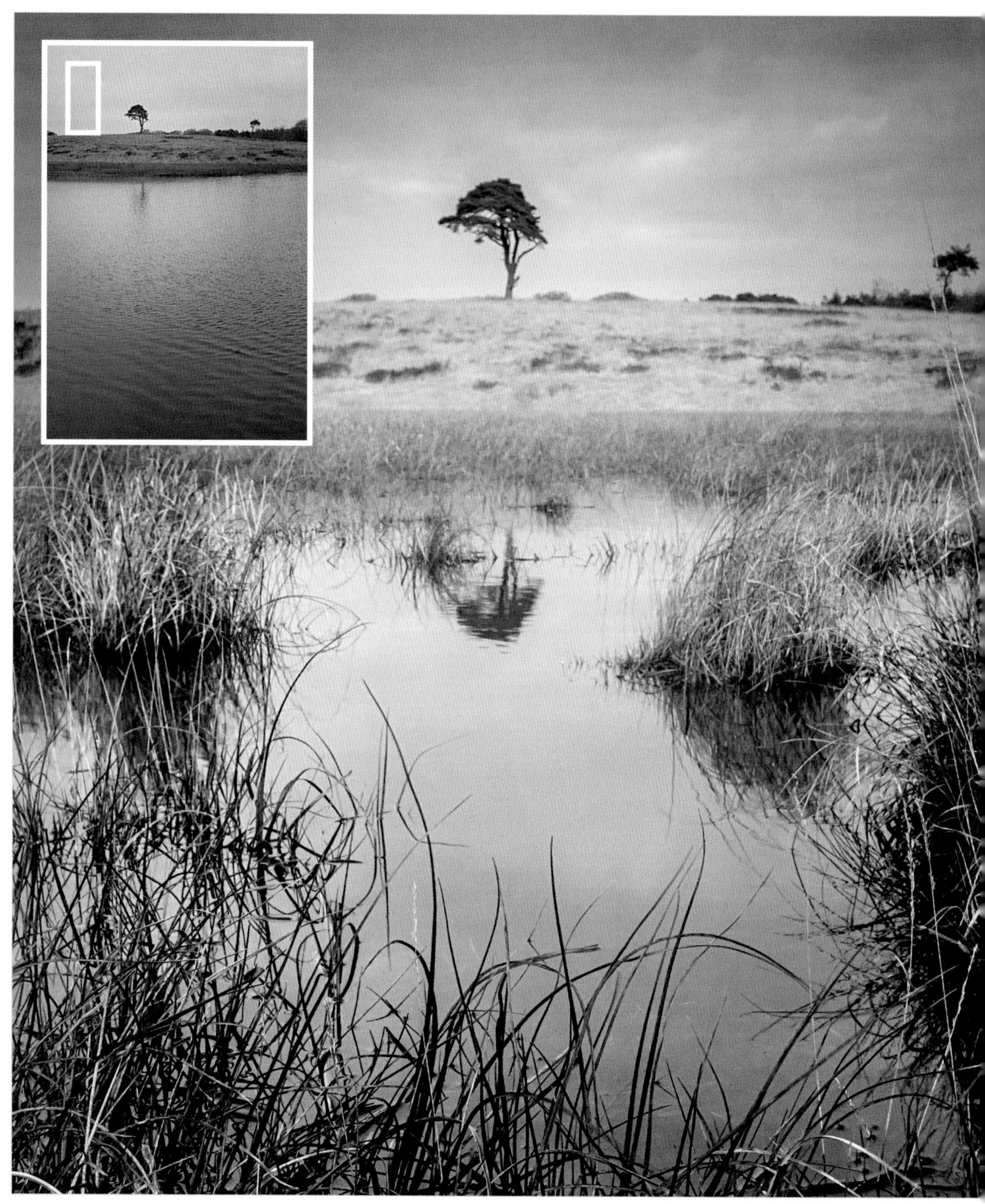

Include interesting foreground interest

Strengthen your compositions by including something of intrinsic interest in the foreground of your image

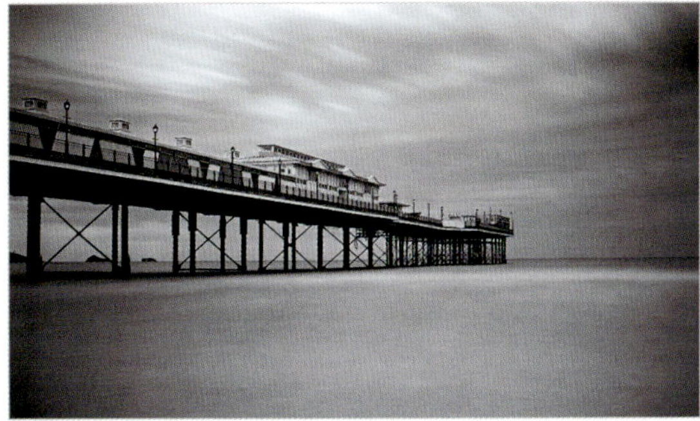

01 Make water look more interesting

When shooting large areas of water you can create the kind of soft, milky effect used by landscape pros simply by slowing your shutter speed (creating a longer exposure). This is a great way of illustrating movement in water — whether you're shooting the sea, waterfalls or fast-moving rivers — but also in dramatic overhead clouds on a windy day. It's this kind of technique that elevates images from simple to stunning.

02 Add some interest

It may seem obvious, but placing something of interest in the foreground of your image really does work — catching the eye of the viewer and leading it onwards through the frame. Shots without foreground interest are very boring. By simply lowering the viewpoint and including something in the foreground, negative space can be filled, and the result is far more pleasing.

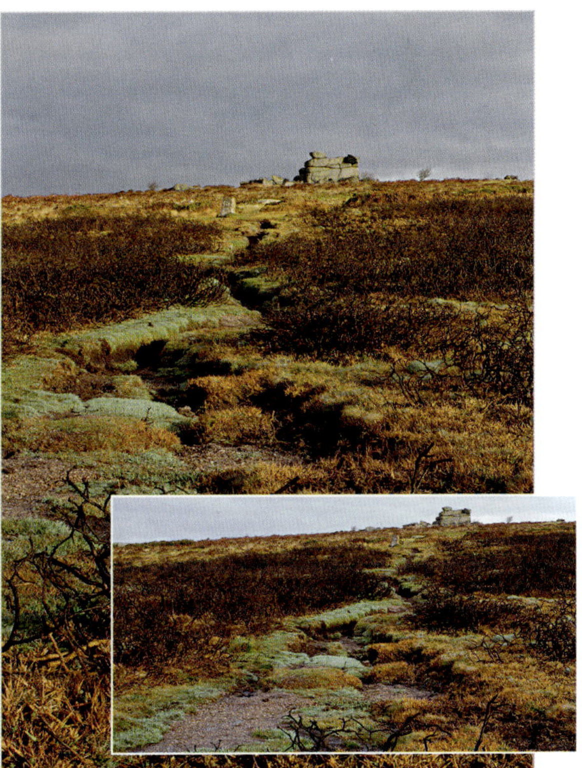

03 Negative space

We've mentioned the term negative space, and despite it sounding like a bad thing, and in some cases it is, there are times when it can be used to create an effective, minimal result. In this monochrome seascape, for example, we've created movement and atmosphere by dragging the camera across as we opened the shutter. This works particularly well in a coastal location like this, where you're trying to capture a large open space.

04 Landscape vs portrait

In landscape photography it's easy to get into the habit of shooting everything in a landscape orientation, that is, with your camera in it's normal shooting position. However, in some situations you'll get better, stronger results simply by turning your camera to a portrait orientation, as shown. Now you can capture an entirely different view of a scene, emphasising vertical lines and features that lead the eye into the image.

Pro landscape tricks

Nature is packed with interesting shapes, forms, patterns
and leading lines. Learn how to use them to your advantage

01 How low can you go?

It really helps to get down low when composing your scenes, as this
exaggerates those leading lines and makes it possible to capture an
original view of a well-photographed scene. Try it for yourself: take an
image from eye level when standing, then get lower to the ground and
shoot again. Take the time to experiment with viewpoints for the very
best results.

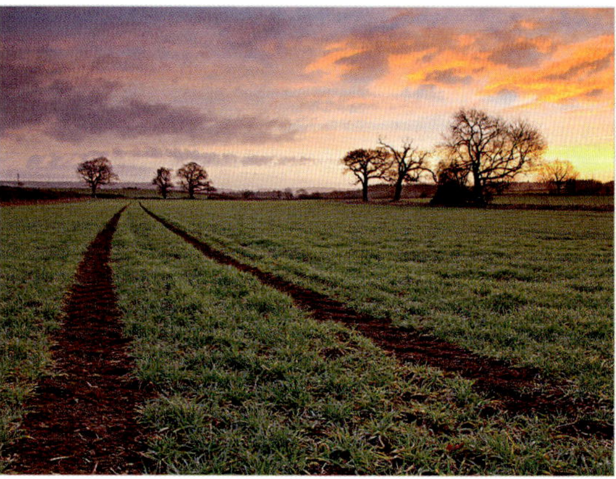

02 Shape and form

Look for shape, form and pattern in the landscape. There are many
natural environments where you can find such things — the beautiful
patterns left in the sand when the tide goes out, for example, or in this
case simple tracks left in a field. To capture this effectively, get down low
and use the rule of thirds to make the image rest easy on the eye.

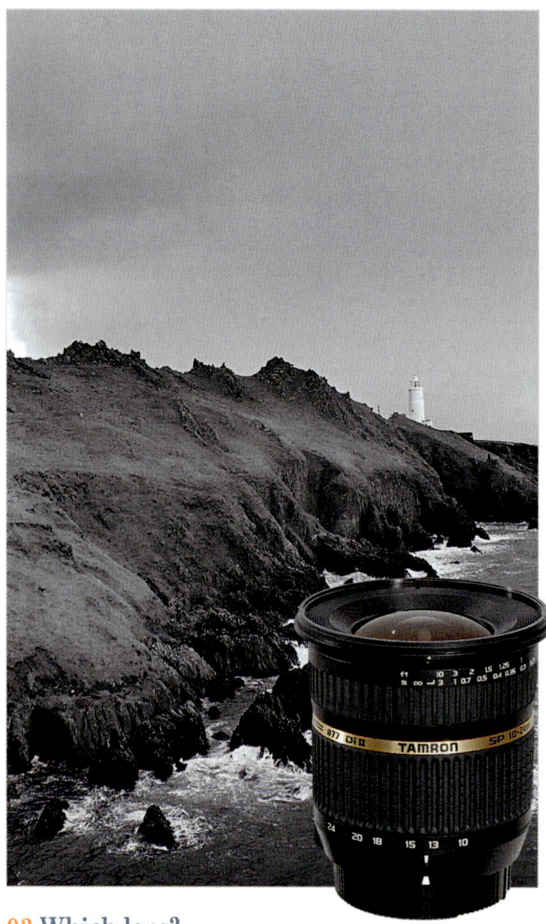

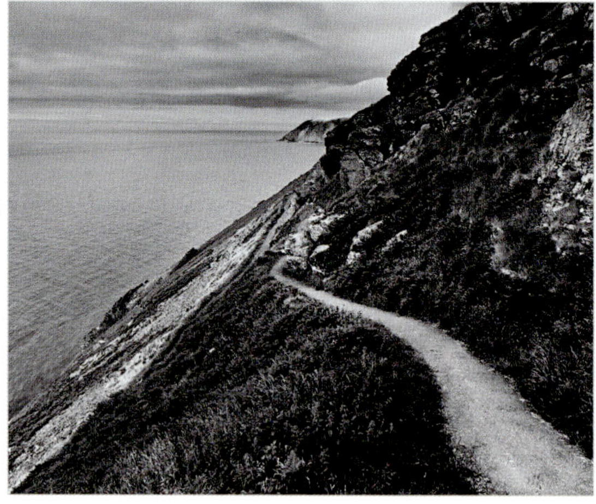

03 Which lens?

On a landscape shoot a wide-angle lens will come in handy. If landscape
photography is something you're keen to get into, then a 10-20mm lens
will be a wise investment. For now though, you can still get good results
with just your kit lens to play with — shoot at the 18mm end to squeeze
as much as you can into the frame.

04 Include leading lines

When shooting landscapes, natural leading lines are an effective way of
drawing the eye through the scene. Look for paths, posts, stone walls,
piers or even streams of sunlight, which can all be used to strengthen
your composition. Notice how these examples draw the eye diagonally
across the scene, creating a more powerful result.

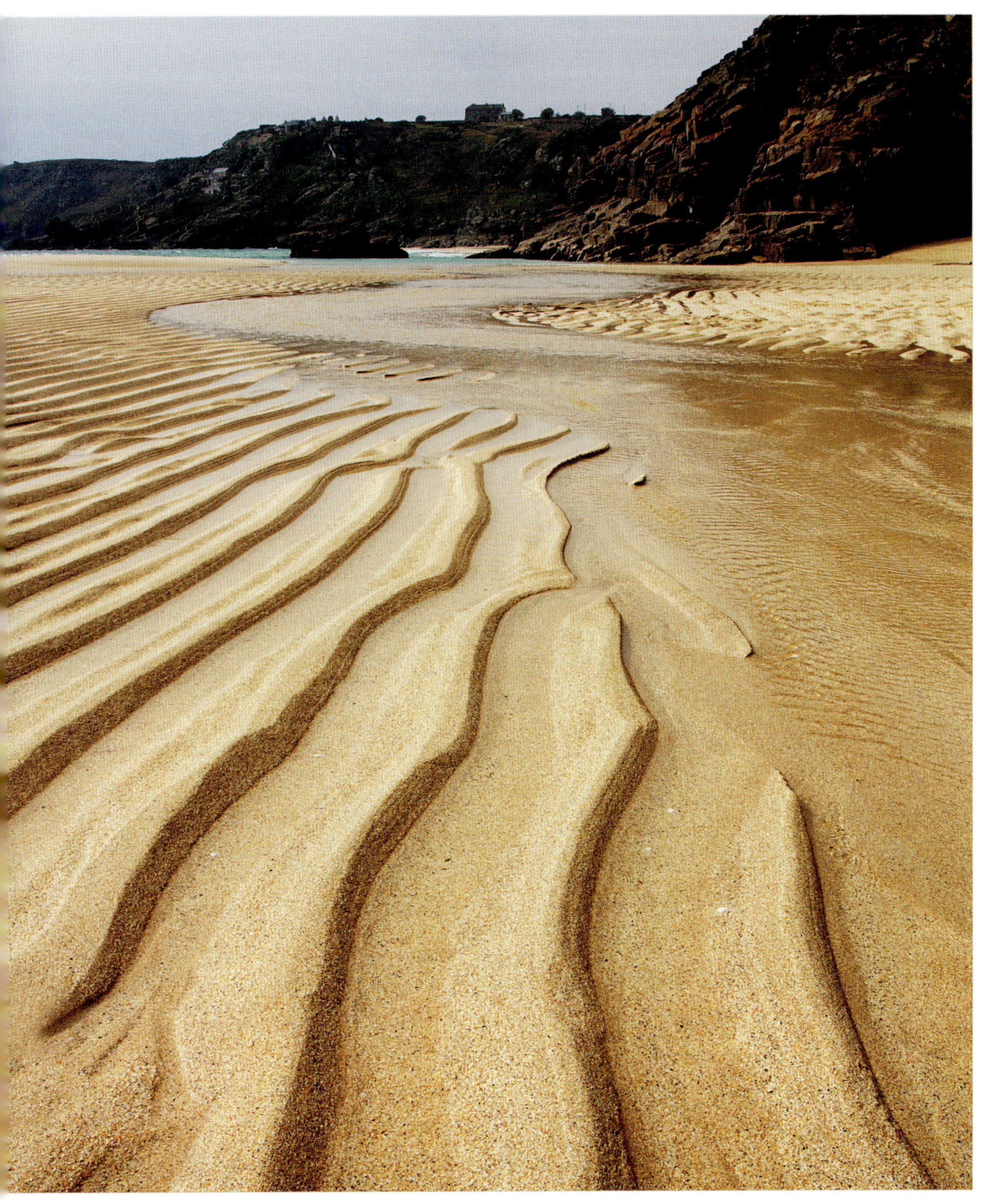

What makes it work?

Here we break a landscape scene down…

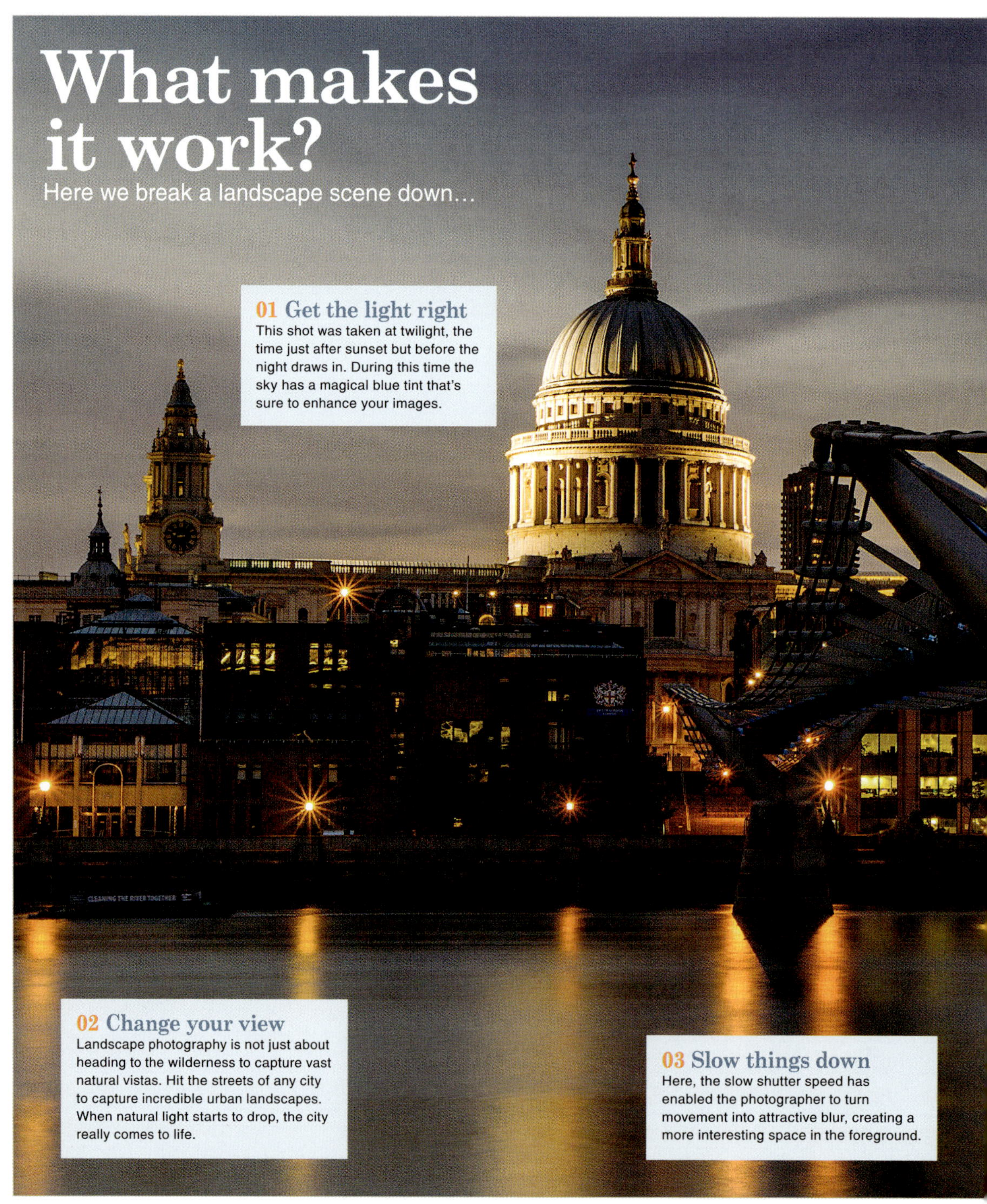

01 Get the light right
This shot was taken at twilight, the time just after sunset but before the night draws in. During this time the sky has a magical blue tint that's sure to enhance your images.

02 Change your view
Landscape photography is not just about heading to the wilderness to capture vast natural vistas. Hit the streets of any city to capture incredible urban landscapes. When natural light starts to drop, the city really comes to life.

03 Slow things down
Here, the slow shutter speed has enabled the photographer to turn movement into attractive blur, creating a more interesting space in the foreground.

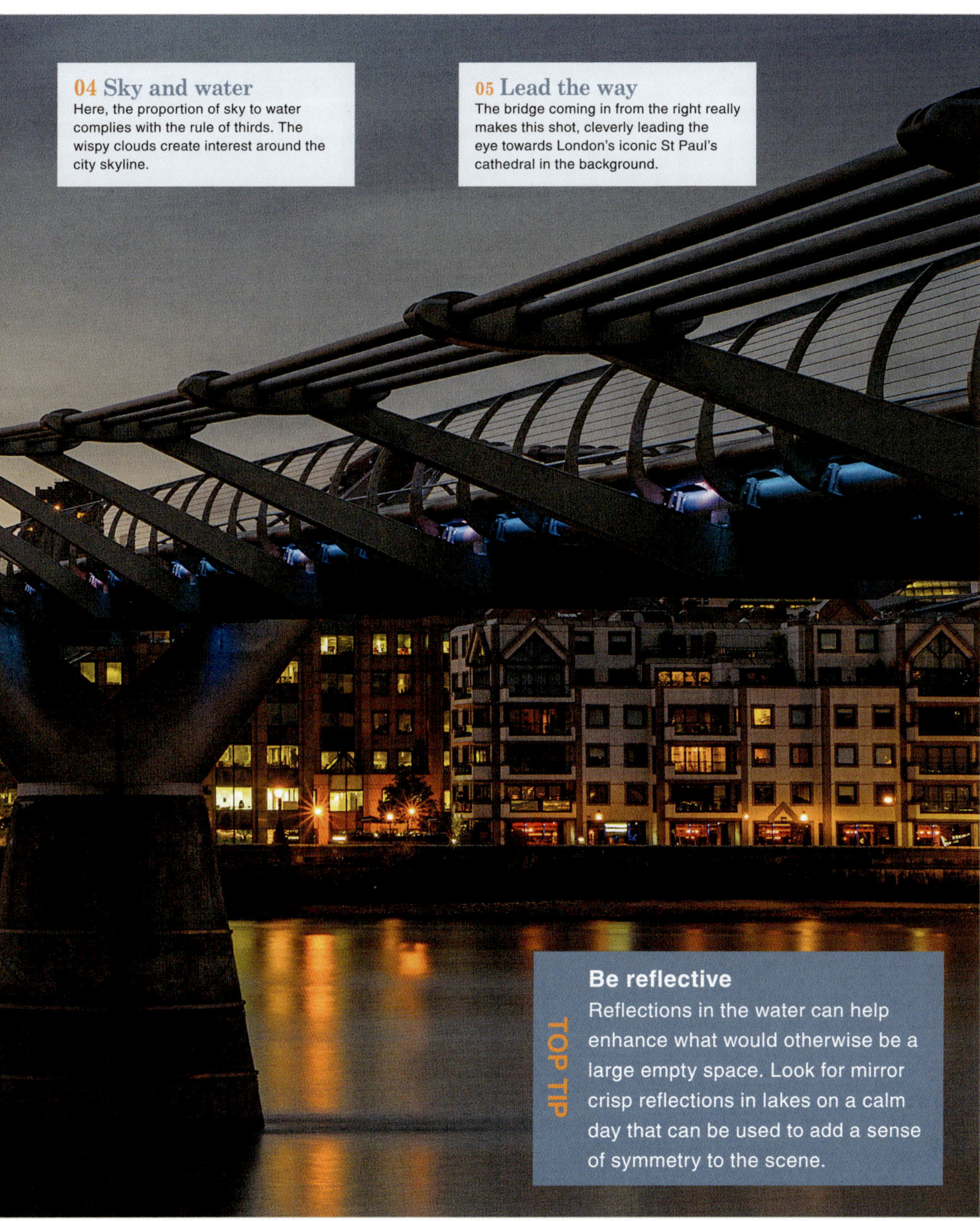

04 Sky and water
Here, the proportion of sky to water complies with the rule of thirds. The wispy clouds create interest around the city skyline.

05 Lead the way
The bridge coming in from the right really makes this shot, cleverly leading the eye towards London's iconic St Paul's cathedral in the background.

TOP TIP

Be reflective
Reflections in the water can help enhance what would otherwise be a large empty space. Look for mirror crisp reflections in lakes on a calm day that can be used to add a sense of symmetry to the scene.

Make the most of natural light

When it comes to landscapes, timing is everything, so ensure great results by being in the right place in the right light!

L ight is a vital part of photography, whatever you choose to shoot, but it's especially important when shooting landscapes. Understanding natural lighting conditions, and being in the right place at the right time to make the most of it, makes the difference between an average image and something truly spectacular.

It pays to be patient — don't expect to pitch up at a local beauty spot, fire off a few frames and then head home. If you stand in the same spot and take pictures all day, you'll get very different results, so you'll need to do your homework. As the sun moves across the sky it will cast varying strengths of light, at varying angles, illuminating the scene in front of you in many different ways. The sun's strength varies from season to season too.

Wondering how to make the most of what Mother Nature throws at you? Here's how to get the best possible results out in the field, whatever the weather…

Shoot in the golden hours

Shoot at first light or dusk for landscape images that really wow

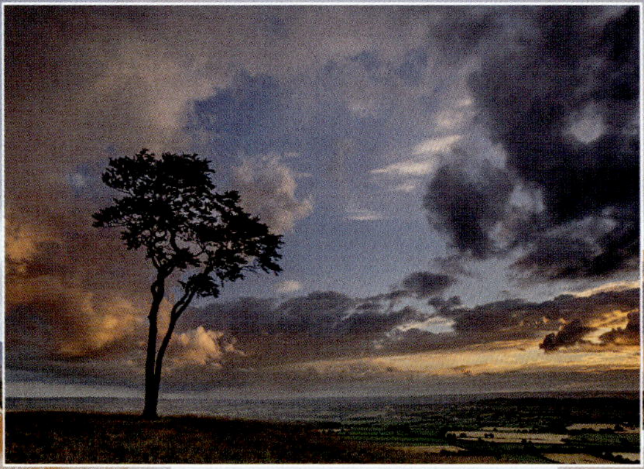

01 Make the most of colour

To make sure you capture the spectacular colours in the sky as the sun rises or sets, first scout the location in the daylight so you can plan your composition in advance. That way you'll be ready and raring to shoot, and are far less likely to miss the magical moment while you fiddle around with camera settings. Take a compass with you, so you know exactly where the sun will rise and set.

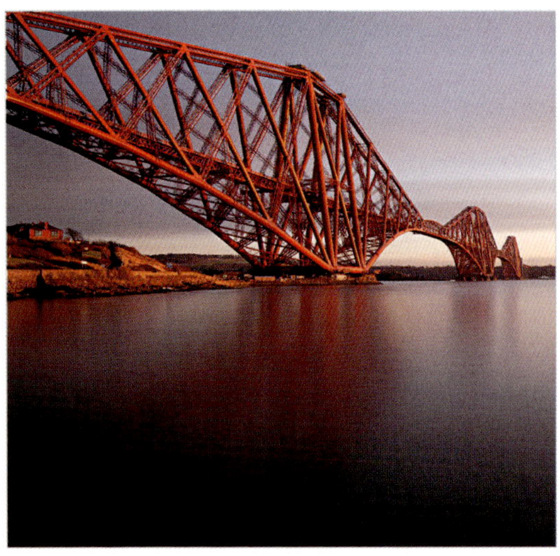

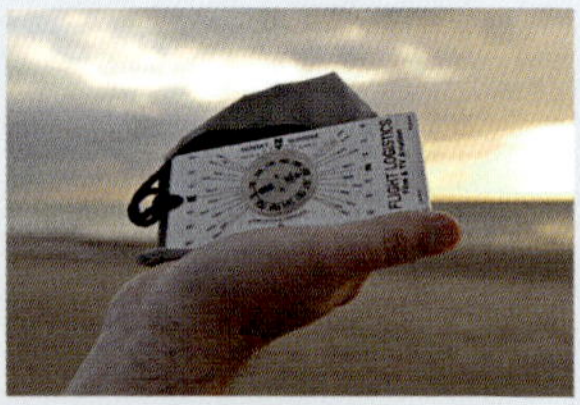

02 When is the golden hour?

The golden hour happens twice a day at sunrise and sunset, and can provide photographers with the best light of the day. To be in with the best chance of capturing it you'll need to arrive at your chosen location and get set up at least half an hour before or after the sunset or sunrise time (which you can easily double-check online).

03 Shoot in diffused light

When the sun is low in the sky it creates a diffused light that is far less harsh than that from the midday sun, enhancing colour and making accurate exposure far easier. The low angle of the sun also helps to exaggerate the shape and form of the land. Try shooting with the sun off to one side and see how it affects the shadows and forms in front of you — shoot into the sun and you'll run the risk of over- or under- exposing your image.

04 Try twilight

Twilight also happens twice a day, just before sunrise and just after sunset. This light is great for cityscapes, as it creates a blue tint in the sky that can look like moonlight. Twilight times vary throughout the year, and change from location to location — the twilight period is shorter if you're closer to the equator. This is because twilight ends once the sun is 18° above or below the horizon.

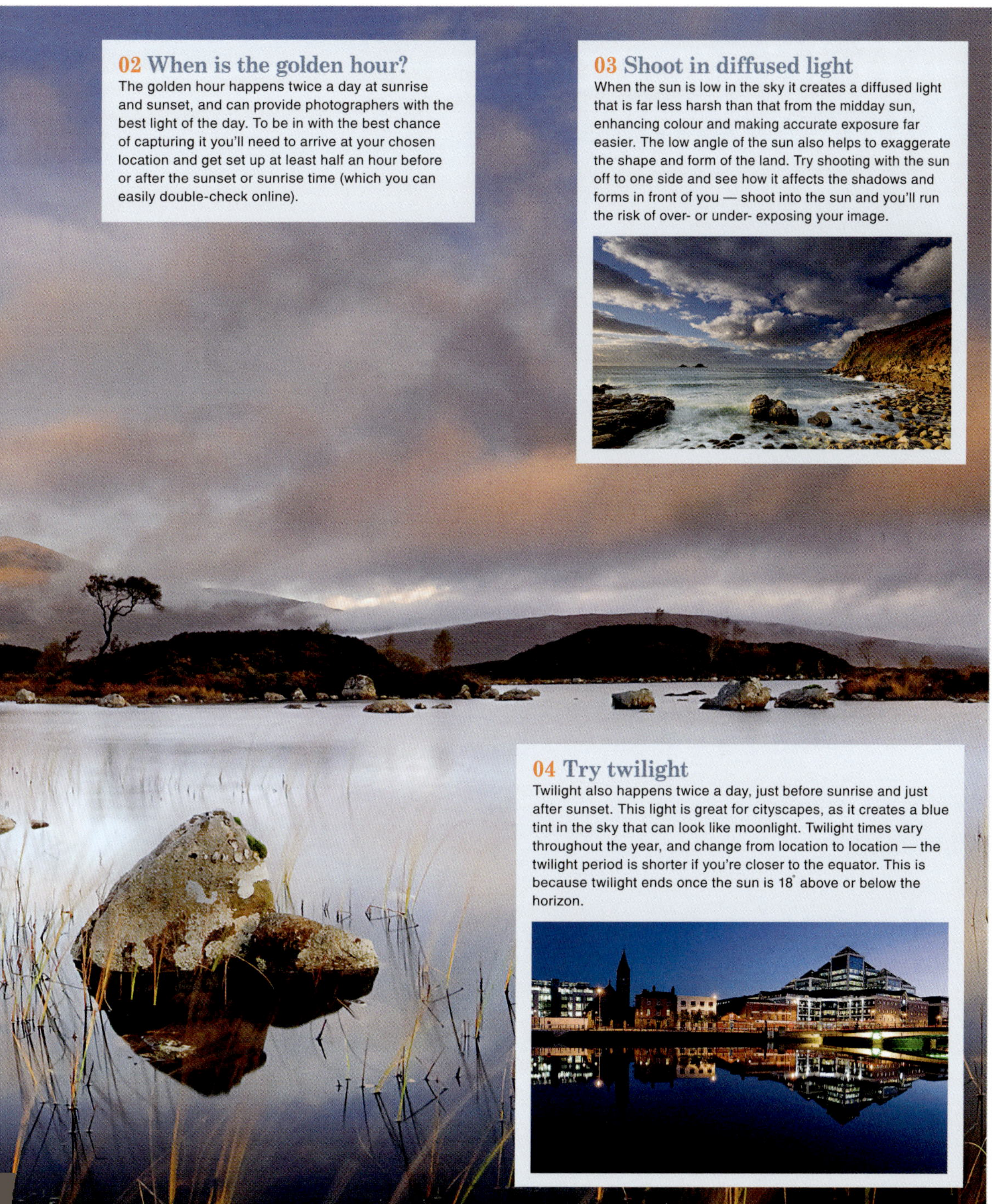

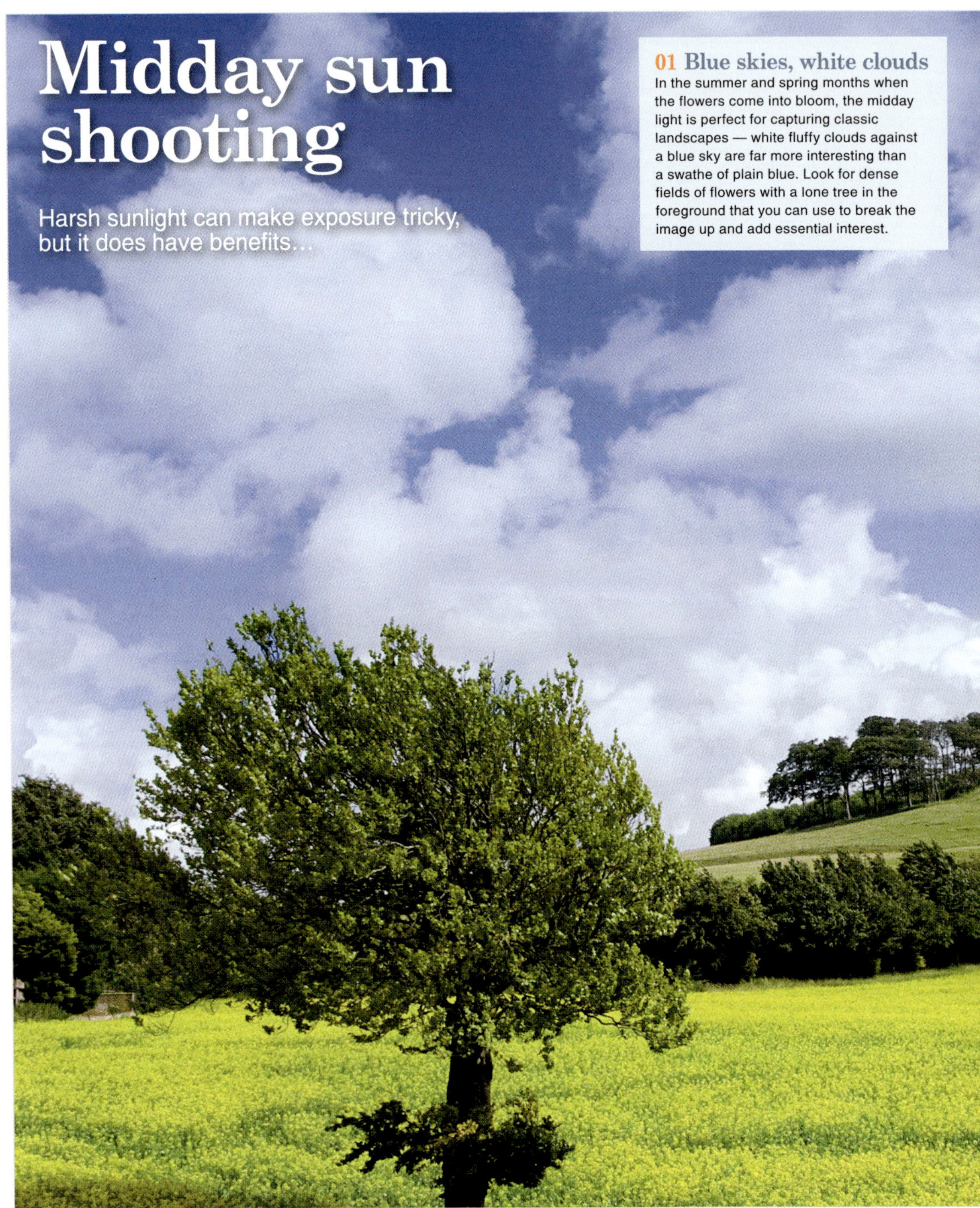

Midday sun shooting

Harsh sunlight can make exposure tricky, but it does have benefits…

01 Blue skies, white clouds

In the summer and spring months when the flowers come into bloom, the midday light is perfect for capturing classic landscapes — white fluffy clouds against a blue sky are far more interesting than a swathe of plain blue. Look for dense fields of flowers with a lone tree in the foreground that you can use to break the image up and add essential interest.

02 What time of day?

In the summer months the midday sun can create very harsh shadows against bright subjects. When the sun is right above you, chances are your camera will over-expose your image, making it too bright. However, if you want to shoot strong, saturated colours this is the light for you — just watch out for exposure, and use your camera's exposure compensation feature to darken the image if necessary (see page 96).

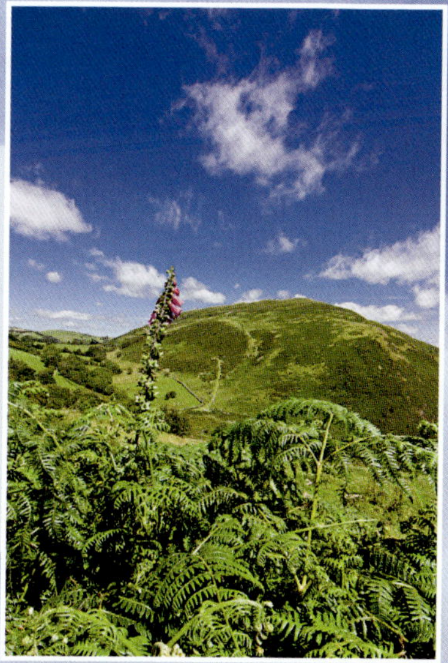

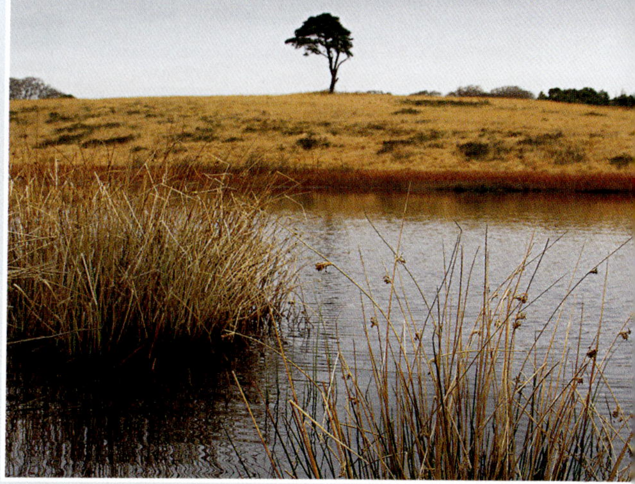

03 The time of year

The time of year you shoot in will make a massive difference to the images you take. Not only will you see varying vegetation, but the light will have varying colours and come from different angles too.

There is no bad time of year to head outside and shoot, but you will need to be prepared for the changing conditions — the midday sun in winter is much cooler and lower in the sky than it is in summer, for example. It can be easier to get dramatic results during the autumn and winter months (despite the inclement weather) — the light is softer and more diffused throughout the day, plus you don't have to wait as long for the sun to set. Of course, this depends on where you are in the world.

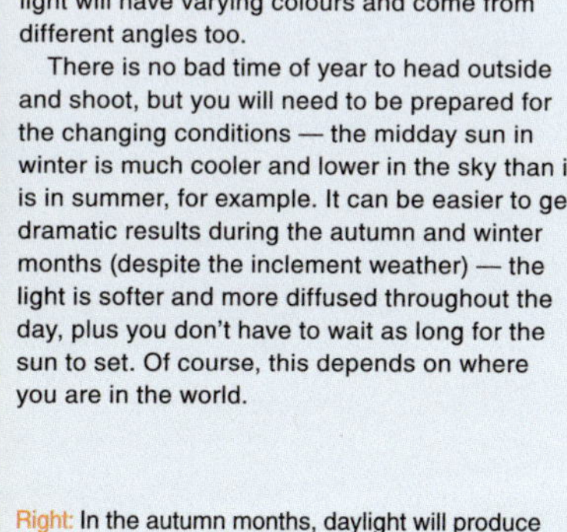

Right: In the autumn months, daylight will produce different results than it would in the summer, and the landscape will contain different tones and colours. Consider this when looking for the perfect location

Shooting in poor light

Light flat? Or shooting at night? Remove the colour from the scene and start seeing in black and white

01 Flat light

The light on overcast, grey days is often referred to as 'flat', resulting in images that lack tone and depth. You needn't pack away your camera on days like this; you simply need to think differently. Flat light is great for black-and-white landscapes, and it makes it much easier to expose your images, as there won't be such a huge difference between a shot's dark and light tones (in its shadows and highlights), which can cause problems on sunny days.

02 Textures in the land

Look out for patterns and textures in the land that you can use to add interest to your shots. Heavy skies with grey, textured clouds will add drama and atmosphere to the end result. If the sky is not heavily textured, include less of it in the frame and instead concentrate more on the form of the land.

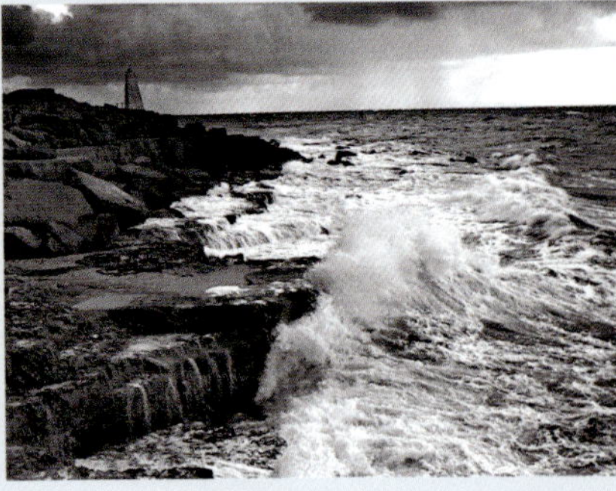

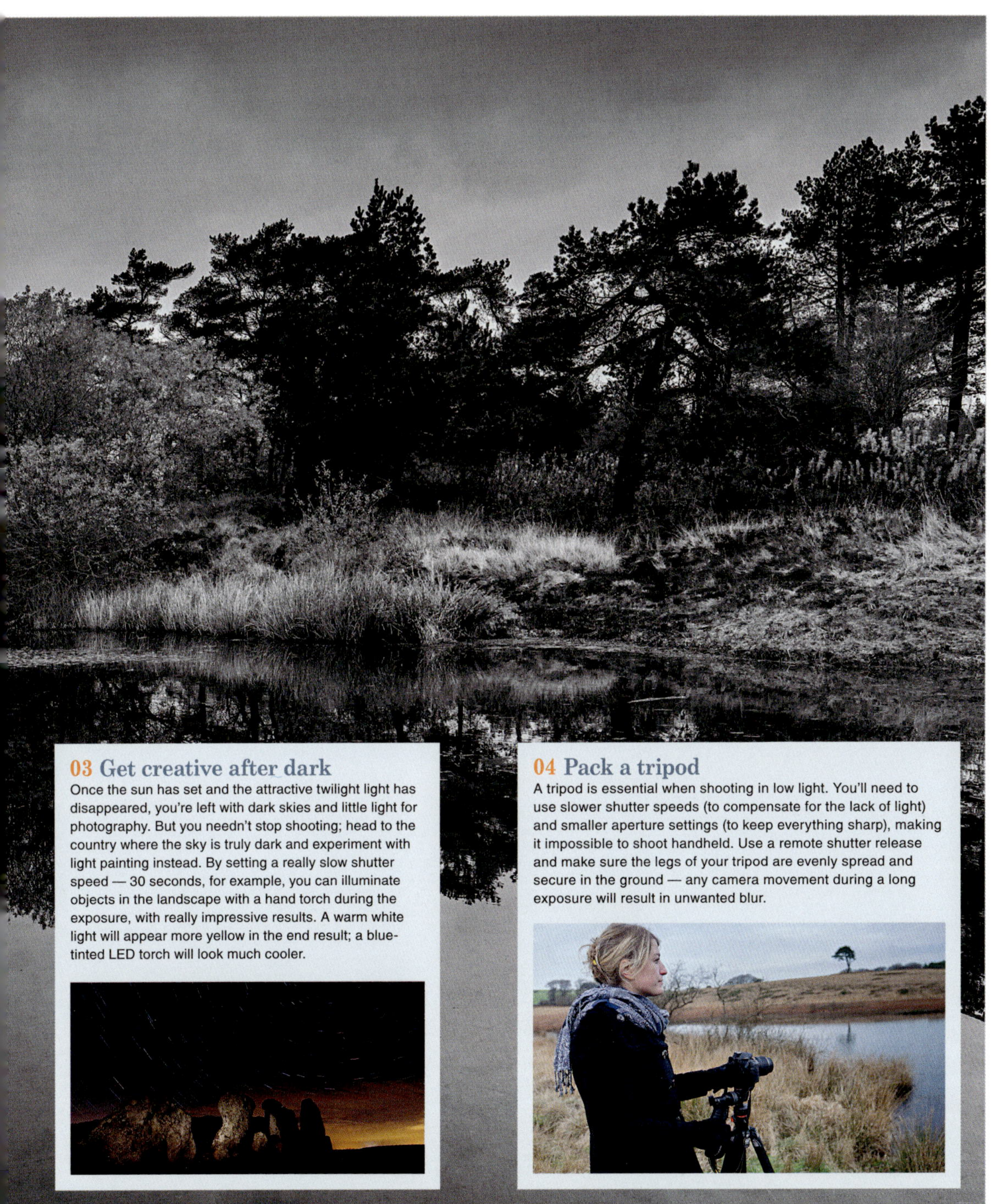

03 Get creative after dark

Once the sun has set and the attractive twilight light has disappeared, you're left with dark skies and little light for photography. But you needn't stop shooting; head to the country where the sky is truly dark and experiment with light painting instead. By setting a really slow shutter speed — 30 seconds, for example, you can illuminate objects in the landscape with a hand torch during the exposure, with really impressive results. A warm white light will appear more yellow in the end result; a blue-tinted LED torch will look much cooler.

04 Pack a tripod

A tripod is essential when shooting in low light. You'll need to use slower shutter speeds (to compensate for the lack of light) and smaller aperture settings (to keep everything sharp), making it impossible to shoot handheld. Use a remote shutter release and make sure the legs of your tripod are evenly spread and secure in the ground — any camera movement during a long exposure will result in unwanted blur.

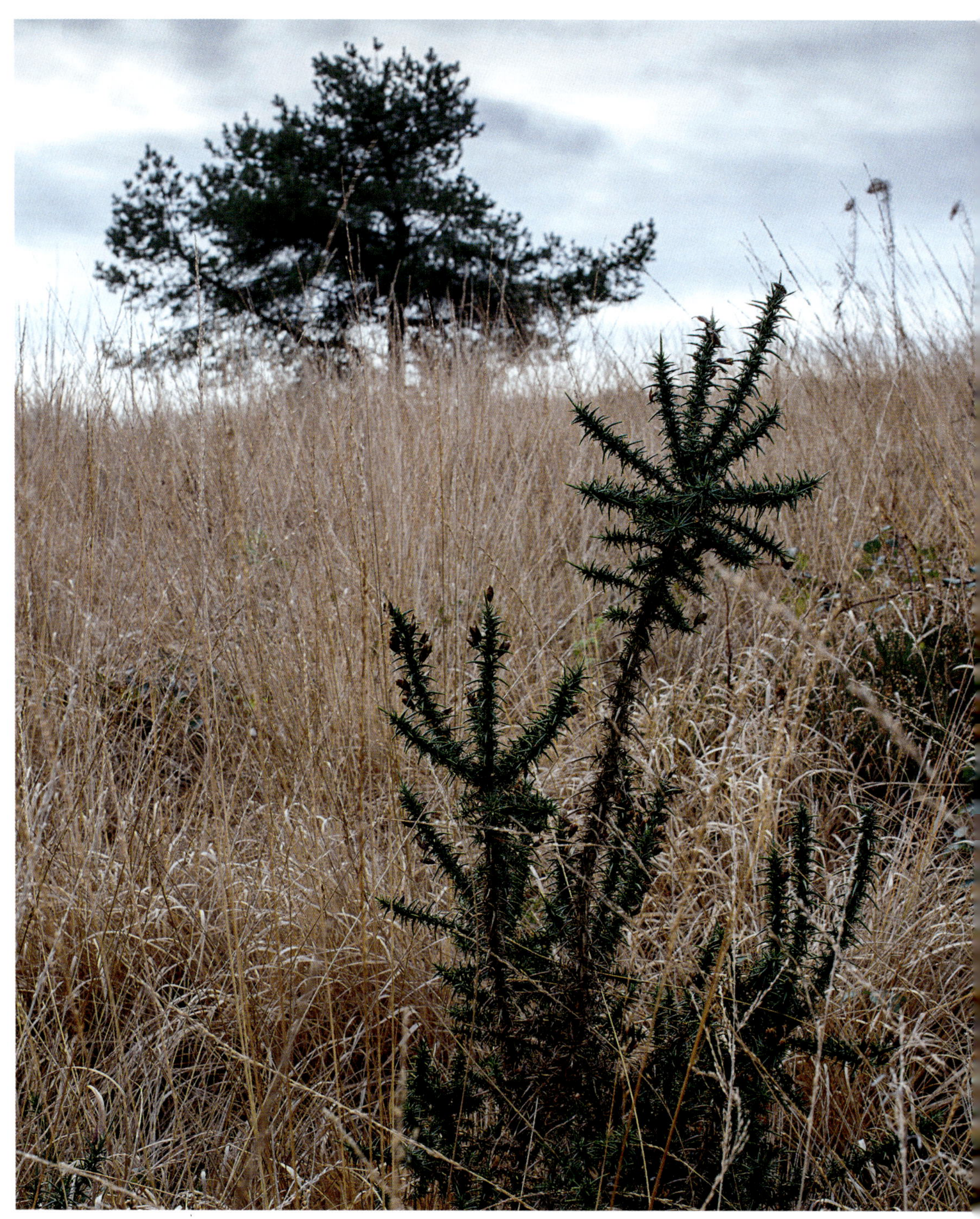

Maximise your depth of field

Discover how to control the focus in your landscapes so that they're sharp throughout the whole scene

Most landscape photographers want everything in their images to be sharp, from the foreground interest to the distant hills, and to do this you need to understand depth of field. To maximise sharpness you must extend the depth of field as far as possible, and to do this you will need to shoot using a small aperture setting (represented, confusingly, by a high number — f22, for example).

One of the simplest ways to do this is to switch your camera to its Landscape scene mode, because this automatically chooses the setting you need to maximise depth of field. However, this automatic setting won't allow you any creative control over the other camera settings — changing autofocus points, for example. The semi-automatic Aperture Priority mode is a useful alternative. In this mode you can select the aperture (f-stop) you wish to shoot at, and the camera will select the correct shutter speed for a decent exposure. In contrast to the Landscape mode, however, you can also control settings such as ISO, flash and autofocus.

When it comes to maximising sharpness, there are other factors to consider — for example, the distance between two subjects in the scene and how close you are to the first subject in the scene. Here, we'll show you how to use Aperture Priority mode to get the very best results in your landscape pictures.

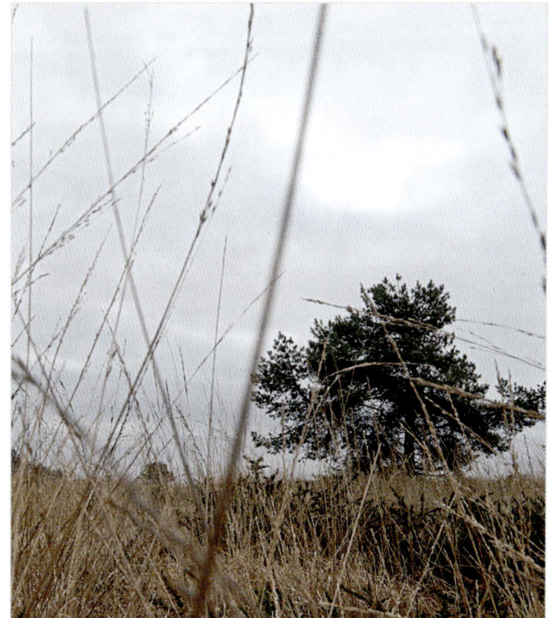

01 Find a location

First, head out and find the right location. For a really great image you'll need a spot from where you can capture something of interest in both the foreground and the background. In our example, we selected a tree in the background with this bush and thorn plant in the foreground. There are lots of textures in the image.

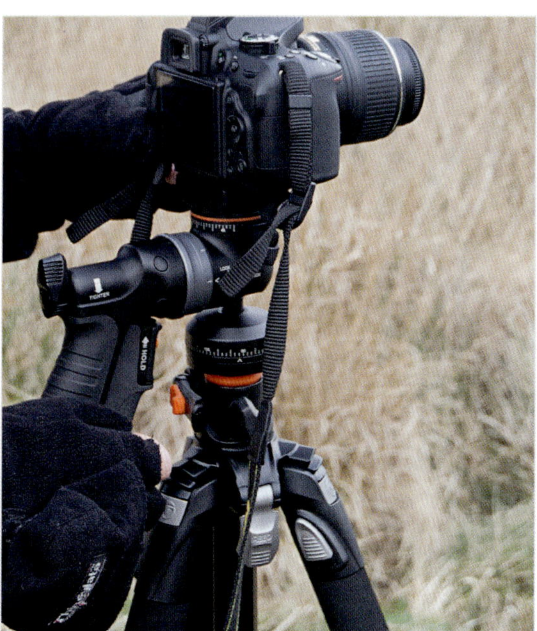

02 Get some support

Mount your camera on a tripod. This means you can ensure sharp shots. By selecting a small aperture you will reduce the amount of light that reaches the sensor, so the shutter speed needed to produce a correct exposure will become longer. Slow shutter speeds make it impossible to get sharp shots handheld.

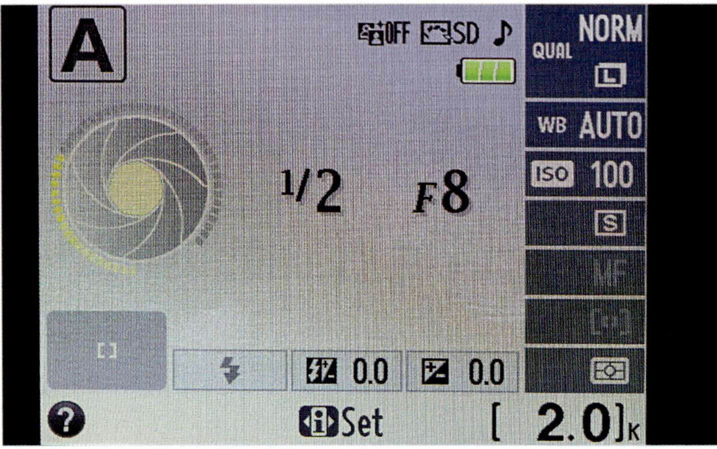

03 All about f-stops

The amount of sharpness in an image is dictated by the size of the aperture in your lens. The aperture is set by selecting one of a number of f-stops (f18, for example) — the higher the number, the smaller the opening. In Aperture Priority mode you select the f-stop you wish to use; the camera will control everything else.

04 Select Av mode

Turn the mode dial to the Aperture Priority setting (marked with the letter A (Nikon) or Av (Canon)). You can now change the aperture using the scroll dial — watch it change in the viewfinder display or rear LCD. Select a high f-stop and the hole inside the lens will let in less light, and maximise the depth of field.

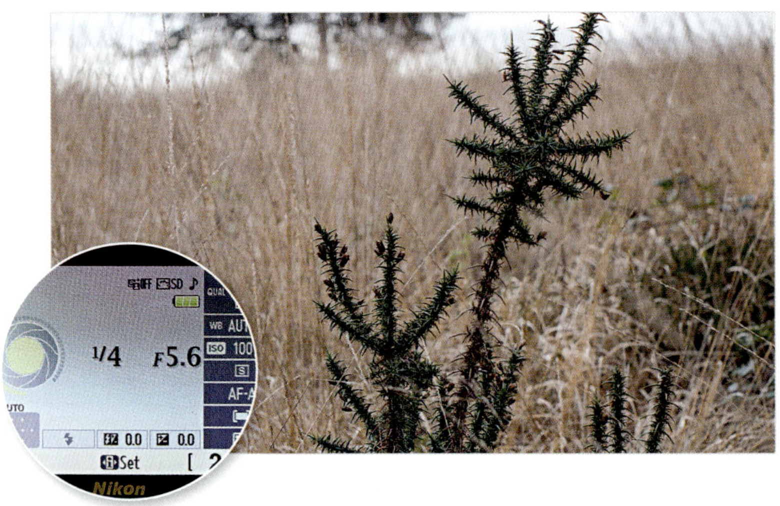

05 An example at f/5.6

Low f-stop numbers — such as f/5.6 — will make the background blur if the lens focuses on an object in the foreground, as shown here. As the hole inside the aperture is at a wider setting, more light will hit the sensor and the resulting shutter speed will be faster. However, at f/5.6 we haven't produced the sharpness we're looking for.

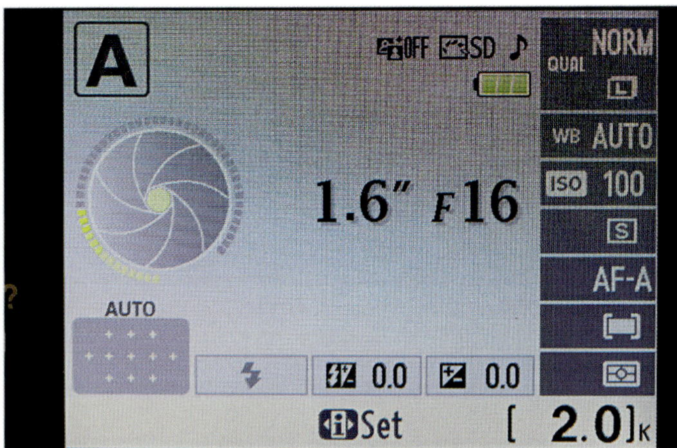

06 Final result at f/16

The higher f-stop numbers close down the aperture hole so more of your image appears in sharp focus. By dialling in an aperture of f/16 the shutter speed will get longer, but because our camera is mounted on a tripod this doesn't matter. Now all that's left to do is focus carefully on your main subject matter and take the shot.

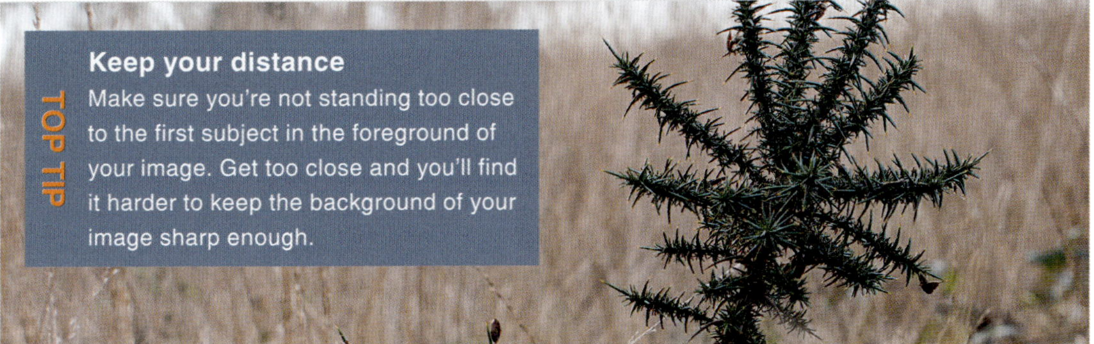

Try manual focus

Instead of letting your camera do the focusing for you, ensure accuracy by using the manual focus setting instead. To do this, attach your camera to a tripod, switch your lens to its MF (or M) setting, then engage the Live View feature on your camera's LCD screen.

Once activated, use the magnify button on the back of your camera to zoom into the scene. Use the back panel control to navigate to the point you'd like to focus on, then turn the front ring on your lens (the focusing ring) until that point appears sharp. Zoom back out to check that you are happy with the result before proceeding to capture the image.

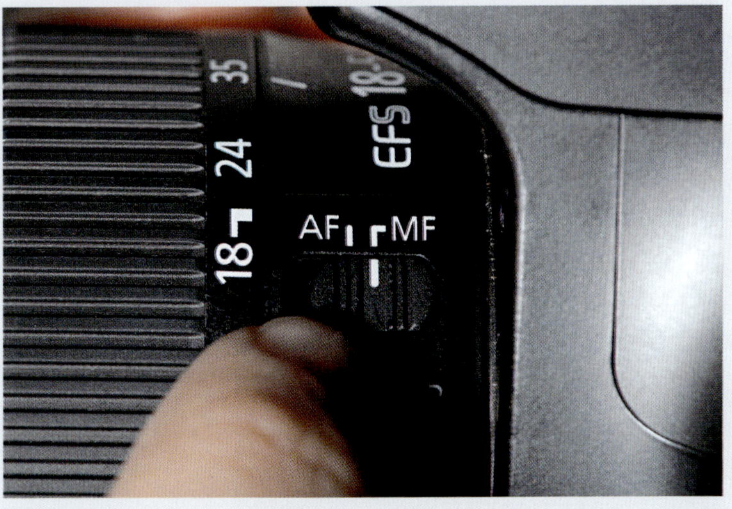

Take control of your exposures

Use your camera's exposure compensation feature to make images lighter or darker as you shoot them

Left to its own devices, your camera will try to guess what camera settings it should use to correctly expose the scene in front of it. However, it's not foolproof — faced with particularly bright or dark areas you'll probably end up with images that are too bright (over-exposed) or too dark (under-exposed). This is because your camera's built-in light meter tries to render everything as something called a midtone (or 18% grey).

But there is a way to override your camera's suggested exposure settings. In basic terms, exposure compensation enables you to make an image lighter or darker by shifting the exposure values one way or the other very slightly. Look through your camera's viewfinder (or on the rear LCD) and you'll see small exposure indicator under the camera settings. You can move the needle on this scale right or left to make the image lighter or darker.

You can also use this feature to do what is known as 'bracketing', where you take multiple images at different exposure settings to ensure you capture detail in a scene's shadows, midtones and highlights, then blend the images together in an image editor later.

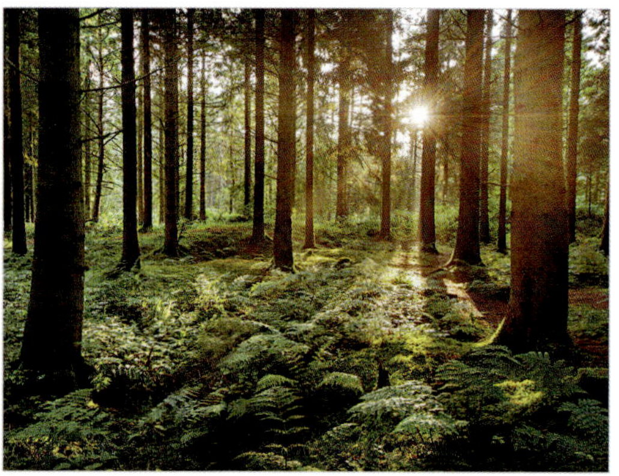

Darken or lighten your images

Master exposure compensation on your camera for perfect exposures every time

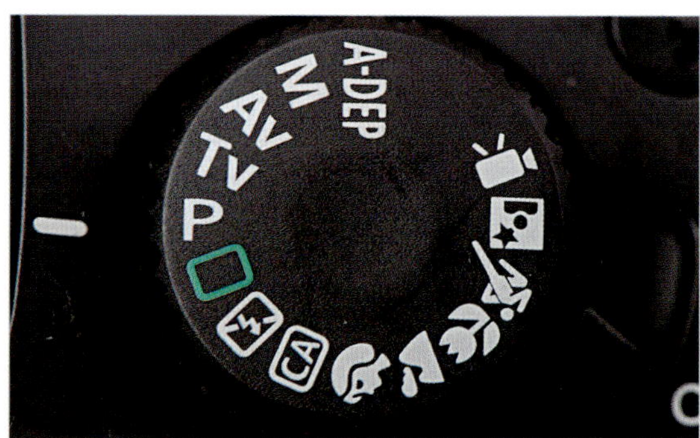

01 Switch to P mode

You cannot access the exposure compensation feature in the Full Auto mode, so for this reason switch your mode dial to its P (Program) setting. This semi-automatic shooting mode suggests settings the camera believes to be correct (aperture, shutter speed, ISO etc.), but enables you to alter key settings should you wish.

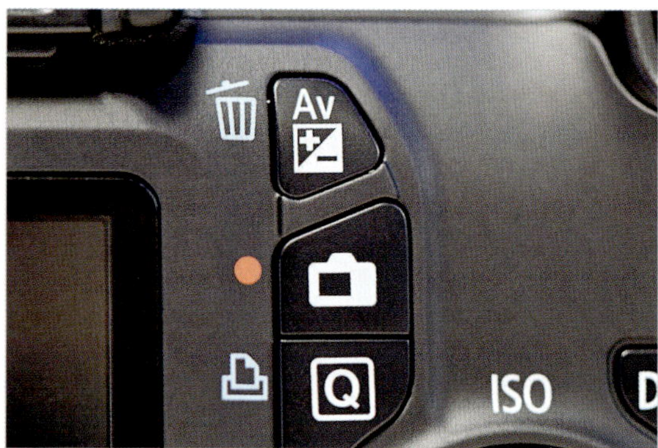

02 Adjust the exposure

To alter the camera's suggested setting, first find and press the +/- exposure compensation button. With the button held down, move the scroll dial left or right (to make the image darker or lighter). The needle on the exposure indicator will move left or right to illustrate the change.

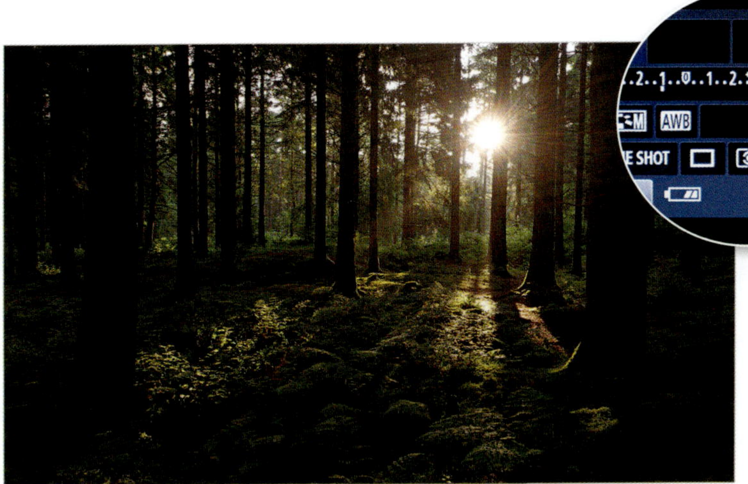

03 Make the image darker

To make the image darker (by what is known as one 'stop', press and hold the exposure compensation button and turn the dial so the needle sits at -1 on the exposure indicator. Reducing it by two stops (-2) will make the image even darker. Hidden detail in the shot's highlights (the brightest areas of the image) should now be revealed.

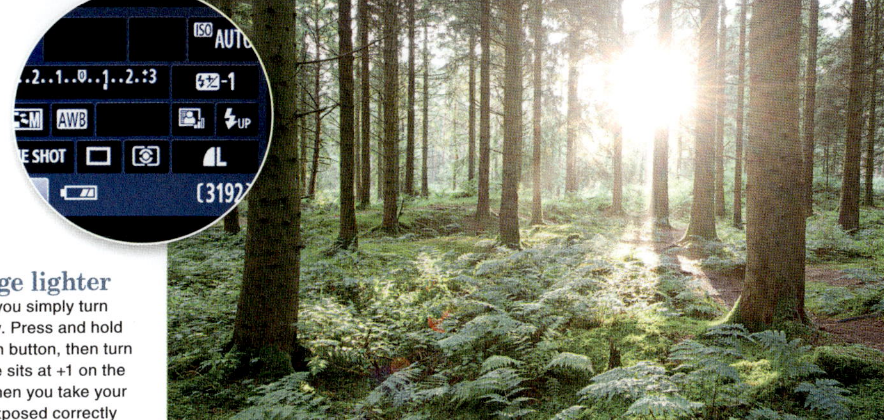

04 Make the image lighter

To make the image lighter you simply turn the scroll dial the other way. Press and hold the exposure compensation button, then turn the scroll dial so the needle sits at +1 on the exposure indicator. Now when you take your shot the shadows will be exposed correctly (and hidden detail will now be visible).

05 Use a tripod

If you want to blend 'bracketed' images together to ensure perfect exposure in tricky shooting situations, a tripod is a must if your images are to match up. With your camera steady, take one image with the needle in the centre of the exposure indicator, then take two more at -1 and +1.

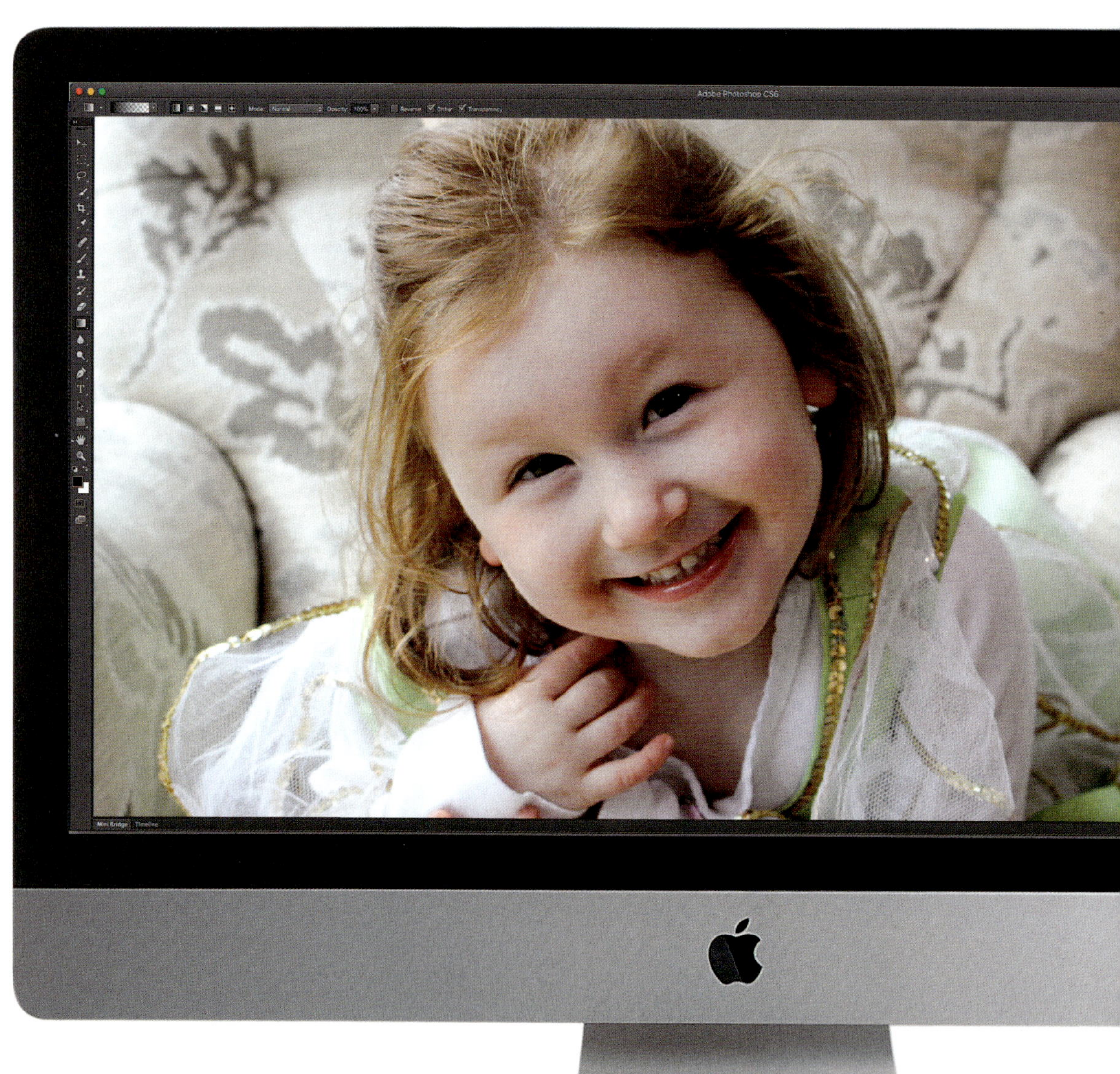

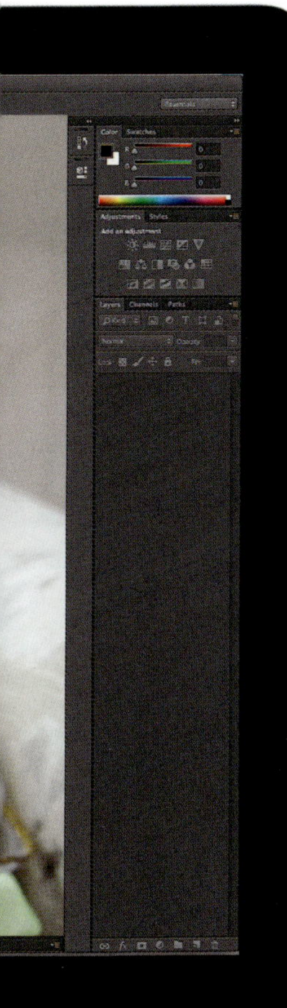

Children

Discover exciting ways to capture the magic of kids, from lighting tips to adding cool effects in-camera and more

90 Easy home lighting
You don't need fancy lights to get great-looking results — discover how to take advantage of the light in and around your home

94 Add drama with camera picture styles
Use your camera's built-in Monochrome picture style to capture classic images in black and white

96 How to avoid unwanted blur
Set up your SLR correctly to avoid unwanted motion blur ruining shots of fast-moving children

98 Capture action packed pictures
Discover how to use your SLR's motordrive modes to ensure you never miss a moment of the action

100 Fun family portrait tips
Use our simple techniques to get the most from your shoot, and get great shots of your kids that you'll treasure forever

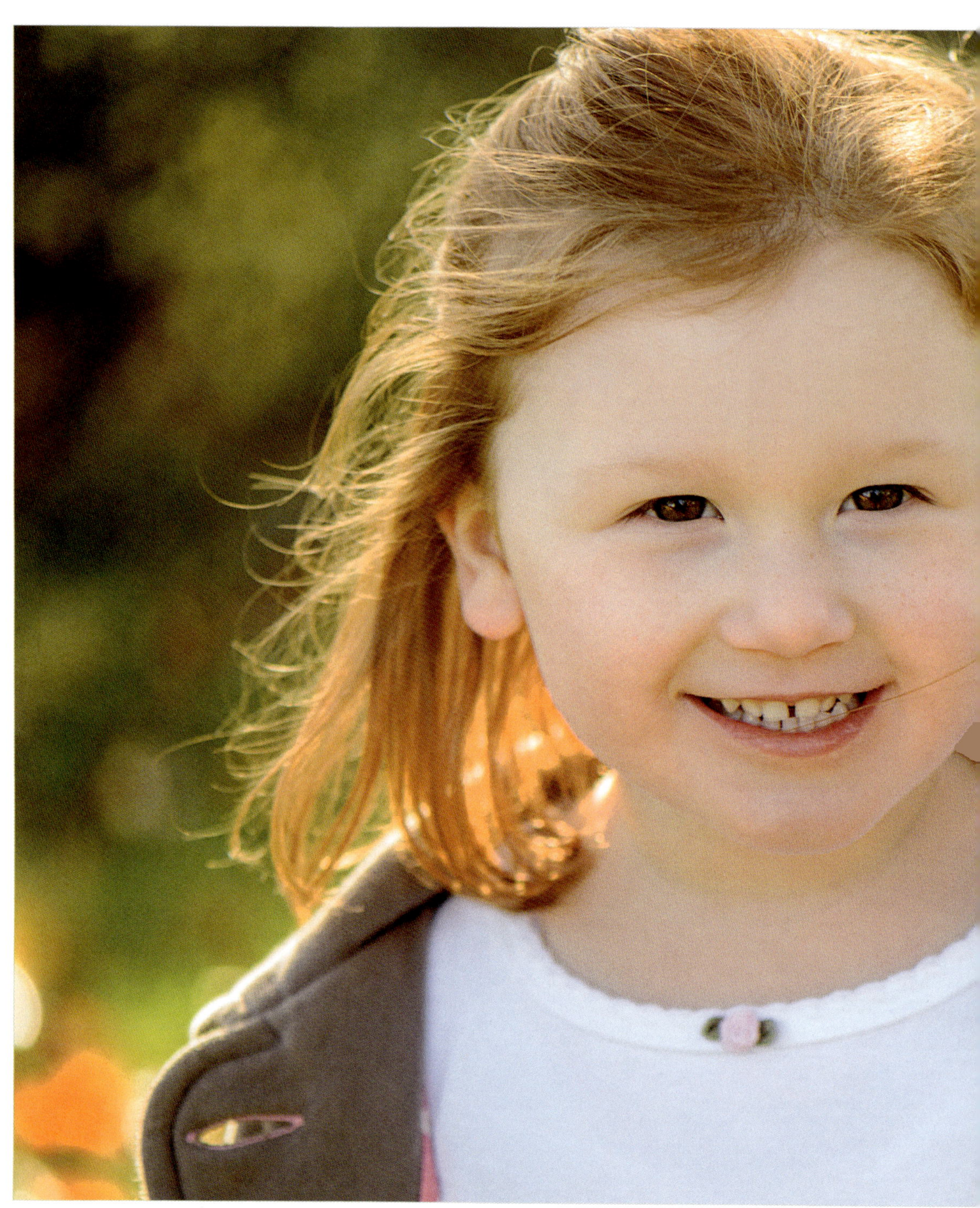

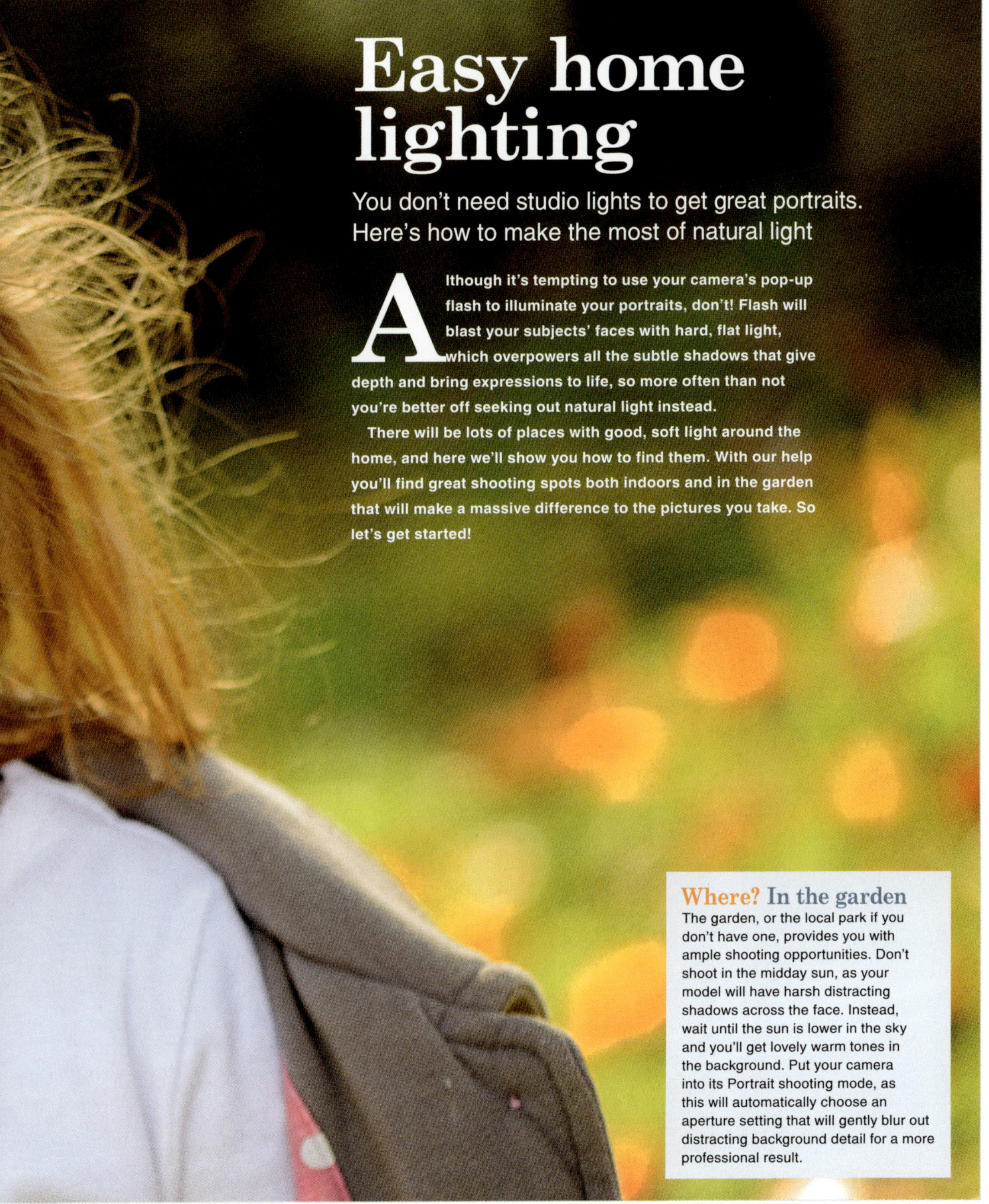

Easy home lighting

You don't need studio lights to get great portraits. Here's how to make the most of natural light

Although it's tempting to use your camera's pop-up flash to illuminate your portraits, don't! Flash will blast your subjects' faces with hard, flat light, which overpowers all the subtle shadows that give depth and bring expressions to life, so more often than not you're better off seeking out natural light instead.

There will be lots of places with good, soft light around the home, and here we'll show you how to find them. With our help you'll find great shooting spots both indoors and in the garden that will make a massive difference to the pictures you take. So let's get started!

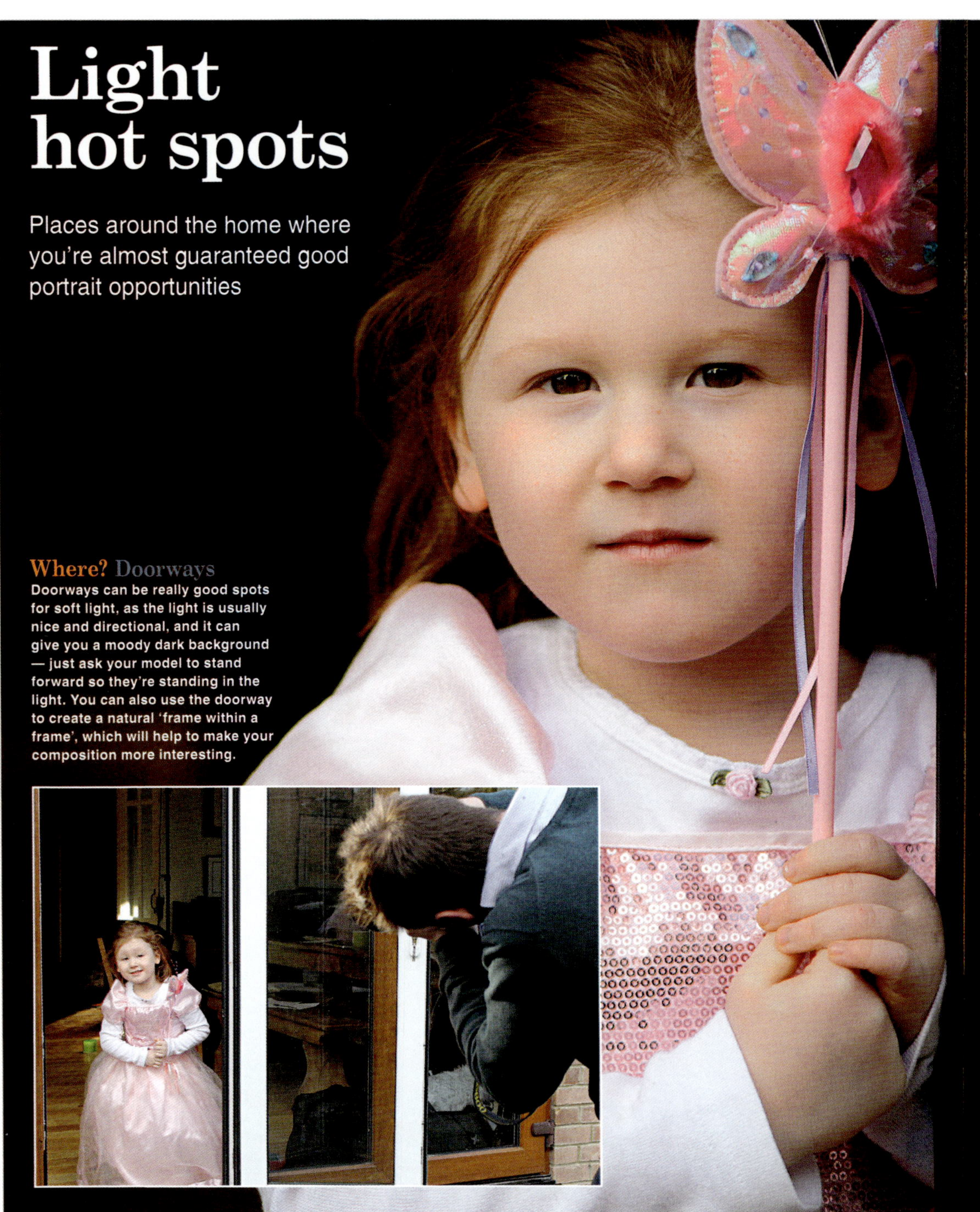

Light hot spots

Places around the home where you're almost guaranteed good portrait opportunities

Where? Doorways

Doorways can be really good spots for soft light, as the light is usually nice and directional, and it can give you a moody dark background — just ask your model to stand forward so they're standing in the light. You can also use the doorway to create a natural 'frame within a frame', which will help to make your composition more interesting.

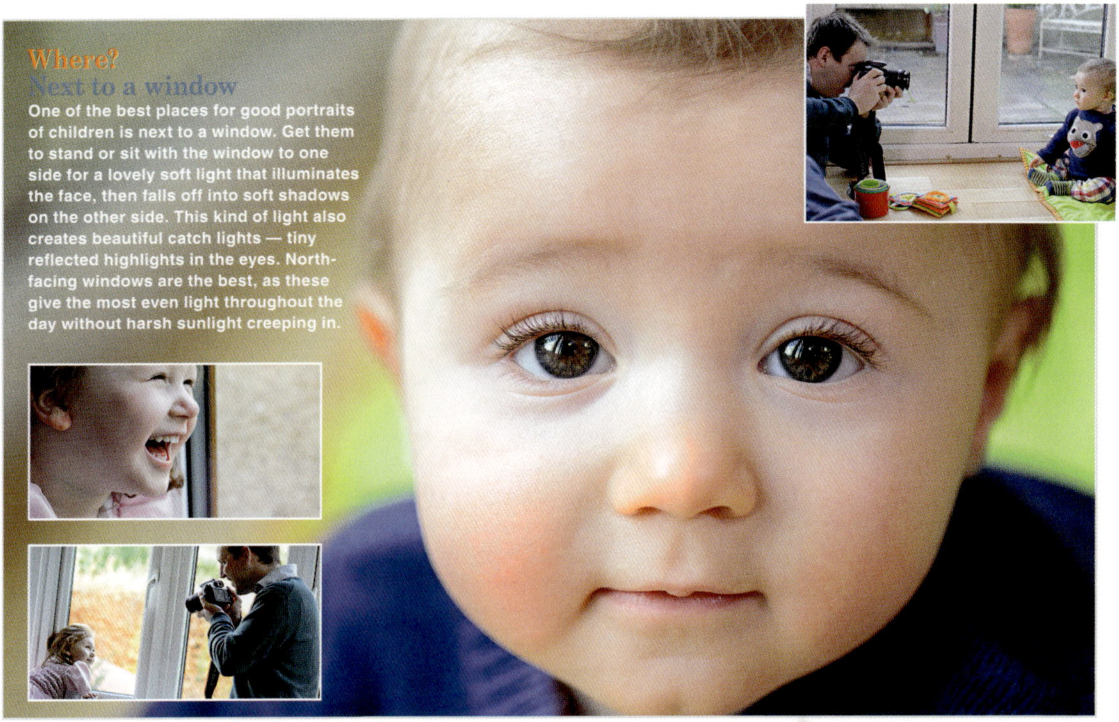

One of the best places for good portraits of children is next to a window. Get them to stand or sit with the window to one side for a lovely soft light that illuminates the face, then falls off into soft shadows on the other side. This kind of light also creates beautiful catch lights — tiny reflected highlights in the eyes. North-facing windows are the best, as these give the most even light throughout the day without harsh sunlight creeping in.

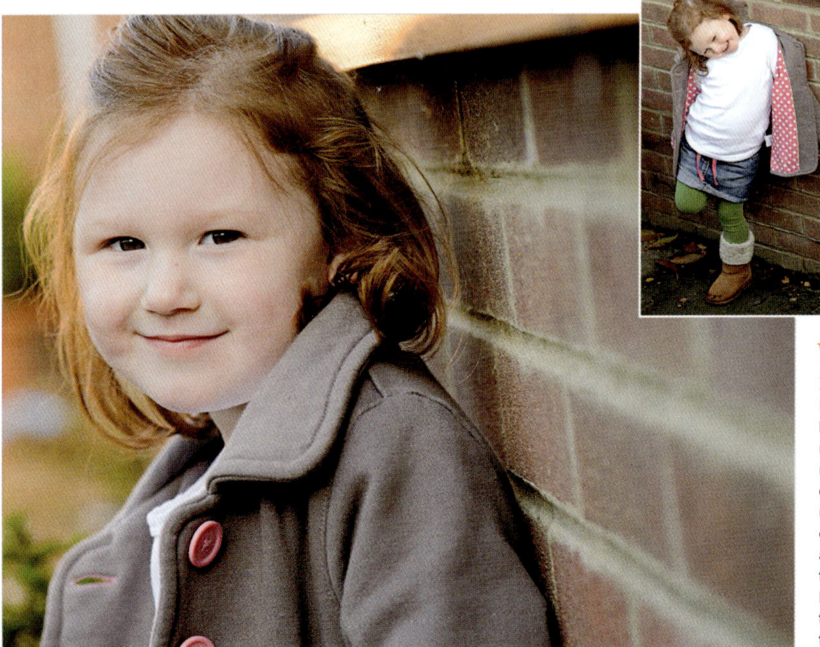

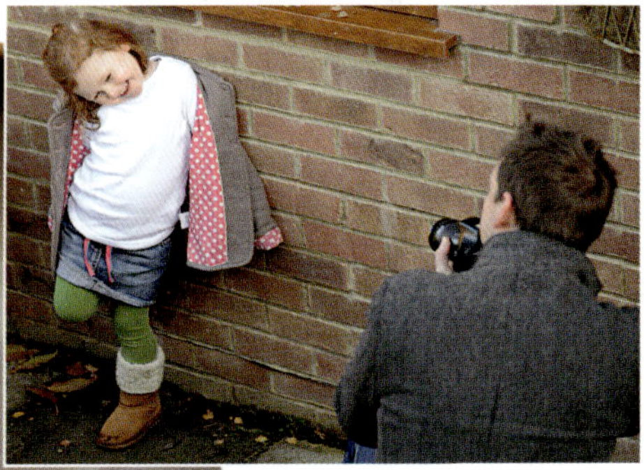

Where? Exterior wall in the garden

Exterior walls can also form great backdrops for portraits, as they naturally block the light from one side, making it more directional. For a nice composition, get your subject to lean up against the wall, then shoot from one side as shown. The wall will act as a natural reflector and create lines that lead the eye towards your subject. Here, we've added depth by capturing the face in sharp focus while letting the background fade gently into blur.

Add drama with camera picture styles

Use your camera's Monochrome picture style to capture classic portraits in black and white

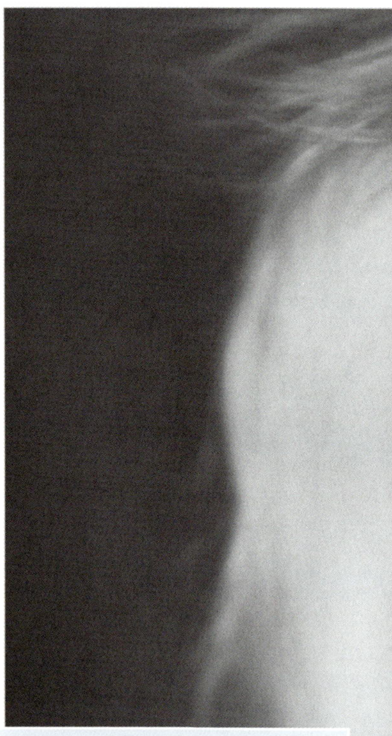

There's something about black-and-white portraits that gives them a timeless, classy feel. By removing a photo's colour you can focus attention on the shape and characteristics of the face, which makes it great for capturing expressions, especially in children.

When it comes to making black-and-white images you have two main options: capture colour images and convert them to black and white using an image editor later; or use your camera's Monochrome picture style to apply the black-and-white treatment as you shoot.

Your camera has several picture styles (or picture controls) built in, including Portrait, Landscape and Monochrome, which adjust capture parameters such as the sharpness, contrast, colour tone and saturation to ensure the best results. They're great for beginners, because they help you to get the most from your subject, whatever you're shooting. Read on to find out more…

How to select a picture style

02 Further tweaks

You can tweak the suggested picture style settings to suit your subject — here we have the option to increase or decrease the sharpness and contrast, for example. You can also add a traditional filter to enhance the image. Here we've selected the Red filter, as this helps to increase contrast.

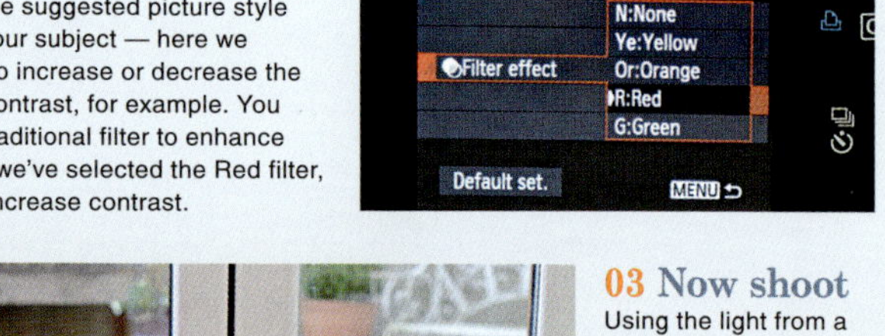

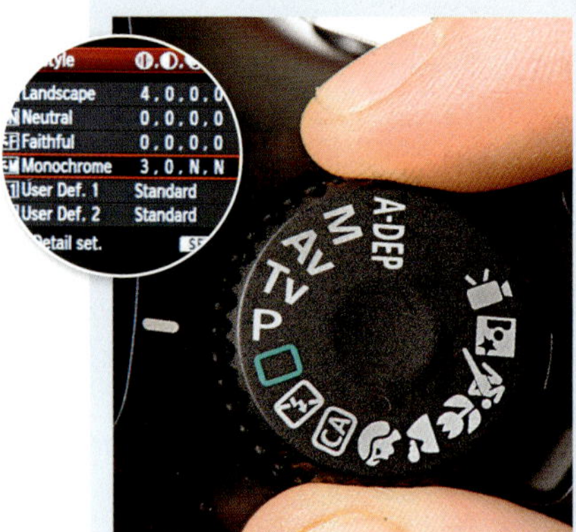

01 Dial P for Program

Switch your camera to its P (Program) shooting mode. Now go to the main menu and navigate to the Picture Style (Canon) or Picture Control (Nikon) drop-down menu. Here you can browse through the different options. To shoot in black and white, highlight and select the Monochrome option.

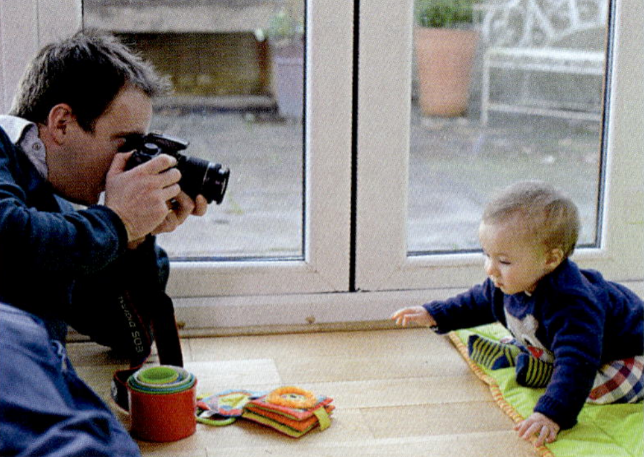

03 Now shoot

Using the light from a window to illuminate your subject's face, compose your image (ensuring the background is clutter-free), then focus carefully on the eyes before taking your shot. If you've shot using your camera's raw quality setting, you can revert your image back to colour later.

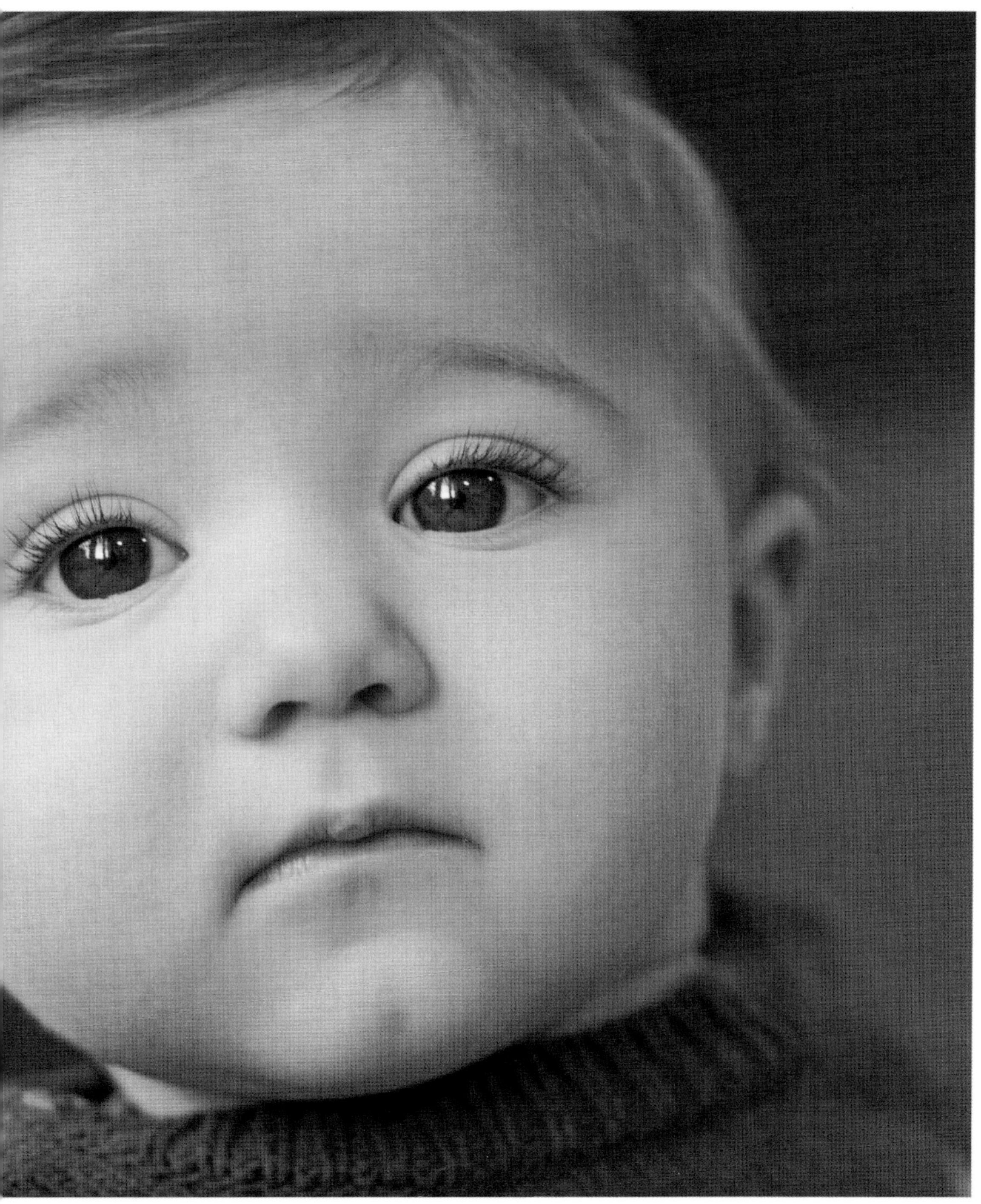

How to avoid unwanted blur

Set up your SLR correctly to avoid motion blur ruining shots of fast-moving children

One of the most important considerations when taking any kind of photograph, but especially portraits, is to ensure your image is captured in sharp focus. After all, it's all too easy to focus inaccurately, or for camera shake to create unwanted blur.

The most common cause of shake is movement in the camera as you take the photo, which results in the entire image looking blurred. This often happens when shooting in low light, because the shutter will need to stay open longer to let enough light in, and even slight movement can ruin a shot. You can minimise blur by mounting your camera on a sturdy tripod, but this is of no use if the blur is caused by movement from within the scene you're shooting, rather than the camera itself.

Photographers sometimes use subject movement for creative effect — blurring the motion of water, for example — but when it comes to portraits, the aim is usually to capture the subject sharply. The problem is, people, and children in particular, rarely stay perfectly still, so you need to set the camera up to record the picture quickly. Here's how…

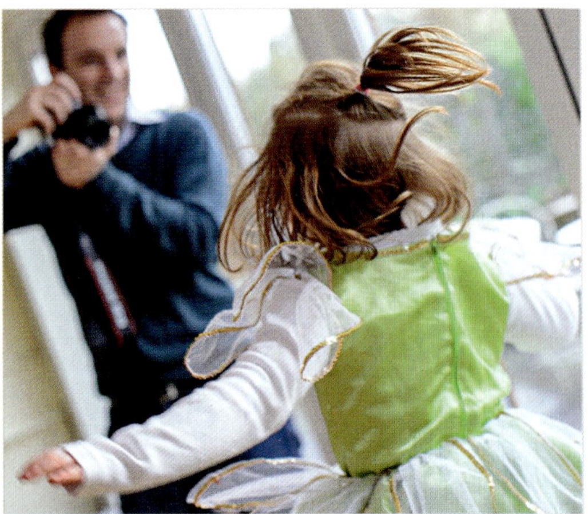

Reduce the risk of camera shake

Five methods you can use to minimise the risk of unwanted blur in your portraits

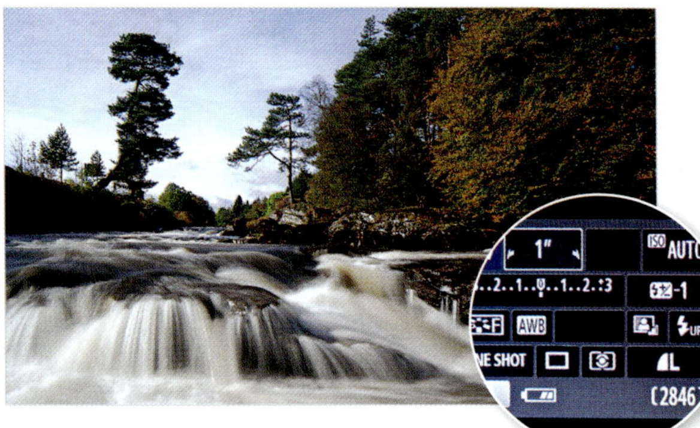

01 Increase your shutter speed

Your camera exposes an image by allowing light to hit the sensor for a set amount of time. This time is dictated by the shutter speed. Speeds can range from hundredths of a second to 30 seconds or more, but unless both the camera and subject are perfectly still, the longer the shutter speed the more chance there is of blur ruining your shot. When photographing some scenes you can use this to your advantage, however. For this image we used a shutter speed of one second with the camera mounted on a tripod.

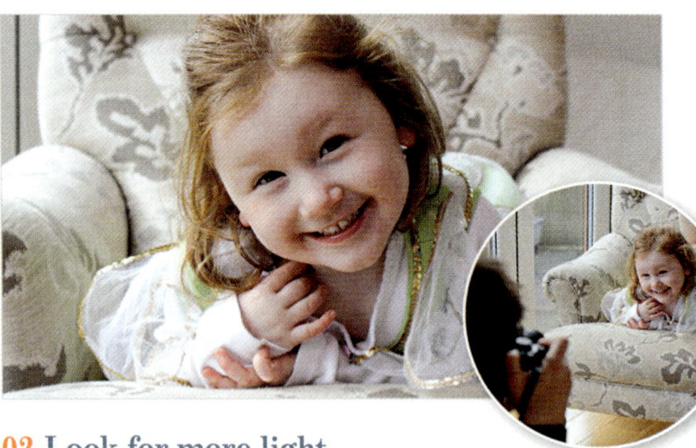

02 Look for more light

If your shutter speed is too slow and your image and subject are blurring, try repositioning them next to a large natural light source. Patio doors, large windows and conservatories can all be used to cast a nice, soft, even light onto your subject. The more light there is, the faster the shutter speed will be, making subject movement less likely to ruin your shot.

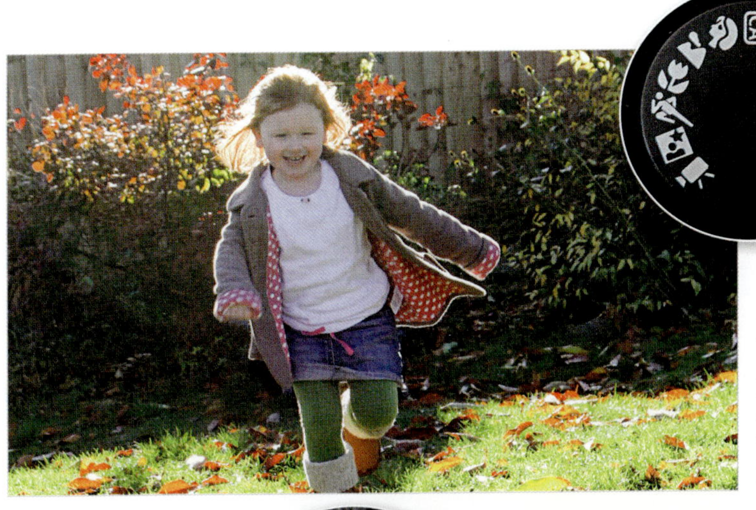

03 Try Sports mode

If you're shooting subjects that you know will move — young children, for example — try switching to your camera's Sports mode. This mode will automatically set a fast shutter speed that will make it easier to capture fast-moving subjects in focus. Autofocus will automatically track the subject while the shutter-release button is half pressed, making this a quick and easy way to capture the action.

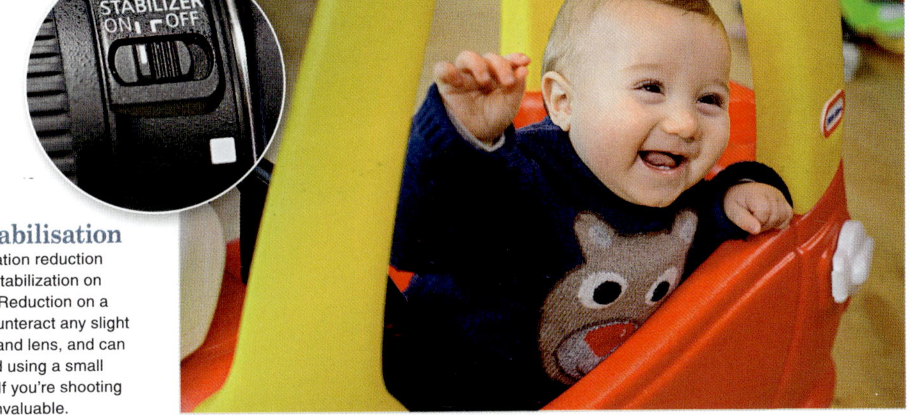

04 Use image stabilisation

Some lenses include vibration reduction technology (IS or Image Stabilization on a Canon; VR or Vibration Reduction on a Nikon), which works to counteract any slight movement in the camera and lens, and can be activated when needed using a small switch on the lens barrel. If you're shooting handheld, this feature is invaluable.

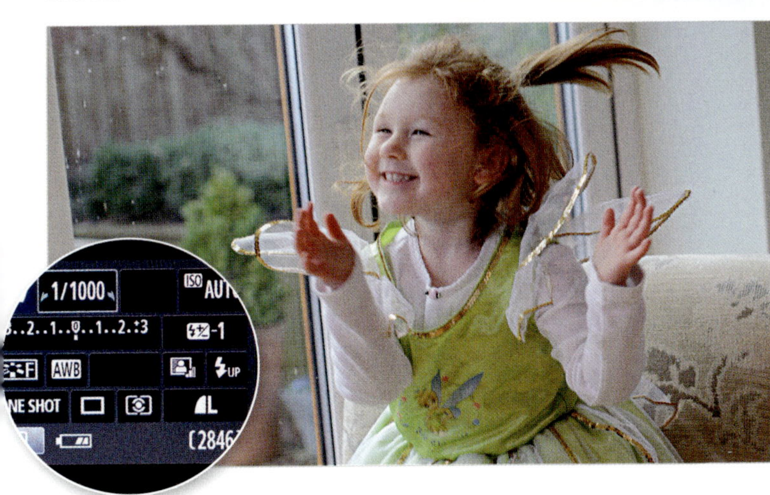

05 Know the optimum settings

For capturing people, we'd recommend you keep your shutter speed above 1/200 sec, but go higher than this (1/1000 sec) if the person is moving fast. Not only will this allow you to hold the camera without risk of camera shake, but it'll also allow for the movement of the person in the photo. You may need to increase the ISO and open the aperture right up to bring in more light. Increasing the shutter speed can lead to a fall-off in image quality, particularly if light levels are low, but it's far better to have a slightly grainy image than one that's blurred and unusable.

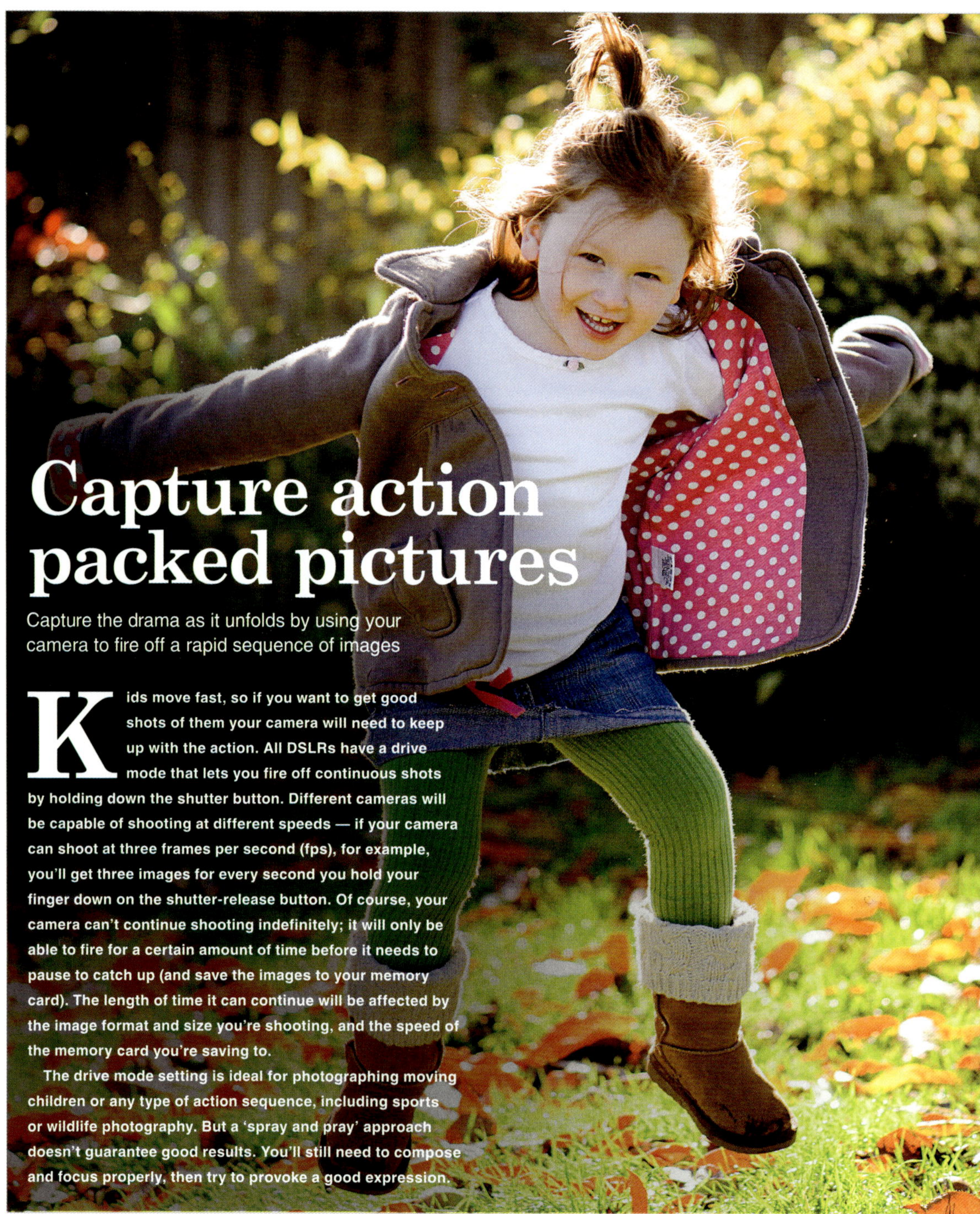

Capture action packed pictures

Capture the drama as it unfolds by using your camera to fire off a rapid sequence of images

Kids move fast, so if you want to get good shots of them your camera will need to keep up with the action. All DSLRs have a drive mode that lets you fire off continuous shots by holding down the shutter button. Different cameras will be capable of shooting at different speeds — if your camera can shoot at three frames per second (fps), for example, you'll get three images for every second you hold your finger down on the shutter-release button. Of course, your camera can't continue shooting indefinitely; it will only be able to fire for a certain amount of time before it needs to pause to catch up (and save the images to your memory card). The length of time it can continue will be affected by the image format and size you're shooting, and the speed of the memory card you're saving to.

The drive mode setting is ideal for photographing moving children or any type of action sequence, including sports or wildlife photography. But a 'spray and pray' approach doesn't guarantee good results. You'll still need to compose and focus properly, then try to provoke a good expression.

Camera, action!

Discover how to get the most from the drive mode options your camera offers

Select a drive mode

With your camera in its P (Program) shooting mode, navigate to the Drive mode menu and select the symbol that looks like a stack of photos on top of each other. Some DSLRs have two continuous burst mode options — standard and high continuous (if you have the latter, it will be marked with a small H next to it). Now you can simply wait for the perfect moment before firing off a burst of shots — five or six should be enough.

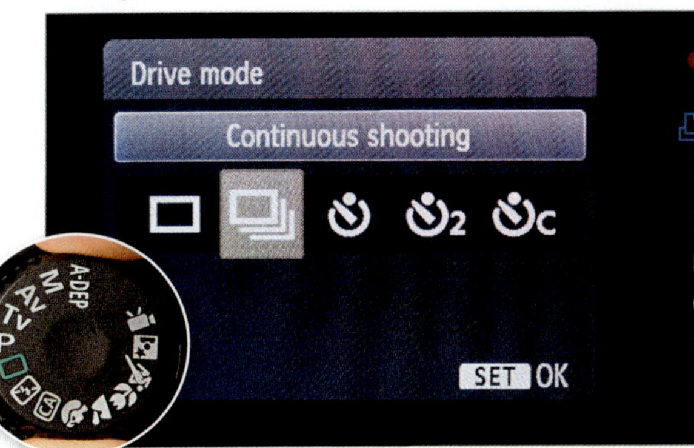

Use sparingly

Of course, taking lots of shots in this way will require more time editing images later, so only use your camera's burst mode when the situation calls for it. When you look back through the shots, accept that not every one will be perfect, but you'll hopefully have at least one good, sharp, well-exposed image in the bag.

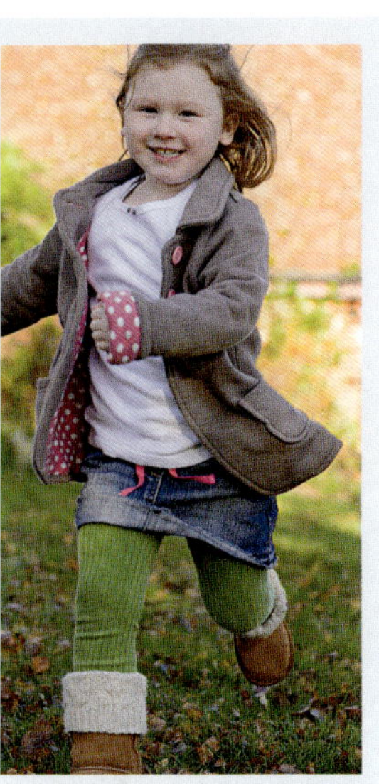

Focus setting

When photographing fast-moving subjects like young children you'll improve your chances of success if you switch your autofocus setting to track your subject as it moves through the frame. On a Canon camera this setting is called AI Servo, and on a Nikon AF-C — simply select the option from the autofocus menu. Half press the shutter-release button to focus once on your subject, then keep it held down to fire off your sequence of shots.

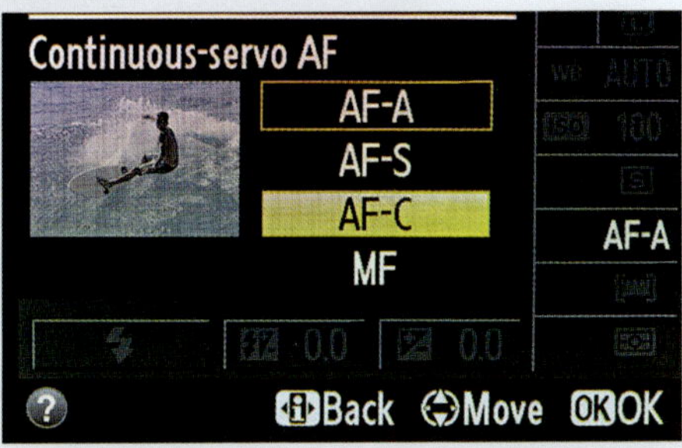

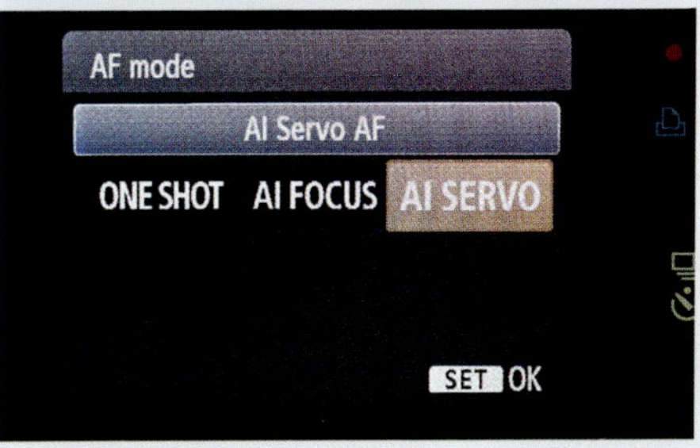

Maximise speed

If you're shooting both raw files and JPEGs at the same time, your camera will slow down when shooting in this mode. For the drive mode to fire at its maximum speed you'd need to set your image quality to its lowest setting, but bear in mind that if you turn the image quality setting right down you won't be able to enlarge your images later. You'll need to find a compromise between speed and image quality.

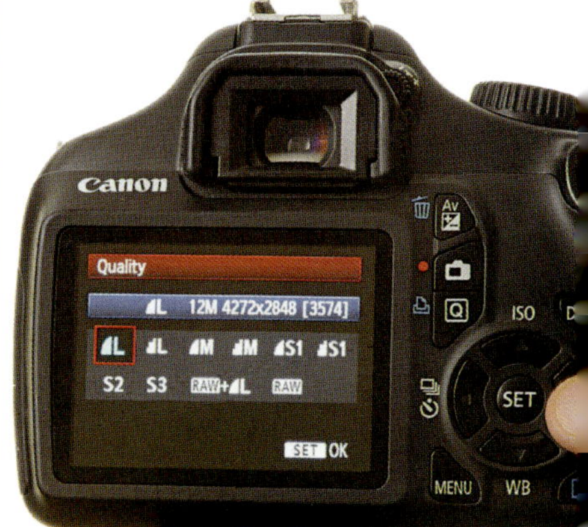

Fun family portrait tips

Use our simple techniques to get the most from your shoot, and get great shots of your kids that you'll treasure forever

Kids usually respond best when they forget they're having their picture taken, so encourage them to run around, play with toys, shout, laugh, pull funny faces, dress up, spin around, jump, throw leaves or absolutely anything you can think of to distract them from the camera and the fact that you're taking pictures. This will lead to some great, fun action shots, and also help to bring out each child's individuality and character. It will also avoid dull, staged and static portraits.

For an interesting angle, ask them to lie down on their tummies and shoot from in front, or get them to roll over and try shooting from above. Still looking for inspiration? Here's a whole host of ideas…

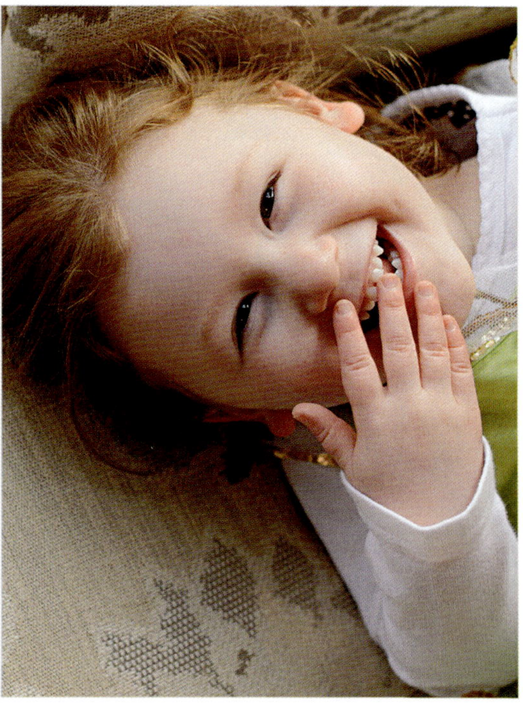

Down with the kids

Get down low and have some fun capturing great portraits of children

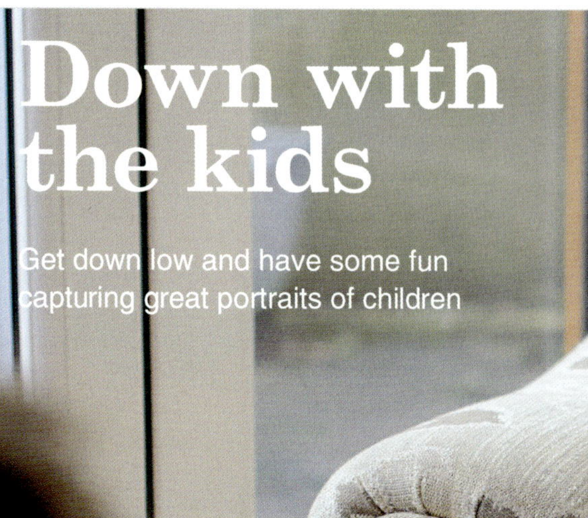

01 Dress sense

Before you start shooting, think about the clothes the children are wearing. Big brand names can be a little distracting, while blocks of colour work well. If in doubt, keep it simple and colourful. While dressing-up clothes are fun, for more natural-looking portraits dress your subjects in their everyday clothes.

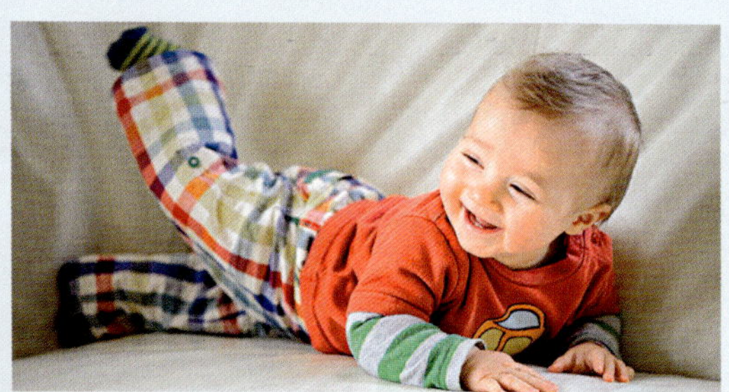

02 Crop for impact

Try cropping out one side of a child's face for a modern, edgy look. To do this, you may need to shift your SLR's focus point so that it sits over one eye, as sharp eyes are the key to a professional-looking end result. Check your images as you shoot by zooming right in on your LCD screen. These kinds of portraits will often look good when cropped into a square shape later.

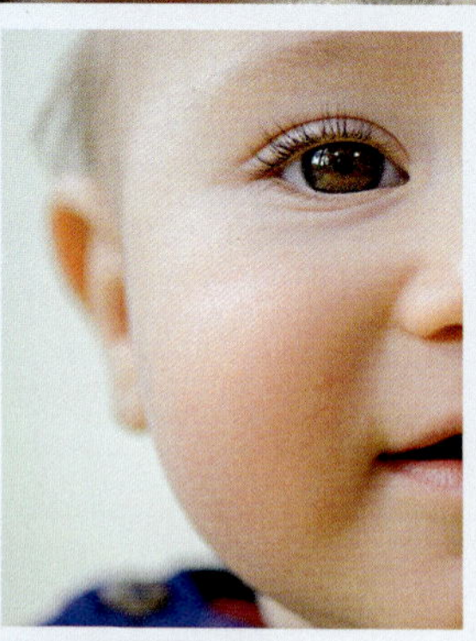

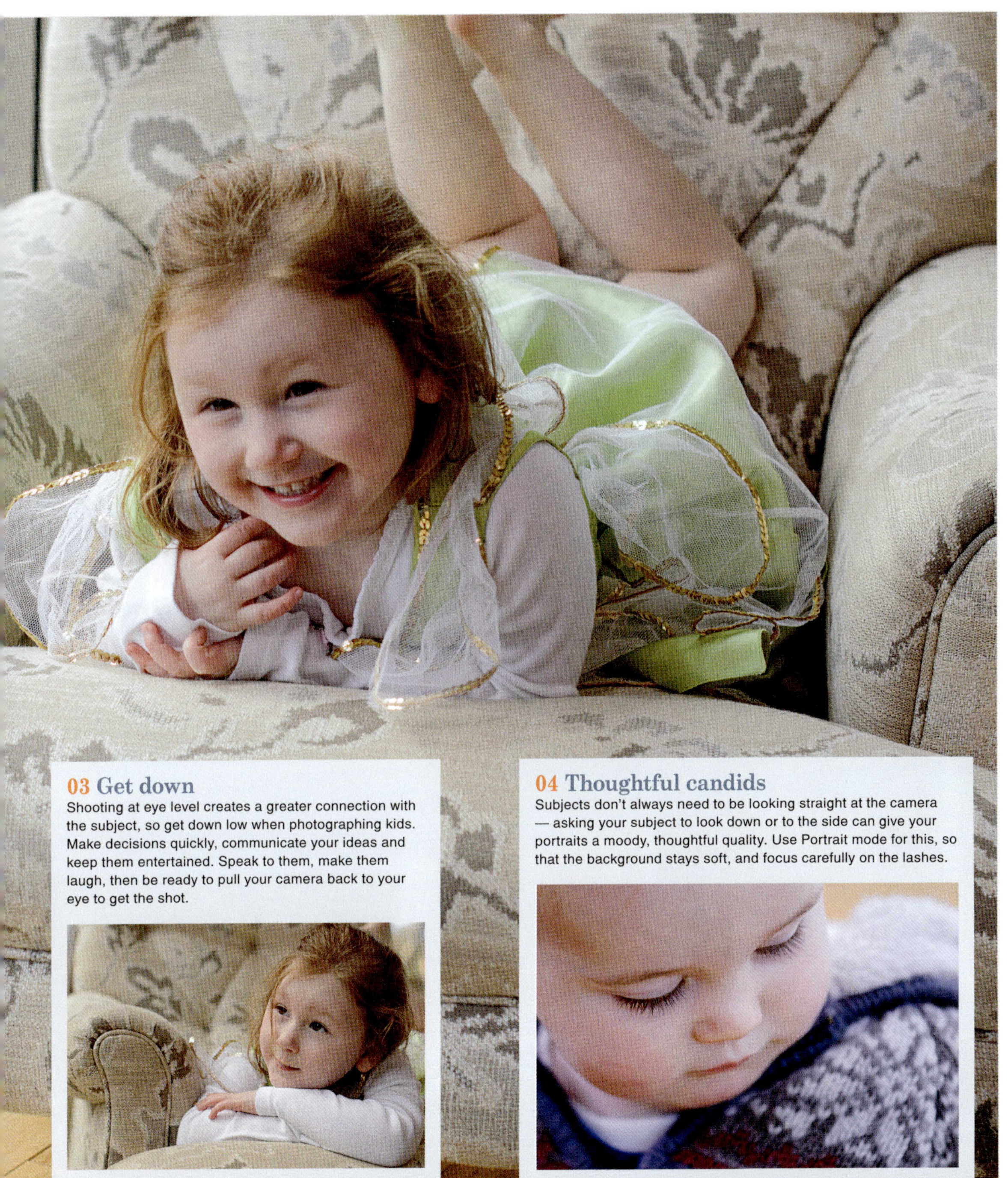

03 Get down

Shooting at eye level creates a greater connection with the subject, so get down low when photographing kids. Make decisions quickly, communicate your ideas and keep them entertained. Speak to them, make them laugh, then be ready to pull your camera back to your eye to get the shot.

04 Thoughtful candids

Subjects don't always need to be looking straight at the camera — asking your subject to look down or to the side can give your portraits a moody, thoughtful quality. Use Portrait mode for this, so that the background stays soft, and focus carefully on the lashes.

Capture the action!

Stay one step ahead to ensure you get your shot

01 On your marks…

Ready, steady, go! When taking action shots like this you'll need to be quick. Make sure you consider the background, ensuring it's not too distracting. It's best to set your focus to its tracking setting, as this will give you the best chance of keeping your shots sharp.

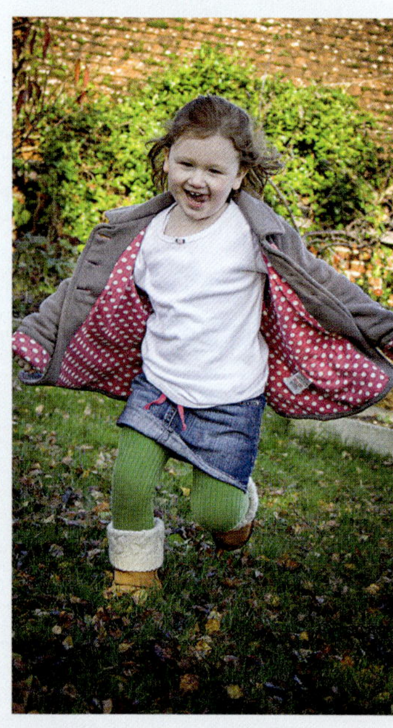

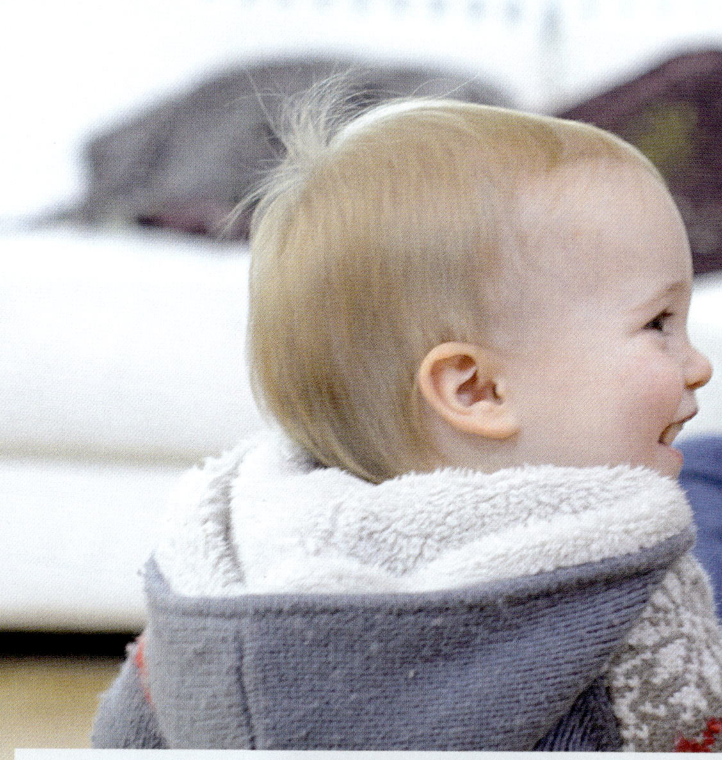

02 Use space

Leaving lots of space (sometimes referred to as negative space) around the subject can give a standard portrait an interesting twist. This approach usually works best with clean, simple or textured backgrounds. Focus on the face, keep the shutter-release half pressed, and then recompose to bring more of the surroundings into the frame. You may need an adult to help with keeping younger children in the right position.

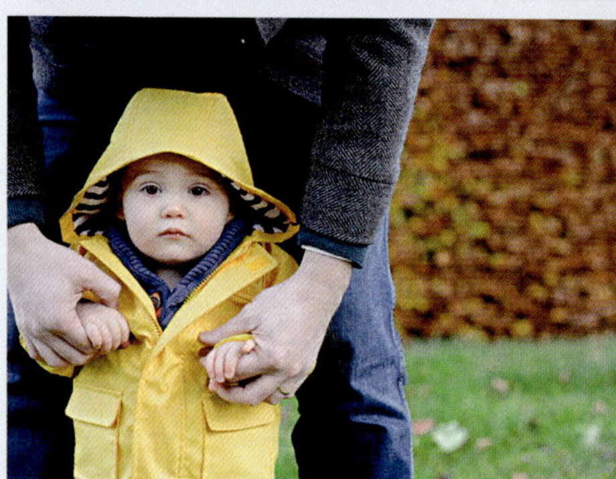

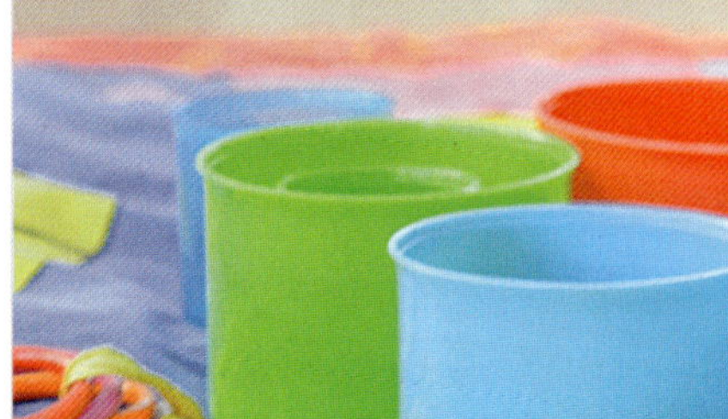

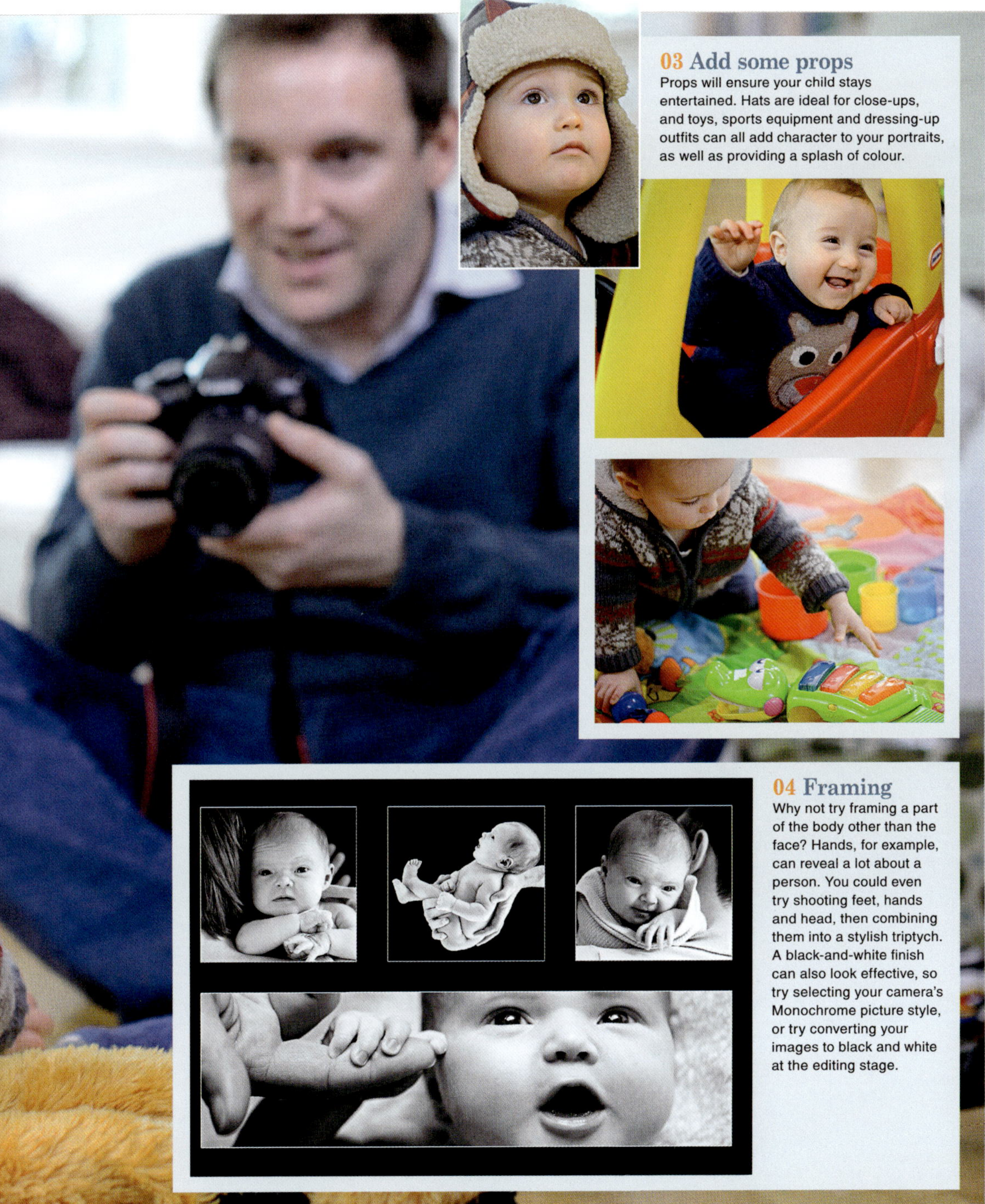

03 Add some props

Props will ensure your child stays entertained. Hats are ideal for close-ups, and toys, sports equipment and dressing-up outfits can all add character to your portraits, as well as providing a splash of colour.

04 Framing

Why not try framing a part of the body other than the face? Hands, for example, can reveal a lot about a person. You could even try shooting feet, hands and head, then combining them into a stylish triptych. A black-and-white finish can also look effective, so try selecting your camera's Monochrome picture style, or try converting your images to black and white at the editing stage.

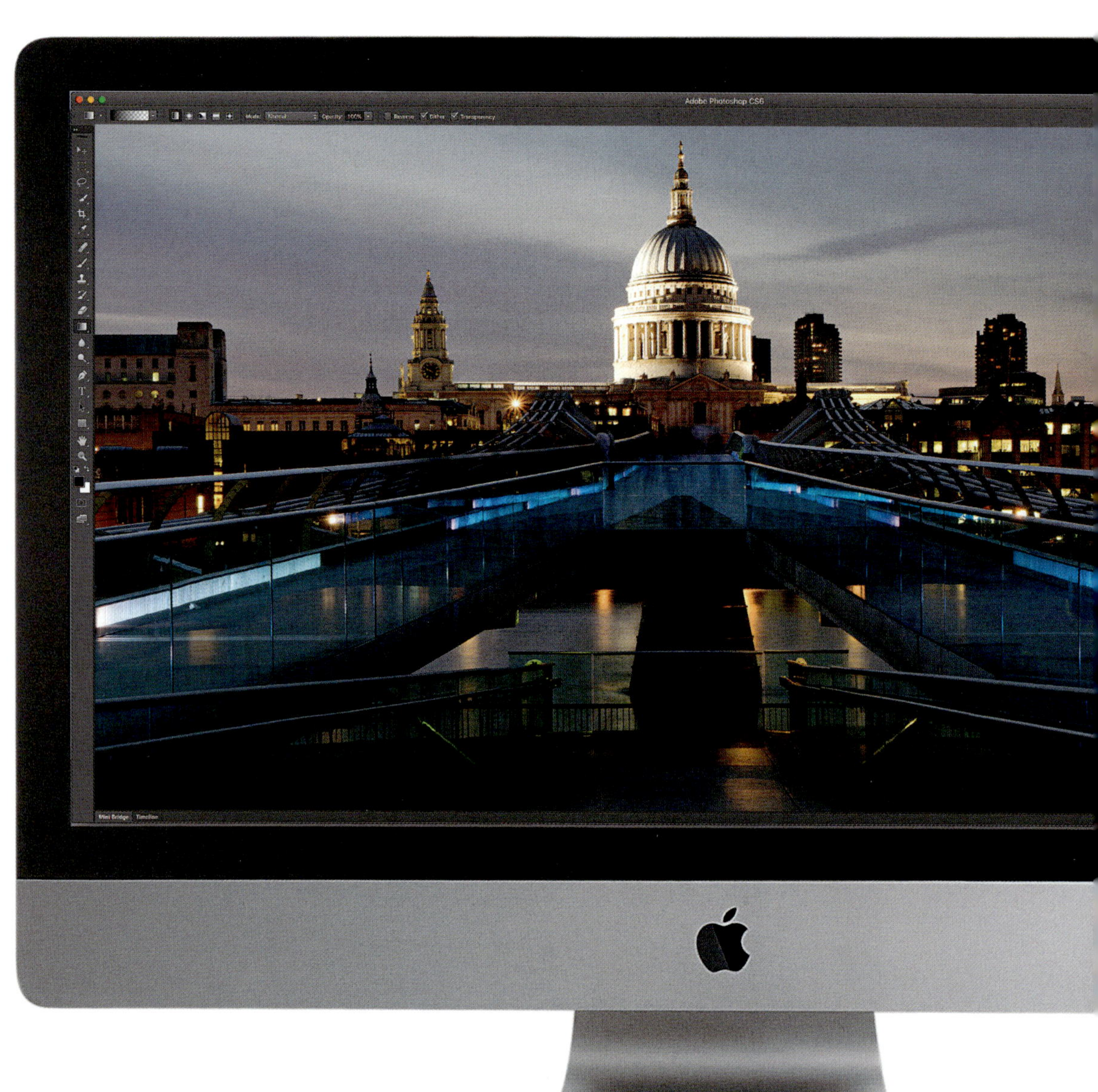

Take Control

Take the next step on your photographic journey by operating your SLR in manual mode and more…

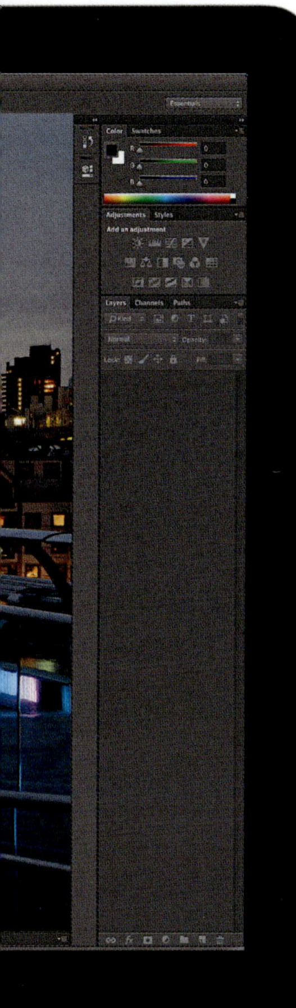

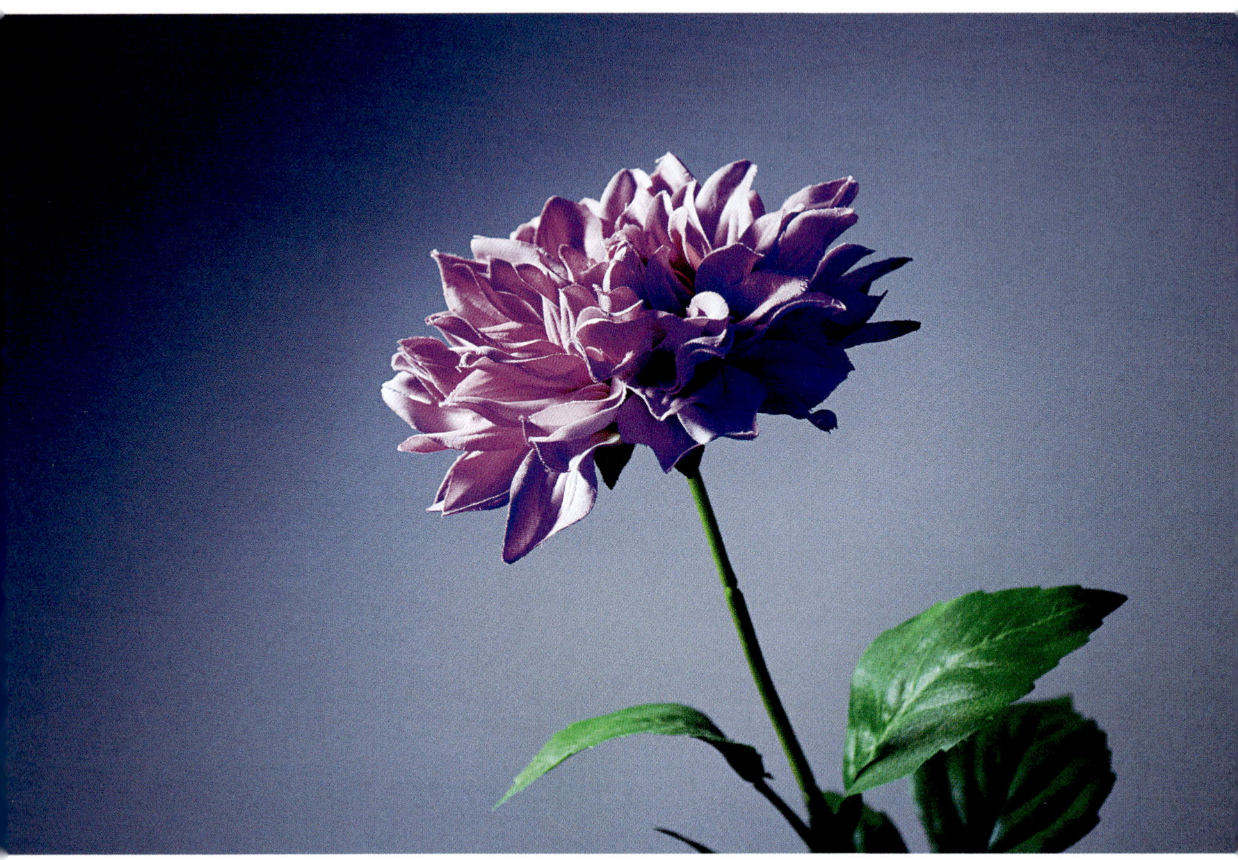

Take control in Program mode

Discover how to take more creative control over the
way your images look by switching to the P mode

Although using the Full Auto mode is great when starting out, you'll find you will come up against limitations, and if you want to progress, you'll need to start controlling the camera yourself. Once you're comfortable with your camera and the various basic shooting modes, you're ready to take the next step by progressing to the creative exposure modes. These are P, A, S (Tv on Canon cameras) and M. They give you control over the three main factors that make up an exposure: aperture, shutter speed and ISO. The easiest of these modes to understand is P, which stands for Program. This works much like the Fully Auto mode in that the camera will figure out the correct exposure for you. But it gives you control over other crucial features, such as ISO.

Program also gives you some influence over the exposure by letting you change the shutter speed with the command dial. For example, if we increase the shutter speed then the aperture gets wider. This kind of exposure, with a fast shutter speed and wide aperture is useful if we want to capture fast-moving action or blur backgrounds.

Program mode also gives you another hugely useful feature: exposure compensation. This feature comes in handy in situations where the camera may have misjudged the exposure and recorded the scene as too bright or too dark, such as in winter snow pictures. All we need to do is hold the exposure compensation button and turn the dial one way or the other to compensate.

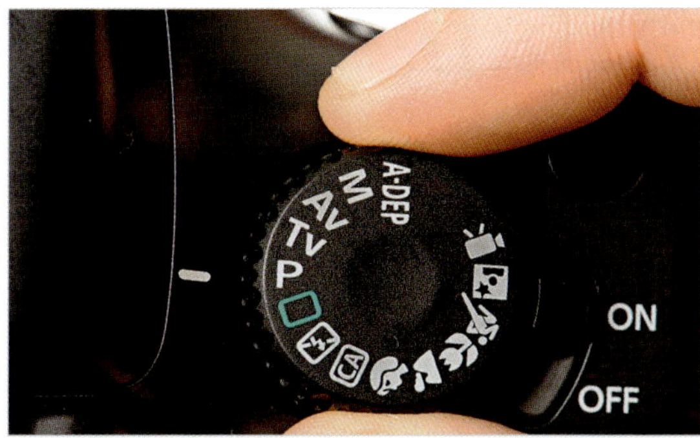

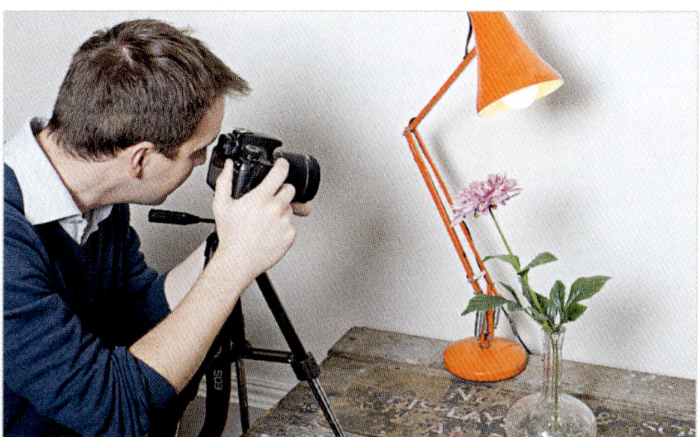

01 Enter Program mode

Put your camera into the Program mode. This can be found on your mode dial symbolised by the letter P, usually next to the Full Auto mode. This will give you extra control over crucial features such as ISO and exposure compensation. It also enables you to shift the aperture and shutter speed.

02 Light your scene

We've selected a still-life setup for this shoot. It can be easier to practise your photography skills on a still life as you can take your time to get the composition and lighting right. We used a lamp to light the main subject, and placed it to the side. This sidelight also creates a shadow in the background that frames the flower nicely.

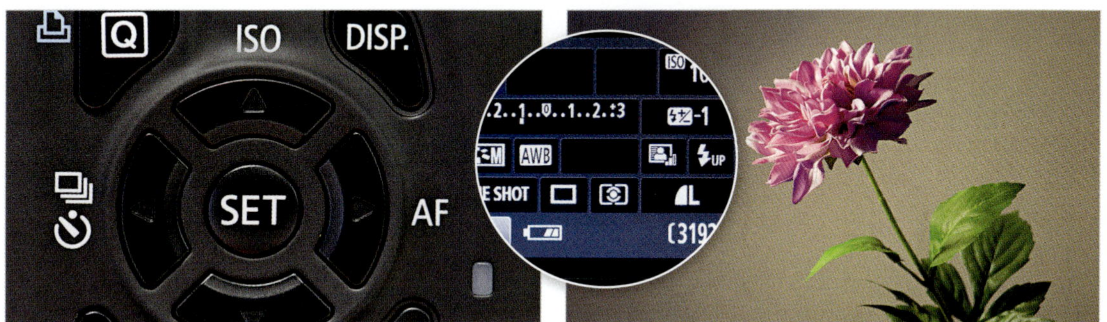

03 Alter the ISO

We're going to mount the camera on to a tripod so we don't need to worry about what shutter speed we're shooting at because camera shake won't be a problem. We don't want to blast our setup with flash light, because we'd get a completely different result. We're going to set the ISO low to 100, which will make the shutter speed longer.

04 Use exposure compensation

Take a test shot. In our example we want to make the background a bit darker so we're going to adjust the exposure compensation. Press the +/- button and turn the scroll dial so that the setting on the back panel LCD or the top plate LCD reads minus one on the meter. Take another test shot and notice the difference the compensation makes.

Useful to know...

With Program, or any of the other creative modes, you have control over the ISO, which determines the camera's sensitivity to light. Lower ISOs such as 100 or 200 make for better quality images, but the lower the ISO, the more light that's needed for a correct exposure. On the other hand, higher ISOs such as 800 or 1600 mean less light is needed, but there's a trade off in image quality, with increased levels of noise.

As well as giving you control over ISO, with P mode you can also choose whether to fire the flash in low-light situations, unlike Full Auto, which will fire the flash whether you want it or not. So for example, if you want to take a shot indoors but you don't want to blast the scene with flat light from your flash, then you have the option to increase the ISO instead.

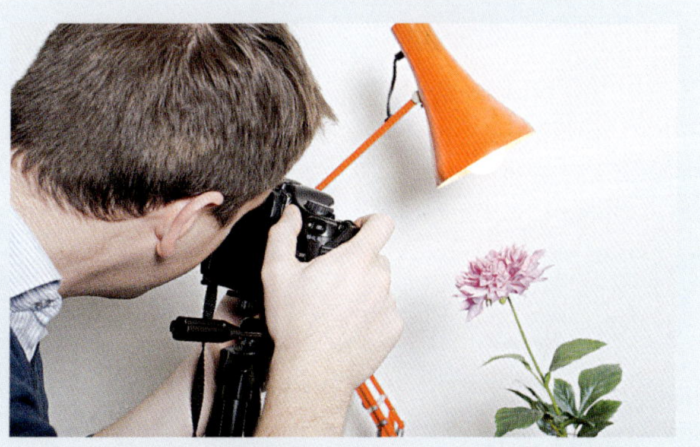

The effects available via picture styles

Select the appropriate picture styles to enhance your images, whatever the subject

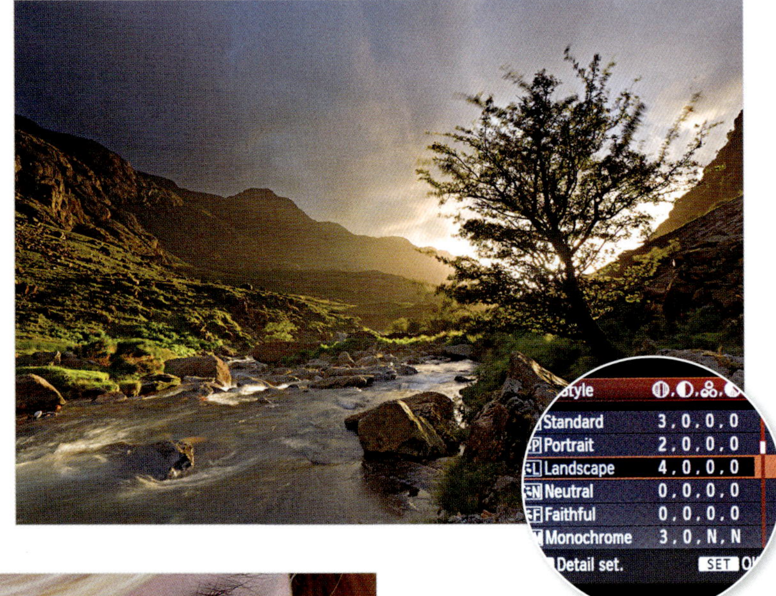

01 Landscape

The Landscape picture style will increase the saturation of the greens and blues in the scene, and also boost the sharpness to enhance detail throughout.

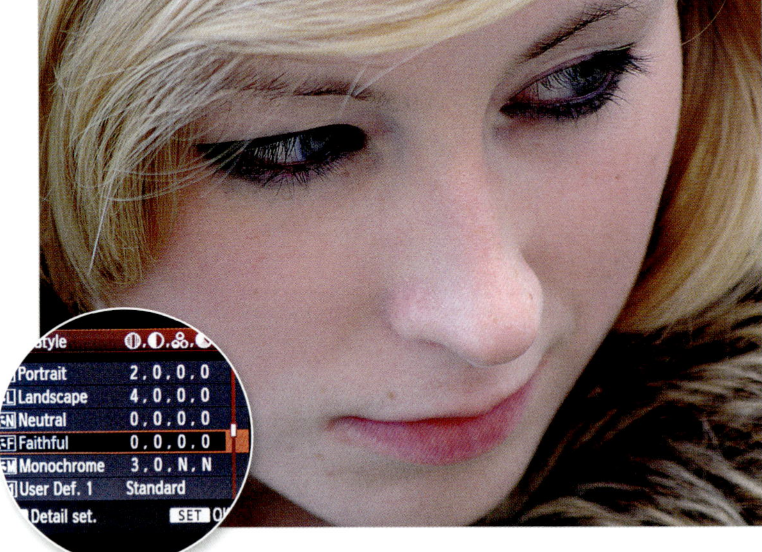

02 Faithful

The Faithful setting will try to reproduce accurate colours in the scene when shot under daylight conditions, so what you see is what you get. It works by decreasing the contrast.

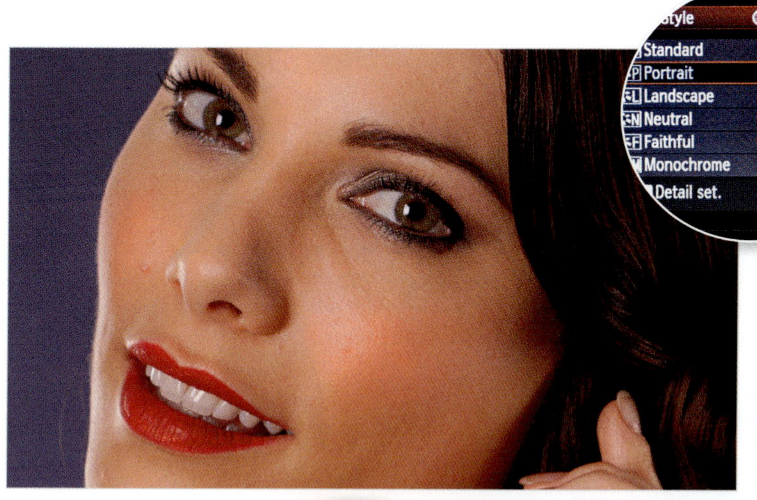

03 Portrait

With the Portrait picture style, edge sharpness is reduced for smoother skin texture. This is done by adjusting the colour tone of the magenta to yellow, and by adding in brightness. Skin tones will appear a lighter pink.

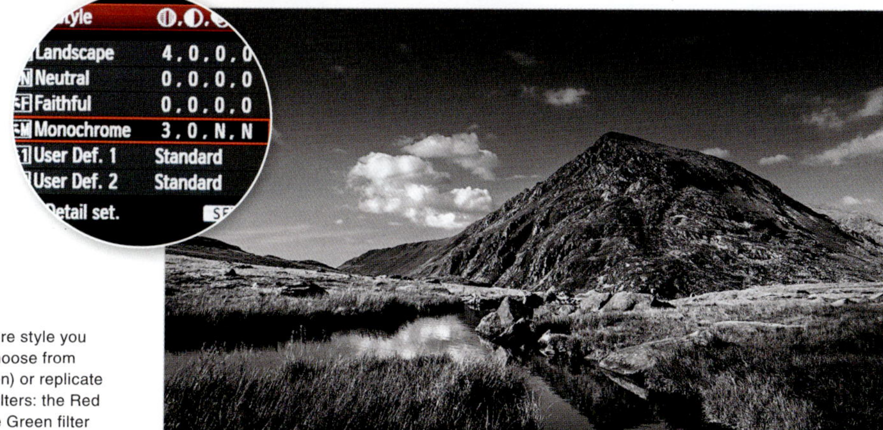

04 Monochrome

With the Monochrome picture style you can also tone the image (choose from Sepia, Blue, Purple or Green) or replicate the look of traditional lens filters: the Red filter increases contrast; the Green filter enhances any green hues.

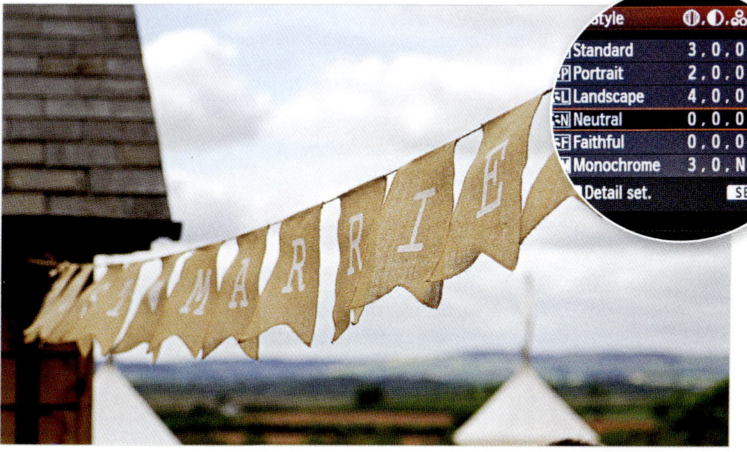

05 Neutral

The Neutral picture style comes in handy when shooting objects or scenes containing vivid colours and subtle shades and tones. It uses a moderate contrast and saturation setting, so there's less risk of colours becoming oversaturated in post-processing.

The mode dial

Take our guided tour around the mode dial and learn
how to select the right shooting mode for your needs

The mode dial is one of the most fundamental controls on your camera. Here you communicate with your DSLR by telling it what you want to control, and what you want it to control. There are many different modes you can select and how you choose to shoot comes down to personal preference.

Some photographers like to fully manually control their camera, where as others like to use the part manual controls. As you get to know your camera you'll soon start to find the way you like to shoot. To make it easier for you to get your head around, we're now going to guide you through the mode dial and the various options…

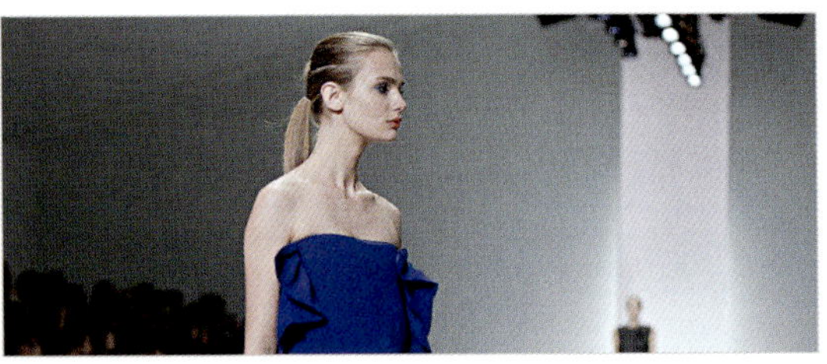

01 Manual Mode

Take control and manually adjust your DSLR. Select the aperture, shutter speed and ISO setting yourself for complete creative control over your images.

02 Aperture Priority Mode

In this setting you can set the aperture and your camera will control the rest of the settings for you. This is useful when the available light or the depth of field is a prime consideration.

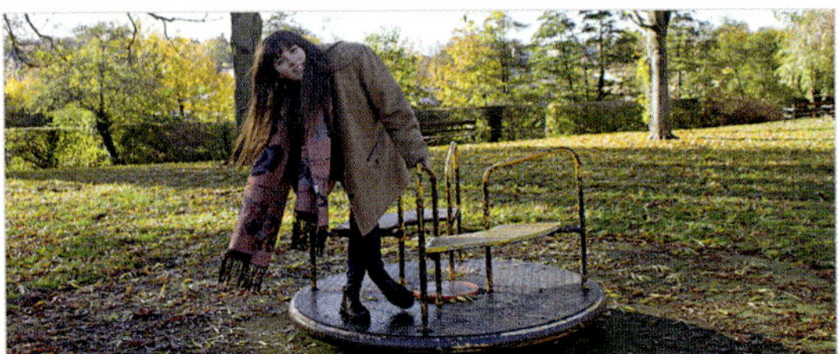

03 Shutter Priority Mode

In this setting you set the shutter speed and your camera will control the rest of the settings for you. This is ideal for action shots in which you want to control the sharpness.

04 Program Mode

The Program mode is an automatic mode that enables you to alter some of the settings such as ISO and exposure compensation. It's handy for weaning beginners away from Full Auto.

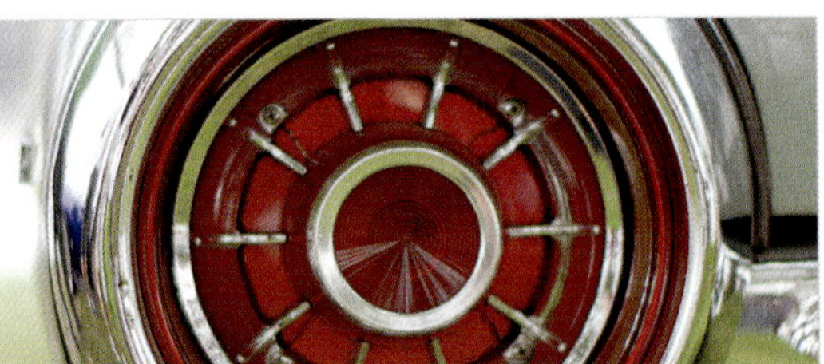
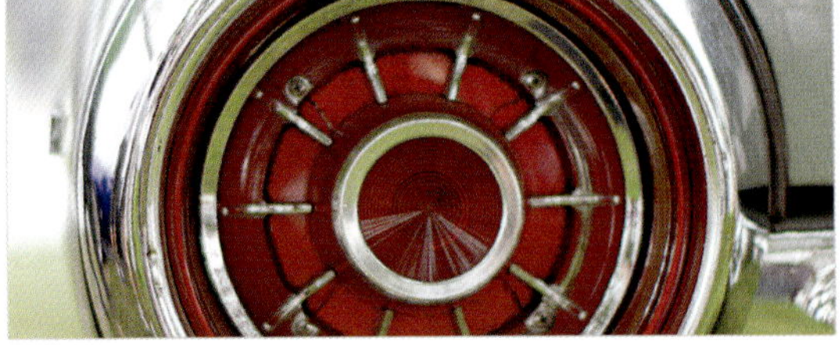

05 Auto mode

All entry-level DSLRs come with a fully automatic mode. With this setting the camera takes control of everything for you. All you have to do is compose and shoot.

06 No Flash mode

This is useful if you don't want to shoot using the pop-up flash in low light. This can be handy if you're in a museum or a gallery where flash light isn't allowed.

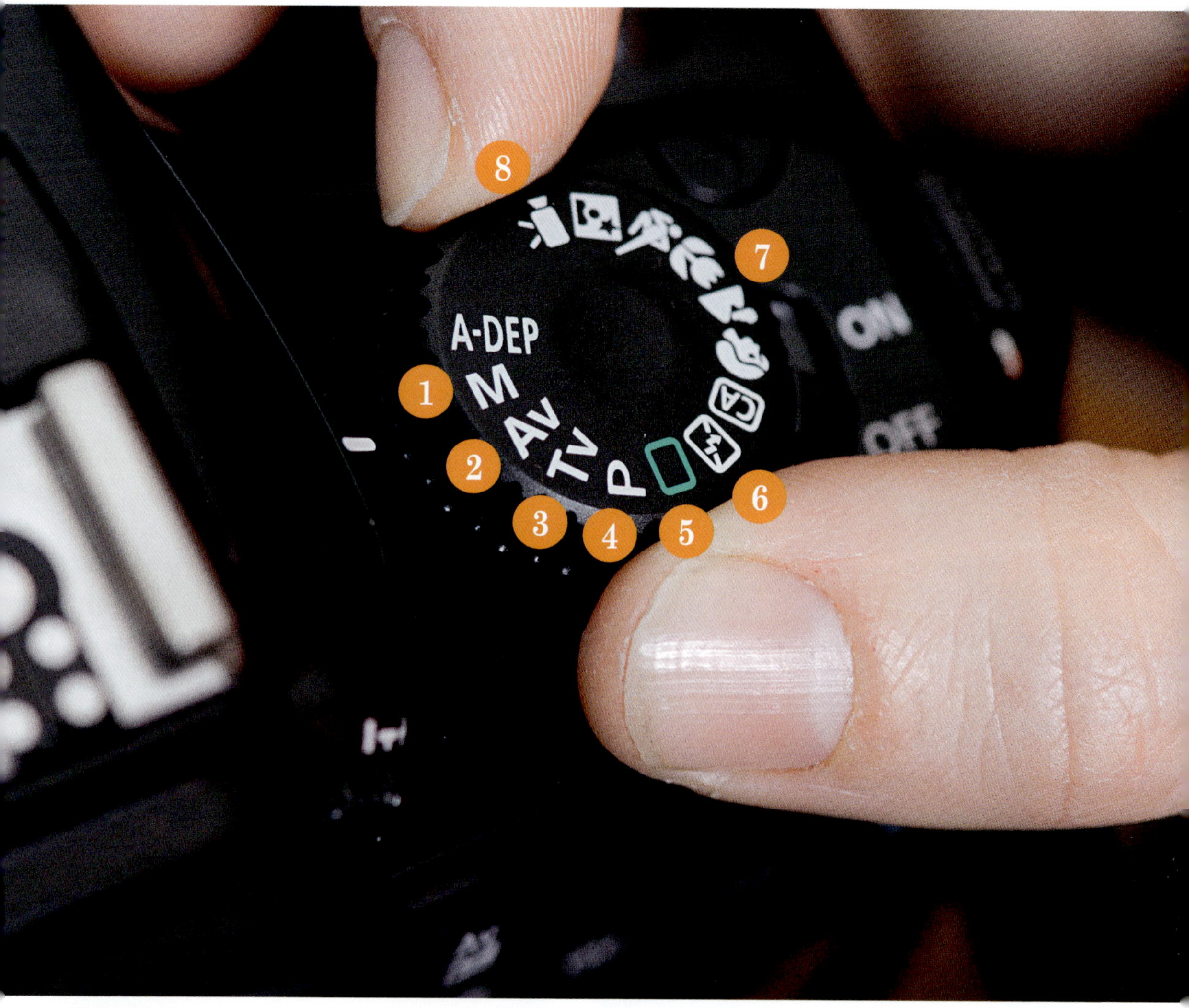

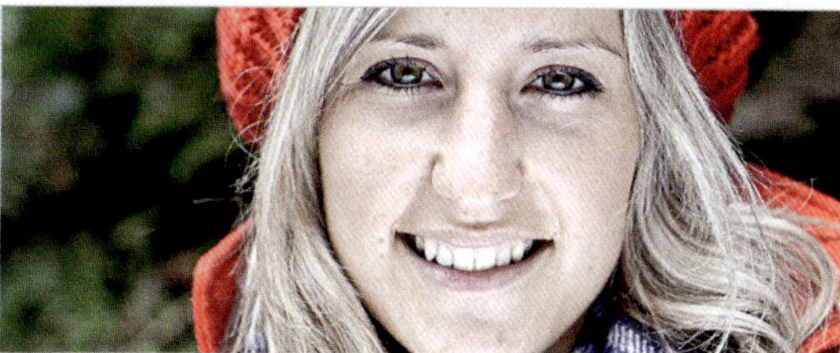

07 The Scene modes

The scene modes are a quick and easy way to customise your camera settings for any given environment. You are limited, however, in what you can do with these.

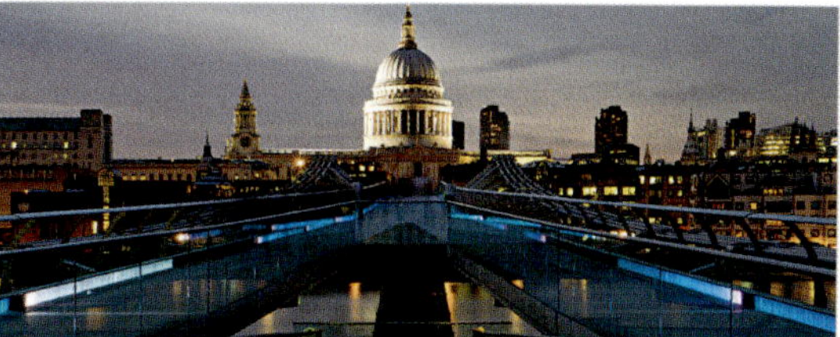

08 Movie mode

Record video footage on your DSLR by switching your camera to the Movie mode. On some models the access to this function isn't on the mode dial and may be on the back of the camera body.

The five main modes

We delve a little deeper into the main shooting modes available on the mode dial

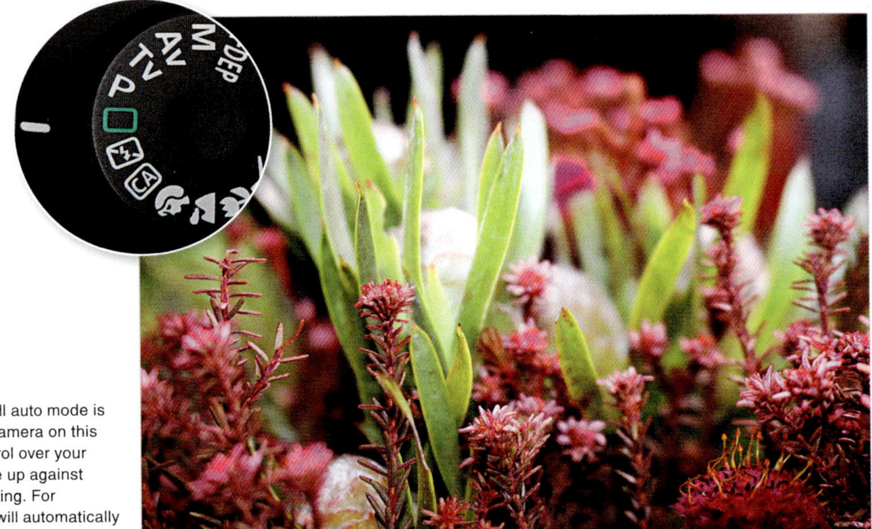

01 Auto mode

On most DSLR cameras the full auto mode is marked as a green icon. The camera on this setting will take complete control over your camera. You will find you come up against limitations when using this setting. For example, in low light the flash will automatically engage when you may not want it to.

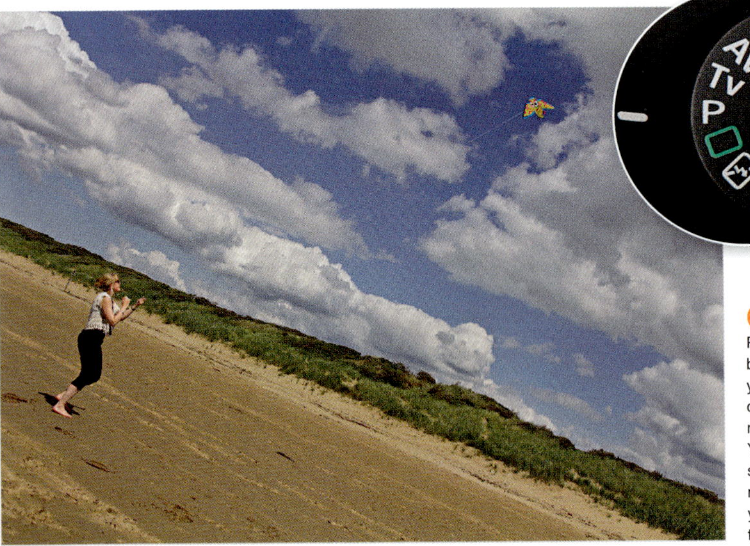

02 Program mode

P for Program, is very similar to full auto, but, as with all the other modes, it gives you control over the ISO and exposure compensation feature. This is useful when you need to make small tweaks to your exposure. You can also make adjustments to the shutter speed setting by turning the scroll dial. The P mode is useful when you're starting out or if you have little time to set up your camera to take a shot.

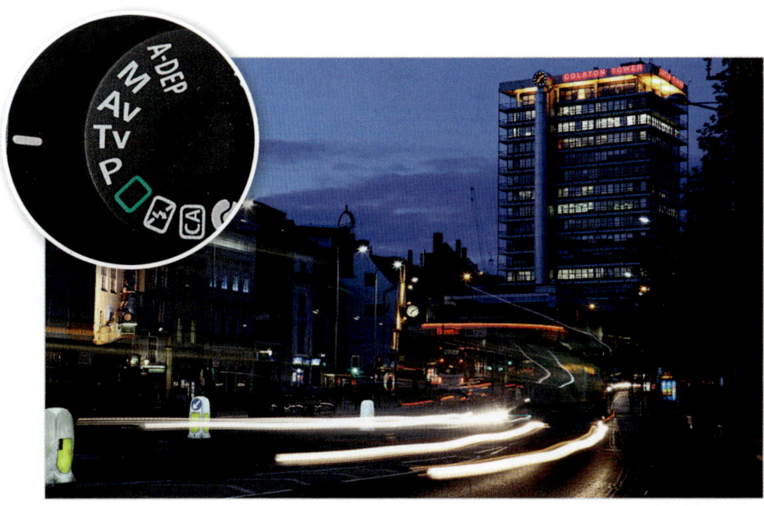

03 Shutter priority mode

Controlling the shutter speed can be useful for creative effects. Setting a long shutter speed can be good for recording blur in moving water or clouds, but you'll need a tripod to keep the camera still. At the other end of the scale, setting a very fast shutter speed is useful for capturing fast-moving subjects. One important thing to note with shutter priority, if the camera calculates that the required aperture falls outside the aperture range of your lens, then the number will flash in your viewfinder. If this happens, you'll need to either change the shutter speed, or adjust the ISO to allow for more or less light.

04 Aperture priority mode

Next to shutter priority is its counterpart: aperture priority. On a Nikon it's called A for aperture, on a Canon it's AV, for aperture value. This mode lets you set the aperture, and the camera will automatically figure out the right shutter speed for a correct exposure. We're able to choose the size of the hole in the lens, and in turn the camera will decide how long the light should be allowed through to the sensor.

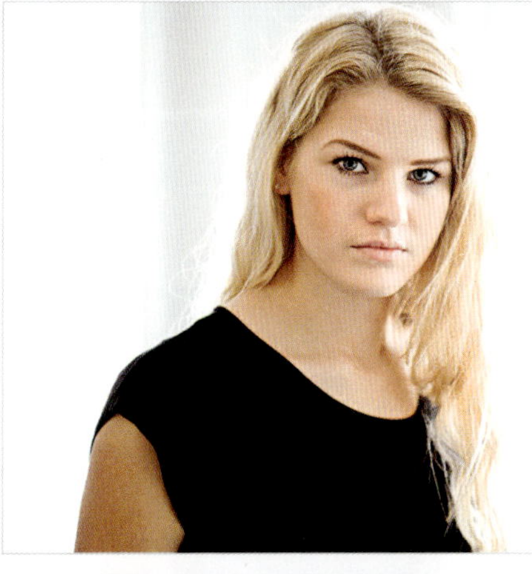

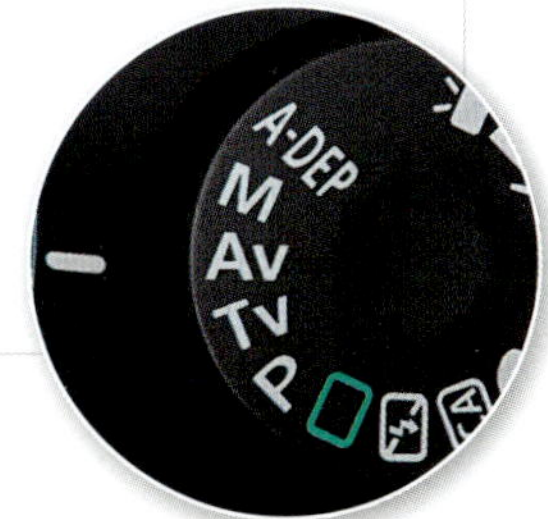

05 Manual mode

The fourth mode is M, which stands for manual. This lets you set both the shutter speed and the aperture. It's useful in environments where the light is controlled, such as in a studio. Manual can also be useful if you want to keep the exposure constant throughout a range of shots. Say for example, if you want to shoot a set of pictures for a panorama, then using manual mode will ensure that all the frames match up.

The basics of exposure

Start to understand the fundamentals of photography and learn how to use aperture, shutter speed and ISO

Although the automatic settings on your DSLR are great when you're starting out, if you want to progress further you'll need to start taking control of your camera. The problem with shooting in automatic modes is that you have no meaningful creative input apart from the composition, and your camera may not select the right settings. So in this tutorial we're going to ease you in, and explain the basics of how exposure works.

There are three elements in a camera that control how much light is let through to the sensor. These are, the shutter speed, aperture and ISO. You should think of these things as a set of scales. You have to balance all three to get a correct exposure. Over the next eight pages we're going to guide you through each element and show you how you can control each. Although this might at first seem quite a lot to think about, once you grasped these basics you'll find your photography can really advance to the next level.

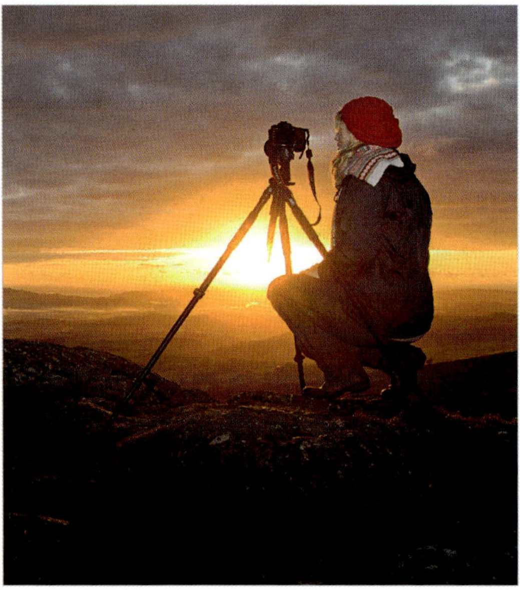

Aperture

Control the plane of focus in your image through the aperture…

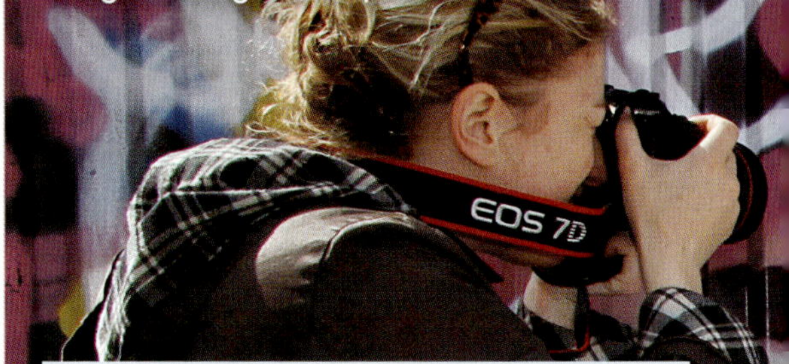

01 What is the aperture?

The aperture is built into the lens and is a bladed circle that opens and closes. This setting effects how much of the scene is in focus. When shooting portraits we tend to keep the person sharp and blur the background. When shooting landscapes we want to keep the entire image sharp. So we can control the aperture and create different effects through this.

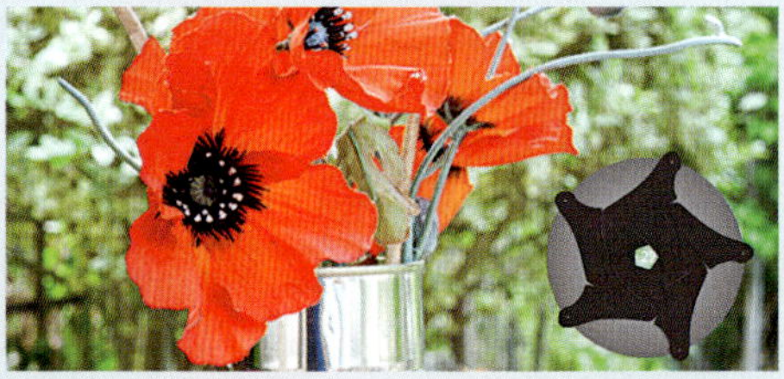

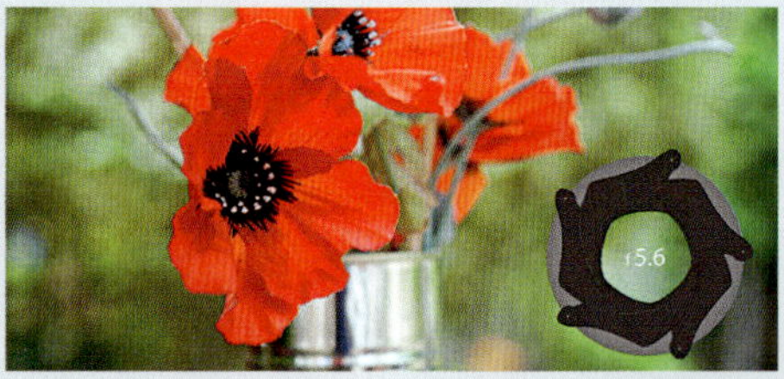

02 Aperture priority mode

You can control just the aperture in your camera with the aperture priority shooting mode. It's marked on your mode dial as A (Nikon) or Av (Canon). It means you set the aperture setting and your camera will work out what the shutter speed setting needs to be, given the ambient light conditions.

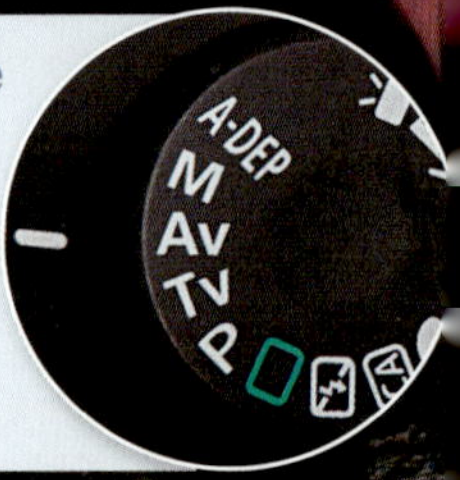

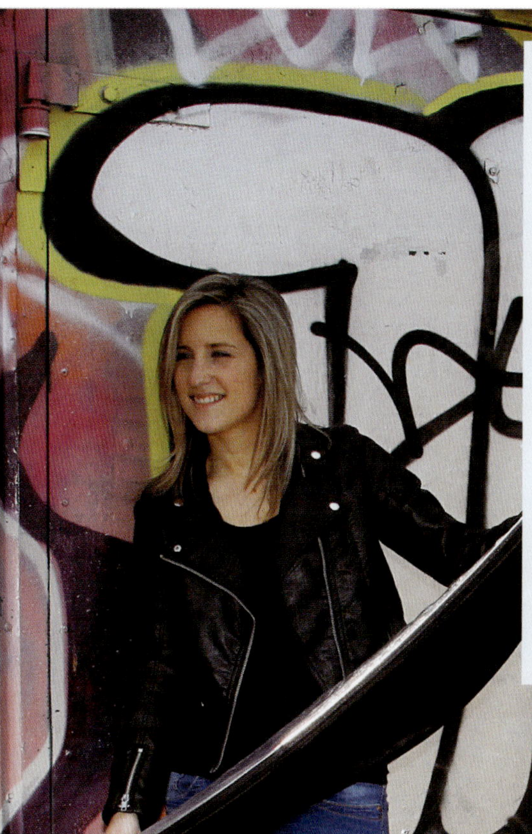

04 F-stops

Photographers measure stops of light through the aperture in f-stops. When starting out the f-stop system may seem a bit confusing. Once you get your head around the numbers it's actually very simple. Your lens has minimum and maximum f-stop numbers. When you increase or reduce the aperture number you are either doubling or halving the light going through to the sensor. For example, if you change the setting from f/8 to f/5.6 then you are doubling the amount of light going through. To make it a bit more complicated our camera goes up and down the setting in thirds of a stop — so for example, from f/8 to f/7.1 is a third of a stop of light. Just remember that low numbers open the hole (need less light) and produce a soft effect, whereas high numbers make the hole smaller (need more light) and keep the scene sharp.

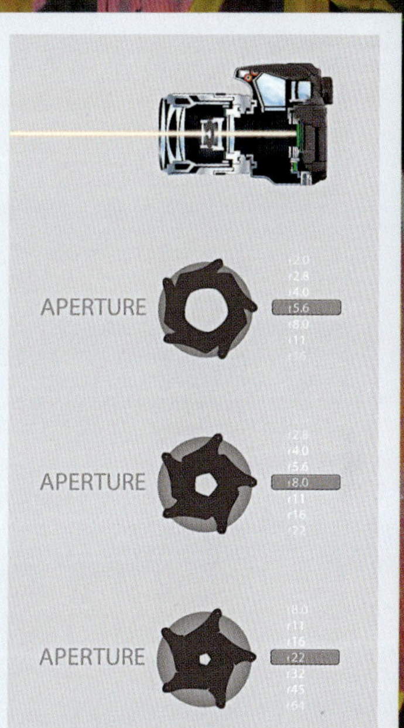

03 Depth of field

If you want to blur and soften the background while keeping your main subject matter sharp then you'll need to use a wide aperture setting, for example, f/5.6. Some lenses open to very wide settings such as f/1.4. You need to make sure you're accurate with your focusing when using your lens at the widest aperture setting, as you have less room for error with getting your main focus point sharp. If you're shooting a portrait make sure the eyes are in focus as these are the most important element. At the other end of the scales if you want to keep your image sharp then turn the aperture setting to a higher number, such as f/16. This is more appropriate when shooting landscapes.

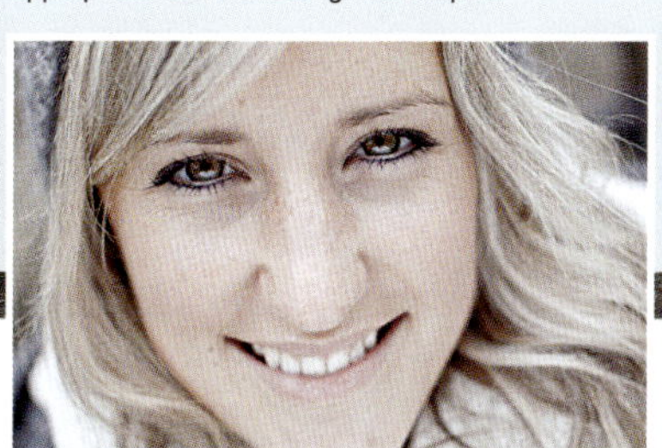

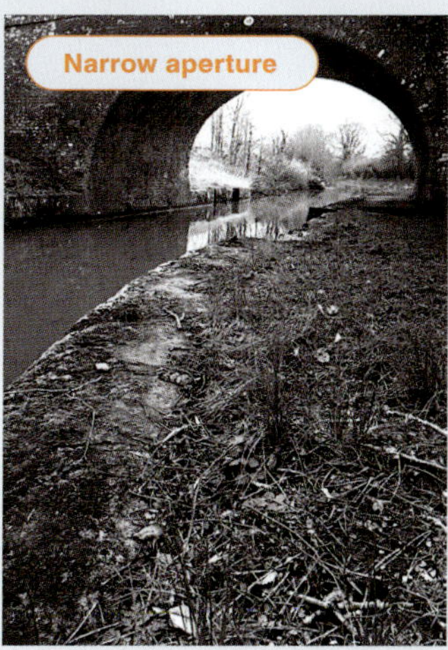

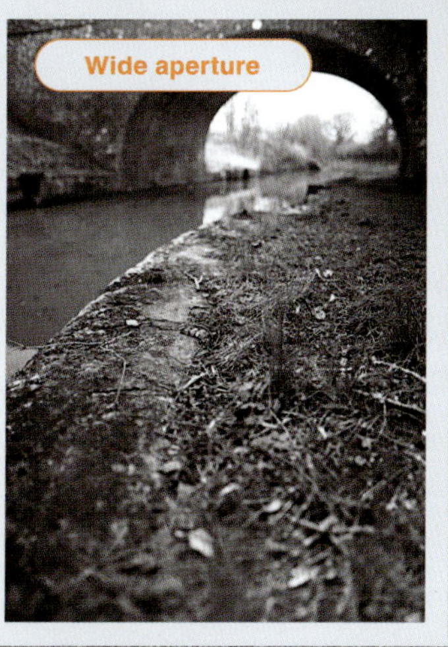

Shutter speed

Control time and movement in your
images using the shutter speed

01 What is the shutter speed?

The shutter is a mechanical part in the camera body that
opens and closes to let light through to the sensor. How
quickly it does this depends on what it is set to. You can set
your shutter to a long setting and this enables you to capture
movement in the scene, or keep the action sharp.

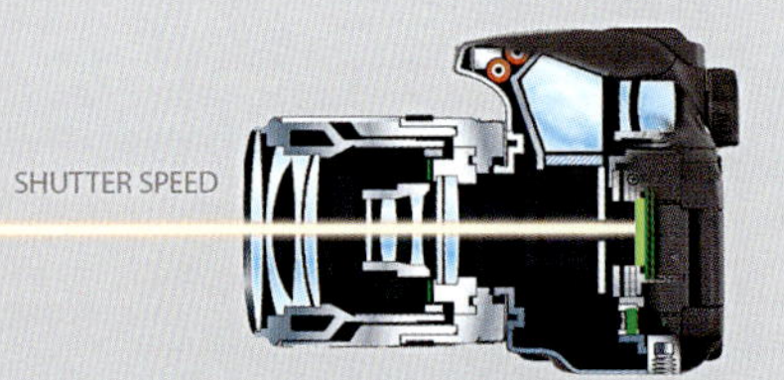

02 How do we measure the shutter speed?

Shutter speed is measured in seconds and fractions of
seconds. For example at 1/500 sec the subject matter is
sharp and frozen. On the other end of the scales if we have
a slow shutter speed, for example 1 second, any movement
in the scene will become blurred. In some examples you can
use this to your advantage. For example, moving water in a
landscape setting becomes smooth and silky, and creates
an effective result. When shooting using a long shutter
speed it's important a tripod supports your camera. You can
hold your camera as long as your shutter speed is reading
1/60 sec or faster.

Left: If the shutter speed is fast
enough it will freeze the action

Below: If the shutter speed is set to
a long exposure, any movement in
the scene will blur

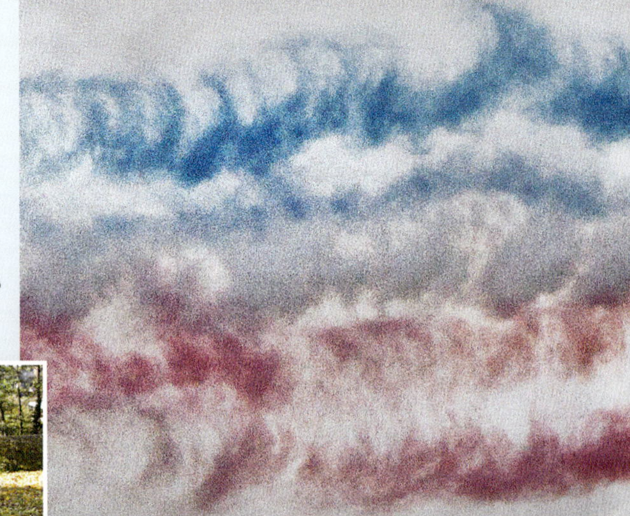

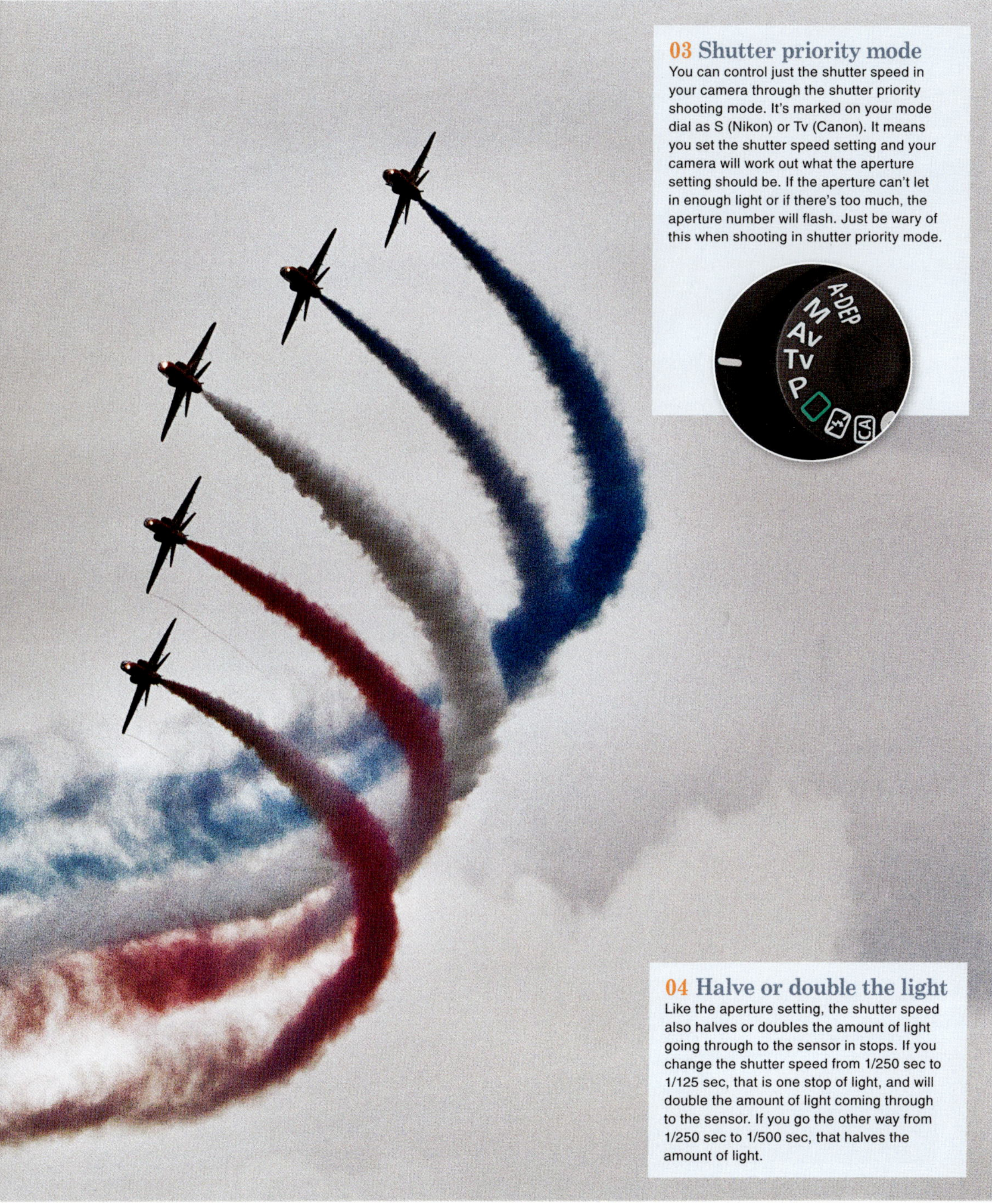

03 Shutter priority mode

You can control just the shutter speed in your camera through the shutter priority shooting mode. It's marked on your mode dial as S (Nikon) or Tv (Canon). It means you set the shutter speed setting and your camera will work out what the aperture setting should be. If the aperture can't let in enough light or if there's too much, the aperture number will flash. Just be wary of this when shooting in shutter priority mode.

04 Halve or double the light

Like the aperture setting, the shutter speed also halves or doubles the amount of light going through to the sensor in stops. If you change the shutter speed from 1/250 sec to 1/125 sec, that is one stop of light, and will double the amount of light coming through to the sensor. If you go the other way from 1/250 sec to 1/500 sec, that halves the amount of light.

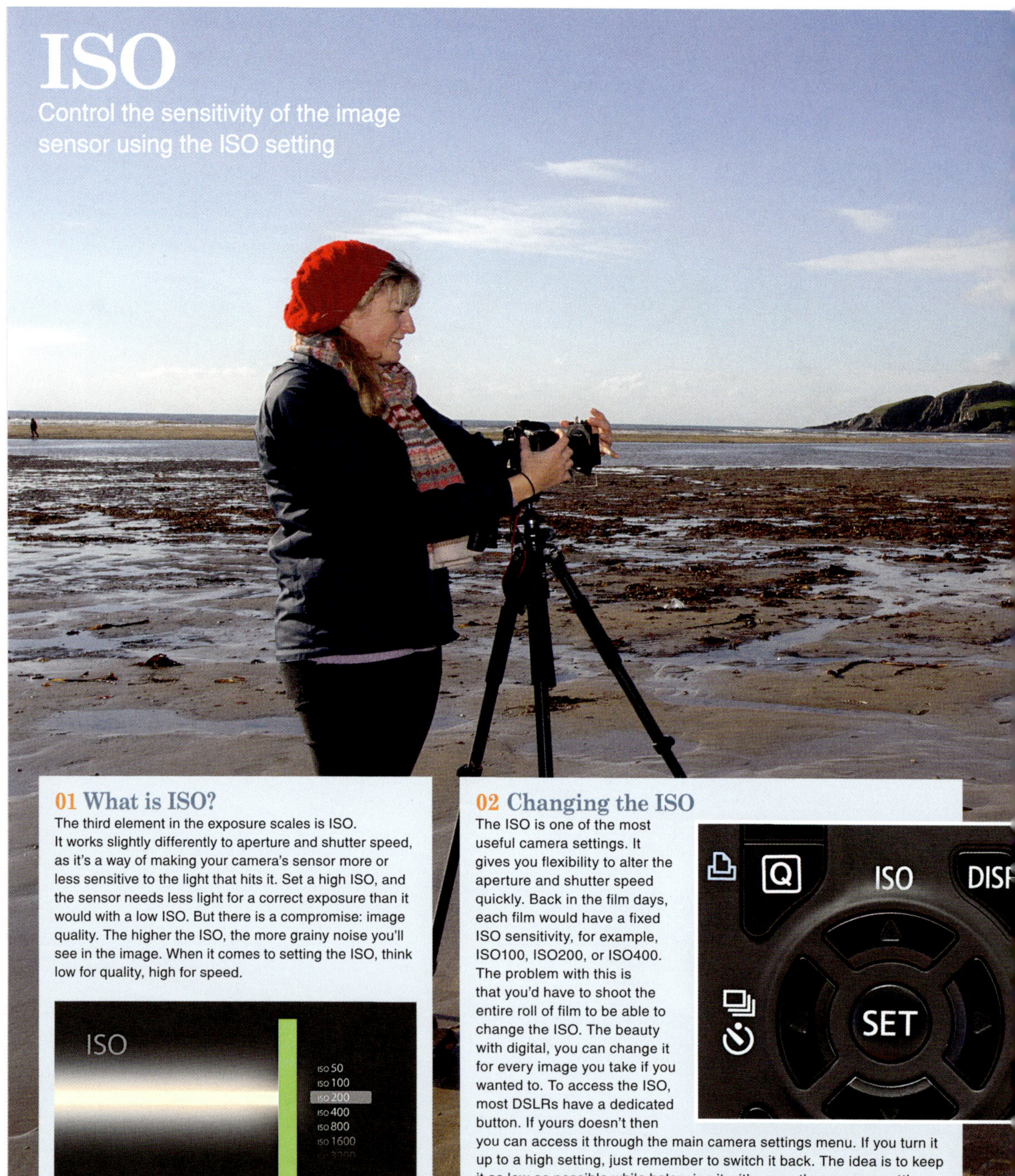

ISO

Control the sensitivity of the image sensor using the ISO setting

01 What is ISO?

The third element in the exposure scales is ISO. It works slightly differently to aperture and shutter speed, as it's a way of making your camera's sensor more or less sensitive to the light that hits it. Set a high ISO, and the sensor needs less light for a correct exposure than it would with a low ISO. But there is a compromise: image quality. The higher the ISO, the more grainy noise you'll see in the image. When it comes to setting the ISO, think low for quality, high for speed.

02 Changing the ISO

The ISO is one of the most useful camera settings. It gives you flexibility to alter the aperture and shutter speed quickly. Back in the film days, each film would have a fixed ISO sensitivity, for example, ISO100, ISO200, or ISO400. The problem with this is that you'd have to shoot the entire roll of film to be able to change the ISO. The beauty with digital, you can change it for every image you take if you wanted to. To access the ISO, most DSLRs have a dedicated button. If yours doesn't then you can access it through the main camera settings menu. If you turn it up to a high setting, just remember to switch it back. The idea is to keep it as low as possible while balancing it with your other camera settings.

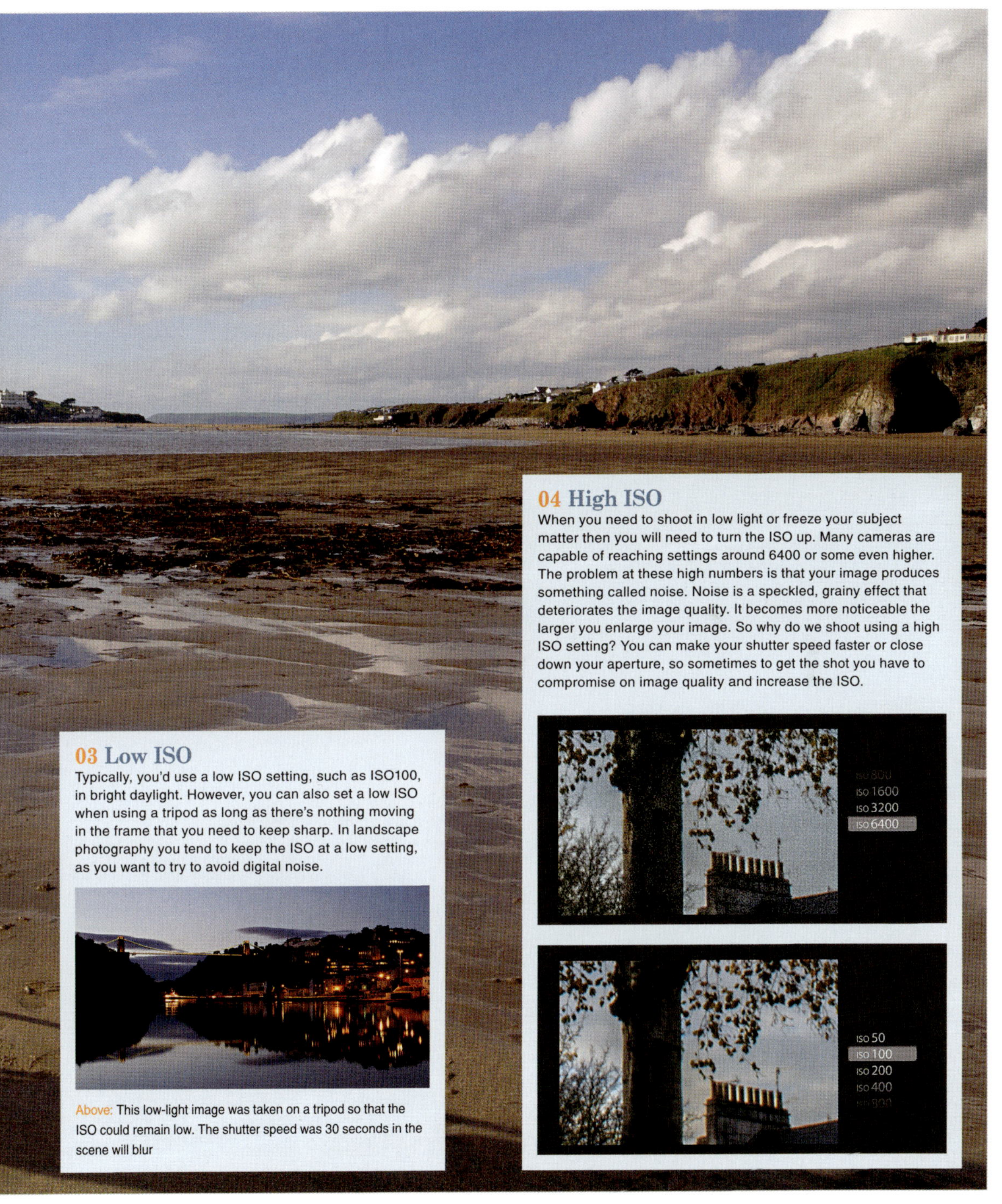

04 High ISO

When you need to shoot in low light or freeze your subject matter then you will need to turn the ISO up. Many cameras are capable of reaching settings around 6400 or some even higher. The problem at these high numbers is that your image produces something called noise. Noise is a speckled, grainy effect that deteriorates the image quality. It becomes more noticeable the larger you enlarge your image. So why do we shoot using a high ISO setting? You can make your shutter speed faster or close down your aperture, so sometimes to get the shot you have to compromise on image quality and increase the ISO.

03 Low ISO

Typically, you'd use a low ISO setting, such as ISO100, in bright daylight. However, you can also set a low ISO when using a tripod as long as there's nothing moving in the frame that you need to keep sharp. In landscape photography you tend to keep the ISO at a low setting, as you want to try to avoid digital noise.

Above: This low-light image was taken on a tripod so that the ISO could remain low. The shutter speed was 30 seconds in the scene will blur

The stop system

Take the three main ingredients and balance them together to complete the exposure triangle using the stop system

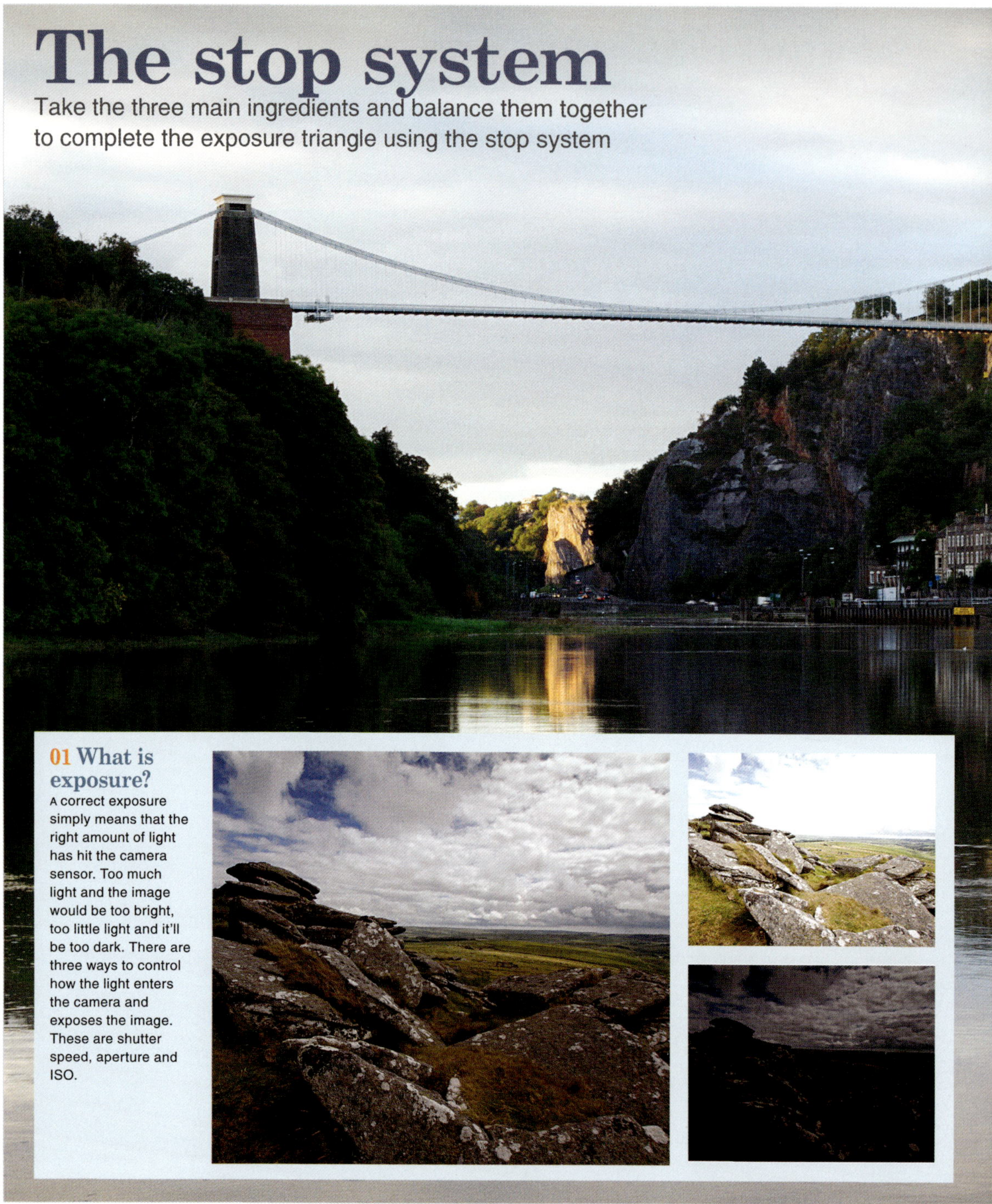

01 What is exposure?

A correct exposure simply means that the right amount of light has hit the camera sensor. Too much light and the image would be too bright, too little light and it'll be too dark. There are three ways to control how the light enters the camera and exposes the image. These are shutter speed, aperture and ISO.

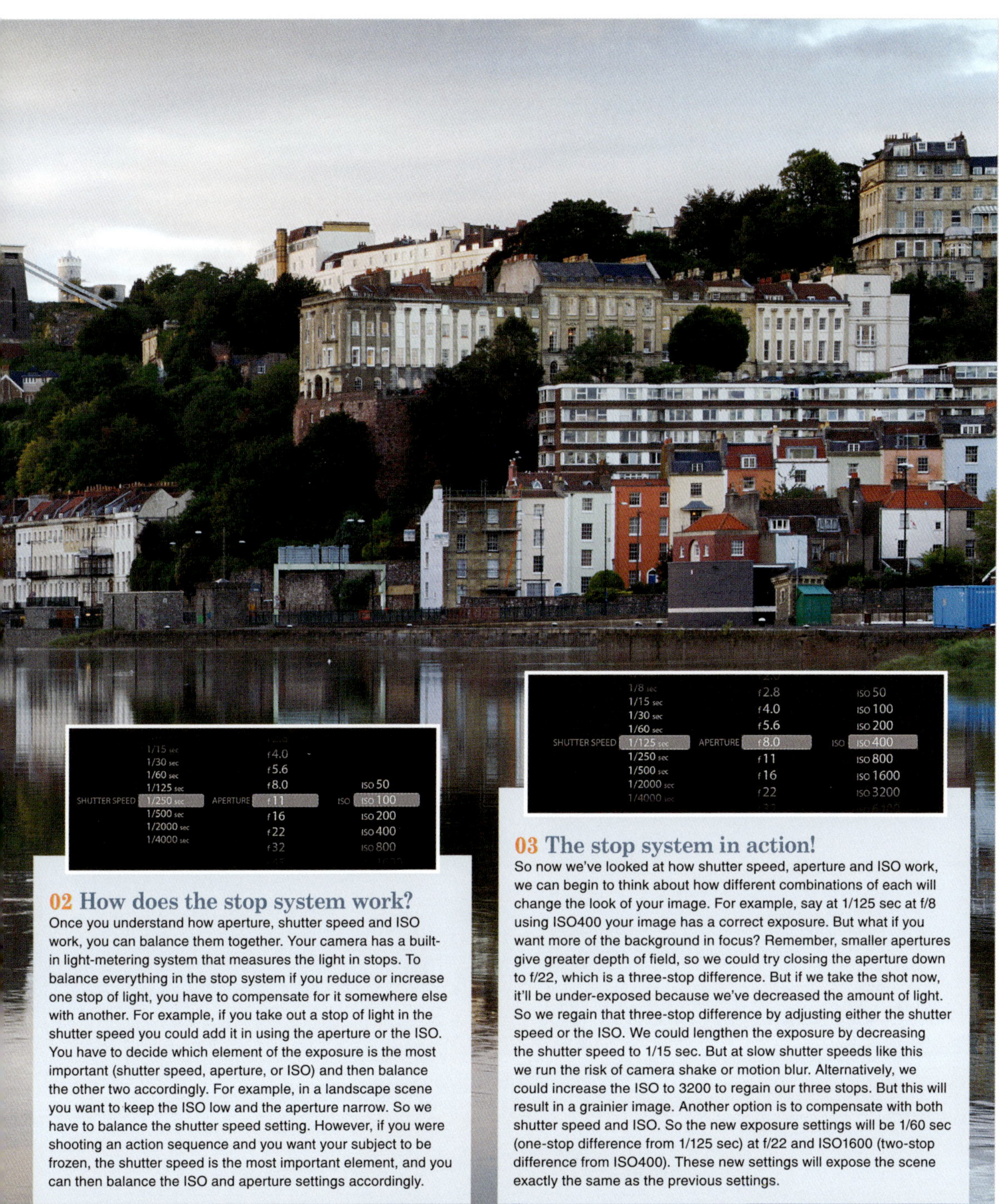

02 How does the stop system work?

Once you understand how aperture, shutter speed and ISO work, you can balance them together. Your camera has a built-in light-metering system that measures the light in stops. To balance everything in the stop system if you reduce or increase one stop of light, you have to compensate for it somewhere else with another. For example, if you take out a stop of light in the shutter speed you could add it in using the aperture or the ISO. You have to decide which element of the exposure is the most important (shutter speed, aperture, or ISO) and then balance the other two accordingly. For example, in a landscape scene you want to keep the ISO low and the aperture narrow. So we have to balance the shutter speed setting. However, if you were shooting an action sequence and you want your subject to be frozen, the shutter speed is the most important element, and you can then balance the ISO and aperture settings accordingly.

03 The stop system in action!

So now we've looked at how shutter speed, aperture and ISO work, we can begin to think about how different combinations of each will change the look of your image. For example, say at 1/125 sec at f/8 using ISO400 your image has a correct exposure. But what if you want more of the background in focus? Remember, smaller apertures give greater depth of field, so we could try closing the aperture down to f/22, which is a three-stop difference. But if we take the shot now, it'll be under-exposed because we've decreased the amount of light. So we regain that three-stop difference by adjusting either the shutter speed or the ISO. We could lengthen the exposure by decreasing the shutter speed to 1/15 sec. But at slow shutter speeds like this we run the risk of camera shake or motion blur. Alternatively, we could increase the ISO to 3200 to regain our three stops. But this will result in a grainier image. Another option is to compensate with both shutter speed and ISO. So the new exposure settings will be 1/60 sec (one-stop difference from 1/125 sec) at f/22 and ISO1600 (two-stop difference from ISO400). These new settings will expose the scene exactly the same as the previous settings.

Manual mode

Take complete control of your exposure, and balance all
of your camera settings by switching to manual mode

For any beginner who wants to advance their skills then understanding how to use the manual shooting mode will really help. The manual mode allows you to control every aspect of your DSLR, from changing the aperture to balancing the shutter speed. The aim is to balance the exposure meter in the middle of the scales so you have a correct exposure. You will find the exposure meter either by looking through the viewfinder — you'll find it on the bottom of the screen — or you can switch on Live View mode and the exposure meter is again at the bottom. Just remember the needle needs to sit in the middle of the scales when the scene is correctly balanced. If there's an arrow flashing to the left then you need to add in more light. If you took the image without changing the setting, all you'd see is a black screen. This is because you haven't got enough light. If an arrow is flashing to the right, this means you have too much light and your image will be completely white.

We'd recommend you start by selecting objects that are static so you have time to work out the correct settings. You'll soon start to become quicker at knowing what to select and how to control everything. We'll take our first shot manually together to make it easier for you through our step-by-step guide. So go and grab your camera and follow along with us!

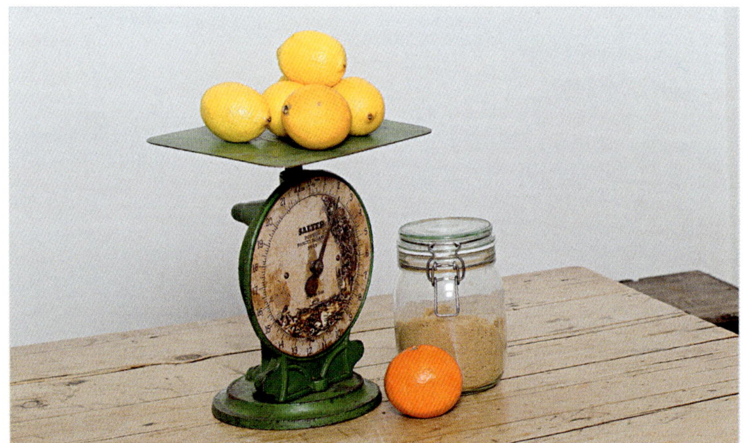

01 Set up the subject matter

Set up a still-life scene in your kitchen. In our example we've used some retro kitchen scales and some fruit. You want to select objects that relate to each other to make your image more interesting. When setting up your objects, look for any distracting shadows and move the object if necessary.

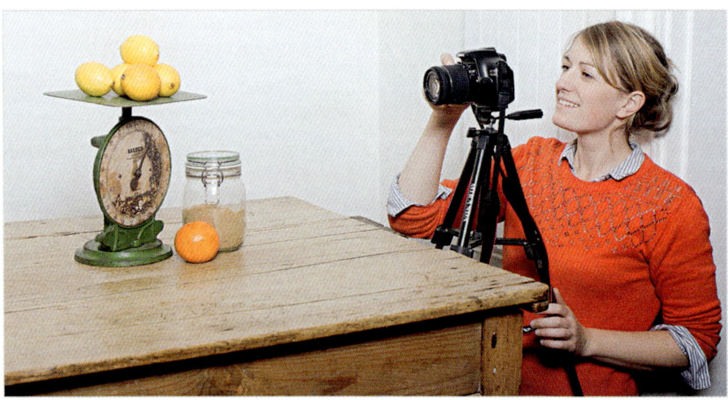

02 Set up the tripod

As we're shooting a still life, there's no movement in the objects, so we want to mount our camera to a tripod. This means we don't need to worry about what our shutter speed is. It also helps when composing the scene as we can keep looking through the viewfinder, or on the Live View screen, so everything sits nicely in the frame.

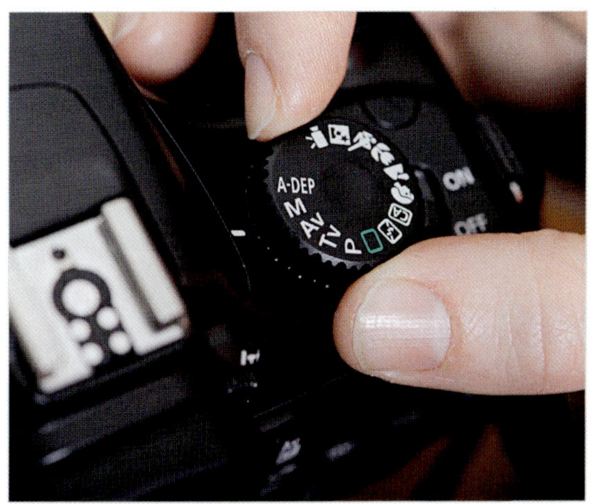

03 Choose manual mode

To access the manual shooting mode on your camera you need to turn the mode dial to M. Now we're in this mode we can control the exposure directly. We need to balance the aperture, the shutter speed, and the ISO sensitivity together. We can adjust these settings individually using the scroll dial and the back panel controls.

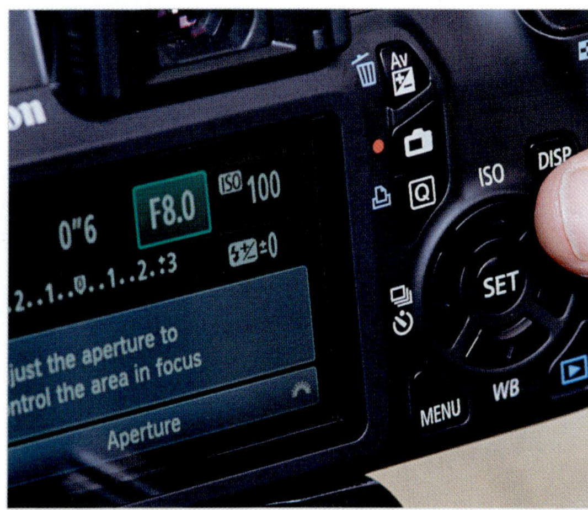

04 Set the aperture and ISO

The first thing we're going to do is set the aperture to f/8. This is so that everything in the scene remains sharp and in focus. We're then going to set the ISO to 100 so that we're shooting at the maximum possible image quality. All that's left to do is balance the shutter speed with these settings so that we have a correctly exposed image.

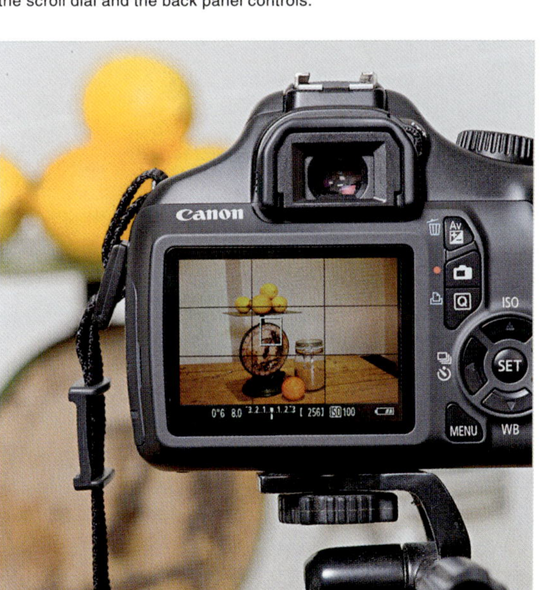

05 Balance the shutter speed

If the arrow is pointing to the left, this means that you need more light, or if it's to the right then you need less. We'd recommend you switch on Live View mode to do this as you can see on the screen if the image is getting lighter or darker. The aim is to balance the exposure meter (at the bottom of the LCD screen) in the centre. In our example our shutter speed is reading 0"6 sec.

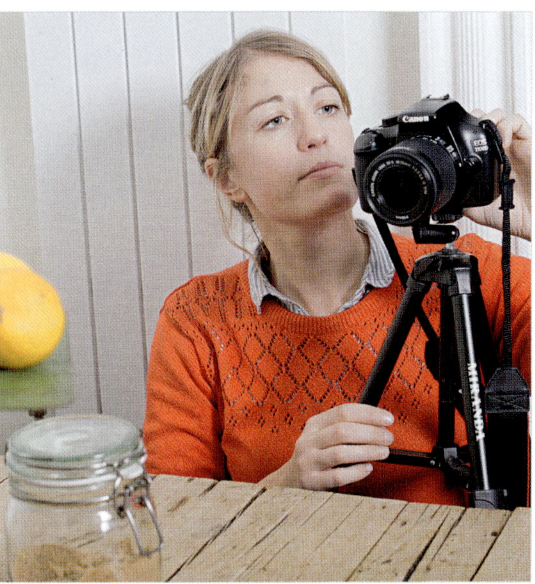

06 Review your photo

Now everything is set up, take a test shot. Don't worry so much about composition in this one — we're just trying to get the exposure right. You then want to review the image. If you're happy with the exposure then you can finish there! If you need to add in more light or take light away then adjust the shutter speed. Keep shooting and reviewing until you're happy.

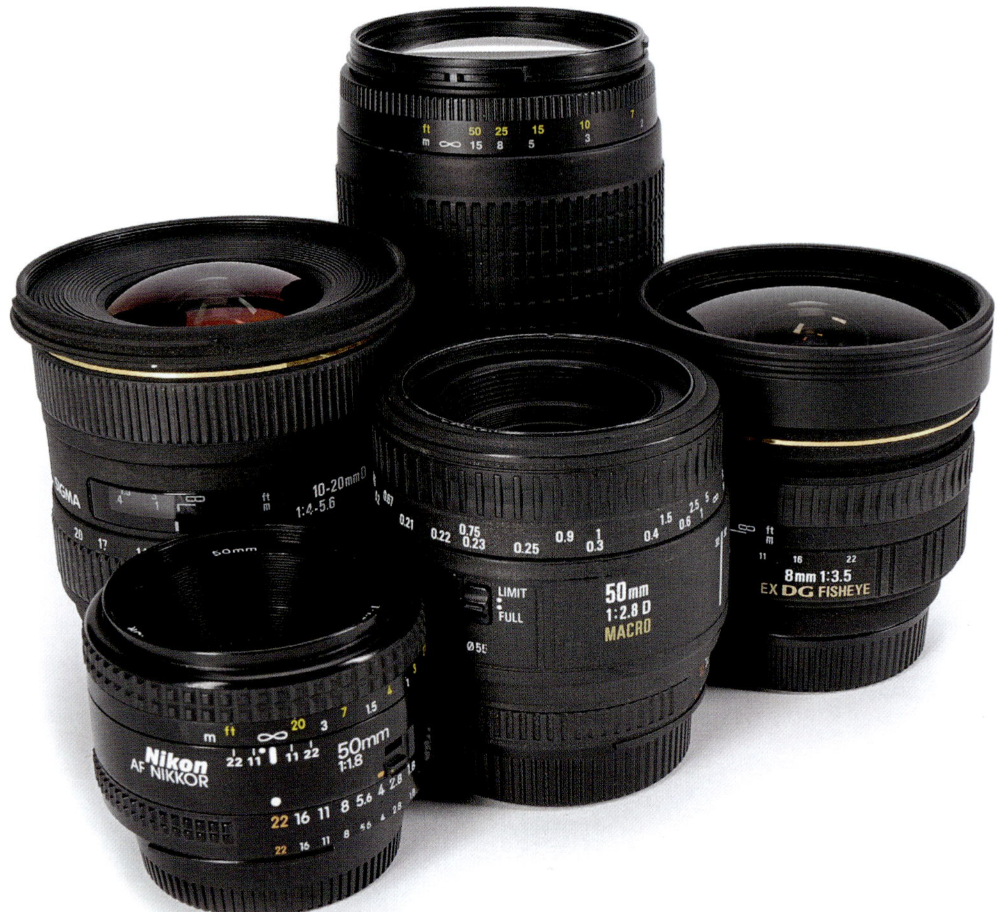

Which lens next?

We help you continue your photographic journey and look
at a range of lenses that will expand your creative options

The lens that comes with your camera is perfectly good for lots of situations, but if you want more options, then there's a whole world of lenses out there of all shapes, sizes and prices. With so many choices, there are a few things to consider when buying a second lens.

When you look at any lens you'll see a number or number range, followed by mm. This is the focal length of the lens. On the standard kit lens the focal range is 18-55mm, which means it can zoom between these two focal lengths. Some lenses are fixed at specific focal lengths, in which case they'll only display one number, for example 50mm.

If you're thinking about a second lens you've probably already found yourself drawn to one type of photography or another, so your preferences will determine the type of focal length you should go for. If, for example, you want to take lots of landscapes then it might be worth buying a super wide-angle lens such as a 10-22mm. This provides a wider field of view than your standard zoom. On the

> *"Primes will generally give you better image quality than similarly priced zooms"*

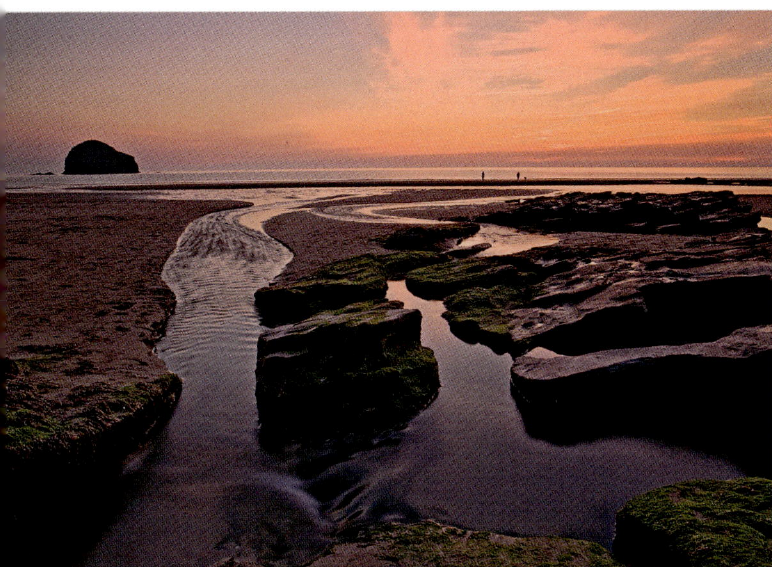

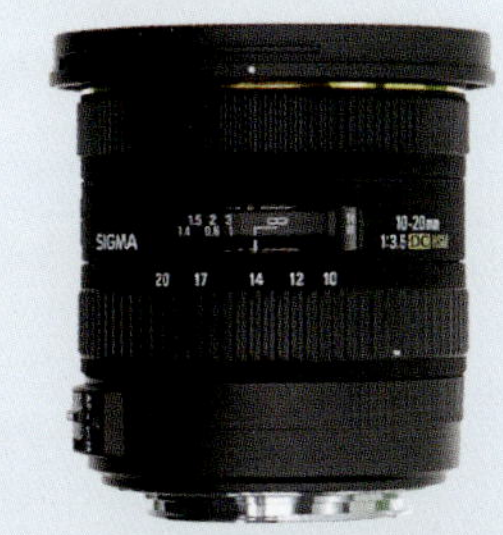

Lenses for Landscapes

The most popular lenses for landscape photography is a wide-angle one. These vary from 10mm to 35mm in focal length. When shooting landscapes generally you want to shoot using a narrow aperture setting so you don't need to worry if your lens is not particularly fast.

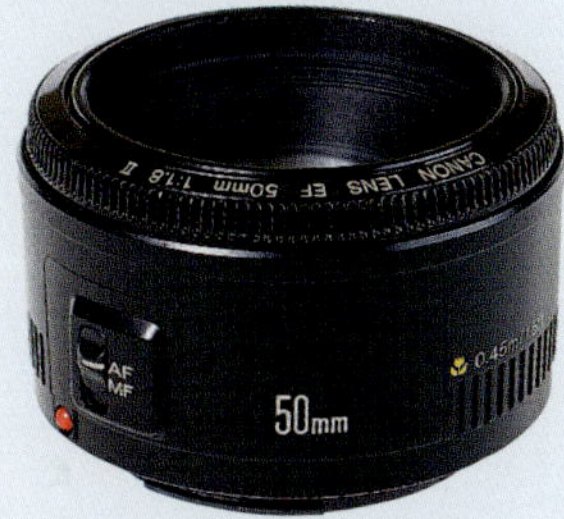

Lenses for Portraits

Fixed focal-length lenses like the one pictured come with wide aperture settings meaning you can create that nice soft blurred background effect. This is good when shooting portraits. The most popular focal lengths for a portrait lens are 35mm, 50mm and 85mm.

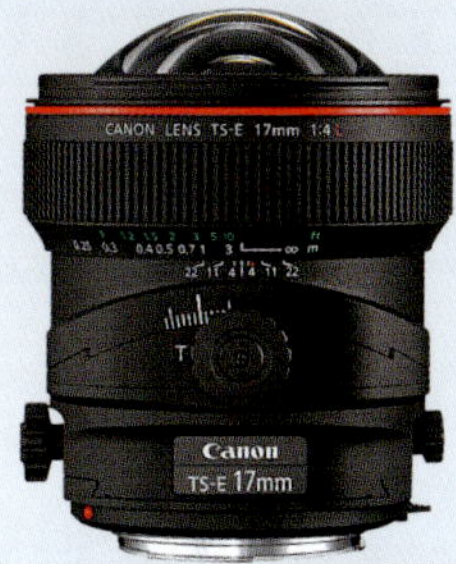

Lenses for Architecture

Tilt and shift lenses are expensive and specialist. However, the image quality from one of these is very high. You can also create the popular miniature effect, when you blur the top and bottom of the image, with one of these.

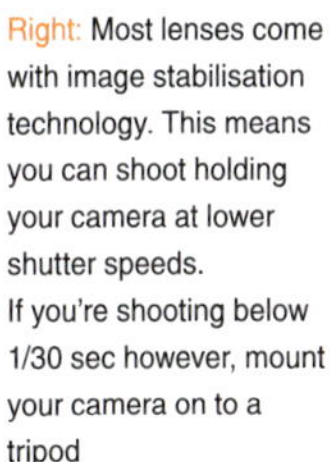

Above: For shooting landscapes you want a wide-angle lens. Something like a 10-22mm is popular with landscape photographers

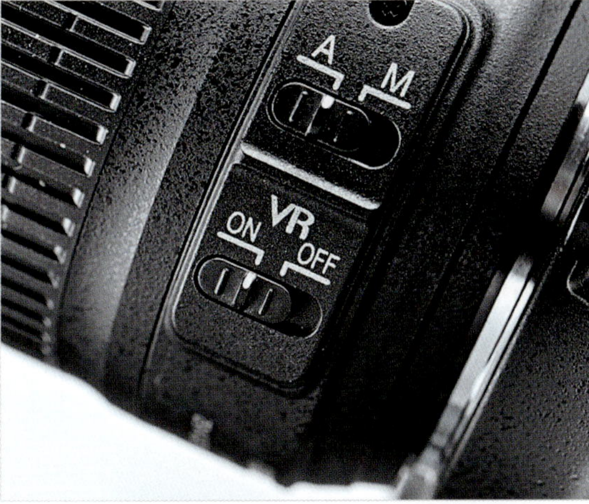

Right: Most lenses come with image stabilisation technology. This means you can shoot holding your camera at lower shutter speeds. If you're shooting below 1/30 sec however, mount your camera on to a tripod

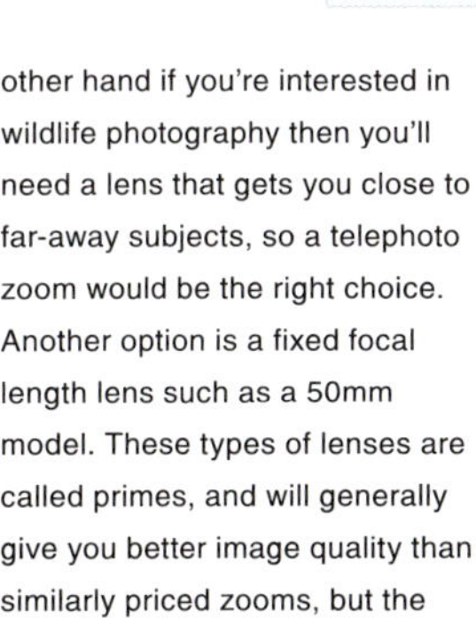

other hand if you're interested in wildlife photography then you'll need a lens that gets you close to far-away subjects, so a telephoto zoom would be the right choice. Another option is a fixed focal length lens such as a 50mm model. These types of lenses are called primes, and will generally give you better image quality than similarly priced zooms, but the trade-off is less flexibility.

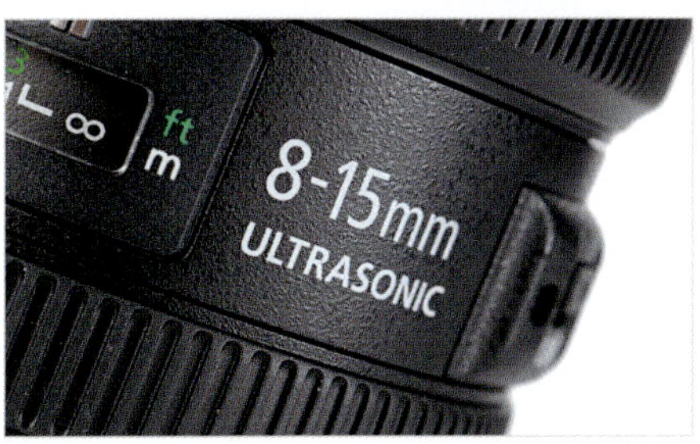

Above: The focal length of your lens is usually written on the side. It will end in the letters mm

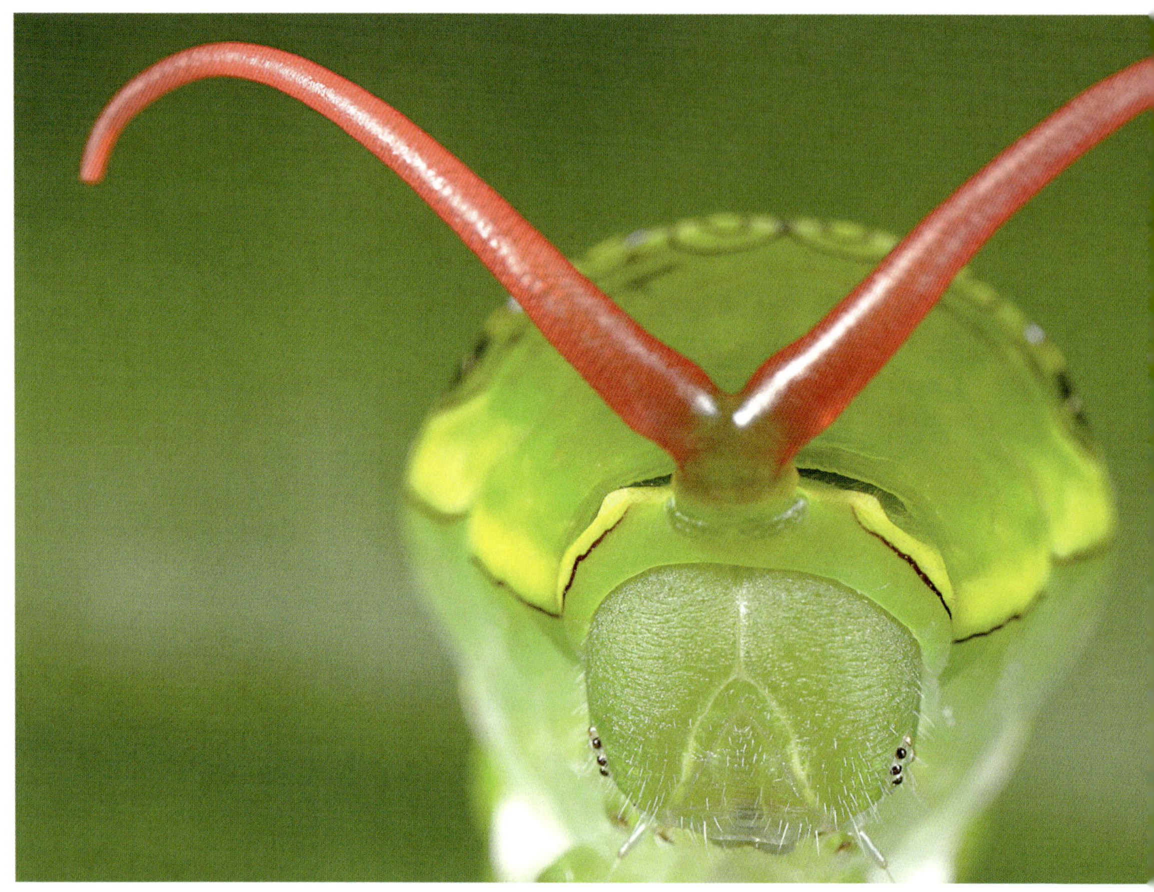

Aperture considerations

It's not all about focal length. There are other factors
to take into account when choosing a new lens

We also need to think about the maximum aperture, also referred to as the speed of the lens. This determines how well the lens performs in low light, and how shallow the plane of focus can get. The maximum aperture will usually be printed on the side of the lens. It'll either be a single number or a range of two numbers. If it's a range, then this means the maximum aperture will change depending on the focal length, with the lower number aperture only available at the lowest focal lengths. Lenses with wider maximum apertures such as f/1.4 or f/2.8 give you greater flexibility by requiring less light, and also allow you to work with really shallow planes of

focus. But these lenses tend to be more expensive.

Of course, price is always a consideration. Lenses vary wildly in performance, and quality lenses aren't cheap, but the good news is that they often hold their value far better than camera bodies, which are superseded every couple of years. So a good quality lens, kept in good condition, can sell for just a little less than it cost when new. So there are lots of things to consider when choosing that second lens. Our advice before parting with your cash is to think carefully about the images that inspire you and the kind of photographs you want to take. So the question you should ask yourself isn't necessarily what lens shall I get next? But rather, what do I want to photograph?

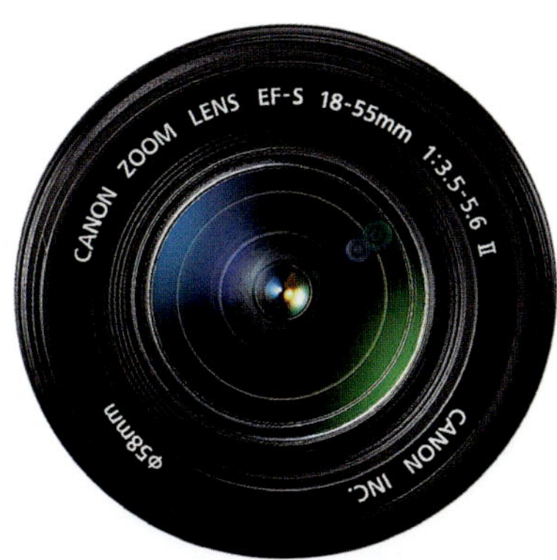

Above: On the front of your lens you can see information about the lens. The numbers on the right show the widest the aperture can open to. It varies depending on where the focal length of the lens is set

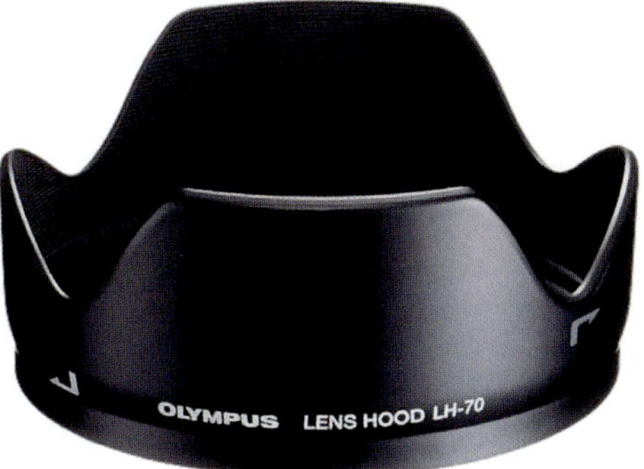

Above: A lens hood protects the end of your lens and helps reduce lens flare, which is when you get a streak and light dots in your image from the light source

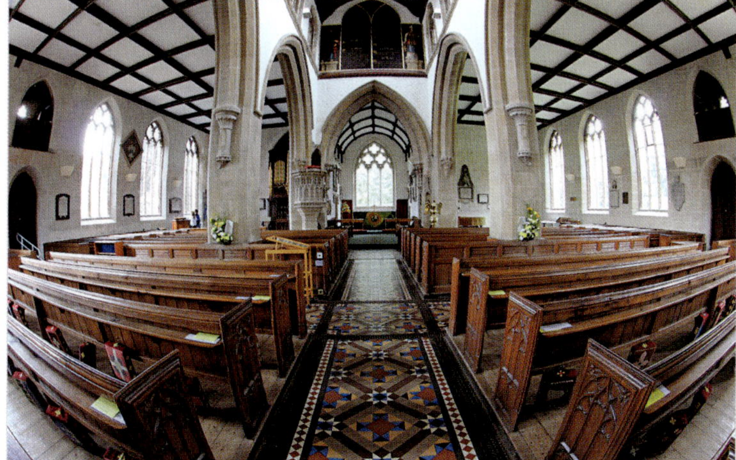

Above: Creative lenses such as a fish eye can be a fun way to produce images that are a bit different

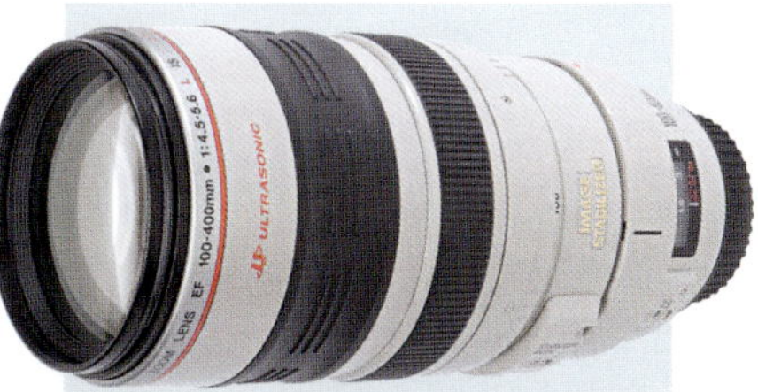

Telephoto

When photographing sports or wildlife, having that extra reach will come in handy. We call these types of lenses telephoto lenses, and you can get ones with fixed or variable focal lengths. Typically, they range from 70mm to 800mm. They can be expensive due to the more complex construction involved.

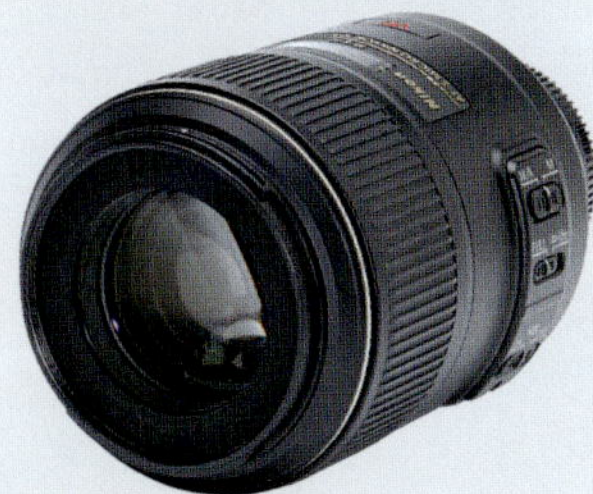

Macro

If you want to photograph objects or creatures at a ratio of one to one or closer then you will need a macro lens. As you're very close to your subject matter you want to shoot using a narrow aperture to keep more of the image sharp in the frame. If you want the whole of the image sharp, photographers use a process called focus stacking. This is more advanced and requires you to blend multiple images together in a software program.

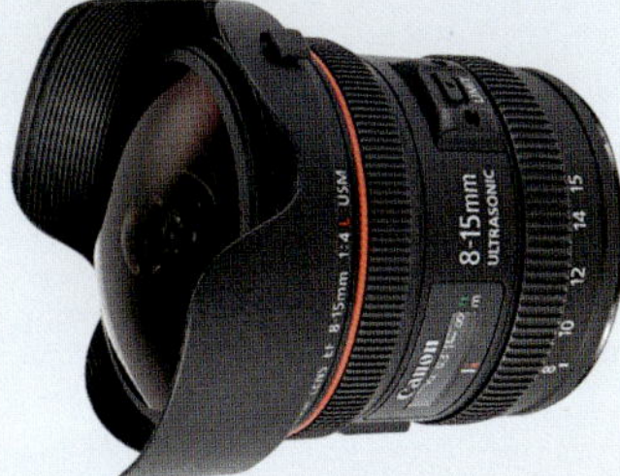

Creative lenses

A fisheye lens is an ultra wide-angle lens that creates a distorted view. Fish eye lenses typically range between 8mm and 15mm in focal length. It's the shape of the glass that creates the effect.

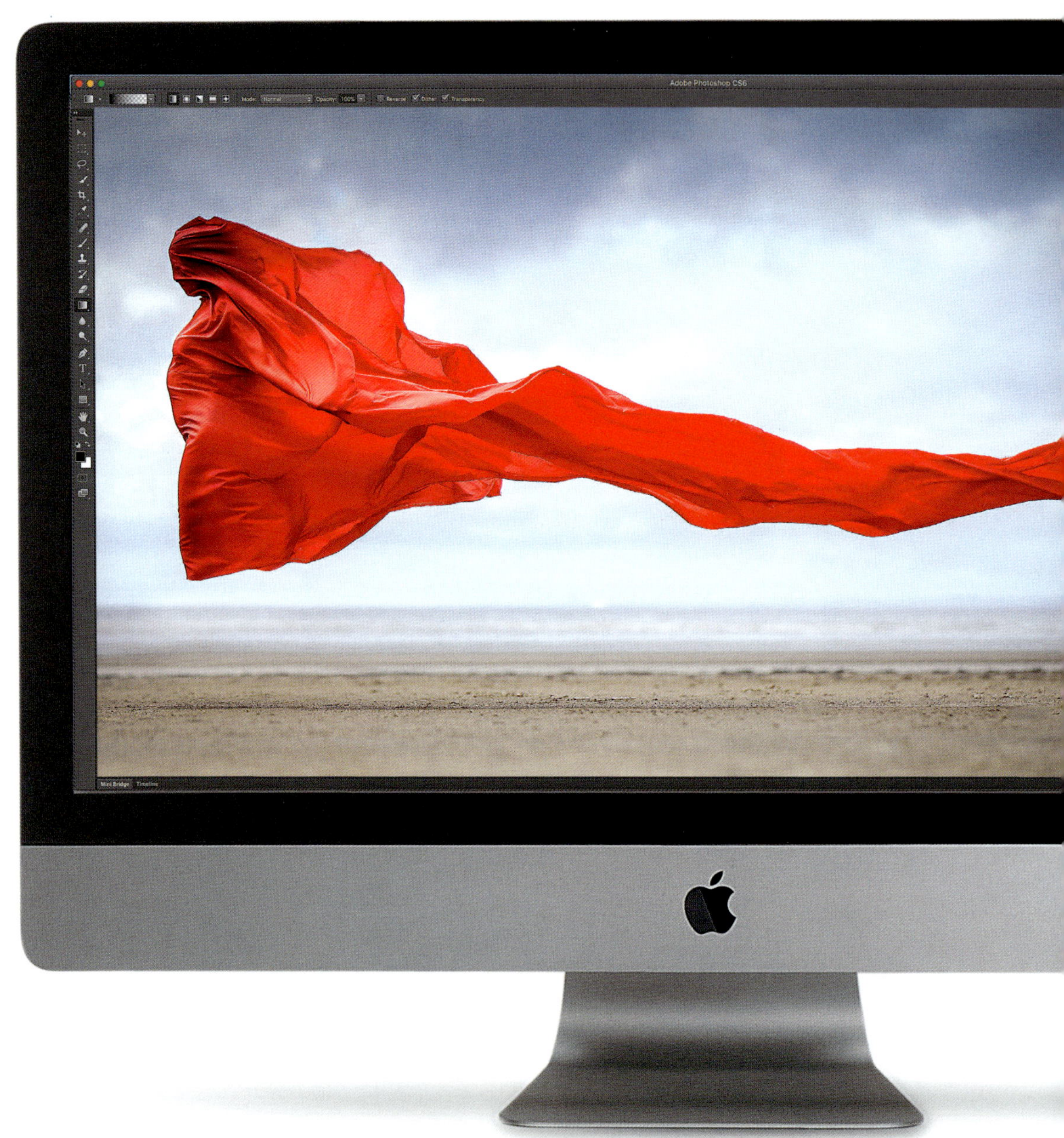

Core Skills

Discover key skills and techniques to take your photography to the next level

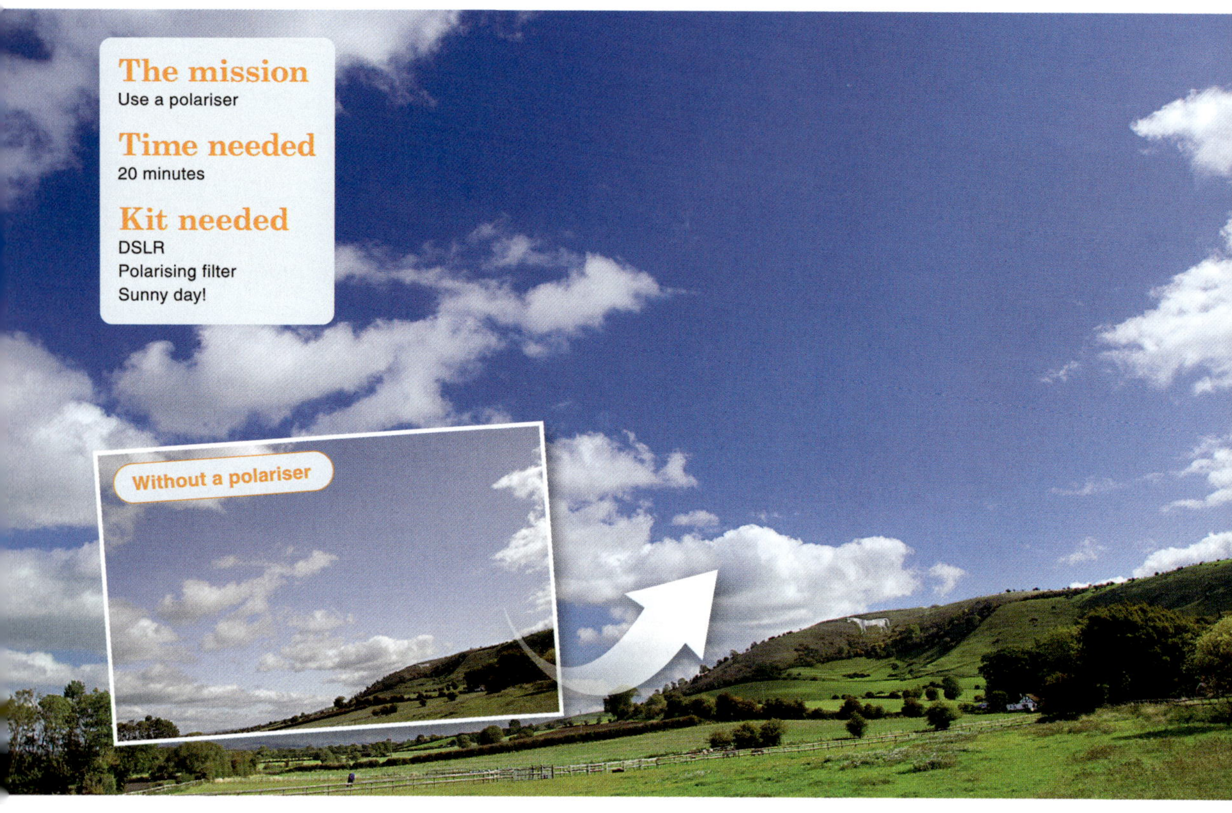

Say hi to a bluer sky!

A polarising filter can completely transform your landscape shots — if you know when and where to use one

Unlike most other filters you can buy for your camera, a polariser does things to the image that you simply can't do in Photoshop. Screwing into the front of your lens, it has the power to make colours look more intense, to cut out unwanted reflections from glass and water and to remove the sheen on everything from painted doors to rocky surfaces.

A polarising filter is especially useful for landscape photography when you're shooting scenes that include blue sky or expanses of water. It's not just useful for boosting colours though. The polariser's effects make it ideal for both black-and-white and architectural photography, as you can achieve better tone and contrast in your images. That means you have more to work with in Photoshop.

Because its effect can be rather hard to predict, a polariser often gives magical results. The filter removes or reduces the amount of polarised light that's reflected from the sky, water or other surface. But as our eyes can't see the difference between normal light and polarised light, you often have to try it to see whether it's going to help the scene you're shooting.

The filter is constructed so that the front of it rotates — the orientation of the glass needs to be adjusted to match the direction of the polarised light. Generally, you turn the filter until you can see the maximum effect possible through the viewfinder. However, in some circumstances, it pays to weaken the effect slightly by turning the filter round a few degrees from this point.

When you're shooting the sky, the effect is most pronounced when the sun is at 90 degrees to the scene, so the filter has little impact if you're standing with the sun behind you. Similarly, the effect is disappointing in overcast conditions.

Using a circular polarising filter

We show you how to transform your shots with this simple but effective camera accessory

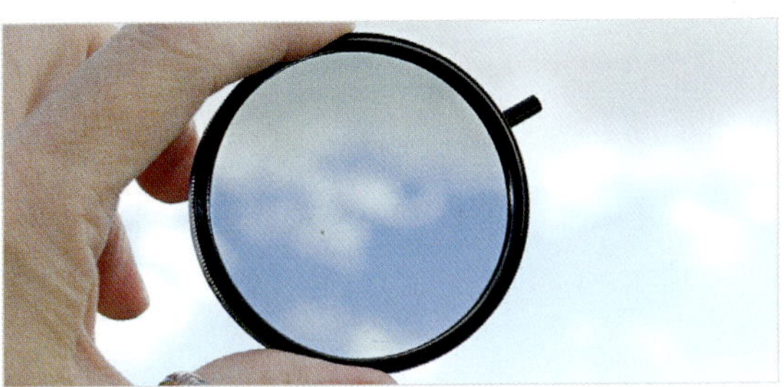

01 Preview the effect

To save screwing the polariser into the front of the lens unnecessarily, hold it up to your eye first. Rotate it to see how it improves the saturation of particular areas of the scene. If you fit the filter, make sure you don't overtighten it — polarisers can be difficult to unscrew!

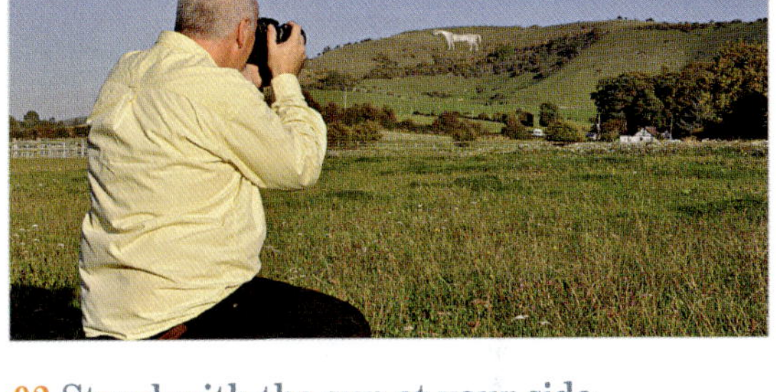

02 Stand with the sun at your side

A polariser's effect is greatest on a sunny day with blue skies, but it also depends on where the sun is in relationship to the scene, and to the camera. You'll get the strongest effect if the sun is to the side of you, so find an angle that allows this, or return at a different time of day.

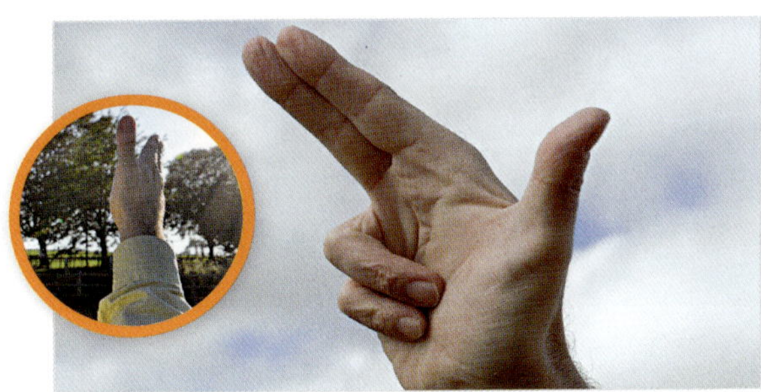

03 Find the sweet spots

To preview which parts of the sky will benefit most from a polariser, make a gun shape with your hand, so your thumb points at 90 degrees to your forefinger. Point your forefinger at the sun and rotate your wrist — your thumb will point to the areas of sky with the most polarised light.

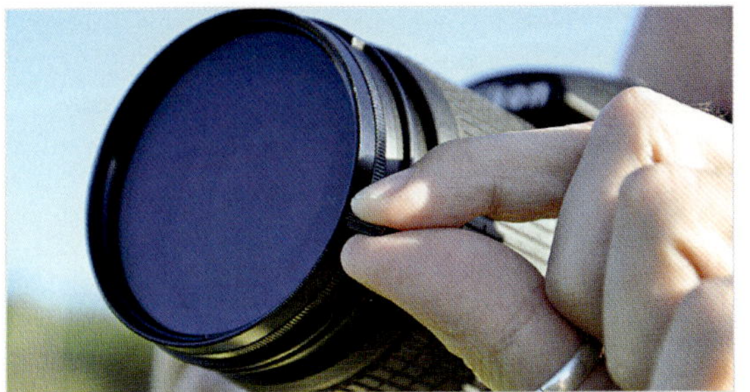

04 Filter your results

It's crucial to turn the front part of the filter, looking at the effect through the viewfinder as you do so, for every shot. It will reduce the amount of light entering the lens by 50-75% (one or two stops), whatever its orientation, so check that the shutter speed isn't too slow, or use a tripod.

Choosing and fitting a polariser

01 Don't be square

You can get polarisers for rectangular slot-in filter systems, but they need to rotate in the mount, so they're usually also round.

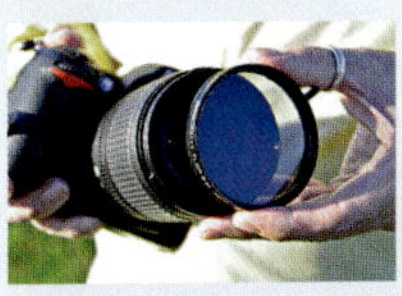

02 Size matters

You need a filter that fits your lens's filter thread. The diameter is often marked on the lens in millimetres and prefixed with a Ø symbol.

03 Get the right type

Be wary of second-hand polarisers. Old linear filters interfere with the autofocus and exposure metering systems of modern D-SLRs.

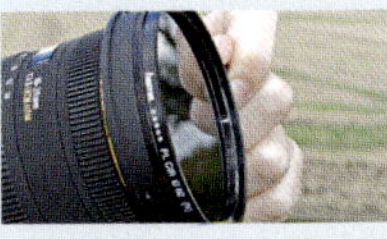

04 Step up

You don't need a different-sized filter for every lens. Buy one in the biggest size you need and use a step-up ring.

05 Wide-angle woes

Polarising filters can give unnatural results on some ultra-wide-angles, so use the filter with more modest wide-angles, or telephotos.

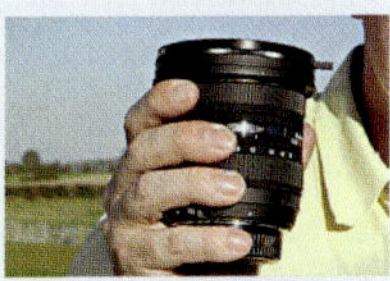

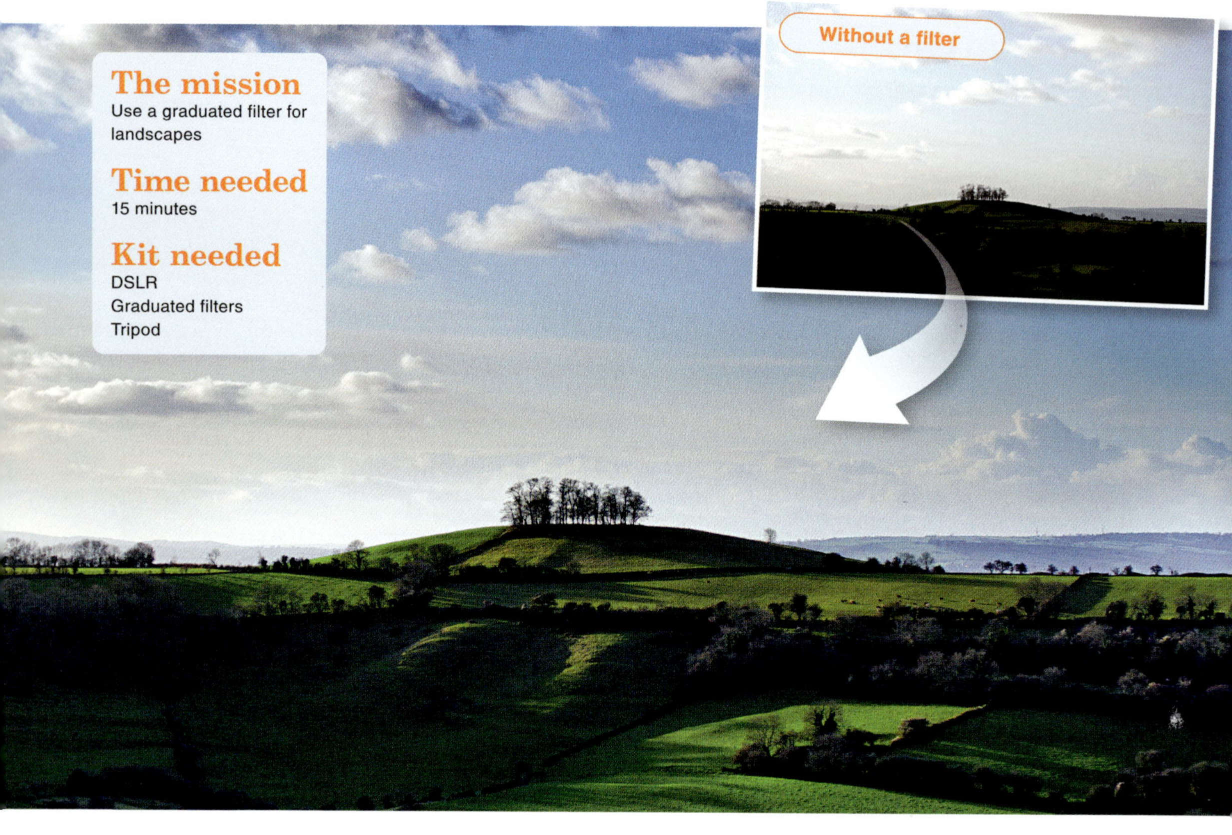

The mission
Use a graduated filter for landscapes

Time needed
15 minutes

Kit needed
DSLR
Graduated filters
Tripod

Control bright skies

Great skies often come hand in hand with big exposure problems, but a graduated filter can make all the difference

Do you struggle to get your skies to come out properly when you're shooting landscapes? Finding the right vista can be the difference between a mediocre image and a masterpiece, but first you might have to overcome a serious, very common issue with the lighting.

All too often, the sky is much brighter than the ground and you can't find an exposure that makes them both come out well. Either the sky is fine but the landscape is underexposed, or you increase the exposure so the landscape looks good, but then the sky becomes overexposed and burnt out.

The answer is a graduated filter. These simple bits of kit are clear at the bottom but darker at the top. This reduces the brightness of the sky but leaves the landscape unaltered. It's not a sudden transition. In the middle is a 'graduated' area, where the darkening effect gradually reduces, hence the name 'graduated' filter. If you want to create the finished effect entirely in-camera, consider a selection of neutral density (ND) and coloured filters for creating blue-sky and sunset effects. However, if you just want to get the brightness of the sky under control and do the rest in Photoshop, a small selection of ND grads is all you need.

These come in different strengths. An ND2 filter reduces the brightness of the sky by 2x (one stop, or 1EV). An ND4 filter reduces the brightness by 4x, or two stops, while an ND8 filter reduces it by 8x, or three stops. Filter strength is sometimes quoted as a decimal, where a 0.3 ND offers a one-stop reduction, 0.6 is two stops and 0.9 is three stops. Used properly, graduated filters can make a huge difference to your photographs. In fact, you'll seldom see a professional landscape photographer without them!

Get more from graduated filters

Using grads is easy — it's choosing and positioning them that takes skill

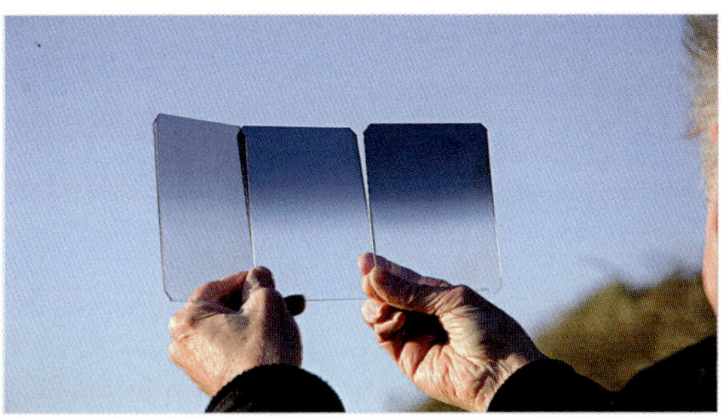

01 Choose your grad

Experience will soon tell you what strength of filter you need. For this scene, a 4x (0.6 ND) filter should be about right. Be careful not to overdo it! What looks good on the LCD display can often seem completely overdone when you check the photo on a computer.

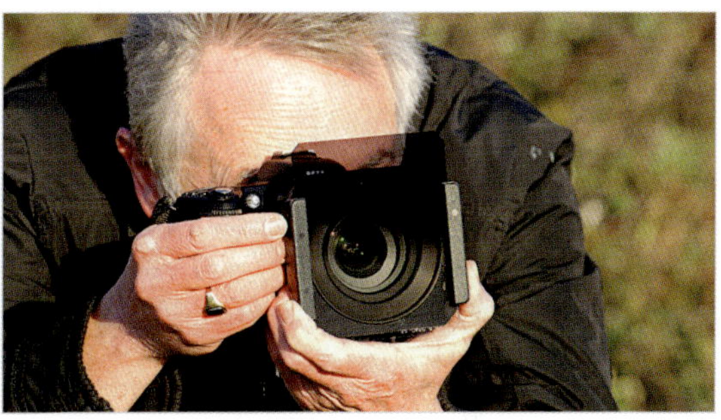

02 Rotate and straighten

When you've chosen the filter, slide it into the holder and then rotate the holder so the grad is parallel with the horizon. Sometimes you can vary this to suit jagged or sloping horizons, but beware — skies that 'graduate' at an angle will look unnatural.

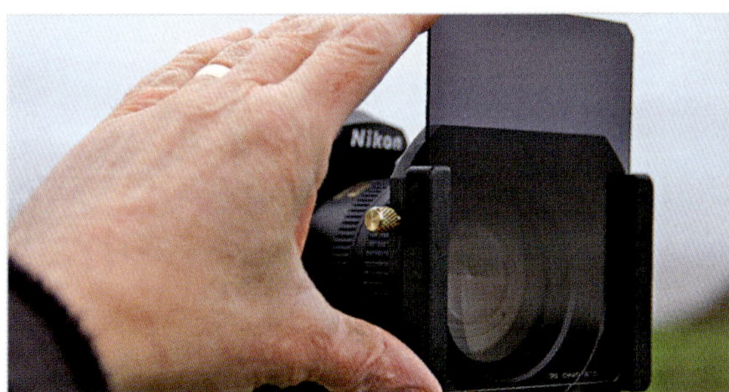

03 Adjust the height

Now move the holder up and down, choosing the position that looks right to you. Having the filter just above the horizon works well because a visible gradation in the sky looks natural, while a darkening effect that starts right on the line of the horizon can look rather odd.

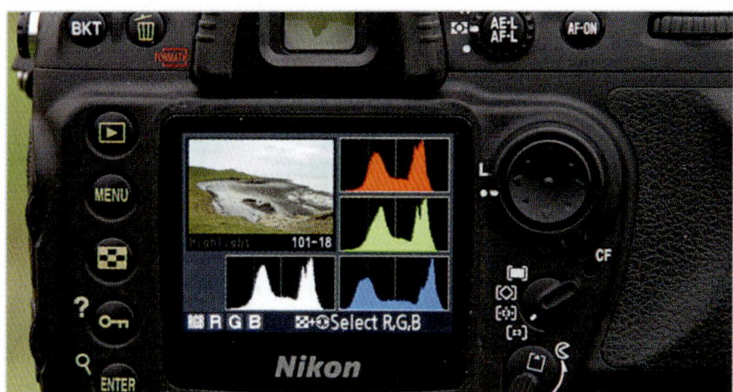

04 Check the exposure

You can shoot using the exposure recommended by the camera with the filter in place, but you might get better results by metering from the foreground, before adding the filter. Either way, check the histogram on your camera and adjust the exposure if necessary.

How to choose and use a grad

01 Suitable lenses

The Nikon 18-55mm kit lens's front element turns during focusing, which is a pain. On others, such as the 18-105mm, it doesn't.

02 Coloured grads

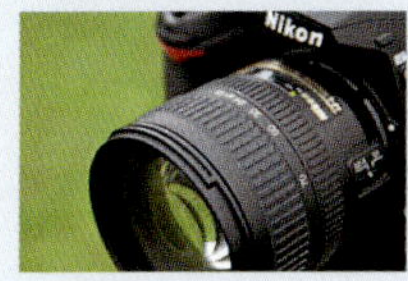

You can use coloured grads to get a final effect in-camera. Alternatively, use an ND grad and add colour in Photoshop.

03 Hard and soft

You can get 'hard' and 'soft' grads for harder or softer transitions. Wider apertures also produce softer transitions.

04 Handheld filters

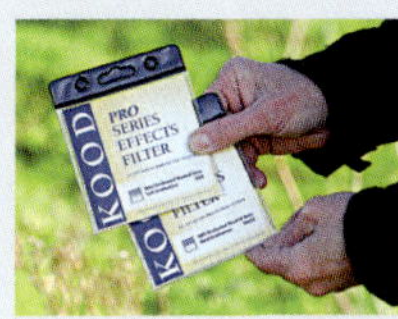

In a rush? Hold the camera with one hand and the filter over the lens with the other. Be careful — grads scratch easily!

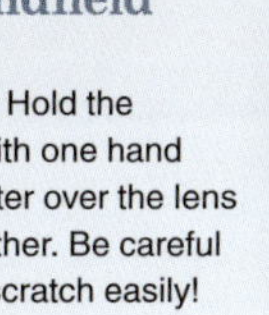

05 Circular grads

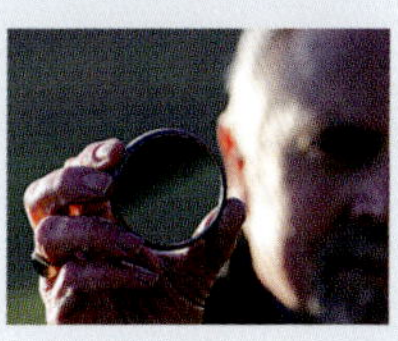

You can get circular grads that screw into the lens's filter ring, but you can't move them up and down, so they're really limited.

Shoot sunsets

As the sun goes down, the light changes to create fantastic
colours — discover how to make sure you're ready

Sunsets make spectacular subjects. The rich colours, dramatic lighting and strong shapes they offer can produce stunning shots with little need for much effort from you. However, you might find that your camera often captures pale imitations of the sunsets you see with your naked eye. The intensity of the colours may have been lost, or the composition might not work. To replicate a spectacular sunset you need to compose your shots properly and adjust the camera settings to make the most of the hues.

The temptation to shoot a sunset when you first see it is overwhelming. But while there's something to be said for getting a shot in the bag quickly, in case the conditions change, it can be worth spending longer over it to make sure you get everything right. Your first attempts might look okay, but you can almost certainly do better.

Your focal length setting and choice of viewpoint will make a big difference to the picture. A quick wide-angle shot might capture the broadest area of sky but won't necessarily give you the best composition. A longer focal length and carefully chosen viewpoint can produce a much more effective result. The sun will be bigger in the frame and you'll have more control over shapes and silhouettes.

The key with camera settings is to make sure you capture the sunset's colours as they are, not how the camera 'thinks' they should be. You might need to adjust the exposure settings to suit the conditions, too, because in extreme lighting situations the camera might not interpret the scene in the way you expect.

These points are all key to getting great sunsets, and you can read on for more information…

Catch the sun

Sunsets disappear quickly, so you need to work fast…

Camera settings are important with sunsets, as you don't want your DSLR to correct things that don't need fixing. We mention White Balance and Picture Controls in this tutorial, but you need to think about ISO settings too. Don't use Auto ISO if you're using a tripod, because you won't need higher ISOs and the image quality will suffer. If you're shooting handheld, though, Auto ISO can be a good safeguard, because light levels (and shutter speeds) can change much more quickly than you might expect.

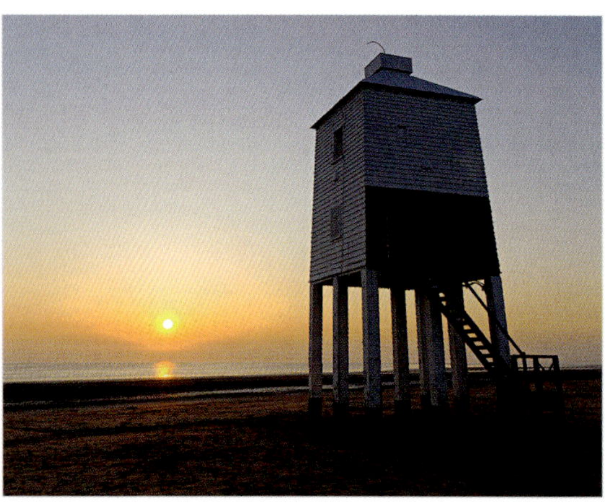

01 Make a first attempt
Conditions will change rapidly, so it's a good idea to get a few shots done quickly first. Here, we've used our zoom lens at its widest focal length and got right up close to the old wooden lighthouse. This has resulted in a dramatic perspective, from tilting the camera upwards, but the sun is quite small in the background.

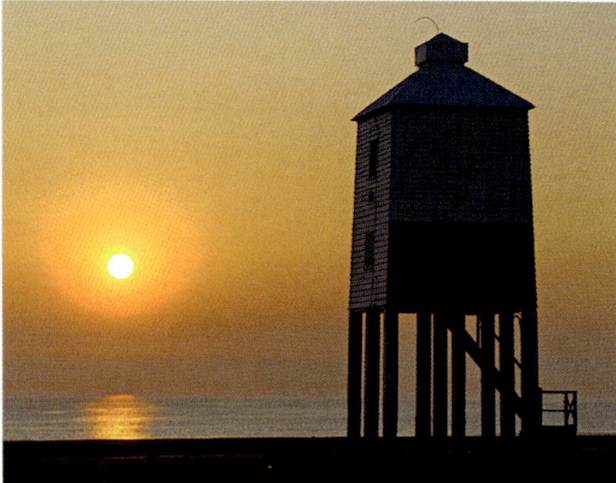

02 Change focal length
Here, we've got a better shot by moving further away and using a longer focal length. The lighthouse is the same size as in our first shot, and is much straighter because we haven't had to tilt the camera. There's a smaller area of sky in the background now, so the sun is larger and we've filled the frame with a rich, orange glow.

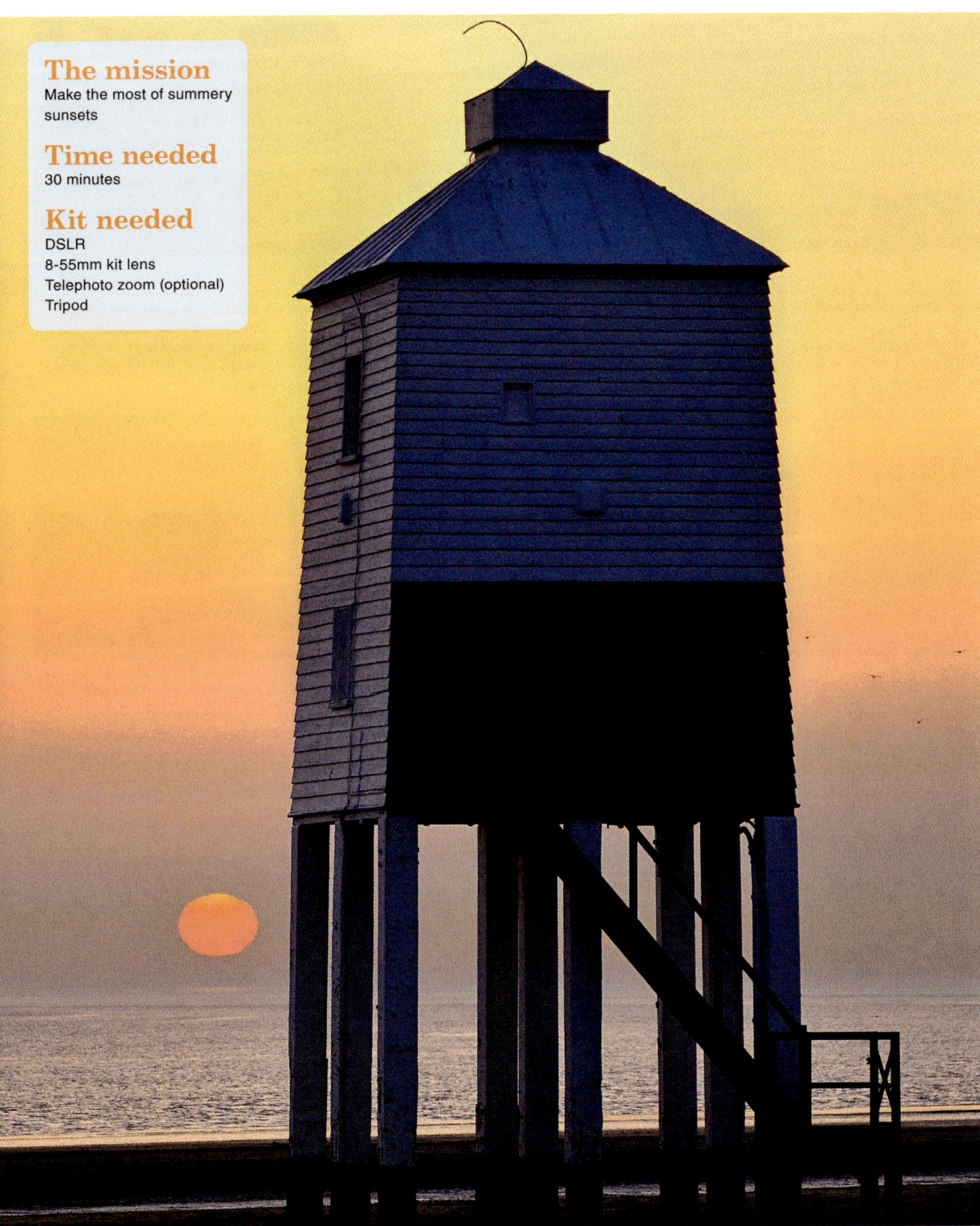
The mission
Make the most of summery sunsets

Time needed
30 minutes

Kit needed
DSLR
8-55mm kit lens
Telephoto zoom (optional)
Tripod

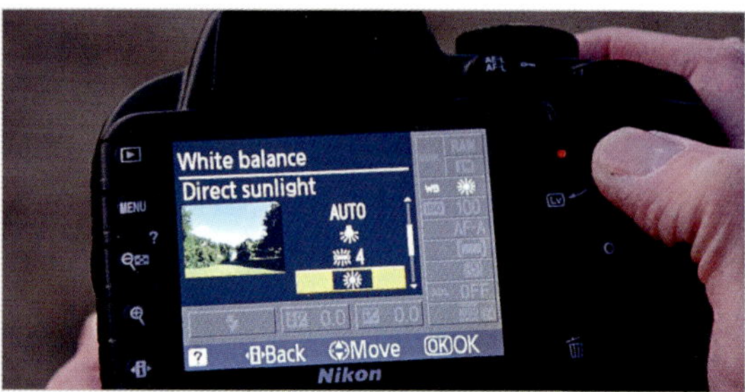

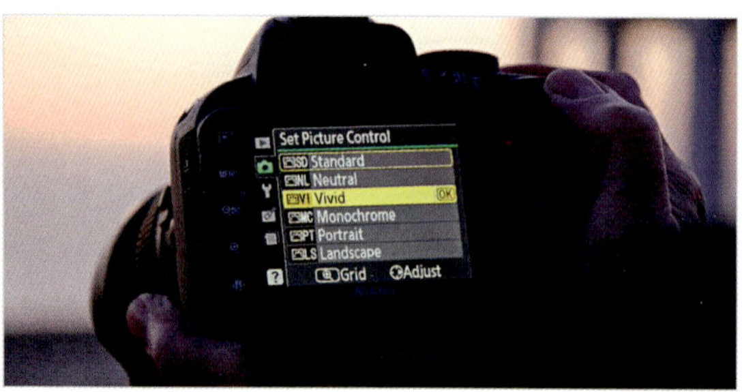

03 Play with White Balance

If you leave the White Balance set to Auto, your camera might attempt to correct what it sees as a colour cast, producing weak or distorted tones. To capture sunset hues as they really are, use the Direct Sunlight White Balance preset. Or, for even deeper, warmer colours, try the Cloudy setting instead.

04 Use Picture Controls

Take a look at your Nikon's Picture Controls. The Standard setting reproduces colours accurately, but switching to Vivid will boost saturation and give extra intensity. Better still, shoot NEF (RAW) files rather than JPEGs. This will give you more scope for changing the White Balance and colour saturation later on.

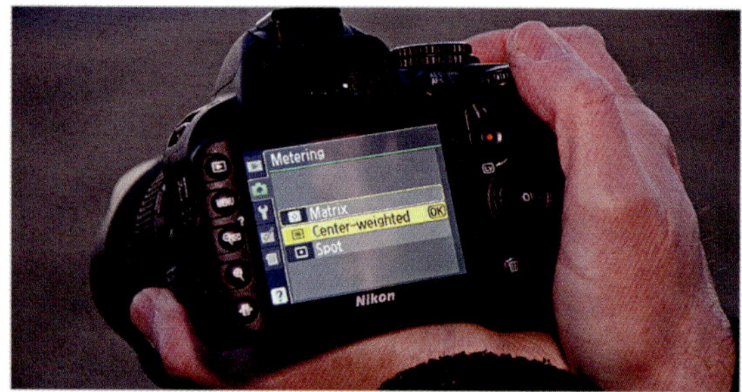

06 Shoot the sun

If you want to include the sun, wait until it's nearer the horizon, when it will be less intense. You'll still need to keep a close eye on the exposure. In extreme conditions, your camera's matrix metering system might not react how you expect, so be prepared to adjust the exposure.

07 Metering modes

Try centre-weighted metering. It's less sophisticated than matrix metering, and more easily influenced by very bright areas, but that's what we want. It's the colour in the sky that's key — foreground objects should be silhouettes. Try spot metering to take a reading from an area of sky.

Do more with RAW

Shooting JPEGs is fine as long as you get the camera settings right. You need to choose the correct White Balance preset and a suitable Picture Control, such as Standard or Vivid. The camera will then process the image according to your settings, discarding 'unwanted' colour data. However, RAW files retain all the colour data captured by the sensor, so you can change your mind later. And if you have Adobe Camera Raw (ACR) you can do a lot more with NEFs.

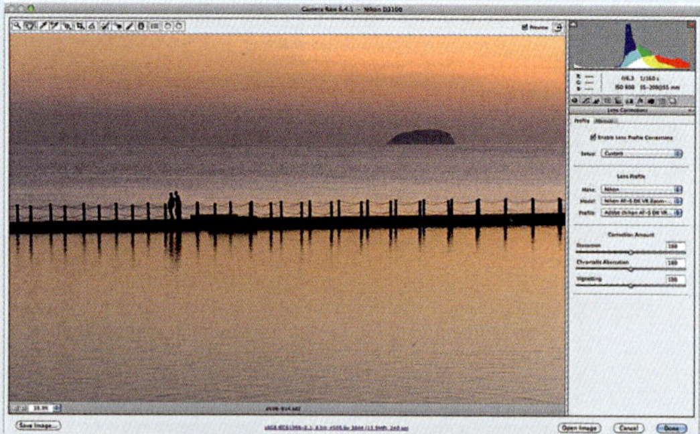

Correct distortion

Nearly all lenses produce some degree of distortion, and this can become very obvious with sunsets, where the horizon needs to be perfectly straight. You can fix any wonky lines manually, using the Lens Correction filter, but Adobe Camera Raw 6.1 (and any later version) comes with automatic correction profiles for most popular lenses.

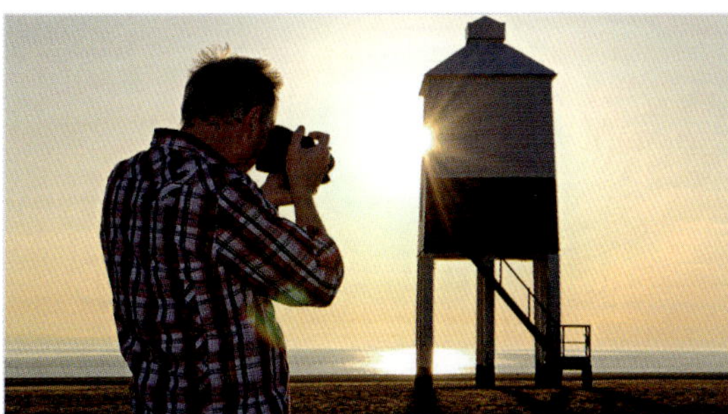

05 Hide the sun

Exposure can be a problem with sunsets, so make sure you check images on the LCD as you take them. If the sun is high in the sky then it might be too intense in the shot, so try hiding it behind another object, such as this lighthouse. You still get rich sunset colours, but without the glare.

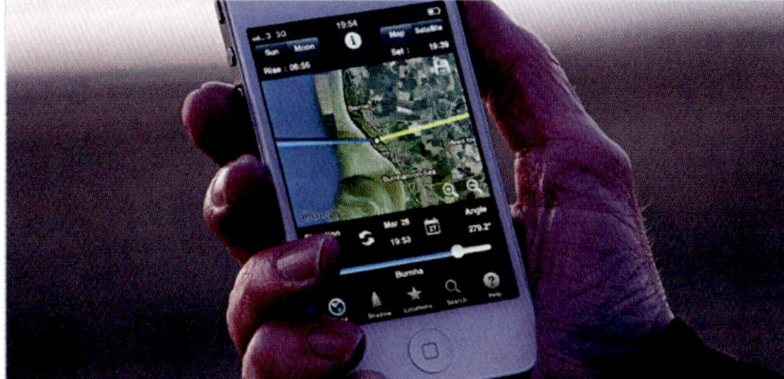

08 Sunset calculators

The secret with sunsets is to be in the right place at the right time. If you have a smartphone you can use a 'sunset calculator', which will tell you what time the sun will set, and at what angle, for any date and location. LightTrac — £2.99 ($4.99) for iOS and £3.01 ($4.99) for Android — is good. You'll still need to arrive early, though, to prepare.

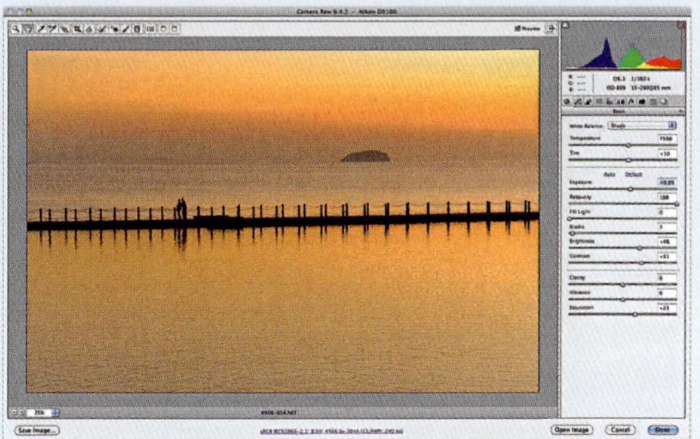

Set White Balance

The colours in the original photo aren't bad (see left), but they don't have the warm glow we're looking for. However, we can cheat by setting the White Balance to Shade in Adobe Camera Raw. We can also boost the saturation. Note that the White Balance presets in ACR are generally a little warmer than those in Nikon DSLRs anyway.

Use your scene

The whole 'sunset' period, from the end of the day to the last glow of twilight, is a prime time for shooting. Don't limit yourself to the few minutes when the sun is actually sinking below the horizon. It's the different tones that will make a shot, and you can use them in many ways.

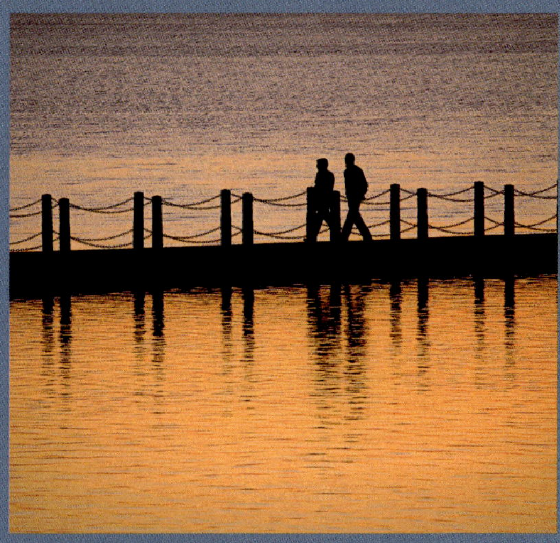

Look for reflections

Water reflects the colours in the sky, so it's like getting two sunsets for the price of one! Sometimes, the surface of the water can produce more interesting patterns and tones than the sky itself. In this shot, the sky has been excluded completely. The interest comes from the different textures in the water on the two sides of the gangway, as well as the simple silhouettes.

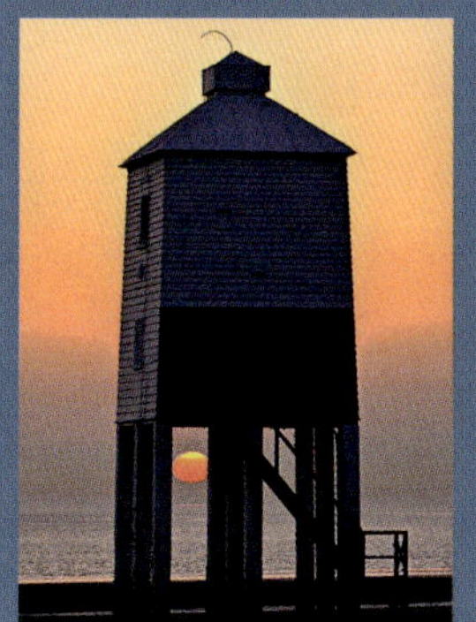

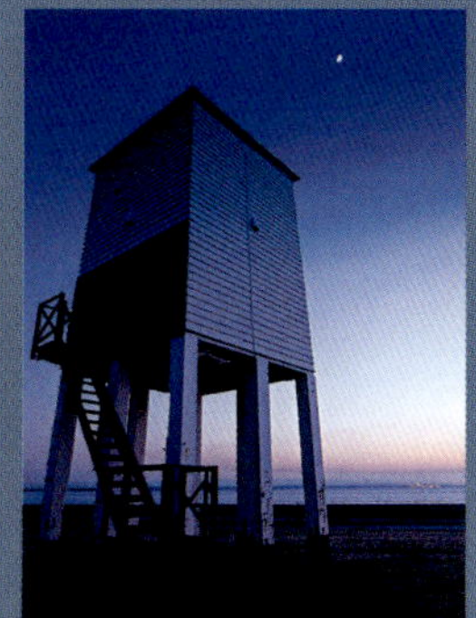

Follow the sun

Magnifying the sun with a long lens will emphasise its movement. Precise alignments such as this one, with the sun perfectly between the wooden legs of the lighthouse, will last for only a few moments.

Stick around

In the hour or so after a sunset, the sky can go through amazing shifts in colour. Stick around and get out your tripod. As it gets darker and exposures get longer, your camera will capture colours and tones you can hardly see.

Take it slow

To get classic pictures at the coast, you need to take things slow,
with a long shutter speed

Timing is key to shooting great seascapes. You need to be there at the right time of day, but just as important is the timing of the exposure. For a raging, stormy sea, a fast shutter speed can be appropriate, but with calmer waters, the best approach is to take it slow. Very slow.

Shutter speeds that are seconds long turn even the gentlest waters into a smooth, silky blur, and the expanse of water takes on a milky white appearance that contrasts with the static rocks.

All landscapes will tend to look their best if you get up at first light, or stay out until dusk. But these dimmer parts of the day are particularly appropriate for milky seascapes, and the low light will give you longer exposures than shooting in the middle of the day. However, a little bit of blur in the water isn't enough to give you the effect you want, which means you either need to shoot after sunset or just before dawn, when the only light is reflected from the sky.

Alternatively, give your camera a helping hand by fitting an ND (neutral density) filter. These dark grey filters (not to be muddled up with graduated neutral density filters, or ND grads) block a percentage of the light entering the camera and enable you to use shutter speeds that are seconds long, even in the middle of the day.

ND filters are available in a variety of strengths. A three-stop ND will increase a shutter speed of 1/4 sec to 2 secs. A 10-stop ND will increase a 1/4 sec exposure to a full four minutes!

As these filters make your camera's viewfinder very dark, they aren't the easiest accessories to use, but our step-by-step guide will show you how to make sure you always come home with a great seascape.

Tame the seas with a super-long shutter speed

Get your settings and location right and you'll be able to capture
stunning long-exposure seascapes

Preparation is vital when it comes to shooting seascapes. You need to do your homework (or know the area well) if you're going to be in the right place at the right time. And as you're working on difficult terrain in low light, you need to have all your kit ready with the right settings to ensure you don't waste any exposures. Shaky shots and wonky horizons are a risk for us all, but if you do all the right pre-shot checks, you'll be able to minimise the chance of these mistakes occurring.

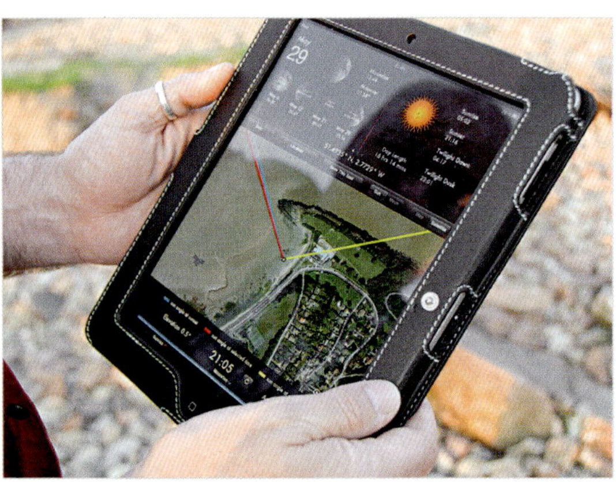

01 Pick your location

Ideally you need somewhere where you can get down near the water as it breaks over the shore. You also need the sun to be low in the sky so it picks out the rocks. For all this information, try a program or app that lets you work out the best time, date and spot to head to. LightTrac, which costs £2.99 for iPad, iPhone and Android phones, is a good choice.

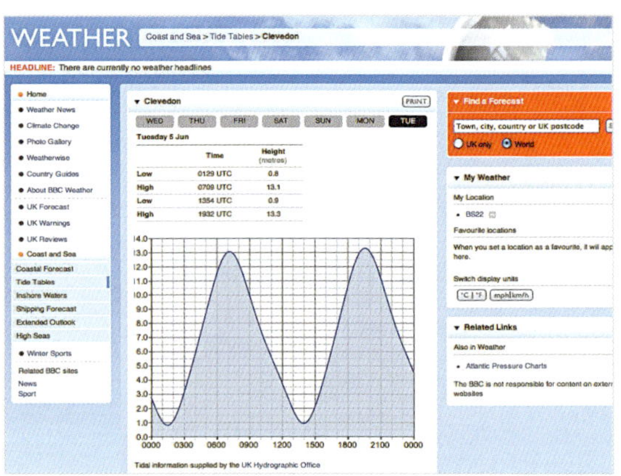

02 Watch the tide

It's no good just turning up at dusk or dawn — you need to check the tides. As a rule, these shots look better if the tide is going out because this ensures that the wet rocks glisten, but you also need the water to be high enough to break against your chosen rocks. UK photographers can visit bbc.in/tide-tables to check the tides online.

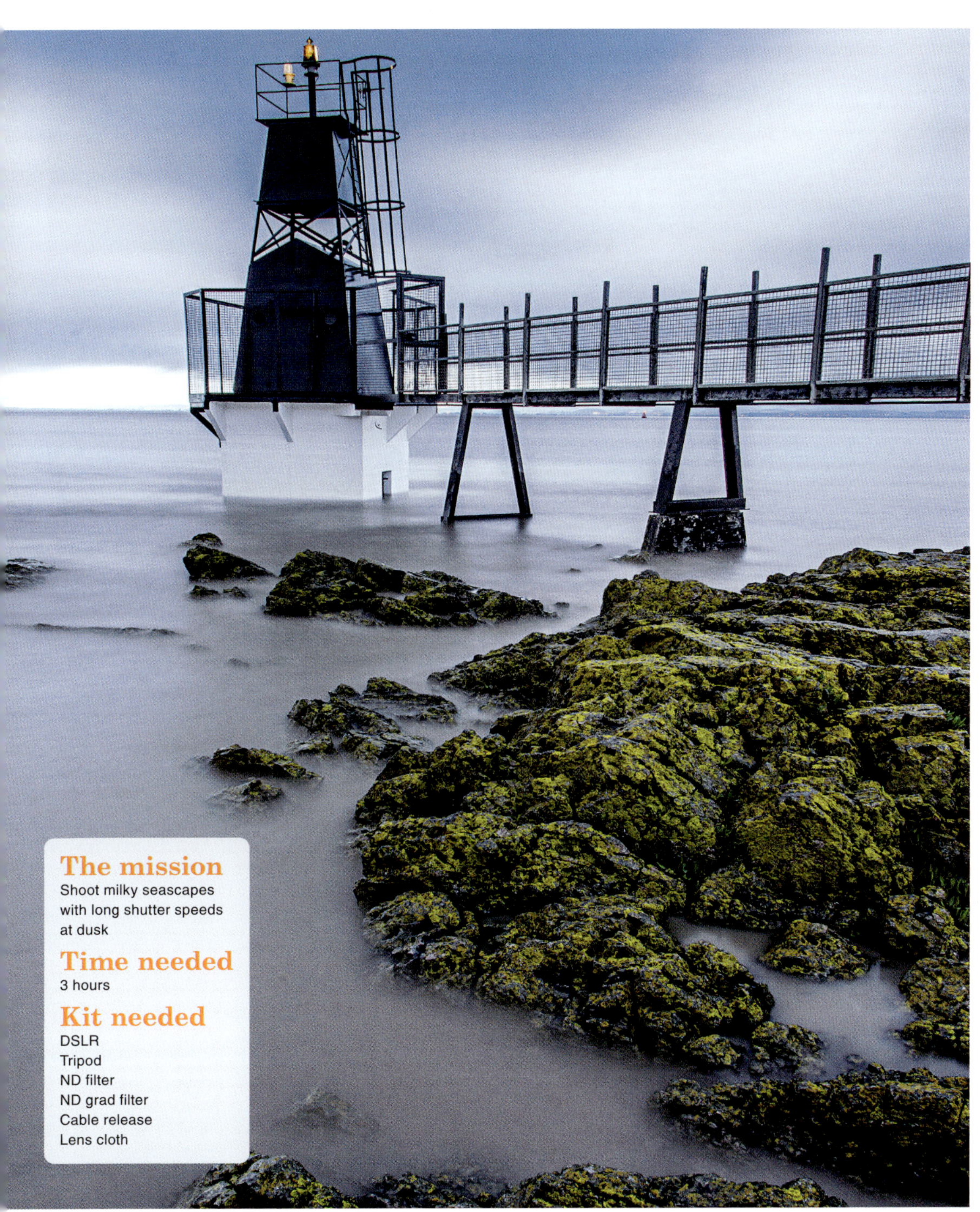

The mission
Shoot milky seascapes
with long shutter speeds
at dusk

Time needed
3 hours

Kit needed
DSLR
Tripod
ND filter
ND grad filter
Cable release
Lens cloth

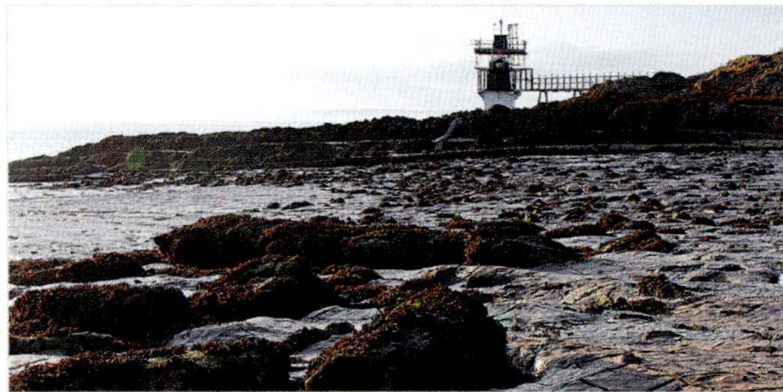

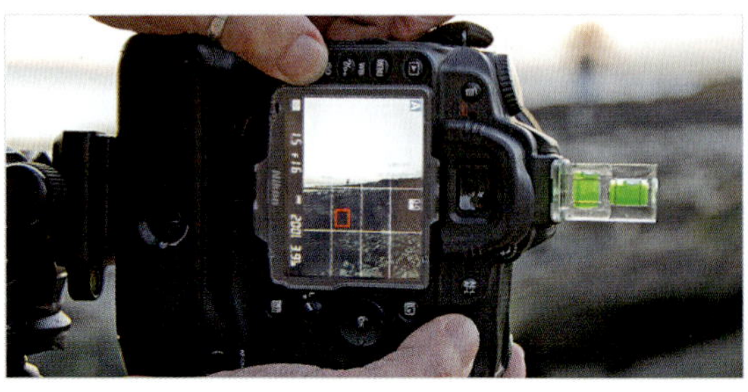

03 Find your foreground

When you get to the location, you need to find the best camera angle, and it's often best to hunt this out without your tripod. You need to find a focal point, such as a headland or lighthouse, as well as a good foreground — getting low helps you make rocks look big in the frame.

04 Keep a level head

Set the camera on the tripod. It's essential that your DSLR is level — a sloping horizon is extremely irritating with seascapes, and this is hard to check as it gets darker. Use a spirit level in the hotshoe, or switch on Live View and use the grid overlay to make sure you get things straight.

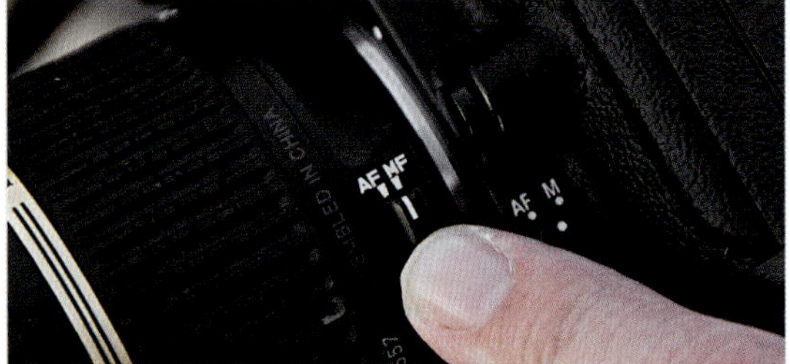

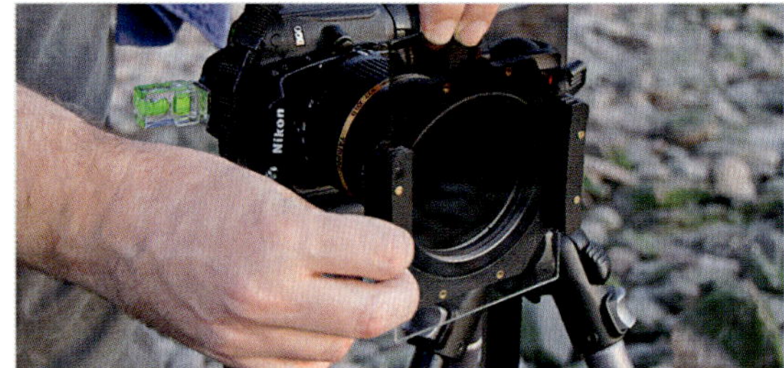

06 Check the focus and lock it down

Take a test shot to check the focus. If everything is sharp, lock the focus by switching off autofocus. Now fit your ND filter. Choose a strength that gets you an exposure that's between 15 secs and 2 minutes long. A variable ND filter (see right) will provide you with a range of shutter speeds.

07 Employ a graduate

With most seascapes, your shots will also benefit from using a second filter — a graduated ND filter that darkens the sky in the top half of the shot and lightens the foreground. A two-stop (0.6) soft-edged graduate is a good all-round choice that will do wonders for most landscape shots.

ND strengths and speeds

ND filters are sold in different strengths, and different scales are used to measure this. Some use an NDxx number, others refer to optical density, and some refer to the light reduction in EV or 'stops'. This table compares the systems and shows how much slower a shutter speed each strength will allow you to achieve.

FILTER	Optical density	Light reduction in stops	SHUTTER SPEED CONVERSION							
			1/4000 sec	1/1000 sec	1/250 sec	1/60 sec	1/15 sec	1/4 sec	1 sec	4 secs
NO FILTER	0	0	1/4000 sec	1/1000 sec	1/250 sec	1/60 sec	1/15 sec	1/4 sec	1 sec	4 secs
ND2	0.3	1	1/2000 sec	1/500 sec	1/125 sec	1/30 sec	1/8 sec	1/2 sec	2 secs	8 secs
POLARISER	Up to 0.5	Up to 1 2/3	1/1250 sec	1/320 sec	1/80 sec	1/20 sec	1/5 sec	1.3 secs	3 secs	13 secs
ND4	0.6	2	1/1000 sec	1/250 sec	1/60 sec	1/15 sec	1/4 sec	1 sec	4 secs	16 secs
ND8	0.9	3	1/500 sec	1/125 sec	1/30 sec	1/8 sec	1/2 sec	2 secs	8 secs	30 secs
ND16	1.2	4	1/250 sec	1/60 sec	1/15 sec	1/4 sec	1 sec	4 secs	16 secs	60 secs
ND32	1.5	5	1/125 sec	1/30 sec	1/8 sec	1/2 sec	2 secs	8 secs	30 secs	2 mins
ND64	1.8	6	1/60 sec	1/15 sec	1/4 sec	1 sec	4 secs	16 secs	60 secs	4 mins
ND100	2	6 2/3	1/40 sec	1/10 sec	1/2 sec	2.5 secs	10 secs	40 secs	160 secs	11 mins
ND256	2.4	8	1/15 sec	1/4 sec	1 sec	4 secs	16 secs	60 secs	4 mins	15 mins
ND400	2.6	8 2/3	1/20 sec	1/5 sec	1.6 secs	6 secs	25 secs	100 secs	6 mins	26 mins
ND500	2.7	9	1/8 sec	1/2 sec	2 secs	8 secs	30 secs	2 mins	8 mins	30 mins
ND1000	3	10	1/4 sec	1 sec	4 secs	16 secs	60 secs	4 mins	15 mins	60 mins

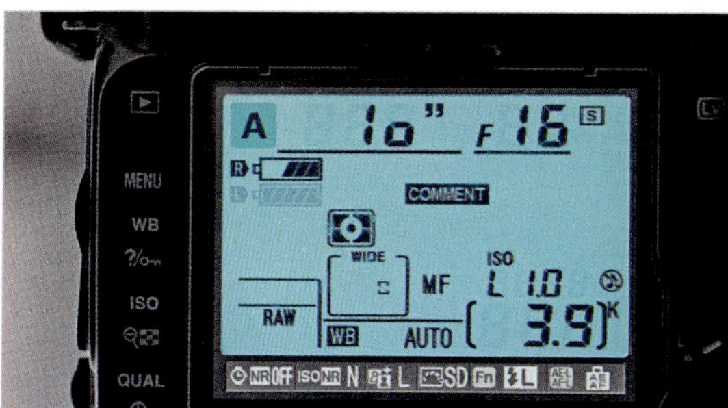

05 Get set to take it slow

To get long shutter speeds, first switch to Aperture Priority mode and set a low ISO of around 100, with a narrow aperture of around f/16. Focus on a point about a third of the way up the frame — depending on the light, you might need to use a torch to light up this point.

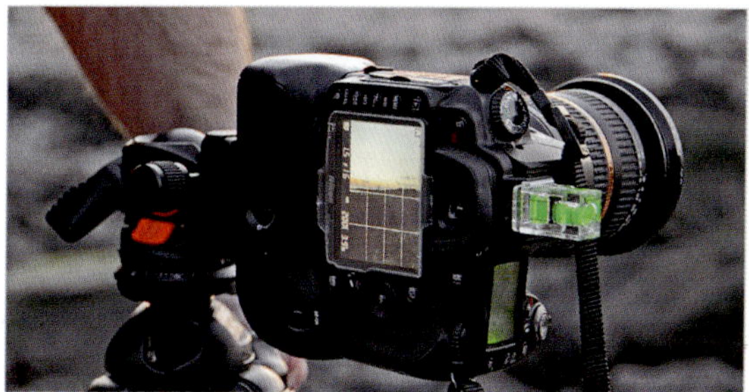

08 Minimise vibrations

With such long shutter speeds, you'll need to use a cable release and Live View to avoid shaky shots caused by the camera's mirror moving as it takes the picture. The combination of long exposures and Live View means your battery won't last long, so make sure you have a spare.

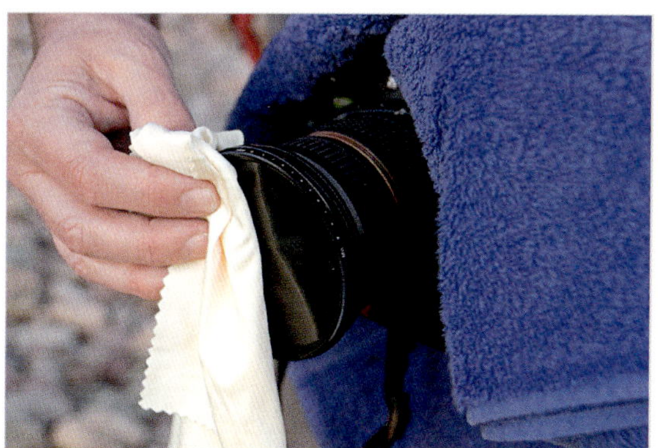

09 Salty spots

Salt spray on the front of the lens is an occupational hazard, and if you don't check for it, it can leave marks on your pictures that can be hard to clone out. Make sure you have a lens cloth at the ready — and a towel, just in case there's a bigger wave that catches you unawares!

Shutter speed choice

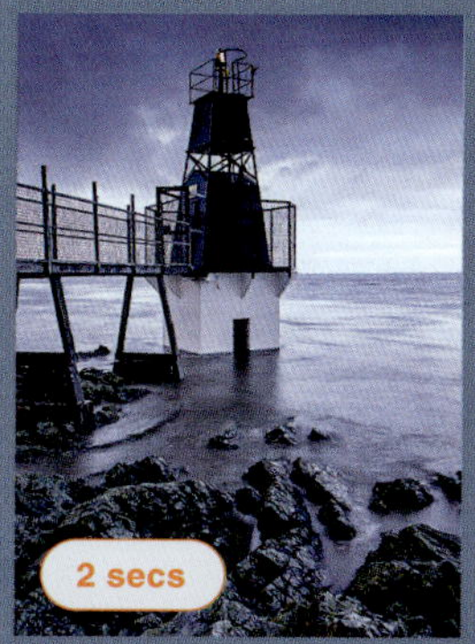

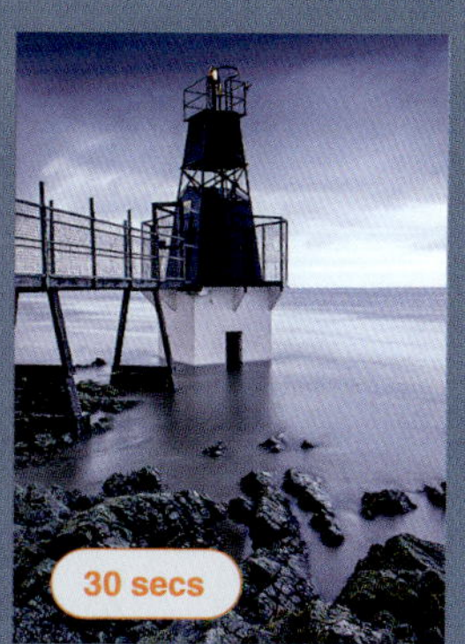

This comparison shot shows graphically that a shutter speed of a couple of seconds is simply not enough to give a good milky water effect. By fitting an ND filter, an exposure of 30 seconds gives a much better effect.

How to pick an ND filter

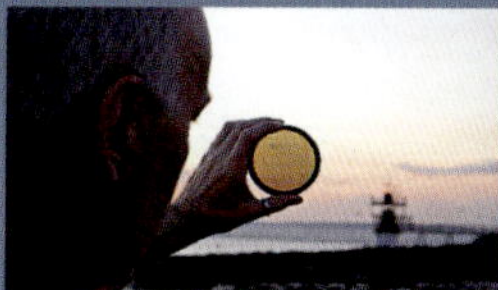

Choose a strength

ND filters come in a huge range of strengths. A one-stop (0.3 or ND2) filter cuts just 50% of light. A 10-stop (ND1000) filter blocks 99.9% of light. The stronger versions are best for seascapes.

Round or square?

Round filters are the best option for ND filters as they prevent any light leaks. However, if you use them in conjunction with ND grad filters, the square slot-in type are a good choice.

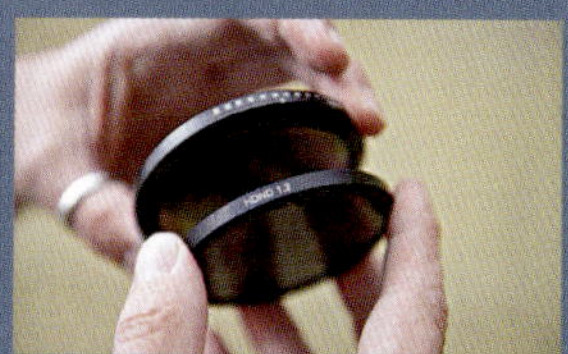

Variable ND filters

Variable ND filters use two polarising filters in one mount. The front ring is rotated to vary the ND's strength. They're popular for shooting video as you can use wide apertures, however bright the light.

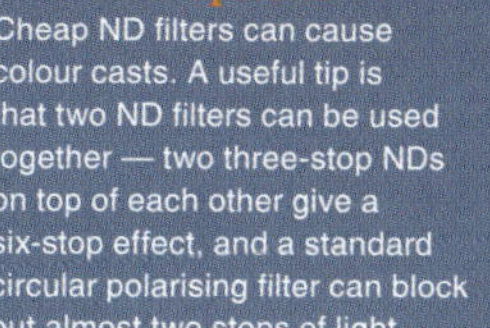

Low-cost options

Cheap ND filters can cause colour casts. A useful tip is that two ND filters can be used together — two three-stop NDs on top of each other give a six-stop effect, and a standard circular polarising filter can block out almost two stops of light.

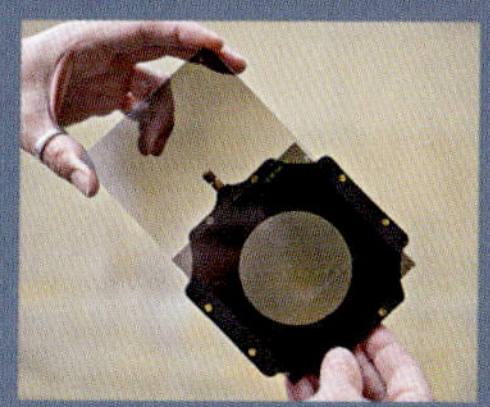

Discover the drama of black and white

Sometimes you need to see the world in black and white!
Let's look closer at our Nikon DSLR's Monochrome Picture Control

We see the world in colour, we respond to colours and today's Nikon DSLRs can reproduce colour with amazing fidelity and depth. So why shoot in black and white? Black-and-white photography can be used to give pictures an 'antique' look, but it has creative benefits too. The lack of colour means it's already one step removed from reality, so that people are more likely to look at the way you've made the photograph and less likely to be distracted by the subject matter itself. Also, if you remove colour from the equation, it becomes much easier to explore shapes, lines and tones and turn them into strong compositions.

This is where your Nikon DSLR can help you. It has a Monochrome Picture Control which turns your photographs into black and white and can help you visualise the world as shades of grey.

We went to Broadway Tower in the Cotswolds to show how this works. The gritty textures and simple shapes made a great subject for black and white, even on a dull and overcast day.

Apart from changing the camera's Picture Control, shooting black and white is technically no different to shooting colour. What you do have to change, rather than settings, is how you 'see' and compose your pictures. Monochrome photography depends on shapes, tones and textures, but most of us are attracted by colour, so it takes a little while to learn how to switch this off — you have to change the mode in your head as well as the one on your camera!

The simplest shapes often make the best subjects, and you should make the most of contrasts in both tone and lighting. Finally, don't expect to get every image perfect in-camera. Even the greatest monochrome-shooting photographers needed a little help in the darkroom…

Setting the tone
Your camera's Monochrome mode doesn't just save time later…

Why set the camera to mono mode when you can simply convert a regular colour image into black and white on the computer? It's because you need a black-and-white 'eye' to shoot good monochromatic shots in the first place, and being able to see the results on the spot is a huge advantage. Shots that work in colour don't necessarily convert well to black and white, but if you only shoot in colour you won't find out how they convert until you get home, when it's too late.

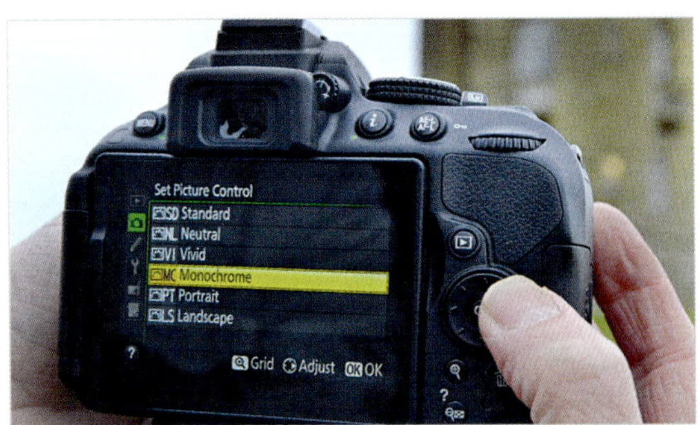

01 Go Mono
Your Nikon's Picture Controls don't change any of the camera's key exposure or focus settings, but they do alter the way the image is processed. With the Monochrome Picture Control selected, your shots will be displayed in black and white (note that it's best to shoot in RAW — see the sidebar overleaf).

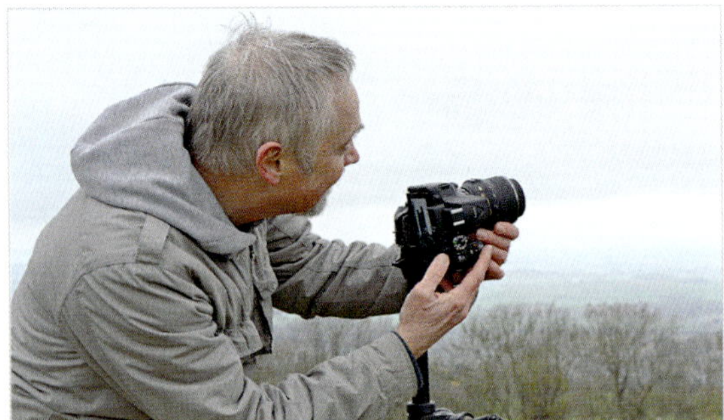

02 Try a tripod
A tripod is not essential, but putting your camera on one does leave your hands free to experiment with the camera settings and the Picture Control options. If you use the viewfinder to compose your shots, you'll still see the scene in full colour, but when the picture appears on the LCD on the back of your Nikon it's in black and white.

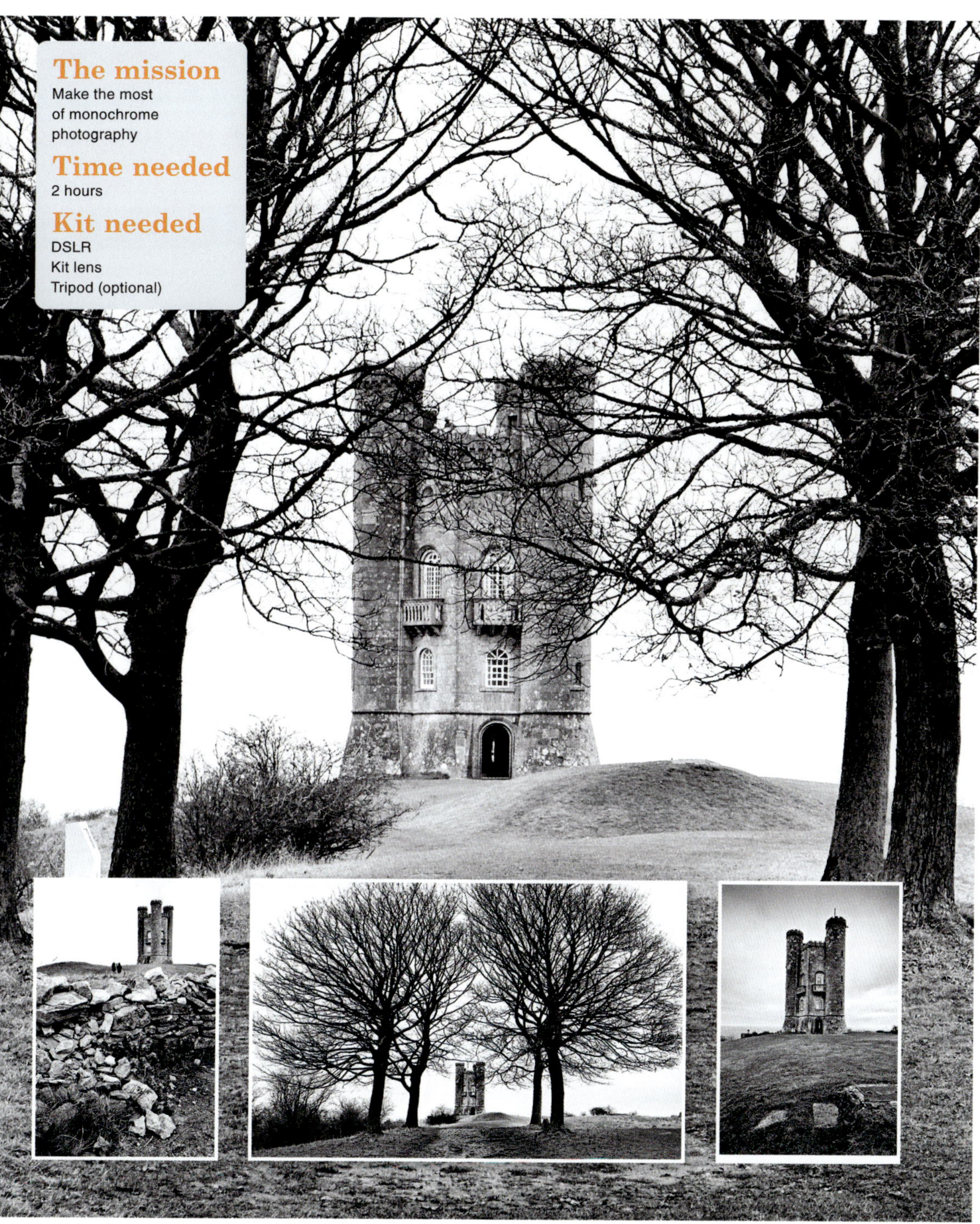
The mission
Make the most
of monochrome
photography
Time needed
2 hours
Kit needed
DSLR
Kit lens
Tripod (optional)

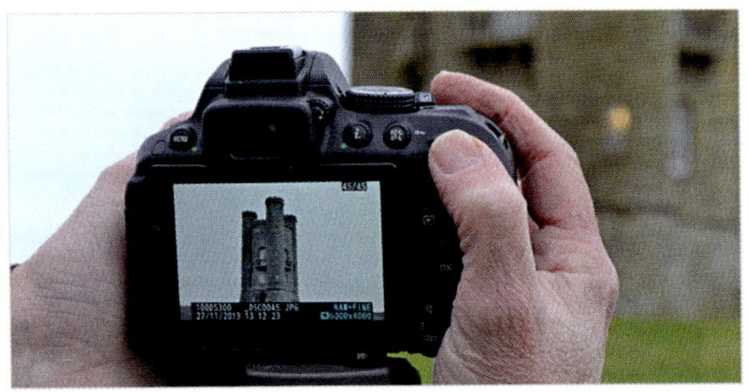

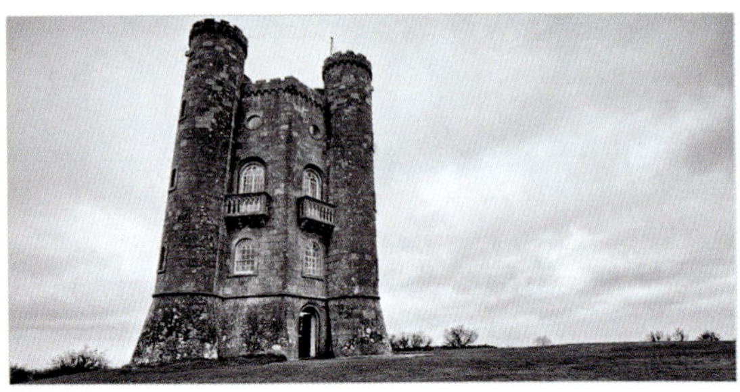

03 Train your eye

This is one of the big advantages of digital black and white photography — straight away, you can see if your shots are working or not. Even better, try switching to Live View mode, because that enables you to compose your pictures in black and white too. Keep an eye on the battery level, though, because Live View drains it faster.

04 Be bold with angles

Black-and-white photography relies on visual impact, so try using your widest lens to get in close for strong angles and perspectives. The converging verticals in this shot have produced a picture with a striking trapezoidal composition. In black and white, shapes and lines become much more important.

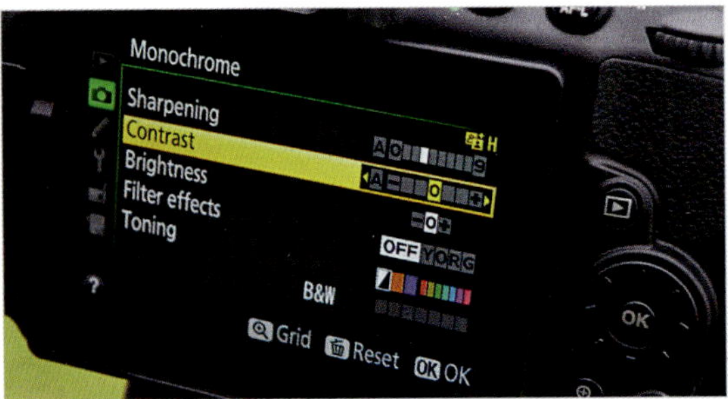

06 Process in-camera

There are so many in-camera options that you may not have time to try them properly while you're shooting, but you can do it later. Newer Nikon DSLRs offer in-camera NEF processing, where you can produce any number of JPEG copies from your RAW files — here are sepia and cyanotype versions of one shot.

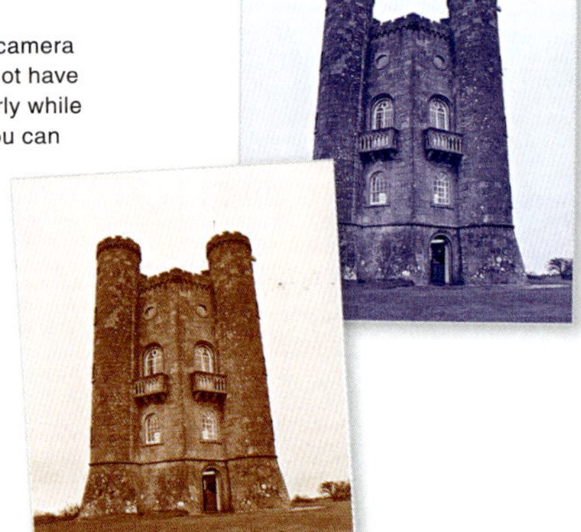

05 Change your settings

On a dull, overcast day, black-and-white pictures can lack contrast, but you can use the multi-selector to access the Monochrome Picture Control's advanced settings. You can increase the Contrast value for a start, but there are also options for adding black-and-white filters and toning effects to add more punch to your shots.

Darkroom experts

You can produce an impressively wide range of black-and-white effects with Photoshop and Elements, of course, but recapturing the elusive 'look and feel' of silver halide films can be difficult, and that's where specialist plug-ins can help. Silver Efex Pro is one of the best around, and it's part of the free Google Nik Collection (www.google.com/nikcollection). Here's how it works…

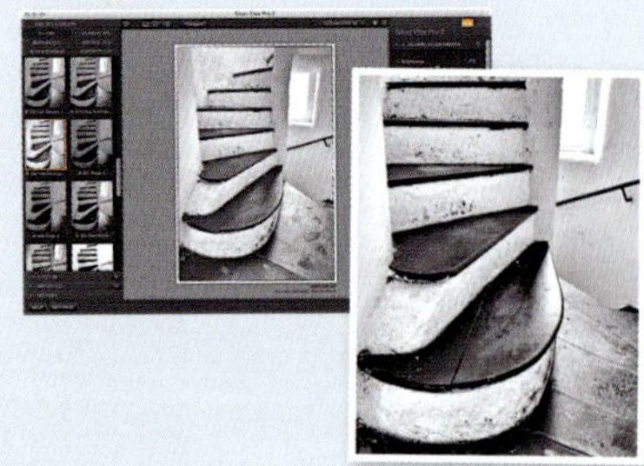

Pick a preset

This panel displays a wide selection of preset black-and-white 'looks', from high-contrast 'push-processed' effects to delicate fine art. The easiest way to use Silver Efex Pro is to start with the preset nearest the effect you want, then adjust the settings manually.

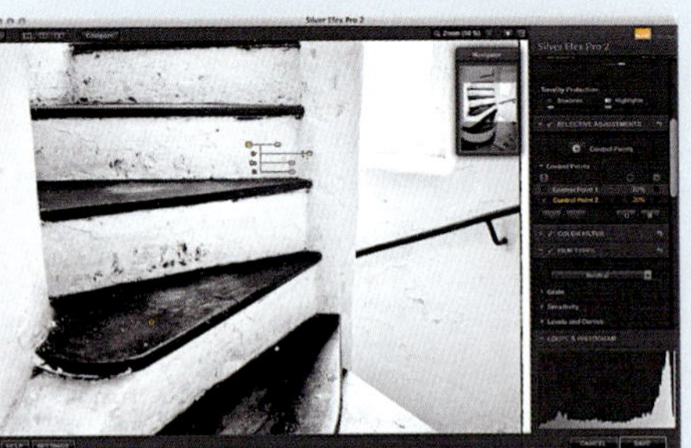

Develop your image

This is done with a set of panels and sliders on the right of the screen. You can use these to change the film simulation (from Kodak Panatomix X to Ilford Delta 3200), contrast, toning and framing effects and even apply dodging and burning effects with quick and simple 'control points'.

Get multiple exposures

Discover how to shoot an in-camera Multiple Exposure for striking blends

A multiple exposure is an image in which two or more exposures are layered on top of each other. In the old days of film cameras, creating such a look was a fiddly process in which you had to disengage the film advance and re-cock the camera's shutter so that two pictures could be taken and sit over one another. Some calculations were needed, too, to ensure the exposure was right.

Today, though, there are several ways to get a multiple exposure, including Photoshop. However, the in-camera option is by far the most rewarding. You can't do it with all DSLRs, but you should be able to with most newer cameras! It's jolly easy to grasp, too, so let's see how it's done…

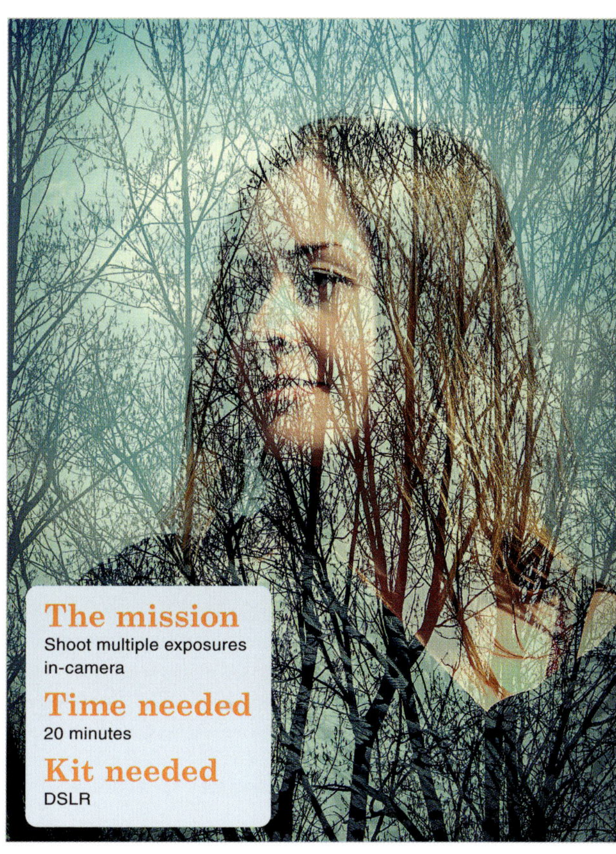

The mission
Shoot multiple exposures in-camera

Time needed
20 minutes

Kit needed
DSLR

Double up on exposures
How to get multiple exposures using just your DSLR

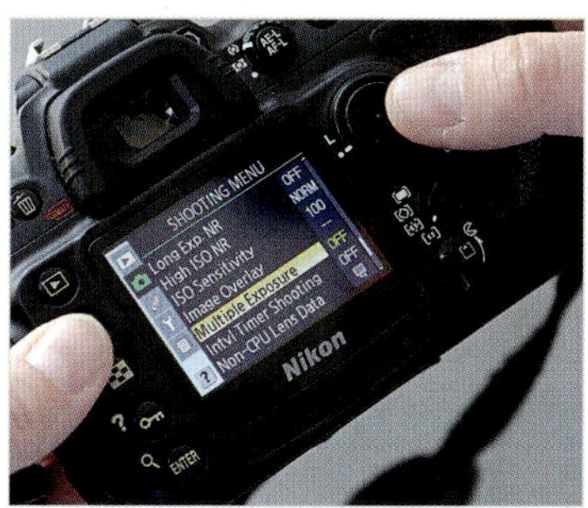

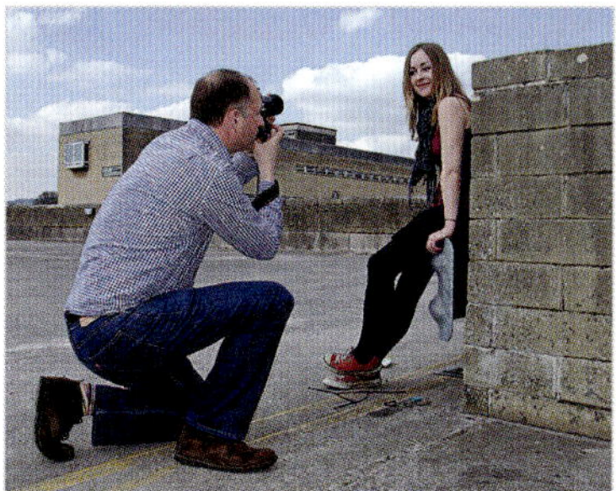

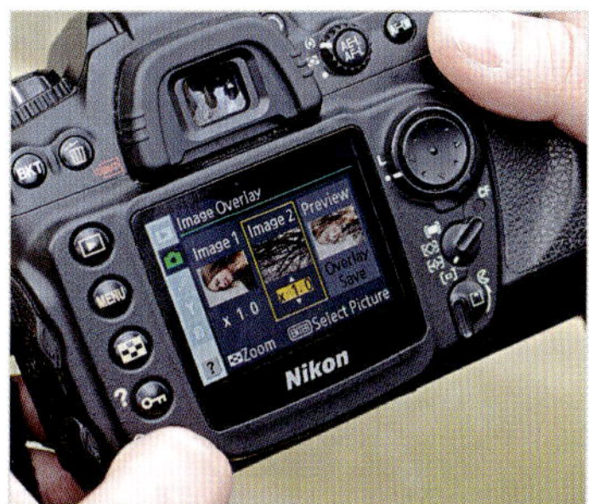

01 Menu settings
Navigate to the Shooting menu, select Multiple Exposure and pick how many shots you want to layer. Activate Auto Gain. Your Nikon's processor can then average out the exposures of each shot, so you don't end up with a badly lit image. Click OK.

02 Set your scene
Some subjects work better than others for multiple exposures. However, the charm of the technique lies in the fact that it's hard to control or visualise how results might look. We're combining a portrait with the urban textures of a car park and surrounding trees.

03 Overlay method
Some Nikon DSLRs have an Overlay function that allows you to blend in-camera images you've already shot. Select Image Overlay from the Retouch menu, scroll to the images you want to merge and press OK. Note that this function only works with RAW (NEF) files.

Shoot the breeze

Make your subjects disappear into thin air for a ghostly portrait effect

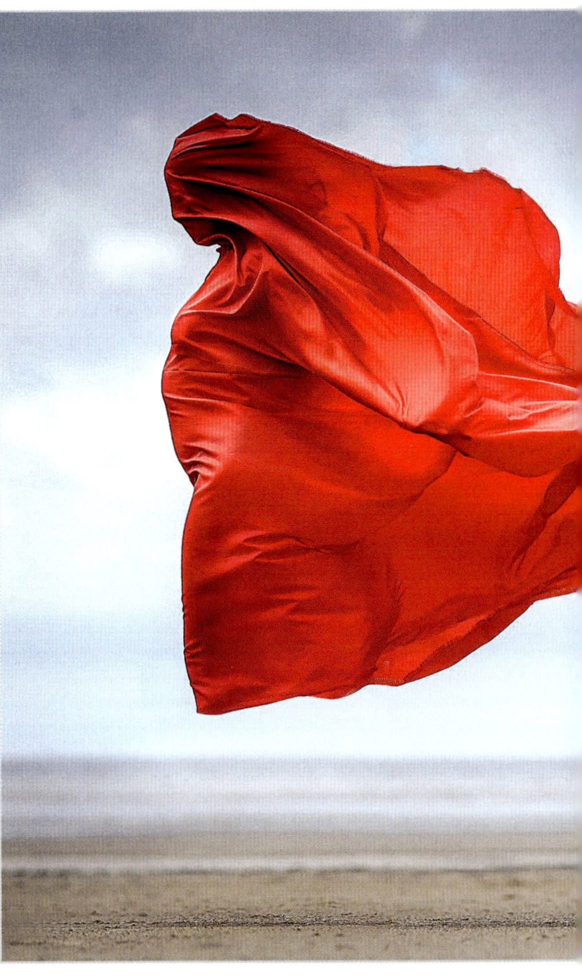

Something as simple as a piece of lightweight fabric can add an incredible burst of colour and shape to your portraits, especially if you can find a windswept location and a willing subject who doesn't mind being buffeted by the breeze. Not only is the fabric fantastic for conventional photos, it can also be used to create beautiful effects, like our ghostly figure. In this project, we'll explain how it's done using a cunning combination of shooting skills and simple techniques in Photoshop.

The fabric in question here is a shiny dress lining material — light enough to get picked up by the wind and thin enough to define the shape of the figure underneath, but also not so transparent that it gives the game away by showing the person in too much detail. After draping the fabric over our subject, we'll use Photoshop skills to remove the legs and replace the area with a portion of the empty scene taken from another frame. Even for Photoshop beginners it's a simple job that takes just a few minutes...

Let the wind blow

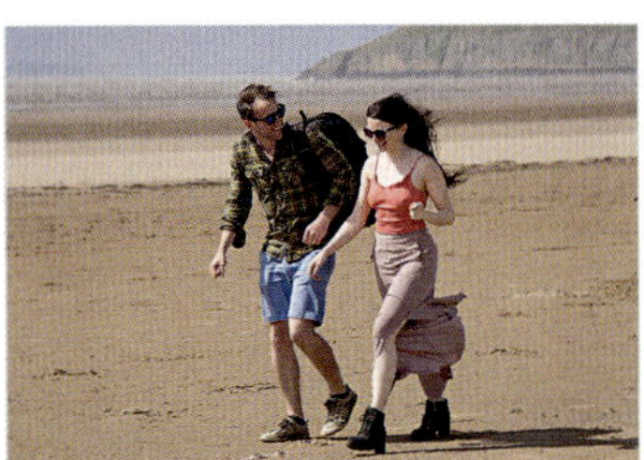

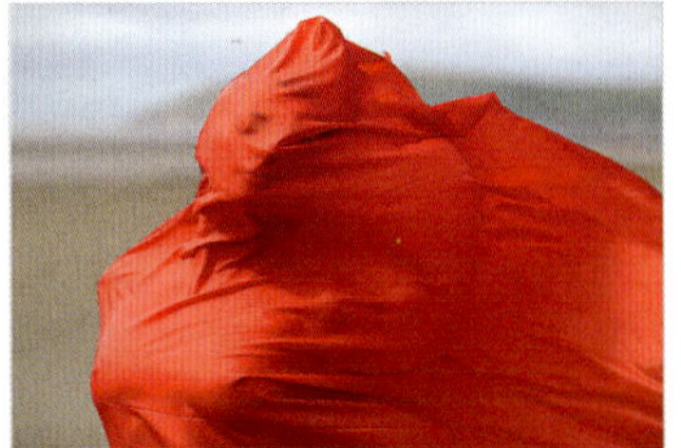

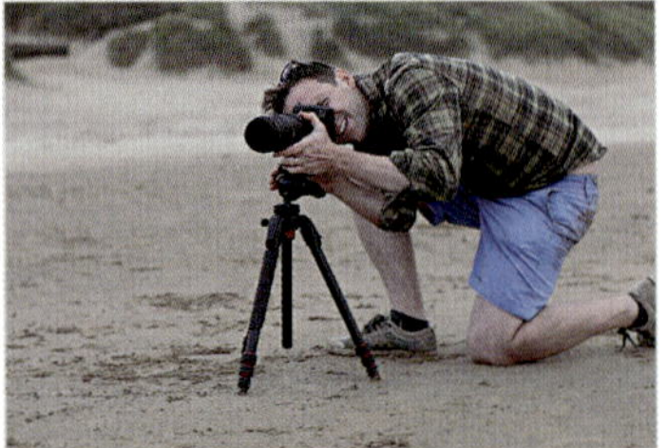

01 Wait for wind
For this project you'll need a willing model and a windy spot to shoot. The space should be wide enough for the fabric to flow, and with enough of a breeze for it to catch in the wind. Hilltops, open fields, high buildings or beaches all work. A simple, uncluttered backdrop is best.

02 Shape the fabric
The fabric needs to be light, but not too transparent. We used dress-lining material — fabric shops sell it fairly cheaply in various colours (our 5x1-metre piece cost less than £20). Once covered, ask the subject to pose so that the fabric shows the shape of the face and body.

03 Use a tripod
We need a tripod to keep the camera position fixed. As for exposure settings, a wide aperture, like f/2.8, gives a nice shallow depth of field and blurs the backdrop. We had our Nikon in Aperture Priority mode at f/2.8, ISO100, resulting in a shutter speed of 1/1600 sec.

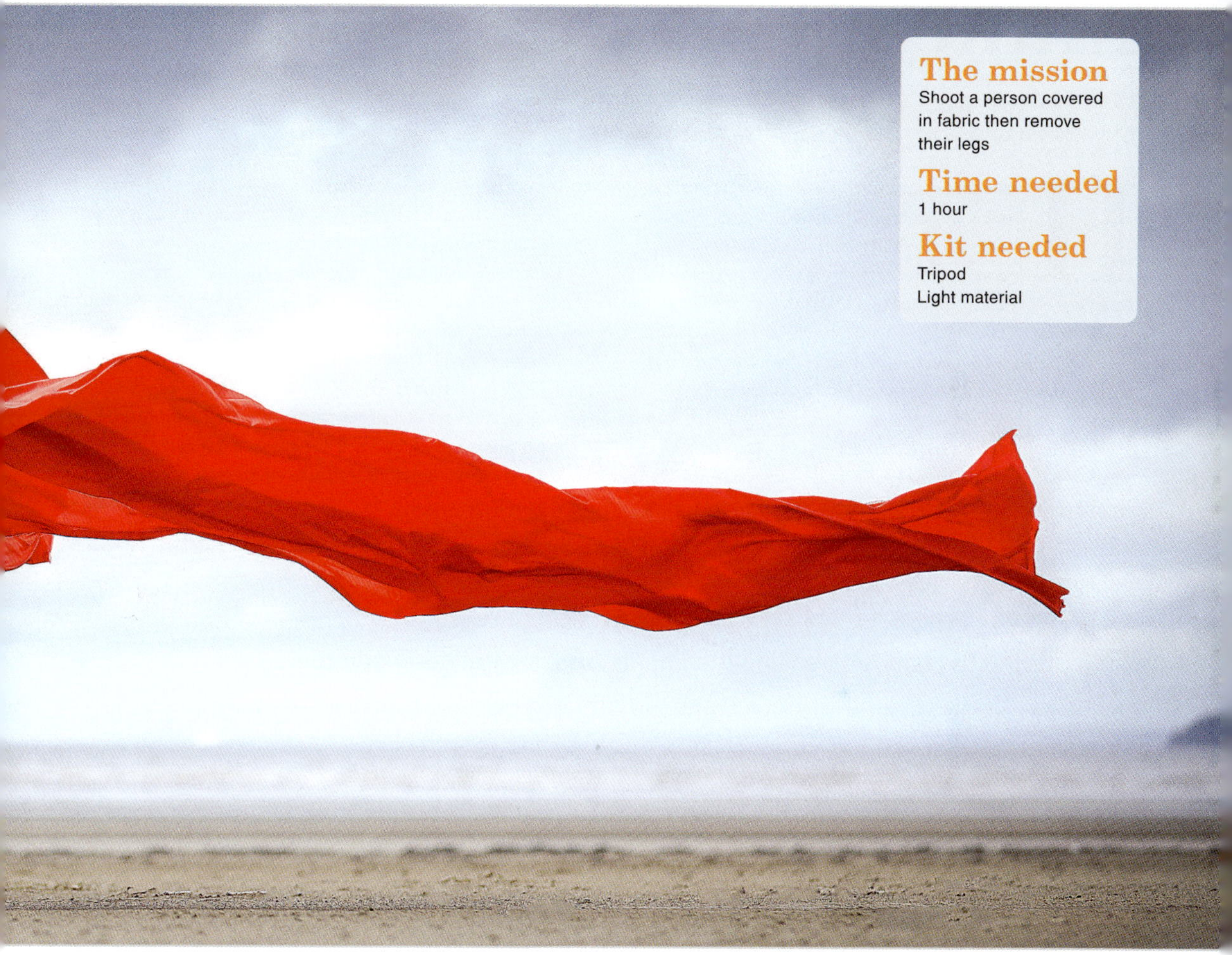

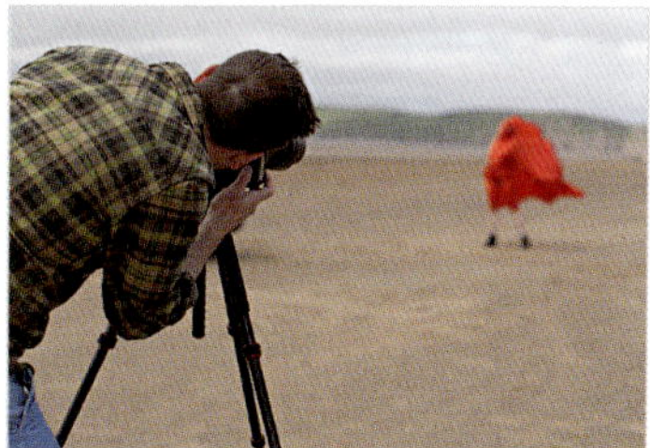

04 Work the poses

After taking a few shots of your subject in various poses (we tried straight-on and side-on), ask them to move out of the frame. Switch to manual focus to stop the focus snapping onto the background, and fire another shot, making sure the exposure matches the other frames.

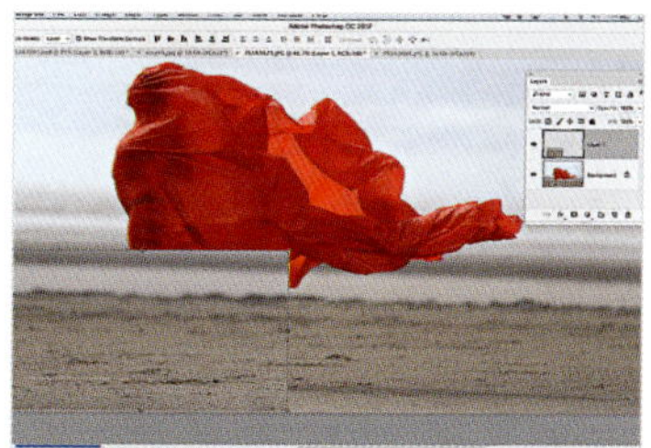

05 Hide the legs

Open your main image and empty frame in Photoshop. Grab the Rectangular Marquee tool and make a rough selection of the empty area that corresponds to the subject's legs. Hit Cmd/Ctrl+C to copy, then go to the other image and hit Cmd/Ctrl+Shift+V to paste in place.

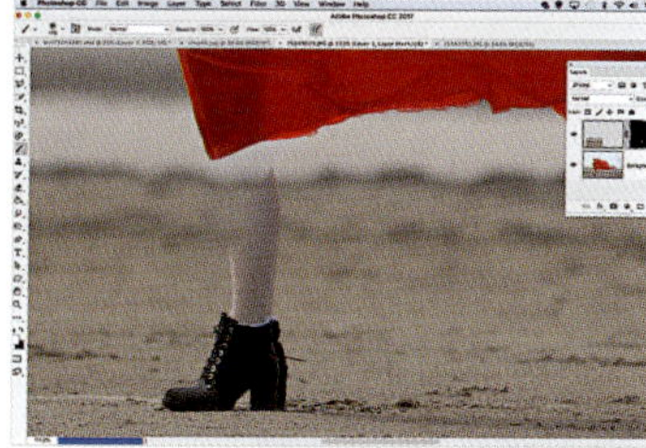

06 Paint a mask

Go to the Layers panel (Window>Layers), hold Alt and click the 'Add Layer Mask' icon to hide the layer behind a full black mask. Grab the Brush tool and set the colour to white then paint over the legs to reveal the empty space. If necessary, tidy any messy patches with the Clone tool.

Make a splash

Learn how to get incredible frozen shots of droplets
of water using your SLR's manual features and a flash

High-speed photography is an easy way to impress friends and other photographers. A quick look for inspiration will often turn up lots of clever tricks, but most involve complex rig setups and specialist equipment. They get good results but are expensive or require a high level of electrical knowledge.

To get started, all you really need is your DSLR, a sturdy tripod, a shutter release and a flash that can be adjusted manually. Oh, and a drop of patience is also essential!

In this project, we're going to look at how to capture a droplet as it splashes through the surface of some water — no mean feat, as this action happens faster than we can see. In order to freeze it, you'll need to deviate from normal focusing and exposure techniques and get to grips with your camera's manual features.

The setup that creates the droplet is essential to a good image, as are the positioning of the camera and flash. Luckily, it's easy to get these right. The most important thing is to shoot in a dark environment — we want to use the flash, rather than the camera's shutter, to expose the image. This is because the pulse of light from the flash will be much faster than your camera's top shutter speed, especially at lower power ratings. Winter evenings are great for this, and shooting in the dark means you should be able to decrease the aperture to f/16, increasing the depth of field and capturing the water droplet in focus.

In this tutorial, you'll learn a number of skills that are key to perfecting manual exposure and capturing subjects in a split second. And don't forget to watch the video guide for extra information and tips on high-speed shots.

Shooting a water splash

From setting the scene to editing the image, here's what you need to do

Here, we're going to shoot simple water droplets breaking a surface. However, you can always try out different fluids, such as milk or emulsion paint, for varying effects. You'll need to fine-tune your

setup for thicker liquids, in order to create the right-size droplets. Experimentation is key. Once you've captured the shot, open the image in Photoshop to tweak tones and colours.

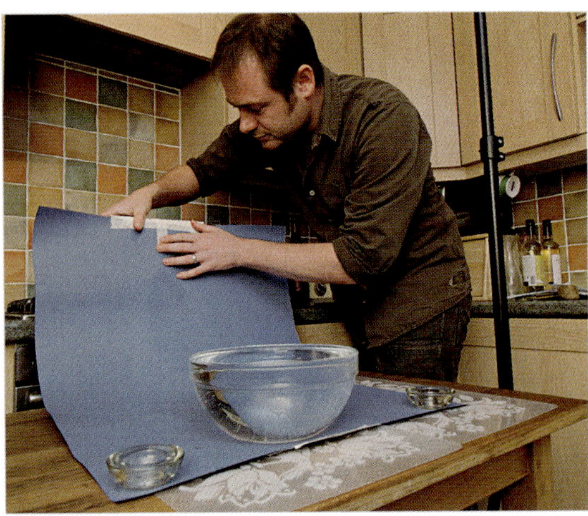

01 Organise the scene

Setup is crucial to getting the shot you want. Start by filling a glass bowl with water. Place this on a coloured sheet of A3 paper that's propped up at the back to create an infinity curve. Next, make a hole in the screw cap of a litre bottle, and use a pin to make a small hole in the side of the bottle. Cover this second hole with tape.

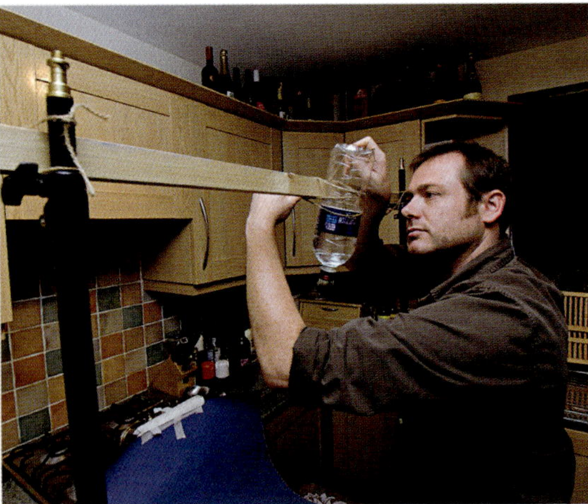

02 Create the water droplet

Half-fill the bottle with water. Place boxes or lighting stands on either side of the bowl, and tape a pole between the two. Attach the bottle to the pole, with the cap pointing down. Peel back the tape and check that the water drops from the cap into the bowl. The higher up the bottle is, the bigger the water droplet will be.

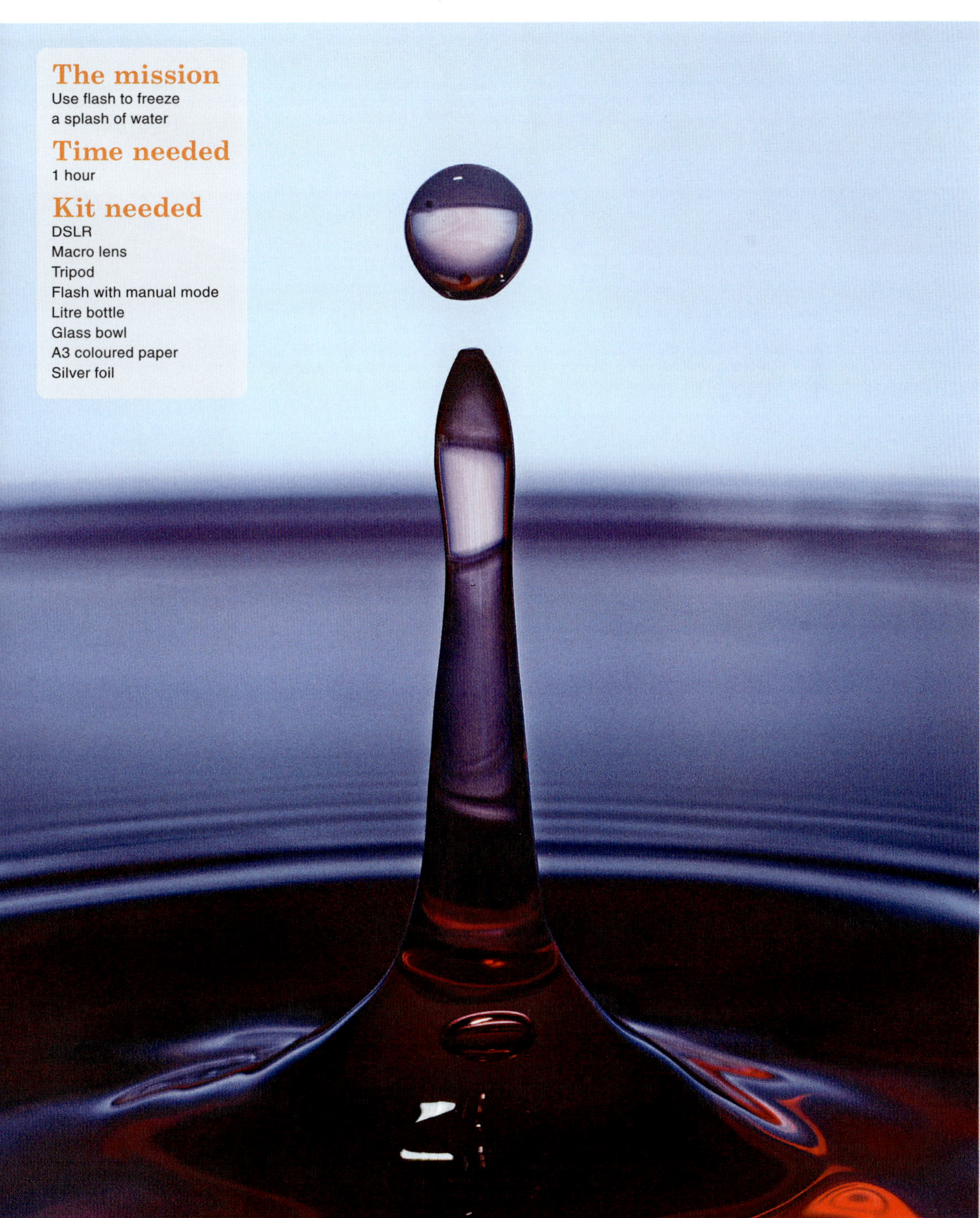

The mission
Use flash to freeze
a splash of water

Time needed
1 hour

Kit needed
DSLR
Macro lens
Tripod
Flash with manual mode
Litre bottle
Glass bowl
A3 coloured paper
Silver foil

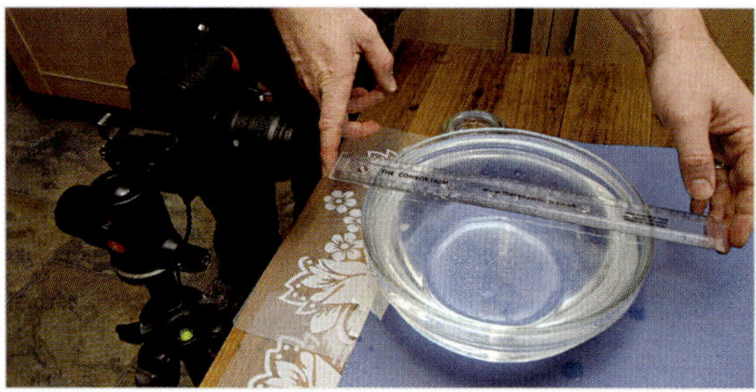

03 Use manual focus

Place your camera on a tripod and angle the body down towards the water bowl by about five degrees. The view of the water should fill the frame. Place a ruler across the bowl and switch the lens to manual, then focus on the point where the water droplet will hit the surface. Switch the camera to manual and decrease the aperture to f/16.

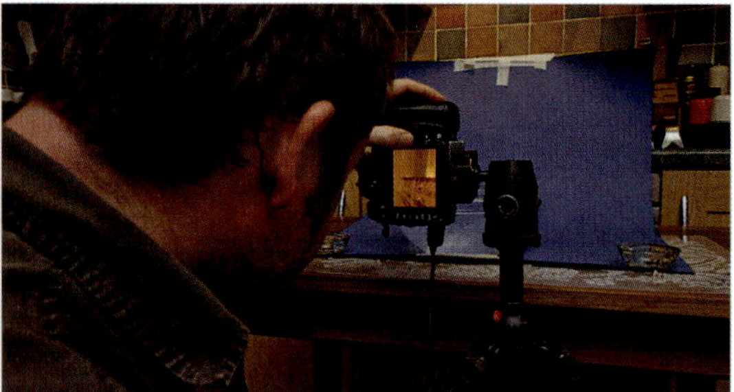

04 Check the focus

Adjust the shutter speed to get a good exposure. Take a shot. Check the image and see how many of the markings on the ruler are in focus. If less than that a centimetre is in focus, increase the aperture to f/22. Connect a shutter release and make sure the room is as dark as possible. Set the shutter speed to 0.5 seconds, or slower.

What you need for high-speed photography

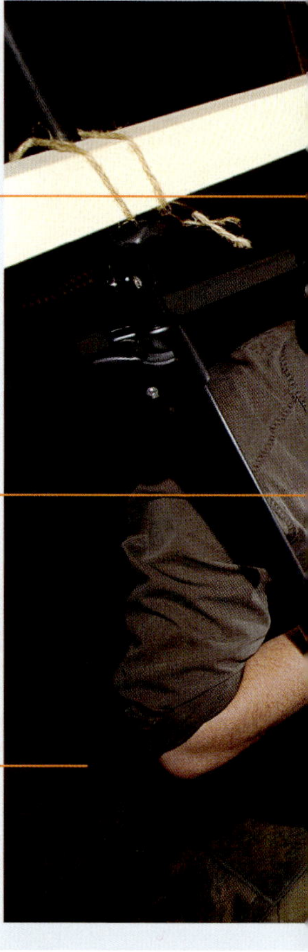

Macro lens

A macro lens such as Nikon's 50mm enables you to get close to the action. With a maximum aperture of f/32 you can get the greatest depth of field possible, too. However, if you don't have a macro lens, don't worry — just position the camera a little further back.

Cable release

A remote control trigger lets you fire the shot without having to touch the camera itself. But its main advantage is that it gives you more flexibility as to where you stand.

Darkened room

Shooting in a darkened room enables you to use the flash to expose your shot. Just make sure there's enough light for you to see what you're doing and gauge when the water droplets are falling.

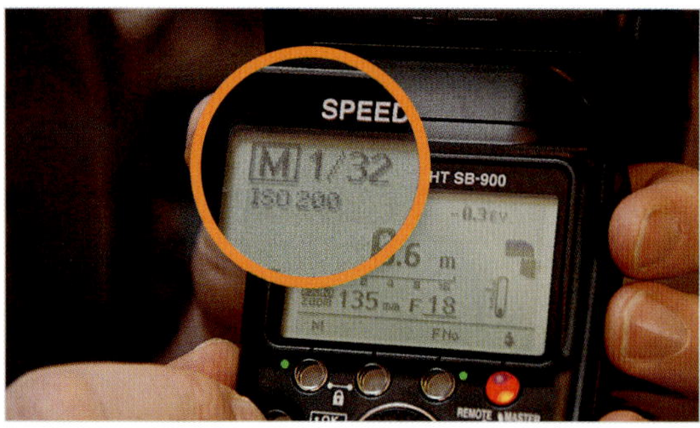

05 Set the flash

Put your off-camera flash to manual and adjust the power to 1/16. We're going to expose our shot by manually firing the flash. Hold the flash about half a metre away at the side of the bowl, fire the shutter, and then press the flashgun's Test button. Review the image — if it looks too bright, reduce the power of the flash to 1/32 and try again.

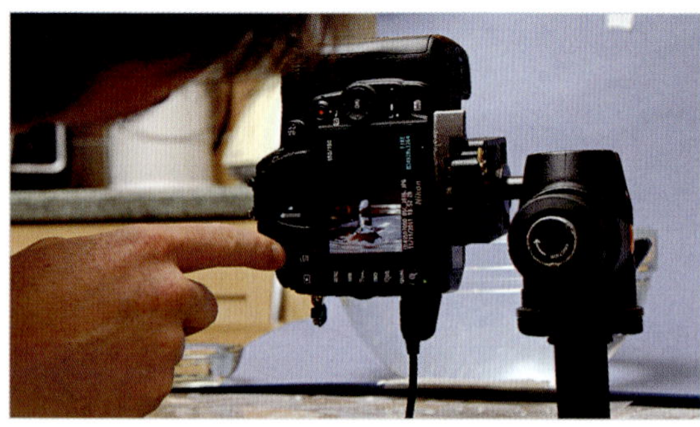

06 Get ready for the shot

Repeat the testing process until you get a good exposure level for the shot of the ruler. At this point, remove the ruler before taking your first test photos. Peel back the tape that's over the hole in the bottle, letting the water out in droplets. The next step takes a bit of trial and error, with timing being the key element.

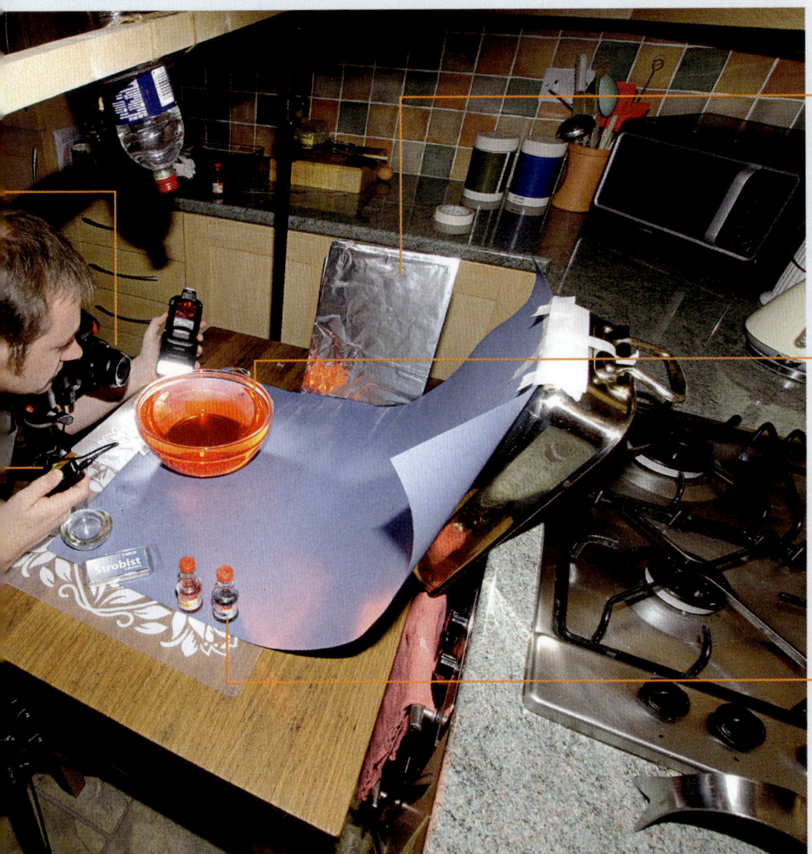

Silver foil
Although not essential, the silver foil acts as a simple reflector, helping to bounce the light from the flash onto the subject. Placing the foil reflector opposite the flash will help to even out exposure and add some much-needed light to the scene.

Water droplet
We've created a simple setup that uses a bottle and gravity to generate water droplets. By covering or uncovering the small hole with tape we can start and stop the droplets easily. Increasing the size of the hole boosts the amount of water released through the cap, but too large a hole will result in a stream!

Food colouring
Food dyes can be added to the liquid to create different-coloured effects. Using contrasting hues, with one in the bottle and the other in the bowl, can also add some visual interest. Just make sure you refresh the water frequently, to avoid a 'muddy pond' look!

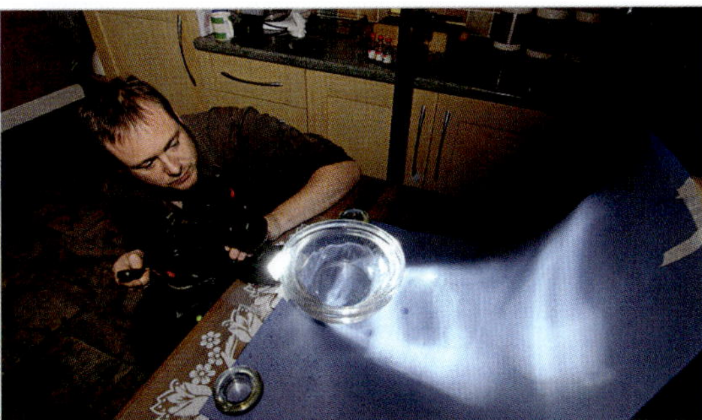

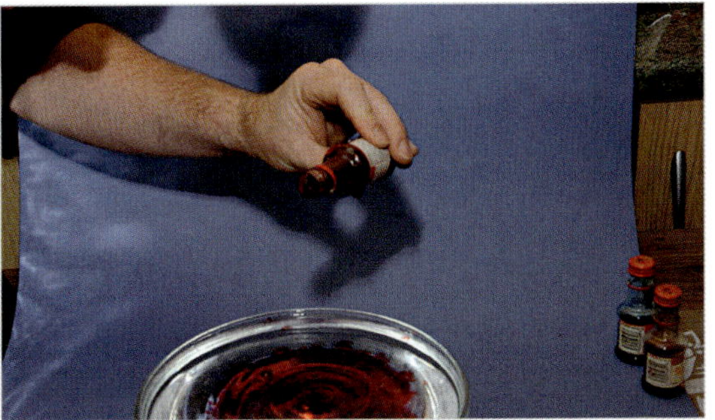

07 Have a play
As the water hits the surface, you'll see droplets form. At this point, release the shutter and fire the flash. Check the back of the camera to see the result. You're aiming to fire the flash at the exact moment when the water hits the surface, so a few attempts will be needed in order to get the timing right — you should find a rhythm between drops.

08 Boost colour and interest
Adding food colouring to the water is a quick way to add an extra something to the image, but you'll have to replace the water after every few drops. Alternatively, put a coloured gel or transparent sweet wrapper over the flash, or get creative and make a multi-coloured snoot to fit over the flash for more interesting colour effects.

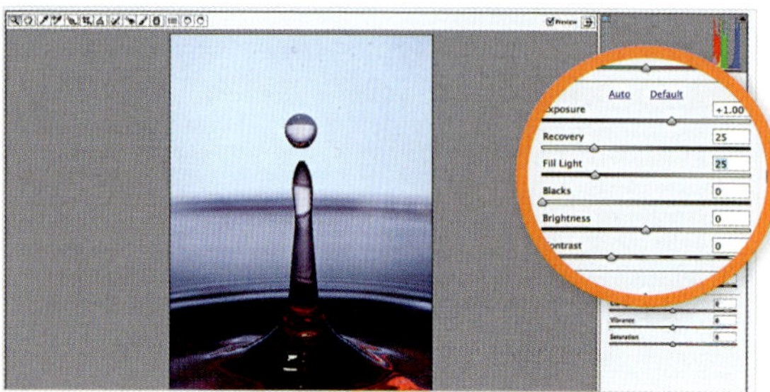

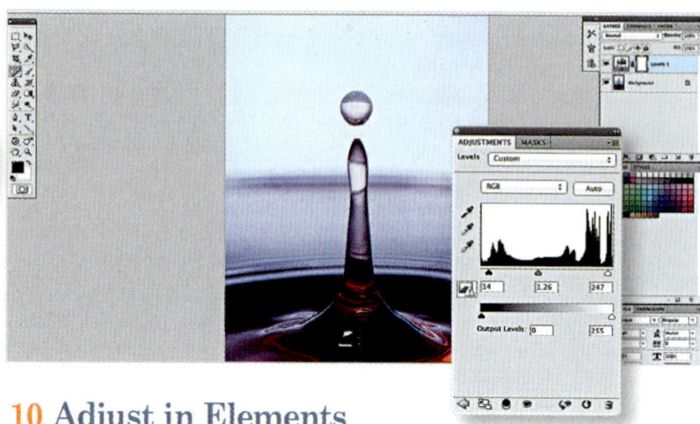

09 Edit your photo in ACR

Select one of the photos and open it in Adobe Camera Raw (ACR). We'll start by improving the exposure. Switch on the Shadow (U) and Highlight (O) clipping warnings and move the Exposure Slider to +0.5. Move the Recover slider to +20 and the Fill Light slider to +25. You should see greater detail in the water droplet.

10 Adjust in Elements

Click the Open Image button to exit ACR. Open Photoshop instead. Create a new Levels Adjustment Layer and move the Shadow and Highlight sliders to meet the edges of the histogram. Our water droplet looks too dark, so we're going to move the middle slider to the left; if it looked too light, we'd move the slider to the right.

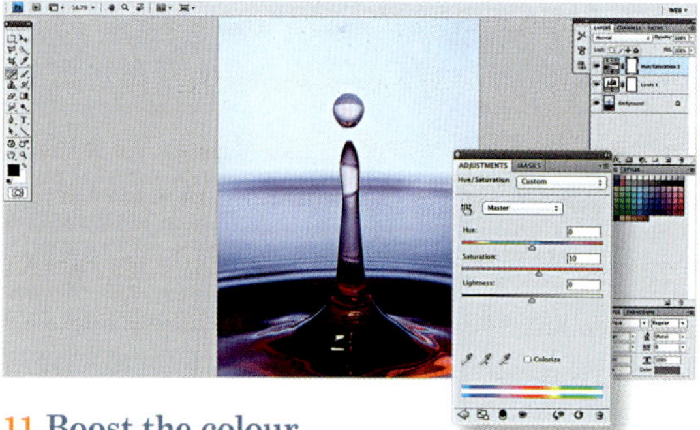

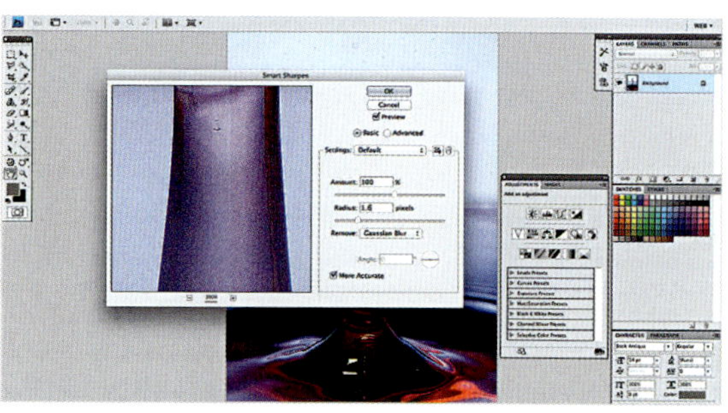

11 Boost the colour

Create a new Hue/Saturation Adjustment Layer. Using the Edit dropdown menu, select Blue and increase the saturation to +15. Then select Green and set it to +10, and finally choose Yellow with a value of +5. Check that the image isn't losing detail, and then boost the Master Saturation to +10. Now click OK.

12 Sharpen the detail

From the Layer options, select Flatten Image, then Enhance > Adjust Sharpness. Increase the Amount to 60% and the Radius to 1.2. Check that Gaussian Blur is selected in the Remove dropdown menu, and that More Refined is ticked. All that's left to do is click OK to finish your final high-speed water droplet image!

Breaking the surface

The beauty of this project is that with just one setup you can get a wealth of effects. We've detailed the 'elongated' water droplet, but here are some other options. The 'crown' on the left is the Holy Grail of high-speed photography — you'll probably only get it once in 50 shots. It's a wide splash, so use the smallest aperture possible. In the middle image, we've placed a low-power flash behind the bowl to really bring out the red food colouring. And on the right the flash is above the bowl, showing red highlights only.

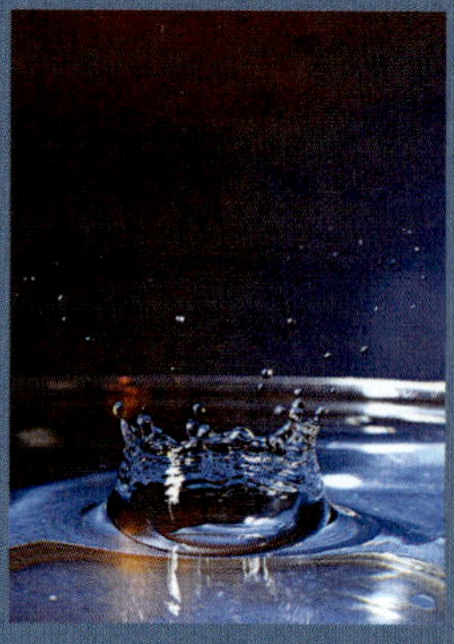

To capture the 'crown' in all its glory, use a tiny aperture such as f/22

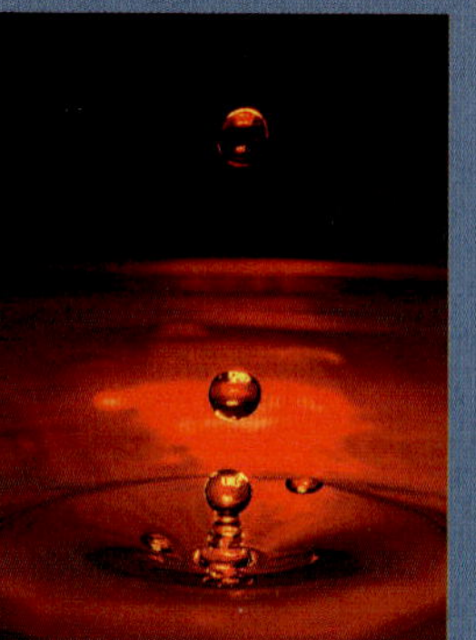

The bright rectangle behind the middle drop is actually the outline of the flash

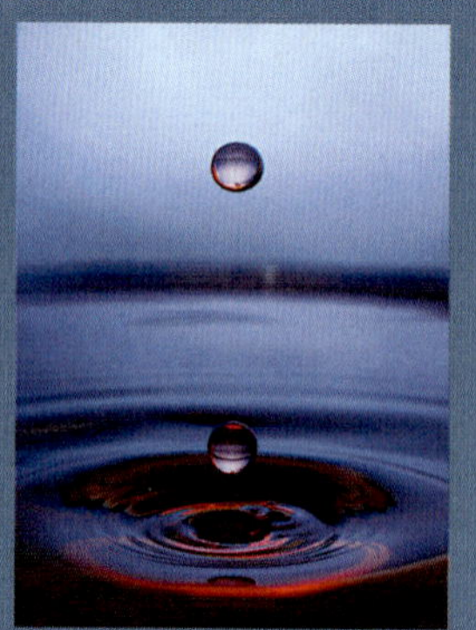

Here, we've picked out some red details against the background of blue card

Go crazy with colour

Capture the quirky hues of cross-polarised light. Let's take a look at how it's done

Believe it or not, the extraordinary colours on show in this vibrant image aren't the result of the overzealous use of Photoshop filters. In fact, they're caused by an optical effect called cross-polarisation.

So how does the result come about? Well, when certain objects are placed between two polarising filters — one on your camera's lens and one covering the light source — the light will behave in an unusual way, revealing wild and wonderful colours that wouldn't normally be visible to the human eye.

While the science behind the effect is complicated, it's actually a really easy technique to get to grips with. Even better, you don't need loads of expensive kit or accessories…

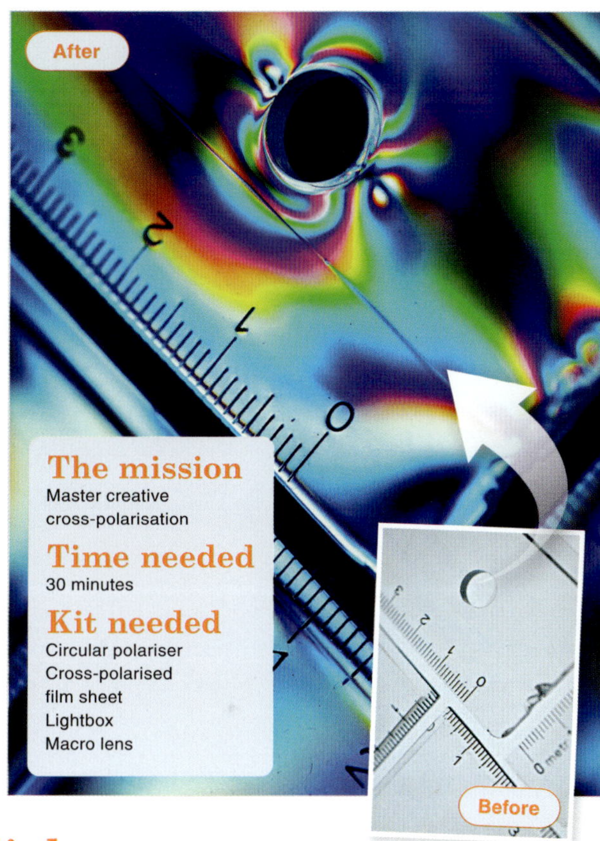

The mission
Master creative cross-polarisation

Time needed
30 minutes

Kit needed
Circular polariser
Cross-polarised film sheet
Lightbox
Macro lens

Capture cross-polarised light

With some basic equipment you can record a complex-looking effect in no time at all

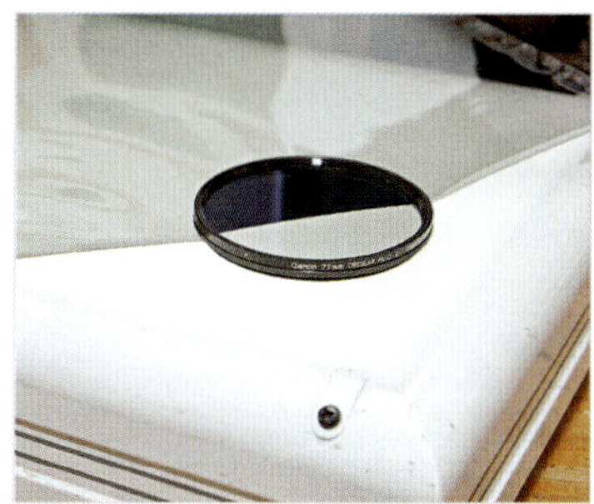

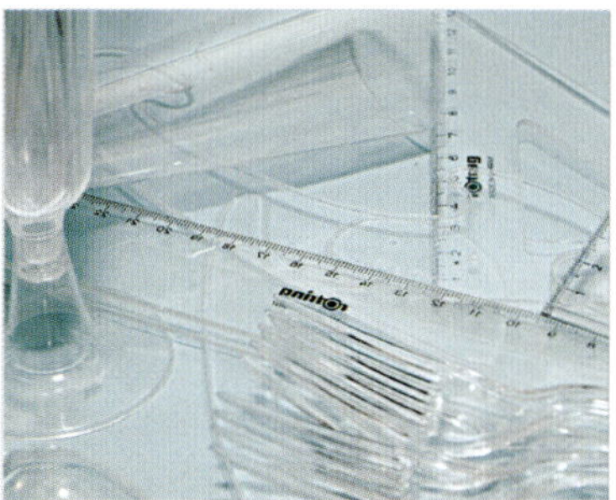

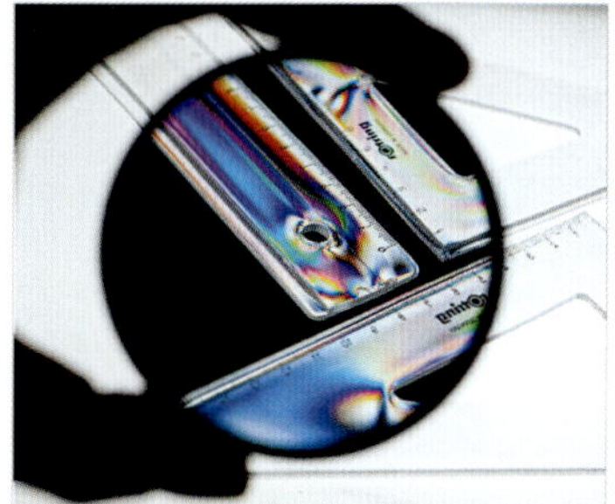

01 Go in a circle
First, get two polarising filters. You'll need a circular one to attach to your lens, and a second to go over the light source. The latter doesn't need to be circular — a sheet of polarising film is fine. We're using an A3 sheet of LEE 239 film on top of a lightbox.

02 Look for plastic
Plastic, especially the injection-moulded variety, works best for this technique because the cross-polarisation effect reveals stress points in all their multicoloured glory. Cutlery, cups, glass and stationery are all cheap, readily available and make perfect subjects.

03 Twist and turn
When you're ready, place the objects on the lightbox and rotating the circular polariser on your camera's lens until you get the desired effect. As you rotate the filter, the intensity of the effect changes — at some points, the white light from the lightbox will become black.

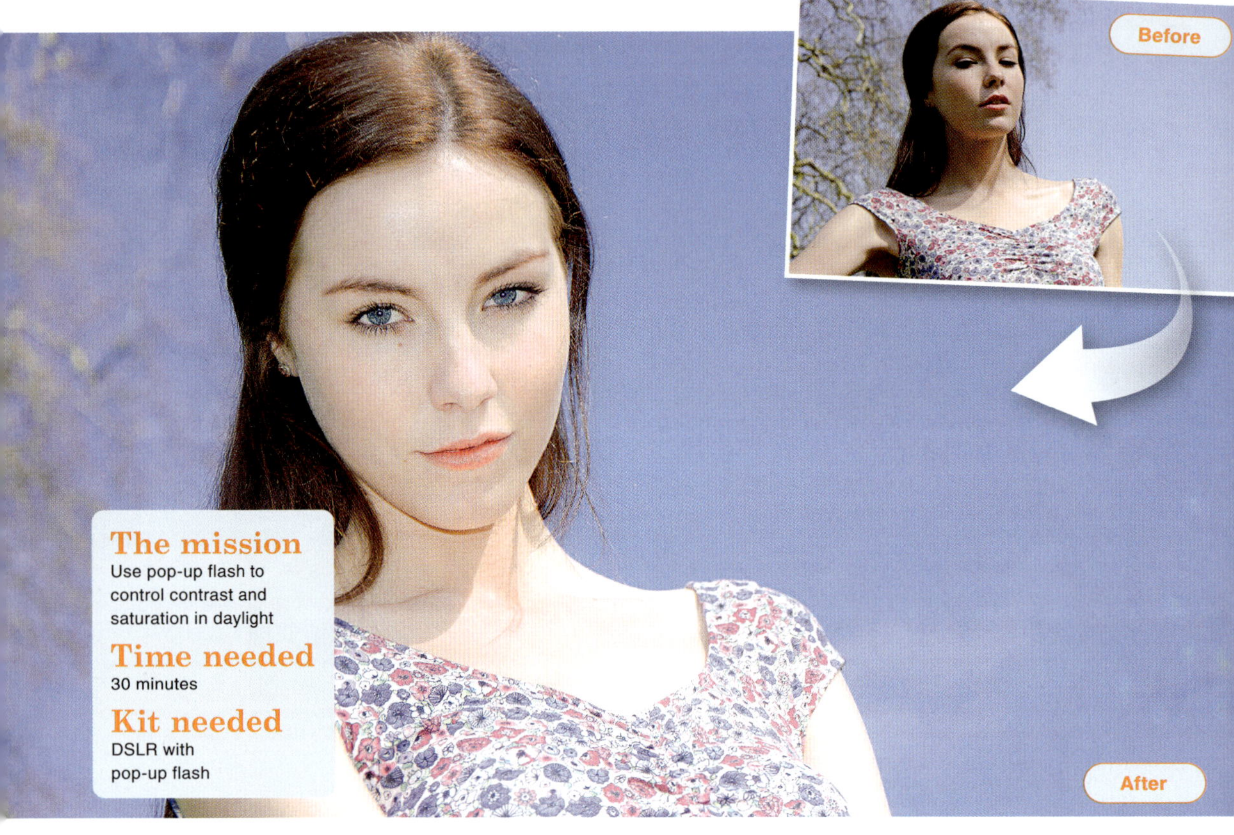

Fill faces with flash

Your built-in flash can work wonders on your portraits, even when you're shooting in bright sunlight. Discover how to use fill flash — and take control of it

Flash can be essential in low light, particularly when you're shooting living subjects. But it often ends up being a necessary evil, killing the atmosphere. Ironically, flash is often of more creative use in the hours of daylight.

Sometimes called 'synchro sun', and better known as 'fill flash', a burst of artificial light can be effective in practically any outdoor situation. What's more, you don't need any specialist kit — you can make do with the pop-up flash that comes built into most popular DSLRs.

The main restriction with the technique is that it only works if you're the right distance away from the right subject. A range of 2-12ft is ideal, so the trick is great for portraits.

In bright sunshine, when you might think there's enough light anyway, flash helps reduce the contrast on a subject, filling in the shadows that make eye sockets look dark and hide other facial

details. On a dull, overcast day, a burst of flash has the opposite effect, adding contrast and making portraits more three-dimensional and colourful. And whatever the weather, the flash also gives a sparkle to people's eyes by adding bright 'catchlight' reflections.

In its most basic form there's little more to the technique than firing the pop-up flash and shooting. You need to be using the right exposure mode, though. Program (P) or Aperture Priority (A) work best if you have autofocus turned on and are using standard evaluative metering.

The beauty of fill flash is that you combine two exposures — one taken using daylight, and the other with flash. By varying the settings you can make the fill flash effect stronger or weaker, which is handy for increasing or decreasing the brightness of the background independently of the subject. Let's see how it's done…

Darken backdrops with fill flash

Tweak exposure compensation to really make your subjects stand out

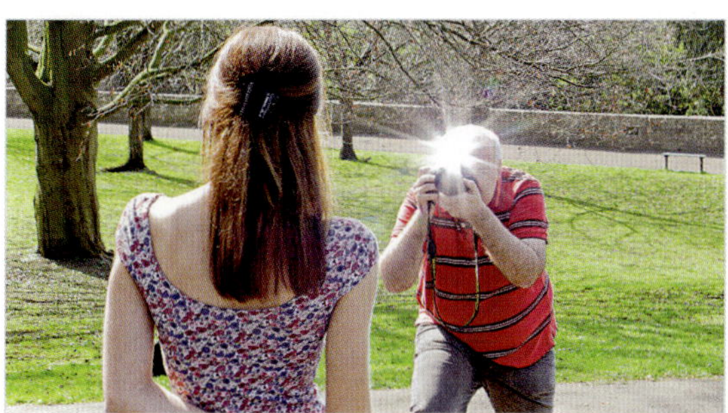

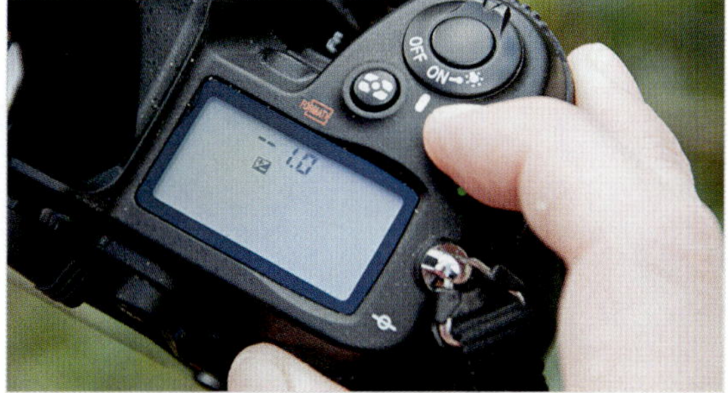

01 Push for pop-up

For fill flash, the easiest exposure mode to use is Program (P). This sets the aperture and shutter speed for you, for a balanced exposure with flash. Use matrix metering, and the AF points so that the camera knows where the subject is in the frame. Now pop up the flash.

02 Step down

Auto exposure is often perfect, but you can play with the settings to make the fill flash effect stronger or more subtle. To make the background look darker — to make a sky look more blue, say — you need exposure compensation. Try -1.0 (one stop underexposed).

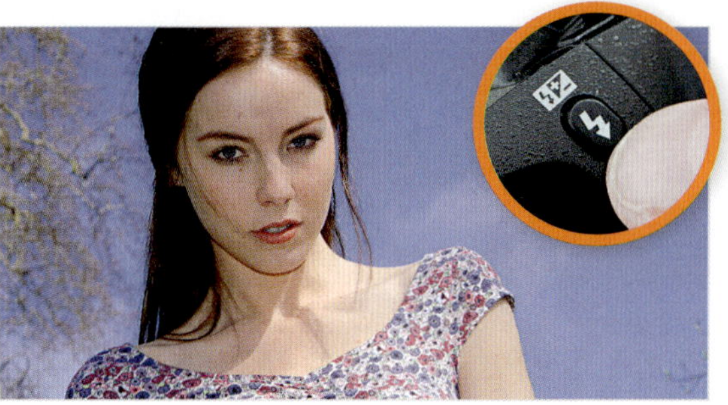

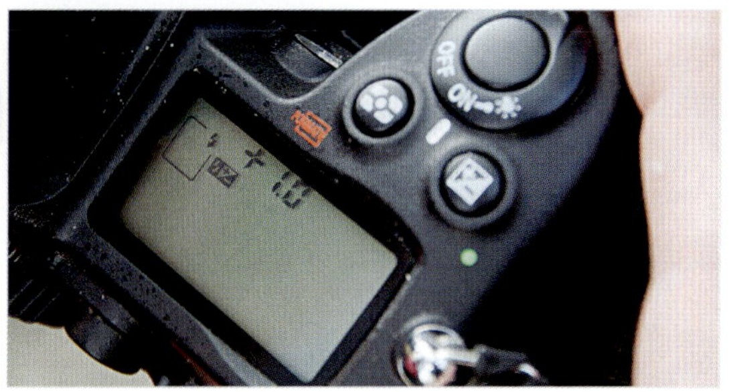

03 Play with power

The exposure compensation will make the foreground and background darker. To ensure that the subject is properly lit, adjust the flash power. Press the flash pop-up button and turn the front dial. On cameras such as the D3100, press +/- Exposure Compensation, too.

04 Finalise settings

Set the Flash Exposure Compensation to +1.0 (one stop over). This is the maximum allowed, although you can turn the power down to -3.0). Take a picture and the subject will be properly exposed but the background will be darkened by the new setting.

Bright ideas for fill flash

01 Take it slow

Leave your pop-up flash set to Slow for better fill flash shots at dusk. Just press the pop-up flash button and turn the dial.

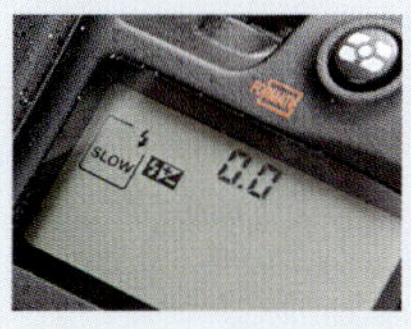

02 Pump it up

To increase the range of the built-in flash, change the ISO. Going from 100 to 800 ups the range from 2.1m to 6m at f/5.6.

03 Watch the hood

Lens hoods can cause problems with fill flash, particularly when you're close to a subject. To avoid shadows, take hoods off!

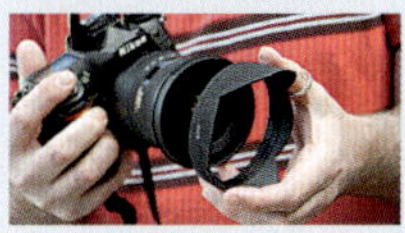

04 Beware of alerts

For more exposure control use Aperture Priority (A). If you see 'Hi' in the shutter speed readout, reduce the ISO or step down aperture.

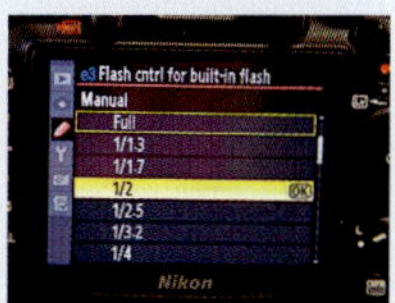

05 Max control

For full pop-up creativity, set 'Flash cntrl for built-in flash' to Manual in the Custom Settings menu. Then expose manually.

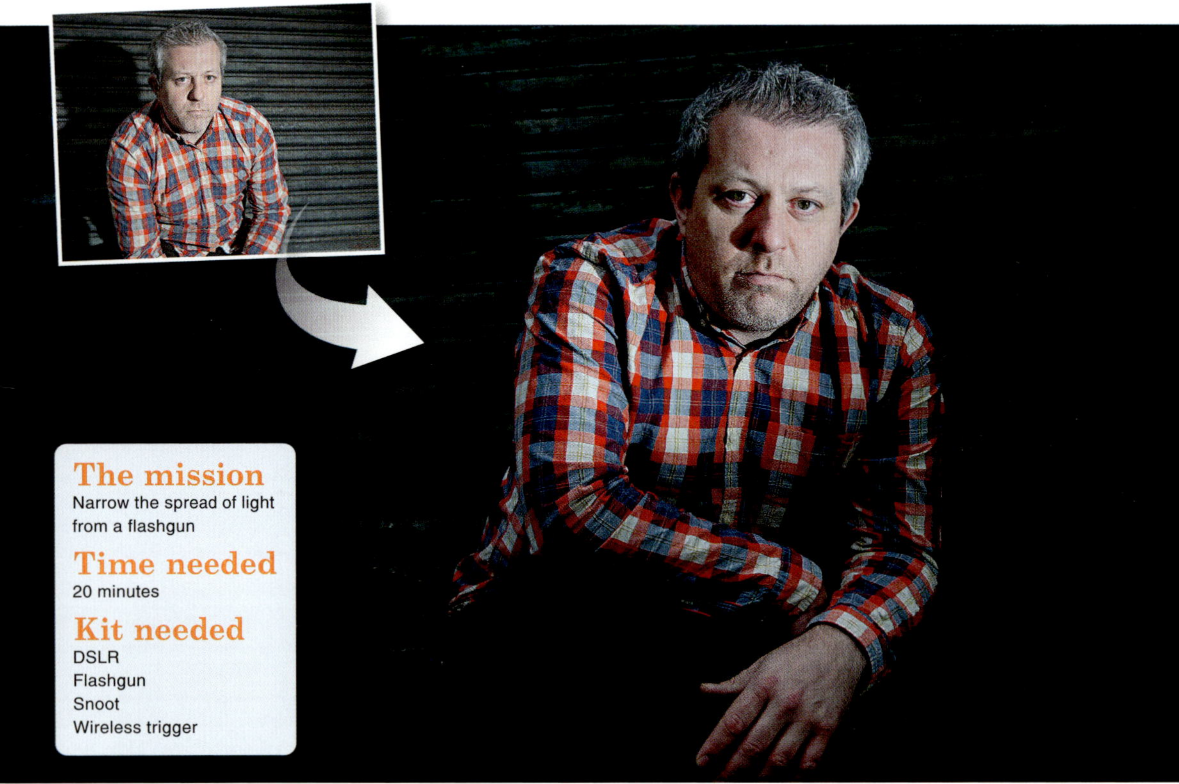

Spotlight on snoots

Create theatrical lighting with your hotshoe flash by controlling the spread of light with a simple add-on tube. Master how to create this dramatic special effect

A flashgun is always a handy tool to have in your camera bag, but it can often be like using a sledgehammer to crack a nut. For this reason, you almost always need extra add-on accessories to turn the flash into a useful creative effect.

The flash accessory with the most unusual name has to be the snoot. This is just a long tube or funnel that attaches to your flashgun, converting it from a floodlight into a spotlight, picking out a small area of the scene.

A snoot is very handy when you are photographing a portraits against a wall. Even though most add-on cstrobes have a zoom head that allows you to narrow the spread of light, the flashgun will still light up the majority of the frame. A snoot restricts the spread to a narrow beam, so that some areas of the frame are not lit at all by the flash. It is an effect that is not just useful for portraits, it can also be used for still-life arrangements, where you only want one thing on your table top to be highlighted.

A snoot is of most use in circumstances where the background is very close behind the subject. If the background is much further away the wide coverage of the flash tube is not an issue, as the light power falls off so sharply with distance. With a portrait, if the wall or backdrop is just behind the subject, the background becomes as well lit as the person. The result is a cold, analytical shot that lacks any atmosphere. Use a snoot and just the person's face is lit, creating a much more theatrical effect.

Commercially made snoots are available to fit most add-on flashguns, but there is no need to spend money on one to get this cool effect, as you can make your own light funnel very easily. Whether you buy one or make one, there are some things to watch out for to get successful results with a minimum of fuss…

Take a moody, spotlit strobist portrait

Set the exposure manually for a dark background, then pop just enough flash for drama!

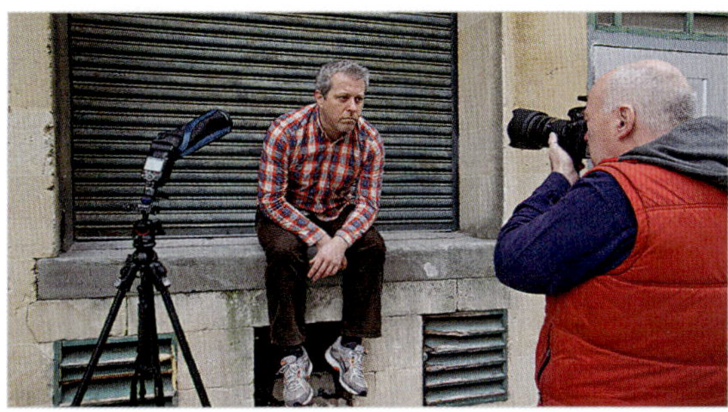

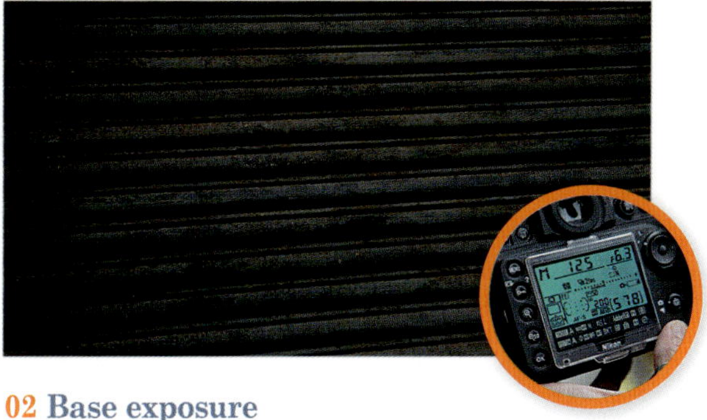

01 Backs against the wall

A snoot is particularly useful when there is little option but for the subject to stand or sit near the backdrop you are using. It is the best option if you don't want the whole background to be as well lit as the person. The theatrical lighting effect is very well suited to male portraiture.

02 Base exposure

With off-camera flash it is wise to use Manual exposure mode, particularly when lighting just a small part of the frame. Settings of 1/125 sec at f/6.3 at ISO200 are a good starting point. Take a test shot of the backdrop without flash (as above) to see that the shot looks dark enough.

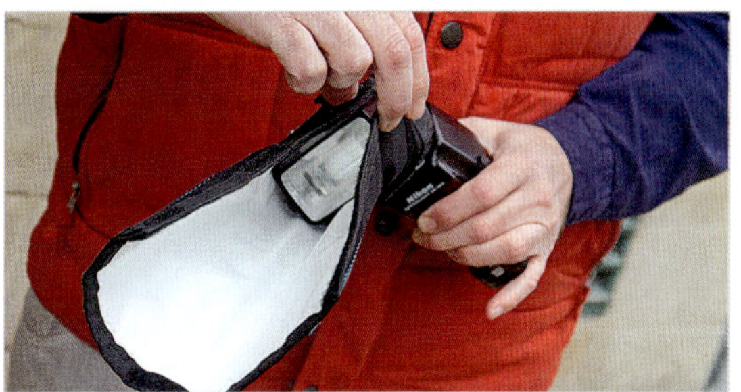

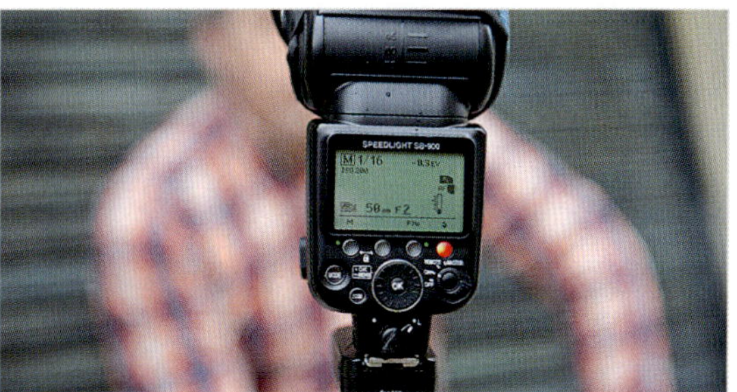

03 That's a wrap!

We used a Large Rogue FlashBender, which wraps around a flashground with an elastic strap and velcro, as our snoot. You also need a trigger for the off-camera flash (see the box on the far right), and something or someone to hold the flash in the right position (we used a tripod).

04 Power control

The exposure for the subject is simply controlled by altering the power output of the flashgun. Use the flash in Manual mode, and start off with a setting of 1/8 or 1/16 power. Take a test shot, and if the subject is too bright reduce the power, or if too dark increase it!

A snoot for every occasion and budget

01 Rogue FlashBender

A portable reinforced nylon solution, held on with a velcro strap. It also doubles as a bounce card and comes in two sizes.

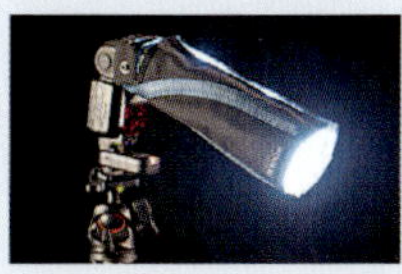

02 Interfit Strobie

A metal snoot with an add-on grid, just one part of a bargain kit of Strobie flash portrait accessories from Interfit.

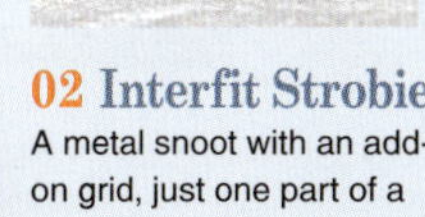

03 Use paper or card

On location, fashion your own impromptu snoot from a rolled up magazine, notebook or newspaper, or a piece of card.

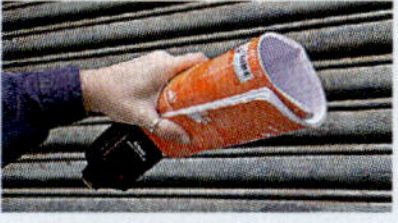

04 Use a tube

This potato chips can was just the right size to make a snugly-fitting snoot for our Nikon SB-900 flashgun. Just cut the end off!

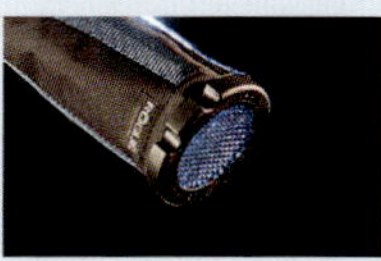

05 Honeycomb grid

A grid or honeycomb narrows the spread of flash light further, and can be used with a snoot. Rogue makes a good set.

Perfect the strobist look

Off-camera flash is one of the easiest ways to get amazing portraits

I f your only experience of using flash is the disappointing result you got with it fitted to the camera's hotshoe, you'll be amazed at how you can transform your photos by simply taking your flash off-camera. You can create a range of lighting effects, from using the flash to fill in the harsh shadows you get in bright sunlight to the much more dramatic results of underexposing the background and employing the flash as your main light source.

This second effect has become popular among a group of photographers known as strobists. They practise the art of off-camera flash and have a vibrant online community, largely thanks to a blog by American photographer David Hobby. His no-nonsense explanations helped demystify the techniques needed to master this art. Here, we show how you can get the strobist look using the automatic TTL exposure metering from your DSLR.

Shoot strobist portraits

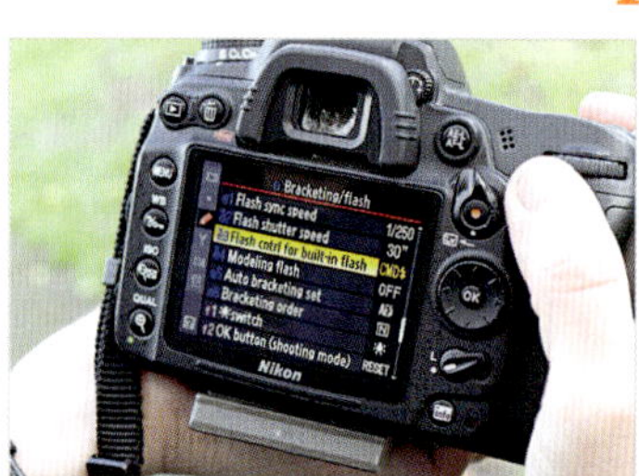

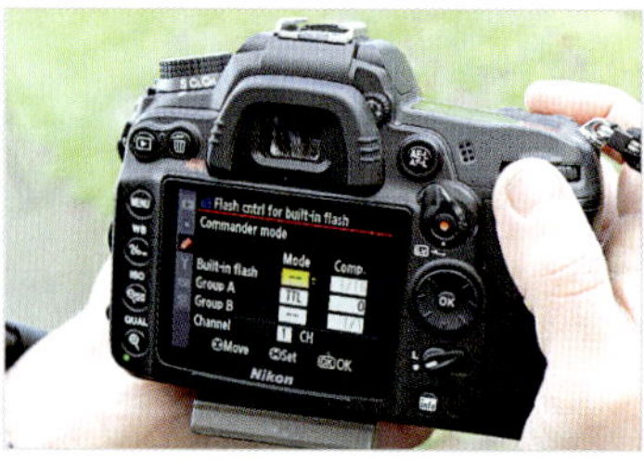

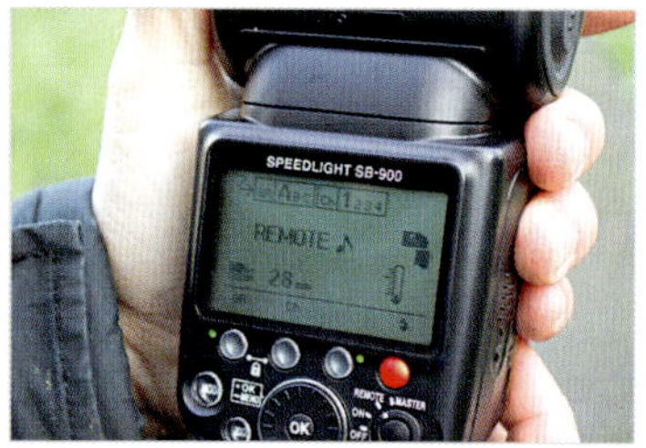

01 Prepare the built-in flash

In the Custom Setting menu, go to Bracketing/ flash, then scroll down to 'Flash control for built-in flash'. Use the navigation pad on the back of the camera to select the Commander setting, then use the same navigation pad to change the built-in flash setting to Off (--).

02 Set the group and channel

You now need to select the settings that will control the off-camera flash. Scroll down to the Group A settings and select TTL. Here you can also change the channel that controls the external flash. In this case, it's Channel 1. Finally, make sure you press OK to apply the settings.

03 Set up the flashgun

On your wireless flashgun, move the main switch to Remote. Select the same group and channel settings you used on the camera. Press the button at the bottom-left of the display and use the dial to set the Group to A. Press the button next to it and use the dial to set the Channel to 1.

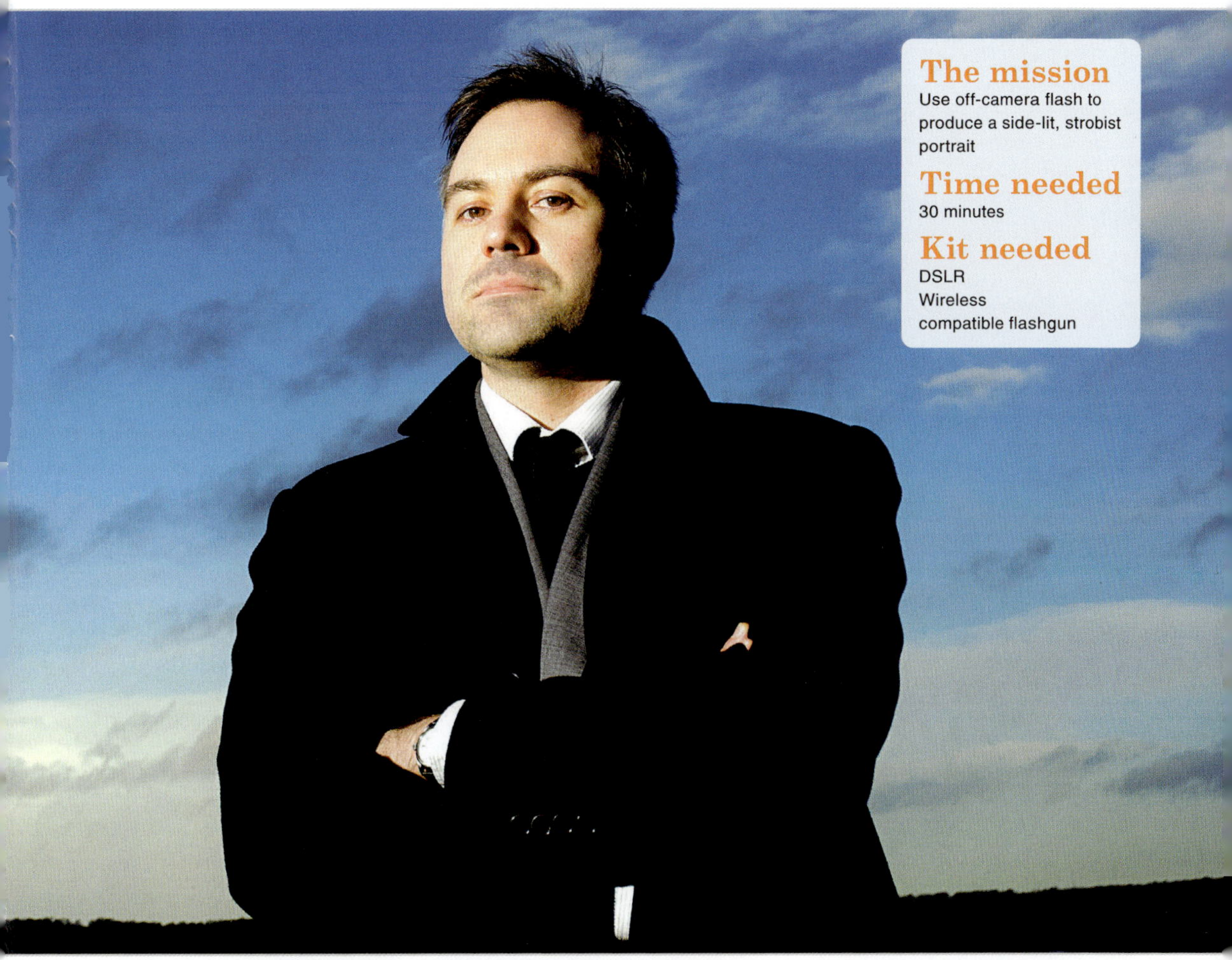

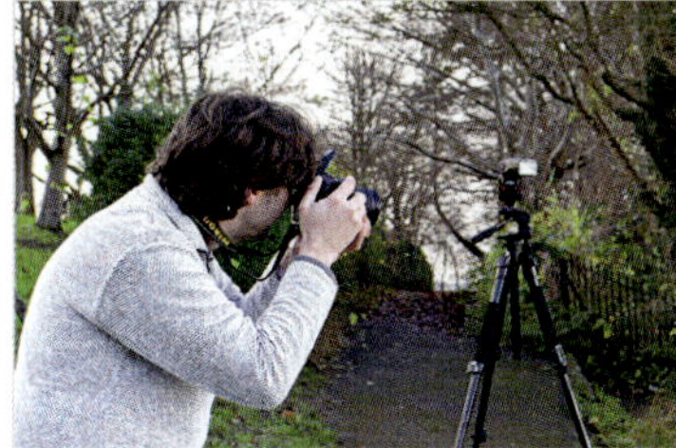

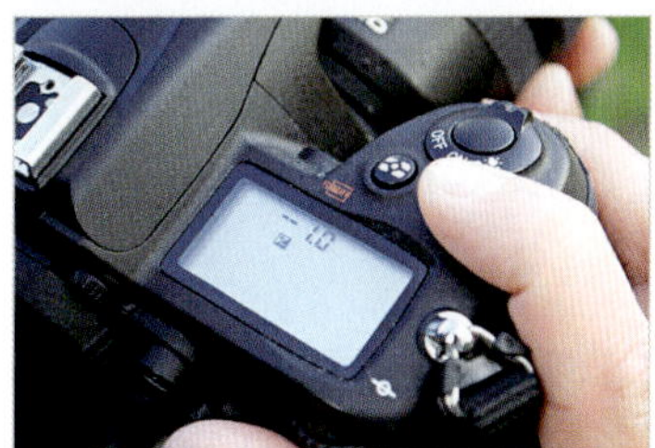

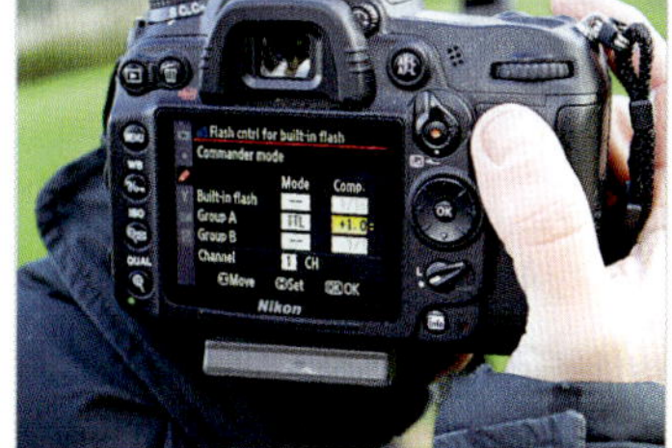

04 Position and soften the flash

Now the basic off-camera settings are done, you can position the flash either on a lighting stand or a normal tripod. For our shot, we're going to place the flash to the left and slightly above the subject to create dramatic side-lighting, making sure the flash is just out of the frame.

05 Underexpose background

With the camera set to f/8 on Aperture Priority mode, take a test shot — the wireless system needs a direct line of sight between the front of the flash and the camera. To give our shot more impact, we'll underexpose the background by setting the exposure compensation to -1 stop.

06 Adjust the flash exposure

This underexposure will affect both the flash and the ambient exposure, so we need to increase the exposure from the flash to properly expose the subject. Go into the Commander setting on the camera and adjust the exposure compensation setting of Group A to +1 stop.

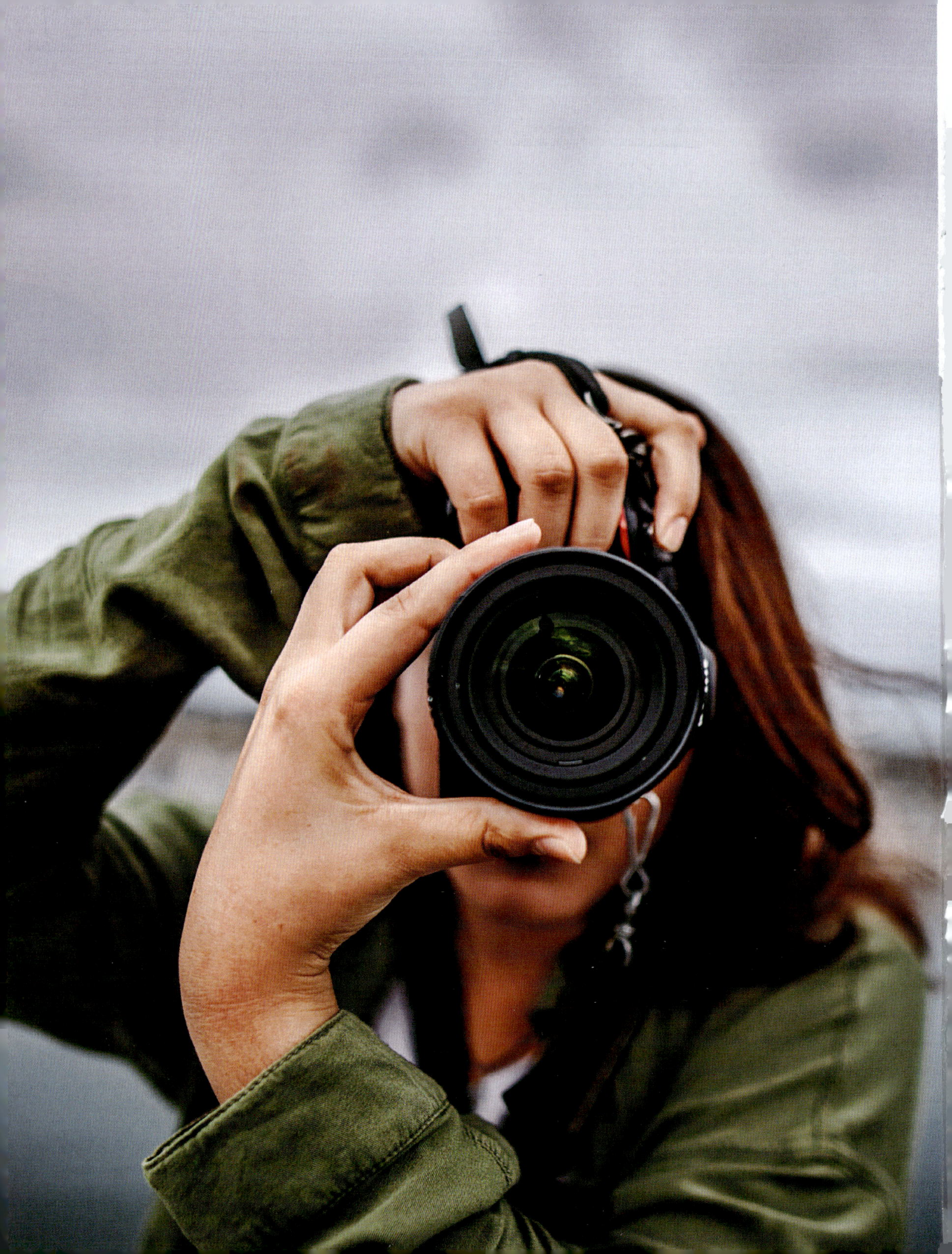